THE DIALECTICS OF DISCIPLESHIP

T&T Clark Enquiries in Theological Ethics

Series editors

Brian Brock
Susan F. Parsons

THE DIALECTICS OF DISCIPLESHIP

Karl Barth, Sanctification and Theological Ethics

Chris Swann

LONDON • NEW YORK • OXFORD • NEW DELHI • SYDNEY

T&T CLARK
Bloomsbury Publishing Plc
50 Bedford Square, London, WC1B 3DP, UK
1385 Broadway, New York, NY 10018, USA
29 Earlsfort Terrace, Dublin 2, Ireland

BLOOMSBURY, T&T CLARK and the T&T Clark logo are trademarks
of Bloomsbury Publishing Plc

First published in Great Britain 2023
Paperback edition published 2025

Copyright © Chris Swann, 2023

Chris Swann has asserted his right under the Copyright, Designs and Patents Act, 1988, to
be identified as Author of this work.

For legal purposes the Acknowledgements on p. vii constitute an extension
of this copyright page.

All rights reserved. No part of this publication may be reproduced or transmitted
in any form or by any means, electronic or mechanical, including photocopying,
recording, or any information storage or retrieval system, without prior
permission in writing from the publishers.

Bloomsbury Publishing Plc does not have any control over, or responsibility for,
any third-party websites referred to or in this book. All internet addresses given in this
book were correct at the time of going to press. The author and publisher regret any
inconvenience caused if addresses have changed or sites have ceased to exist,
but can accept no responsibility for any such changes.

A catalogue record for this book is available from the British Library.

Library of Congress Control Number: 2023939079

ISBN: HB: 978-0-5677-0877-9
PB: 978-0-5677-0882-3
ePDF: 978-0-5677-0878-6
ePUB: 978-0-5677-0881-6

Series: T&T Clark Enquiries in Theological Ethics

Typeset by Newgen KnowledgeWorks Pvt. Ltd., Chennai, India

To find out more about our authors and books visit www.bloomsbury.com
and sign up for our newsletters.

CONTENTS

Acknowledgements	vii
List of Abbreviations	ix
Preface	x

Chapter 1
INTRODUCTION — 1
- 1.1 The discipleship turn — 2
- 1.2 Discipleship in the post-Christian West — 8
- 1.3 Resourcing discipleship from Barth — 12

Chapter 2
BARTH AND HIS CRITICS ON DISCIPLESHIP — 17
- 2.1 Discipleship in Barth's theology of sanctification? — 17
- 2.2 The critics on discipleship in Barth — 20
- 2.3 Bonhoeffer and Barth's 'turn' to discipleship — 29
- 2.4 Discipleship in Barth and Barth's discipleship — 33

Chapter 3
THE PROBLEM AND PROMISE OF DISCIPLESHIP IN *CD* IV/2 §66 — 43
- 3.1 Christology and the context of discipleship in Barth — 43
- 3.2 Sanctification as Christ-centred discipleship — 47
- 3.3 Which Christocentrism? Whose discipleship? — 61
- 3.4 A 'Lively Christology' for discipleship — 74

Chapter 4
THE DIALECTICS OF DISCIPLESHIP — 83
- 4.1 Discipleship and freedom — 84
- 4.2 Discipleship as formed reference — 92
- 4.3 Discipleship, sanctification and moral discernment — 98

Chapter 5
DISCIPLESHIP AND THE ANALOGY OF GRACE IN *CD* IV/2 §66 — 105
- 5.1 Discipleship and the shape of correspondence — 106
- 5.2 Correspondence as discipleship? — 113
- 5.3 Discipleship, correspondence and theological ethics — 123

Chapter 6
DISCIPLESHIP AND ANALOGY FROM *ROMANS* II TO
THE CHRISTIAN LIFE — 127
   6.1 The identity and agency of the church in *Romans* II and *Church Dogmatics* IV — 130
   6.2 Ethics and the analogy of grace in *Romans* II and *The Christian Life* — 144

Chapter 7
THE IMPLICATIONS OF DISCIPLESHIP FOR MORAL AGENCY — 155
   7.1 The 'actualistic concreteness' of the church in *CD* IV/2 — 156
   7.2 Mortification and discipleship-shaped moral agency — 161
   7.3 Solidarity and difference in the discipleship-shaped church — 167

Chapter 8
THE IMPLICATIONS OF DISCIPLESHIP FOR MORAL ACTION — 171
   8.1 The 'indirect directness' of moral action in *CD* IV/2 — 173
   8.2 Good works and discipleship-shaped moral action — 176
   8.3 Discipleship and practical reasoning — 185

Chapter 9
THE IMPLICATIONS OF DISCIPLESHIP FOR MORAL SUFFERING — 189
   9.1 Discipleship, 'active passivity' and moral suffering — 190
   9.2 Grace, character and discipleship-shaped suffering — 197
   9.3 Discipleship and the 'ambiguities of liberation' — 201

Chapter 10
WITH, AGAINST AND BEYOND BARTH ON DISCIPLESHIP — 209
   10.1 *With* Barth on discipleship — 210
   10.2 *Against* Barth on discipleship — 212
   10.3 *Beyond* Barth on discipleship — 216
   10.4 The theological significance of discipleship — 222

Bibliography — 229
Index — 239

ACKNOWLEDGEMENTS

I am delighted to acknowledge the generosity and support of many. To begin with, I acknowledge the Wurundjeri people of the Kulin nation, owners of the unceded land upon which I live and work. I pay my respects to their Elders, past, present and emerging.

This book finds its origins in my doctoral study at St Mark's National Theological Centre in Canberra. I am deeply grateful for St Mark's as a community of learners, scholars and worshippers. I particularly want to thank my supervisors, Geoff Broughton, Andrew Cameron and David Neville. Geoff first recognized, and then frequently reminded me, that engaging with Barth was the thing that gave me energy. Andrew provided an invaluable sounding board as well as a long leash in the formative stages of my research. But this book would certainly not have been published without David's gentle and firm persistence in encouraging me to make something of my research. Alongside those at St Mark's, I am honoured by the attentive and insightful responses of my doctoral examiners, Martyn Percy, Brian Brock and Geoff Thompson, who have helped me deepen and sharpen my thinking in much needed ways. I am also indebted to the editors of this series, Brian Brock and Susan Parsons, who have championed my work, and Anna Turton and Sinead O'Connor from Bloomsbury, who have stewarded it so deftly.

I gratefully acknowledge the financial support of the Australian Government Research Training Program. This work was completed while I have been employed by City to City Australia, who have been generous with study leave and remarkably tolerant of my preoccupation with matters only tangentially related to our core business of training and resourcing church planters. Many others contributed along the way by providing feedback and input, prayer, speaking timely words, and offering kindness, support and patience. This includes Andrew Errington, Chris Porter, Rebekah Earnshaw, Sam Freney, Mike Allen, Melonie and Piers Bayl-Smith, Georgina and Hugh Dircks, Megan and Phil Curlis-Gibson, Andrew Katay, Mark Morley, Tim Foster, Michael O'Neil, Len Firth and Angela Cook. I am thankful above all for the friendship of each of these people.

Personally, I am conscious that the support and love of my parents and my wife's parents is incalculable and unreserved. Although not limited to the time when there were two simultaneous PhDs under way in our household, I remain particularly thankful for the ever-generous support and willingness of Mike and Diane Lauer to wade into the mess to care for our children, do dishes and mow the lawn.

Finally, thank you to my wife, Natalie, and my children, Benjamin and Abigail. Individually and together, you are God's gifts to me for my own discipleship and sanctification. You make me more human.

Several chapters in this book incorporate material published elsewhere. The preface has been expanded as Chris Swann, 'A Tale of Two Bedrooms? The Problem and Promise of Karl Barth's Theology of Discipleship' in St *Mark's Review* 251.1 (2020): 20–36.

Chapter 4 is adapted from Chris Swann, 'Discipleship on the Level of Thought: The Case of Karl Barth's Critique of the Religion of Revelation', chapter 10 of *Revelation and Reason in Christian Theology*, edited by Christopher C. Green and David I. Starling (Bellingham: Lexham Press, 2018). Chapters 5 and 9 include material reworked from Chris Swann, 'Karl Barth on the Dignity and Crown of Suffering: Reimagining the Fourth Age for Discipleship', chapter 6 of *Embracing Life & Gathering Wisdom: Theological, Pastoral, and Clinical Insights into Human Flourishing at the End of Life* edited by Stephen Smith, Edwina Blair and Catherine Kleeman (Macquarie Park: SCD Press, 2020).

ABBREVIATIONS

CD   Barth, K. *The Church Dogmatics*. 4 vols in 13 parts. Translated by Geoffrey W. Bromiley. Edinburgh: T&T Clark, 1956–75. Unless indicated, all citations from *The Church Dogmatics* are to this edition and are included in the body of the text.

KD   Barth, K. *Die kirchliche Dogmatik*. 4 vols in 13 parts. Zürich: Theologischer Verlag Zürich, 1938–65.

Inst.   Calvin, J. *Institutes of the Christian Religion*. Translated by Ford Lewis Battles. Edited by John T. McNeill. 2 vols, Library of Christian Classics. Philadelphia: Westminster Press, 1960.

PREFACE

'I don't want to boast, but it really was my text.' So wrote Barth, referring to the text of the *Barmen Declaration* (1934) – or, more precisely, to the six articles that form its theological core.¹ Few theological statements of the twentieth century can claim the ecclesial and ecumenical significance of the *Barmen Declaration*. Adopted by the Confessing Church (and many others thereafter), it made Christ central to the church and the Christian life and translated this centrality into a vision of discipleship with far-reaching political and ethical implications in its original context. And as Karl Barth was later to reminisce, he drafted it (or at least brought it to near-final form) in his bedroom at the Basler Hof Hotel in Frankfurt with the aid of some strong coffee and Brazilian cigars while his two Lutheran collaborators slept the afternoon away. Eberhard Busch records Barth's quip about that afternoon: 'The Lutheran Church slept and the Reformed Church kept awake.'²

This book investigates the theological significance of discipleship within the vision of sanctification that Barth develops in *Church Dogmatics* IV/2 §66, with an eye to its potential as a resource for Christian living in post-Christian contexts like the late-modern West. While the details of what transpired in that hotel bedroom in Frankfurt are subject to at least some degree of exaggeration, it poses the question: How could we fail to listen to what the chief architect of the *Barmen Declaration* has to say about discipleship when he gives himself the time to consider the theme at length?

However, if this bedroom looms in the background of this thesis, another bedroom likewise casts its shadow over it. This other bedroom was the single room at Princeton Theological Seminary shared by Karl Barth and his secretary Charlotte von Kirschbaum in 1962. Once again, the full details of what transpired in this bedroom – and what precisely it represents – are not possible to retrieve, and the way it is interpreted is subject to exaggeration (and not a little guesswork). Nevertheless, I find it impossible to pass over or ignore this second bedroom. Although it is not the main focus of this book, the questionable relationship between Barth and Charlotte von Kirschbaum can hardly be set aside – especially

---

An expanded version of this preface, including material from Chapters 2 and 10 of this book, first appeared in Chris Swann, 'A Tale of Two Bedrooms? The Problem and Promise of Karl Barth's Theology of Discipleship', *St Mark's Review* 251.1 (2020): 20–36.

1. Cited in Eberhard Busch, *Karl Barth: His Life from Letters and Autobiographical Texts*, trans. John Bowden (Eugene: Wipf & Stock, 2005), 245.

2. Eberhard Busch, *Karl Barth*, 245.

in the current context of a wide-ranging and urgent public conversation about gender inequality in society and the church, and in light of the fresh prominence given their troubling relationship by the personal correspondence from 1925 to 1935, which Christiane Tietz has recently rendered into English for the first time.[3] This presses the inevitable question: What could someone with such a questionable personal record of discipleship have to say about this theme that is worth hearing?

Which bedroom tells the real story of Barth's discipleship – and by extension Barth's theology of discipleship? Which way should Barth's legacy be interpreted? Should the bold political stance enshrined in the *Barmen Declaration* overshadow his questionable interpersonal relationships? Or should the troubling reality of his personal conduct cast suspicion on his theology, and perhaps also his politics? Of course, such a way of putting the matter is itself irresponsible. Neither the story of Barth's own discipleship – which is inescapably the story of *both* bedrooms – nor the story of Barth's theology of discipleship, can be treated like this. No politics, no matter how noble, can justify a powerful man using his position and 'significance' to use women. Few things could be clearer. Nevertheless, this does not automatically render his theology of discipleship meaningless. We may have to judge Barth's own discipleship a failure – although perhaps a more mixed, less moralistic conclusion is fairer to what we know and what continues to remain unknown (even allowing for the new evidence from their early correspondence). Even theologians may see and speak more truly than they are able to live. At the same time, the mixed legacy of Barth's own discipleship must be allowed to raise questions about his theology of discipleship (just as it must raise questions about his theology of marriage and family). The questions raised by these fresh revelations will need to be the subject of further research. By drawing attention to them here, I acknowledge their overarching significance for receiving Barth and invite readers to bear them in mind in what follows.

Taken together, however, these two bedrooms create a prima facie case for investigating the theological significance of discipleship in Barth's most sustained exposition of the theme in *Church Dogmatics* IV/2 §66. Barth 'turns' quite suddenly and dramatically to the theme of discipleship in the midst of developing a radicalized but still recognizably Reformed doctrine of sanctification. In doing this, he develops a properly theological, materially christological and consequently deeply practical vision of following Jesus, the living Lord who is central to Christians not just theoretically but as a gracious and authoritative moral presence. The theological intuitions represented by Barth's vision of discipleship supply rich resources for a novel constructive contribution to the contemporary conversation that has sprung up around this theme in the late-modern, post-Christendom West. Whether or not there is a 'Barmen moment' facing the churches today, Christians need to recognize that 'Jesus Christ, as he is attested for us in Holy Scripture, is the

---

3. Christiane Tietz, 'Karl Barth and Charlotte von Kirschbaum', *Theology Today* 74.2 (2017): 86–111.

one Word of God which we have to hear and which we have to trust and obey in life and in death.'[4] To the extent that it may help us in this task, Barth's theology of discipleship needs to be investigated, recovered and lived.

---

4. *The Theological Declaration of Barmen*, Article 1, in *The Book of Confessions: The Constitution of the Presbyterian Church (USA), Part I* (Louisville: Office of the General Assembly, 2004), 249.

Chapter 1

INTRODUCTION

A popular Christian ministry manifesto opens by announcing: 'We don't have a missional problem in the Western church. We have a *discipleship problem*.'[1] Another goes further:

> Of all the things we have chosen to remember over 2,000 years ... we have somehow managed to all but forget the essential gospel mandate to make disciples of the nations! How is this possible? How have we effectively managed to purge from church practice all but the faintest traces of one of the most central purposes and practices of the original church?[2]

These two authors are not alone in suggesting that a crisis of discipleship lies at the root of the problems the church is facing – from its growing cultural irrelevance to its lack of fruitfulness (and clarity) in mission. This emphasis on recovering discipleship is understandable. Discipleship boasts an explicit biblical pedigree and contains much promise. The theologian Philip Ziegler observes that 'when we make discipleship our theme, we ask, How ought we to characterize a human life that, having been justified, redeemed, and reconciled to God *by* Jesus Christ, is now given time and place in which to live anew *in* and *with* Christ?'[3] It therefore seems hardly surprising that a vigorous conversation has sprung up around the theme of discipleship, fuelled by a sense of its urgency in the present moment. Discipleship offers to connect Christology and soteriology to ecclesiology and Christian living – and to do so in a profoundly concrete and practical way.

Nevertheless, the language and imagery of discipleship has not always been accorded significant place in theological reflection on Christian identity and self-understanding. The contemporary emphasis on discipleship, as well as the

---

1. Mike Breen, *Building a Discipling Culture: How to Release a Missional Movement by Discipling People Like Jesus Did* (Greenville: 3DM Publishing, 2016), Kindle edition.
2. Alan Hirsch, *Disciplism: Reimagining Evangelism through the Lens of Discipleship* (Centreville: Exponential Resources, 2014), 1.
3. Philip G. Ziegler, 'Discipleship: Militant Love in the Time that Remains', in *Militant Grace: The Apocalyptic Turn and the Future of Christian Theology* (Grand Rapids: Baker Academic, 2018), 188.

historic interest the Anabaptist tradition has displayed in it, is unusual – at least within Protestant theology. Moreover, within the New Testament the language of discipleship is most prominent in the Gospels, virtually disappearing outside Matthew, Mark, Luke and John. As Eduard Schweizer points out, the verb 'to follow' (*akoloutheo*) only appears once outside the Gospels.[4] Especially within Protestant theologies of the Christian life, the theme has not typically been incorporated into mainstream treatments in any integrated or systematic way.[5] Bucking this trend, discipleship is both prominent and thoroughly integrated in Karl Barth's theology of sanctification as he articulates it in his *Church Dogmatics* IV/2 §66. Barth's integration of discipleship into his vision of sanctification has far-reaching consequences for Christian living – especially in the context inhabited by Christians and churches in the late-modern West.

This book investigates the significance of discipleship in Barth's theology of sanctification with an eye to its value as a resource for Christian living at the particular historical and social moment inhabited by the churches in the late-modern, post-Christian West. In order to establish the conceptual reference points for this investigation, we must understand the appeal of the discipleship motif, briefly explore the cultural context in which it has emerged to prominence and consider how to explore Barth's exposition of discipleship in order not only to do justice to it on its own terms but also to constructively furnish resources for theological ethics.

1.1 The discipleship turn

In John Webster's important essay 'Discipleship and Calling', he sets out two broad approaches to developing a theology of the Christian life – conceived in terms of 'that form of human existence which is brought into being and upheld by the saving work of God'.[6] There is the more traditional approach, in which 'the main lines of the theology of the Christian life [are] structured around the Pauline and Johannine theology of union with and life in Christ'.[7] Within Protestant theology, Webster explains, this traditional approach has frequently involved appeal to an *ordo salutis* (order of salvation) that connects the saving work of God to the life of believers in a sequence of moments. These moments can be narrated as a history, forming the backbone of every believer's spiritual autobiography. The Christian life is therefore a matter of what results from the accomplishment of God in salvation. The Christian life is the 'What shall we do?' that follows the announcement of

---

4. Eduard Schweizer, *Lordship and Discipleship* (London: SCM Press, 1960), 12, 77.

5. Ziegler traces the mixed fortunes of the theme in the tradition in 'Discipleship: Militant Love', 188–92.

6. John Webster, 'Discipleship and Calling', *Scottish Bulletin of Evangelical Theology* 23.2 (2005): 133.

7. Webster, 'Discipleship and Calling', 134.

God's achievement in raising Jesus in Acts 2.37. The fact that the Christian life is framed here as a question, the yet-to-be-determined human response to God's action in Christ, ought not be missed. It is only slightly uncharitable to observe that for many in the Protestant tradition – especially among its popular advocates – the Christian life is a problem. A theology of the Christian life must struggle against the intuition that it is unnecessary (given the decisive action of God in salvation) or 'unevangelical' (a moralistic add-on to soteriology). In the latter case, it looks not so much to God as to human activity in applying the moral principles of Scripture, imitating Christ's example or drawing inspiration from biblical imagery. Ivor Davidson sums up the challenges here well:

> The history of the doctrine of sanctification is strewn with evidence of theology's enduring capacity to treat holiness as something other than the gospel. All of them persist in contemporary forms. There is the subtle (or not-so-subtle) danger of a quasi Pelagian preoccupation with salvation by works. Can we articulate a theology of sanctification that does not collapse into a form of moral self-improvement, the pursuit of favour with God for special devotion? There is the danger of condemning the world to which God has committed himself. Can we think of sanctification in a way that does not celebrate flight from the material order? God has pronounced that order primordially good; in the resurrection of Jesus, he has pledged its ultimate redemption from evil's effects. There is the danger of a privatized spirituality. Can reflection on sanctification avoid obsession with individual experience, personal milestones, the acquisition of gifts or achievements as private spiritual capital? Can it talk adequately about the gospel's vocation to life together, the declaration of a new social order in the church, the summons to a people, not just isolated selves, to bear witness to the world?[8]

David Fergusson vividly describes the functional Pelagianism that often afflicts attempts to relate the action of God and the active human response in a temporal sequence: the 'Christian life is somehow jump-started by an act of divine justification but learns to proceed thereafter on its own Spirit-assisted combustion'.[9] Within such a view (rarely reflectively adopted), Christ provides the basis for the sanctified life – and, through the Spirit, some degree of assistance in living it; but he is far from unambiguously present to or active as Lord in it. In Miroslav Volf's evocative image, Christ may supply divine 'performance enhancement' for Christian living, but his agency is hardly primary in it.[10] Different from the Pelagian

---

8. Ivor J. Davidson, 'Gospel Holiness: Some Dogmatic Reflections', in *Sanctification: Explorations in Theology and Practice*, ed. Kelly M. Kapic (Downers Grove: InterVarsity Press, 2014), 190.

9. David Fergusson, 'Reclaiming the Doctrine of Sanctification', *Interpretation* 53.4 (1999): 383.

10. Miroslav Volf, *A Public Faith: How Followers of Christ Should Serve the Common Good* (Grand Rapids: Brazos, 2011), 32.

tendency in much traditional thinking about sanctification is an inclination to limit Christ's concern to one aspect of the Christian's morality at the expense of others – typically their private rather than their public lives. Whether fed by an incipient Gnosticism or simply a matter of the church uncritically taking on aspects of secular, managerial culture, this inclination yields a lopsided theology of the Christian life in which human moral action is unnecessary in some spheres and 'unevangelical' in those where it is deemed necessary.

The alternative approach identified by Webster dwells on the synoptic theme of discipleship. Once a minority report in Protestant theology, an emphasis on the concept if not the language of discipleship has recently become a major point of convergence and conversation. Beyond its natural home in New Testament studies, the theme of discipleship is a current focus of interest and attention from across a range of disciplines: theological ethics, practical theology and particularly practical ministry.[11] It is not too much to speak of a contemporary discipleship 'turn'. People representing a bewildering variety of perspectives seem to be gravitating increasingly to discipleship. It is of interest to advocates of the so-called Benedict Option – a particular politically and culturally conservative version of the well-worn trope of appropriating the medieval practices of Christian

---

11. Among theological ethicists, Brian Brock, Alister McFadyen, Mark Thiessen Nation and Glen Stassen have all fruitfully explored the theme of discipleship – frequently in conversation with Dietrich Bonhoeffer. See Brian Brock, 'Bonhoeffer and the Bible in Christian Ethics: Psalm 119, the Mandates, and Ethics as a "Way"', *Studies in Christian Ethics* 18.3 (2005): 7–29; Alister I. McFadyen, 'The Call to Discipleship: Reflections on Bonhoeffer's Theme 50 Years On', *Scottish Journal of Theology* 43.4 (1990): 461–83; Mark Thiessen Nation, 'Discipleship in a World Full of Nazis: Dietrich Bonhoeffer's Polyphonic Pacifism as Social Ethics', in *The Wisdom of the Cross: Essays in Honour of John Howard Yoder*, ed. Stanley Hauerwas et al. (Grand Rapids: Eerdmans, 1999), 249–77 and Glen H. Stassen, *A Thicker Jesus: Incarnational Discipleship for a Secular Age* (Louisville: Westminster John Knox Press, 2012). More recently, Michael Banner has championed the concrete specification of discipleship laid out in Benedict's Rule as paradigmatic of the shape and promise of Christian ethics in his *Christian Ethics: A Brief History* (Chichester: Wiley-Blackwell, 2009), 10–22. And Stanley Hauerwas has frequently returned to the theme of discipleship and its conceptual cognates in his theological ethics. See, for example, Stanley Hauerwas, 'Discipleship as Craft, Church as Disciplined Community', in *The Christian Century* (2 October 1991): 881–4. Among practical theologians, discipleship has received attention from writers as diverse as the Roman Catholic theologian Terrence Tilley and those drawing more from the Anabaptist tradition such as Lee Camp, David Augsburger and Geoff Broughton. See Terrence W. Tilley, *The Disciples' Jesus: Christology as Reconciling Practice* (Maryknoll: Orbis, 2008); Lee C. Camp, *Mere Discipleship: Radical Christianity in a Rebellious World* (Grand Rapids: Brazos, 2008); David Augsburger, *Dissident Discipleship: A Spirituality of Self-Surrender, Love of God, and Love of Neighbor* (Grand Rapids: Brazos, 2006); Geoff Broughton, *Restorative Christ: Jesus, Justice, and Discipleship* (Eugene: Pickwick, 2014).

formation for a contemporary context – just as it was of interest to practitioners of the New Monasticism before it.[12] An increasing number of mainstream Protestant theologies make discipleship an important category, if not the organizing principle when it comes to the Christian life.[13] Discipleship likewise continues to receive attention from those more explicitly indebted to the Anabaptist tradition, often in combination with some version of postliberalism or postmodernism.[14]

The contemporary convergence on discipleship treats it as more than simply illustrative. Instead, as Webster argues, discipleship is taken to highlight the eschatological character of Christian existence – and, we might add, its proximity to Christ. 'Discipleship means dislocation; and that dislocation is in an important sense a permanent characteristic of the Christian condition.'[15] What is more, it arguably reframes the typical Protestant way of configuring the relationship between soteriology and the Christian life. Rather than the result of Christ's work, the Christian life is ingredient with it. Disciples are not simply those for whom Christ has done something, which they receive in faith and then wonder about how it may apply to their behaviour. Instead, they are those who, called by Jesus, have given their allegiance to him. His way becomes theirs as they accompany him, are instructed by him, and as he sends them out. Their sanctification is therefore intimately tied to his presence and activity. As such, discipleship has become the theme for a lively and ongoing conversation. But what accounts for the appeal of discipleship? Why has it become so resonant now?

---

12. The leading advocate of the Benedict Option is Rod Dreher, *The Benedict Option: A Strategy for Christians in a Post-Christian Nation* (New York: Sentinel, 2017). While focused on a North American context, Erik C. Carter's 'The New Monasticism: A Literary Introduction', *Journal of Spiritual Formation and Soul Care* 5.2 (2012): 268–84, provides a good overview of the earlier movement, pinpointing Jonathan R. Wilson's *Living Faithfully in a Fragmented World: Lessons for the Church from MacIntyre's 'After Virtue'* (Harrisburg: Trinity Press International, 1997) as a watershed text.

13. Discipleship is a key coordinate, for example, in the vision of Christian living that Reformed theologian Michael Horton develops in *The Christian Faith: A Systematic Theology for Pilgrims on the Way* (Grand Rapids: Zondervan, 2011). And the question of discipleship, if not always the language, animates James K. A. Smith's entire 'cultural liturgies' project in *Desiring the Kingdom: Worship, Worldview, and Cultural Formation* (Grand Rapids: Baker Academic, 2009), *Imagining the Kingdom: How Worship Works* (Grand Rapids: Baker Academic, 2013) and *Awaiting the King: Reforming Public Theology* (Grand Rapids: Baker Academic, 2017).

14. Representatives of those informed by postliberalism include the examples already cited of Hauerwas, Camp and Augusburger, whereas neo-Anabaptists owing more to postmodernism include Nathan R. Kerr, *Christ, History, and Apocalyptic: The Politics of Christian Mission* (Eugene: Cascade Books, 2009) and Ry O. Siggelkow, 'The Nothingness of the Church under the Cross: Mission without Colonialism', *Anabaptist Witness* 1.1 (2014): 103–19.

15. Webster, 'Discipleship and Calling', 134.

Glen Stassen's vision of 'incarnational discipleship' exemplifies many features of this way of situating the Christian life with respect to Christ. Although Bonhoeffer is frequently and understandably invoked as the precedent for the contemporary focus on discipleship – and Stassen does devote substantial attention to him – it is the *Barmen Declaration* that he sees as paradigmatic. Citing it, Stassen develops a three-dimensional vision of discipleship. Its first dimension is a 'thick' Jesus – that is, a commitment to Jesus' historical reality as central for both theology and ethics. Stassen fleshes this out in terms of paying 'extensive attention to the teachings and actions of Jesus' in order to resist any tendency to interpret 'Jesus in terms of a vague ideal or principle; or as teaching ideals too high to actually be put into practice; or ... [limiting] Jesus' teaching to internal church relations among individuals but not applicable in the rest of life.'[16] Its second dimension is an emphasis on 'the lordship of Christ or sovereignty of God throughout all of life and all of creation.'[17] Jesus is a constant point of reference for a Christian life viewed in terms of discipleship, not simply its point of departure. As New Testament scholar Eduard Schweizer discerned in his classic work on the connection between Christ and the Christian life, lordship and discipleship go together.[18] The third dimension of Stassen's vision is its emphasis on the call of discipleship to liberation from 'worldly' powers and authorities that enslave and entangle through ideologies like nation, race and greed. What this means for 'incarnational' disciples is 'repentance from letting some other lord, ideology, or nationalism take over their ethics and their loyalties'.[19]

Other approaches to discipleship vary in their details, but all concur with Stassen that discipleship makes Jesus central for Christians in practice and not just in theory. Such is the promise of discipleship for many. It summons Christians to resist the temptation to separate Christ from the Christian life. Christ cannot remain distant from the moral life of his disciples. He is present to them, freely and sovereignly directing them in ways that resist the tendency to distance or abstract him from the moral life – for instance, by making him merely an example or inspiration for it.[20] As Terrence Tilley contends, 'discipleship is Christology and soteriology in practice'.[21] To insist on discipleship is to insist that Christians side with Jesus, and that this allegiance must be manifested tangibly. At the turning point of Mark's Gospel, Jesus highlights the implications of failing to grasp this: 'Those who are ashamed of me and of my words in this adulterous and sinful generation, of them the Son of Man will also be ashamed when he comes in the glory of his

---

16. Stassen, *A Thicker Jesus*, 20–1.
17. Stassen, *A Thicker Jesus*, 16.
18. Schweizer, *Lordship and Discipleship*.
19. Stassen, *A Thicker Jesus*, 21.
20. Davidson highlights the common tendency here to 'compromise the uniqueness of Christ's person, implying that he is better than the rest of us only by degree'. Davidson, 'Gospel Holiness', 208.
21. Tilley, *The Disciple's Jesus*, 25.

Father with the holy angels' (Mk 8.38). Discipleship cannot be merely a matter of notional or purely intellectual allegiance with no visible, bodily, behavioural expression – costly as that may be. As Bonhoeffer points out, such a fantasy is only nurtured by the kind of 'cheap grace' that wants to claim the name 'Christian' without attentiveness to Christ and his distinctive way: 'Christianity without the living Christ is inevitably Christianity without discipleship; and a Christianity without discipleship is always a Christianity without Jesus Christ.'[22]

In making Christ's active presence and lordship its theme, discipleship also highlights the 'permanent dislocation' of Christians. Disciples will be distinctive – and even dislocated – insofar as Christ's call to follow him relativizes their existing allegiances and priorities. Disciples are *called* to Christ and therefore called *away from* other, competing allegiances. The encounters with Jesus gathered together in Matthew 8.18–23 (and its parallel in Lk. 9.57–62) all stress that the call to follow Jesus takes priority, cutting across mundane concerns with self-preservation, cultural expectations about the honourable discharge of familial duties and much else besides. Therefore, Christian disciples are 'an assembly of migrants, answerable finally to the law of another city,' in Rowan Williams's apt metaphor.[23] In the terms employed in 1 Peter, they are 'aliens and exiles'. Importantly, this is not a matter of merely inward allegiance or religious affiliation (as though that could be a merely private matter in the first century). It is necessarily tangible and social, manifesting in transformed behaviour and patterns of relating.[24] Those who view themselves as aliens, exiles and migrants like this are called to 'abstain from the desires of the flesh that wage war against the soul' and to 'conduct [themselves] honourably among the Gentiles' so that those who malign them may come to praise God – whether willingly or begrudgingly, now or at Christ's return (1 Pet. 2.11–12). The notion of being a disciple – a follower – of Jesus, and owing loyalty to him, is particularly well calibrated to highlight the 'permanent dislocation' Christians can expect to experience in any culture and context. It speaks of their distinctiveness both negatively and positively. Negatively, they abstain from the desires of the flesh. Positively, they conduct themselves honourably.

This emphasis on discipleship recommends itself in particular when it comes to the questions surrounding this 'permanent dislocation' – how should Christians be distinctive in any given context? And what kind of formation will yield this? As we will see, discipleship discourse promises to address such questions of distinctiveness and formation. Webster speaks for many when he remarks, 'Where discipleship has become a strange idiom … we may take that as a sign that the

---

22. Dietrich Bonhoeffer, *Discipleship*, Dietrich Bonhoeffer Works (English edition), volume 4 (Minneapolis: Fortress Press, 2001), 58–9.

23. Rowan Williams, *Why Study the Past? The Quest for the Historical Church* (Grand Rapids: Eerdmans, 2005), 41.

24. Miroslav Volf explores this dimension of the teaching of 1 Peter in 'Soft Difference: Theological Reflections on the Relation between Church and Culture in 1 Peter', *Ex Auditu* 10 (1994): 15–30.

church may be disregarding its eschatological condition and fitting itself too snugly into the world.'[25] Medi Ann Volpe pinpoints the challenge with respect to formation when she suggests that the process of producing disciples requires more than simply informing the mind or policing behaviours (or some combination of the two): 'Our failure consistently to practice "true discipleship" suggests that there is more to Christian identity than the honing of our intellectual and moral skills.'[26] Behind their divergences over how exactly this distinctiveness is to be parsed and what the most promising strategies are for generating it, every contributor to the contemporary discipleship conversation is cognisant of the lack of fit between Christians and their context – especially in the late-modern West – and most also agree that this lack of fit is in some sense *necessary* rather than accidental, *permanent* rather than contingent or limited to particular historical circumstances.

Disciples no longer belong to the world or their context or even themselves. They belong to Christ, the one who calls them to himself. In Pauline terms, 'if anyone is in Christ, he is a new creation; old things have passed away, and look, new things have come' (2 Cor. 5.17). Emphasizing the theme of discipleship promises to help theological ethicists, practical theologians and ministry practitioners to do justice to the lack of fit in the present that results from this newness. So it highlights the accompanying cultural astringency of Christian community and living: 'If the world hates you, understand that it hated me before it hated you' (Jn 15.8). Those whose imaginations are steeped in the language and logic of discipleship are, it is supposed, best prepared to embrace this crucial aspect of Christian identity. David Augsburger puts this well: 'It is said that authentic disciples of Jesus, in following the way of the cross, are already dead, so no one can kill them; they are already citizens of a new regime, so the current regime does not control them.'[27] Such is the appeal of the discipleship motif in thematizing the language of 'permanent dislocation'. This appeal is a significant factor in explaining why those who are serious about the dual challenge of maintaining adequate Christian distinctiveness and attending with due seriousness to Christian formation are turning to the motif of discipleship. Few other images seem as well-calibrated for helping Christians recognize and respond to the reality of their 'permanent dislocation'.

1.2 Discipleship in the post-Christian West

The appeal of the discipleship motif itself helps account for the contemporary turn to discipleship. However, something further needs to be said about why this

---

25. Webster, 'Discipleship and Calling', 134–5.

26. Medi Ann Volpe, *Rethinking Christian Identity: Doctrine and Discipleship* (Oxford: Wiley Blackwell, 2013), 13. For Volpe, this 'more' involves an adequate wrestling with the reality and power of sin – and the resources the Christian story attunes us to, beyond our own efforts – to deal with it.

27. Augsburger, *Dissident Discipleship*, 191.

turn is happening now, at this particular point in the late-modern West. For many, discipleship has become *the* decisive theme that makes sense of the Christian life, upholds the significance of the church and binds together theology and practice in a coherent and comprehensive Christian ethics. While many would not go this far, the widespread interest in discipleship, the resonance of the theme and the prominence it has assumed beyond the bounds of Anabaptist-inspired theology suggest that something makes this historical and cultural moment particularly receptive to it. Indeed, the contemporary turn to discipleship owes its energy to more than the intrinsic appeal of the language and imagery of discipleship in thematizing the 'permanent dislocation' of Christian existence. A specific sense of 'present crisis' adds fuel to the fire, and helps account for why discipleship is so frequently emphasized now. Crucially, there is a convergent sense that the West today has become post-Christian – although the diagnosis of the causes of this and the church's prognosis differ within the discipleship conversation.

Post-Christian is a phrase hovering between different senses. For example, it can suggest moving beyond the historical reality named by Christendom. In many Western societies, the cultural centrality, privilege and influence of the Christian faith, institutions and sensibilities is increasingly a past rather than a present reality. This is tied to more than numbers of church attenders or those claiming Christian affiliation in surveys, which are symptoms of the movement to a post-Christian phase. The cultural historian of religion Callum Brown ambitiously proposes to chart this movement with regard to Great Britain in his *The Death of Christian Britain* (2001). There, Brown narrates 'a story not merely of church decline, but of the end of Christianity as a means by which men and women, as individuals, construct their identities and their sense of "self".'[28] Brown argues that Christianity's loss of traction at this discursive, identity-forming level has happened in a rapid and dramatic way since the 1960s. Further, he proposes that it is this fundamental shift that lies behind the church's decline in terms of institutional affiliation and attendance, intellectual influence in society, functional impact on civil society (whether through government or the 'third sector') and missionary expansion. Many in the contemporary discipleship conversation conceive of the current social context more or less in these terms, although frequently it is the longer, more gradualist narratives of Alasdair MacIntyre and Charles Taylor that are preferred over Brown's thesis of a rapid and dramatic change of direction in late-modern societies.

Writing in a North American context, Rod Dreher, author of *The Benedict Option*, appears to have perfected the art of sounding the alarm about the 'end of Christendom' understood in this sense. No doubt, Dreher's book is a piece of popularism – and one that is already past its zenith. But the ecclesiastical and ethical programme it calls for, as well as the cultural analysis it draws upon to motivate this call, reflects some of the most important trends evident in a surprisingly diverse

---

28. Callum G. Brown, *The Death of Christian Britain: Understanding Secularization, 1800–2000* (London: Routledge, 2001), 2.

array of contemporary theologians, pastors and church leaders. Specifically, Dreher grants great prominence to the language and concept of discipleship as part of a necessary and urgent 'strategy' that Christians and churches must adopt given the apocalyptic crisis into which he believes (late) modern culture is plummeting. The church, Dreher argues, must recover a discipleship-shaped self-understanding. This means becoming a visible counterculture as it renounces and abstains from the corrupt and corrupting social context it finds itself in, 'thickening up' its distinctiveness by retrieving various ancient and medieval practices to flesh out its social and/or geographical isolationism:

> A church that looks and talks and sounds just like the world has no reason to exist. A church that does not emphasize asceticism and discipleship is as pointless as a football coaching staff that doesn't care if its players show up for practice. And though liturgy by itself is not enough, a church that neglects to involve the body in worship is going to find it increasingly difficult to get bodies into services on Sunday morning as America moves further into post-Christianity.[29]

Markedly different in tone and politics, but convergent in rooting the call to discipleship in a diagnosis of the collapse of Christianity's cultural dominance (again in North America) is Lee Camp's *Mere Discipleship*. To be sure, Camp does not regard Christendom's end as yet arrived – at least in the United States. In fact, Camp sees Christianity as deeply entangled with American culture in ways that generate a variety of problems for the church. Specifically, he detects in this entanglement the presence of 'particular ways of thinking about Jesus that obscure (if not set aside) his teaching'.[30] These include the ascendancy of an ends-means rationality that is invoked to excuse thoroughly anti-Christian tactics in pursuit of the high ideals of the Christian faith. Violence and deception are legitimized as the means supposedly necessary to promote 'Christian' ends such as the protection of religious freedom (as they were in the Cold War's international crusade against Communism).[31] Likewise, Camp detects in this entanglement a tendency to separate doctrine and ethics, belief in Christ and following the way of Christ. Rendered as purely interior and spiritual, Christian faith is treated as irrelevant to matters of this-worldly concern.[32] Even more problematically, Camp contends that the widespread assumption in North America is that it is Christianity's 'task to be in control, to run the world, to make things turn out right'.[33] As a result, the defining Christian narrative of 'downward mobility' – in which Christians, like Christ, set aside power and privilege for the sake of others (see, e.g. Phil. 2.5–11; 2 Cor. 8.9) – is stood on its head. In contradiction to the basic Christian intuition

---

29. Dreher, *The Benedict Option*, 121.
30. Camp, *Mere Discipleship*, 26.
31. Camp, *Mere Discipleship*, 41–2.
32. Camp, *Mere Discipleship*, 43–4.
33. Camp, *Mere Discipleship*, 45.

that history – and the very revelation of God – finds its focus in a powerless, crucified Jew in an obscure corner of the Roman Empire, Christendom sees 'the power brokers [as] the only major players in human history'.[34] Acting as salt and light in society requires commandeering and submitting to the powers that be.

Seen in this way, the movement to a post-Christian context can only be a good thing. This is because in Christendom, Camp argues, ' "Christianity" has become a vaccination protecting us from discipleship'.[35] The diagnosis of Christendom's decline therefore comes to take on a different – and more positive – meaning in the hands of those like Camp who hope that its collapse will pave the way for the recovery of true discipleship.[36]

Understood like this, the post-Christian social context of the West may be evaluated more positively and less like a 'crisis'. For example, in *Living Faithfully in a Fragmented World* (1997), Jonathan R. Wilson discerns an opportunity for the church in the social marginalization and demise of the historic power and cultural prestige of Christianity in the West. With Camp, he concedes that 'the church in Western culture is in grave danger of compromising its faithfulness to the gospel'. But he contends that within this danger there is concealed 'a wonderful opportunity for faithful witness to the gospel, as the church reexamines its own life and witness and discovers once again the power of the gospel of Jesus Christ to redeem humanity'.[37] Ian Barns's rendering of the Australian scene likewise highlights the opportunity and challenge of the present social context. He begins by observing the increasing prominence of moral questions 'that go beyond the usual concerns of economic development, distributive justice, and due process' in Australian public policy debate.[38] Examples he cites include questions about Indigenous land rights, euthanasia, the environment and human sexuality. His assessment of the implications of this for the church is worth quoting:

> The re-emergence of such questions presents Christians with new opportunities to give public expression to our spiritual and theological convictions. Such opportunities have been scarce in the predominantly utilitarian culture of postwar Australia. Yet the 'deeper agenda' also poses a major challenge because in this erstwhile 'Christian' country, Christianity is perceived to have long occupied a privileged position from which it has oppressed non-Christian

---

34. Camp, *Mere Discipleship*, 45.

35. Camp, *Mere Discipleship*, 37.

36. Camp is not alone in harbouring such hopes. Malcolm Muggeridge, for example, sees the collapse of the cultural dominance of the church as an opportunity for the church's Lord to appear now free of this worldly trappings. Malcolm Muggeridge, *The End of Christendom* (Grand Rapids: Eerdmans, 1980).

37. Wilson, *Living Faithfully in a Fragmented World*, 1.

38. Ian Barns, 'Towards an Australian Post-Constantinian Public Theology', in *Faith and Freedom: Christian Ethics in a Pluralist Culture*, ed. David Neville and Philip Matthews (Adelaide: ATF Press, 2003), 175.

minorities and coercively imposed its views in areas such as sexual morality. Is it possible for Christians to commend the message of Jesus Christ as a public vision without implying a return to a position of cultural dominance?[39]

According to Barns, the best hope for the church is a discipleship programme that foregrounds Christian distinctiveness and attends to the task of formation: 'the task of renewing the politics of the kingdom … will involve overcoming the habits of Christendom'.[40] In connecting the 'end of Christendom' to a recovery of discipleship, Barns represents a significant strand within the contemporary conversation. He also attests to an emerging consensus that, alongside the intrinsic appeal of the discipleship motif, something about the present situation makes discipleship particularly pertinent to recover and emphasize. Together with the intrinsic appeal of the New Testament discipleship motif, this sense of inhabiting a post-Christian context – however that is defined and evaluated – helps account for the contemporary turn to discipleship. It is this context that frames the need to retrieve and then constructively develop Barth's integration of discipleship in his theology of sanctification.

1.3 Resourcing discipleship from Barth

This book develops the theological significance of discipleship in Barth's theology of sanctification with an eye to its resonance with the contemporary turn to discipleship. My contention is that Barth's richly theological and materially christological rendering of discipleship and sanctification can make a significant contribution to this conversation. Barth's 'turn' to discipleship can resource an intervention in the contemporary discipleship conversation. So how do I propose to investigate and retrieve Barth's 'turn' to discipleship? Constructively, how will I do this in a way that uncovers its potential as a resource for Christian living – especially where this must move not only with but also against and beyond Barth?

In investigating the significance of discipleship in Barth's theology of sanctification, I am picking up on the cues provided by Kimlyn J. Bender in his thorough and careful study of the christological determination of Barth's ecclesiology.[41] Bender suggests that 'future studies of Barth's ecclesiology may well need to address his critical yet undeniable retrieval of themes most generally associated with (though not in every case exclusive to) the free church tradition and shaped by his own Swiss Reformed context'.[42] Among these themes Bender highlights 'Barth's emphasis on *discipleship* as a central aspect of the Christian life'.[43] More, he highlights its inextricable entanglement with the crucial notion of

39. Barns, 'Towards an Australian Post-Constantinian Public Theology', 175–6.
40. Barns, 'Towards an Australian Post-Constantinian Public Theology', 188.
41. Kimlyn J. Bender, *Karl Barth's Christological Ecclesiology* (Aldershot: Ashgate, 2005).
42. Bender, *Karl Barth's Christological Ecclesiology*, 284.
43. Bender, *Karl Barth's Christological Ecclesiology*, 285.

'correspondence' (*Entsprechung*), itself the most obvious verbal marker of Barth's programmatic insistence on conceiving human action as analogical with divine. As Gerald McKenny puts it in his important study of Barth's ethics, *The Analogy of Grace* (2010), 'the *telos* of God's grace is realized, when human beings in their action become the image of God'.[44] More forceful still is Helmut Gollwitzer's summary: 'The gospel ... is aimed toward a bodily, worldly realization. That against which and for which God struggles, according to the gospel, is that against which and for which – with appropriate distance of the creature from the Creator – we, too, must struggle.'[45]

Beginning with Bender's call to attend to free church themes and especially discipleship in Barth – and alert to the centrality of 'correspondence' in his theological ethics – I focus on what Barth says about discipleship, how he says it and how he connects it with the ecclesiology and vision of Christian living that emerges from §66. I do this in order to uncover Barth's underlying theological intuitions as well as his goal in emphasizing discipleship in the way that he does. In this, I am self consciously following John Webster's direction with regard to the study of Barth's moral theology:

> What is required more than anything else is detailed study of Barth's writings which, by close reading, tries to display the structure and logic of his concerns without moving prematurely into making judgements or pressing too early the usefulness (or lack of it) of Barth's work for contemporary moral theology.[46]

I take very seriously Webster's warning about making premature judgements – although my aims in investigating and seeking to retrieve Barth's treatment of discipleship are not purely antiquarian or descriptive. Quite the contrary. I investigate Barth's approach to discipleship with a constructive agenda. I want to establish the extent to which it may provide a resource for Christian living in post-Christian contexts. In keeping with the way theologians like Webster and Oliver Crisp have described the broad and diverse project of theological retrieval, I regard Barth's treatment of discipleship less as a problem to be explained in contemporary terms and more as a resource for speaking into the contemporary conversation.[47] My project therefore is an attempt to do what Webster describes

---

44. Gerald McKenny, *The Analogy of Grace: Karl Barth's Moral Theology* (Oxford: Oxford University Press, 2010), 208.

45. Helmut Gollwitzer, 'The Kingdom of God and Socialism in the Theology of Karl Barth,' in *Karl Barth and Radical Politics*, 2nd edn, ed. George Hunsinger (Eugene: Cascade, 2017), 52.

46. John Webster, *Barth's Moral Theology: Human Action in Barth's Thought* (Grand Rapids: Eerdmans, 1998), 1.

47. See, John Webster, 'Theologies of Retrieval', in *The Oxford Handbook of Systematic Theology*, ed. John Webster et al. (Oxford: Oxford University Press, 2007), 583–99; Oliver D. Crisp, *Retrieving Doctrine: Explorations in Reformed Theology* (Milton Keynes: Paternoster Press, 2010), vii–xiv.

and to 'stand with the Christian past which, precisely because it is foreign to contemporary conventions, can function as an instrument for the enlargement of vision' in the present.

Barth has a richly theological and unexpectedly practical vision of discipleship. The properly theological – and especially christological – character of Barth's vision of discipleship emerges most clearly when it is read in the context of his revision of Calvin's theology of sanctification and with an eye to Luther and Barth's own Lutheran interlocutors. After some preliminary engagement around the the theme of discipleship in Barth and his critics in Chapter 2, I carry out this reading in Chapter 3, employing the motifs George Hunsinger has shown to be operative in structuring Barth's thought. The three motif pairs Hunsinger identifies are: actualism and particularism, objectivism and personalism and realism and rationalism.[48] I trace how each of these motif pairs functions in Barth's account of sanctification to further specify his Christocentrism – which in itself is not adequate as a label for Barth's (or any other) theology, as a number of scholars have argued.[49] To be sure, John Yocum is right to highlight the potential limitations of such 'motif study'. As he puts it, 'expounding Barth in terms of motifs runs the risk of turning attention away from the material dogmatic matters with which Barth's work is centrally concerned'.[50] If the identification of motifs becomes an end in itself, then the danger is not only that they become a distraction from the task of understanding Barth's theology but also that it detaches the criteria of assessment from the substance of his theology. It can incline us, in other words, to focus on and judge Barth's thought according to its form rather than its content. Interesting as that form is, this must be avoided.

I draw on Hunsinger's motifs primarily to specify how Barth's Christocentrism impacts his development of the doctrine of sanctification. At the same time, I resist the temptation to treat the identification of these motifs as an end in itself – as though recognizing their presence and function in Barth's account of sanctification was all there was to be said about it, or worse as though 'the beauty of the internal structure of the *Dogmatics* was its own validation'.[51] I am convinced that recognizing the motifs is a starting point for generating a closer examination of the contours of Barth's account of discipleship. Consequently, I allow them to direct me back to the theological shape, content and texture of Barth's theology of sanctification, which I analyse closely in Chapters 3 and 4. In Chapter 5, I then focus on how discipleship comes to explicitly anchor and give shape to Barth's crucial notion of correspondence in §66. This is a

---

48. George Hunsinger, *How to Read Karl Barth: The Shape of His Theology* (Oxford: Oxford University Press, 1991), chapters 1 and 2.

49. On the inadequacy of 'Christocentricism' by itself as a distinguishing feature of Barth's theology, see Bruce L. McCormack, *Karl Barth's Critically Realist Dialectical Theology: Its Genesis and Development, 1909–1936* (Oxford: Oxford University Press, 1995), 453–5.

50. John Yocum, *Ecclesial Mediation in Karl Barth* (London: Routledge, 2016), xvi.

51. Yocum, *Ecclesial Mediation in Karl Barth*, xvi.

significant innovation and advance within Barth's own theological ethics. As such, my examination of it is the heart of this book. After placing this innovation within the broader arc of the development of Barth's ecclesiology and ethics from *Romans* II to *The Christian Life* in Chapter 6, I devote Chapters 7, 8 and 9 to evaluating the consequences of Barth's integration of discipleship into his theology of sanctification. Specifically, I interrogate the distinctive vision of moral agency, moral activity and moral passivity (or suffering) that emerges in the remainder of §66 and bears fruit in §67 and §68. In Chapters 10 and 11, I turn to the constructive task proper, dwelling on where we may fruitfully work with, against and beyond Barth in harnessing his discipleship-shaped theology of sanctification as a resource in the present context.

Numerous studies have highlighted the historical, political, polemical and interpersonal contexts of Barth's theology. In addition to the need to contextualize Barth's work on discipleship in these terms, its place within his intellectual development must also be reckoned with. Bruce McCormack has rightly alerted all who work on Barth's late (post-1936) theology to the reverberations of Barth's 'correction' of the doctrine of election in *CD* II/2, located as it is *within* his presentation of the doctrine of God and therefore at the head of all God's works *ad extra*.[52] The implications of this 'correction' are a controversial matter in contemporary Anglophone Barth studies. However, its significance is impossible to miss in Barth's revision of sanctification.[53] In §66.2, Barth explicitly brings his understanding of election to bear on his thinking about holiness, with profound consequences.

Notwithstanding the importance of attending to the various contexts of Barth's thinking about sanctification and discipleship, his most pertinent and timely contribution to the contemporary discipleship conversation is when it appears most alien to it. This fundamentally aligns with liberation theologian Gustavo Gutiérrez's observation about Barth's theology more generally: 'The one who

---

52. See, McCormack, *Karl Barth's Critically Realist Dialectical Theology* and 'Grace and Being: The Role of God's Gracious Election in Karl Barth's Theological Ontology', in *Orthodox and Modern: Studies in the Theology of Karl Barth* (Grand Rapids: Baker, 2008), 183–200. For its impact on Barth's ethics, see Paul T. Nimmo, *Being in Action: The Theological Shape of Barth's Ethical Vision* (London: T&T Clark, 2007). For an overview and assessment of its implications, see the interlocking essays in Simon Hattrell, ed. *Election, Barth, and the French Connection: How Pierre Maury Gave a 'Decisive Impetus' to Karl Barth's Doctrine of Election* (Eugene: Pickwick, 2016).

53. One of the fullest – though undoubtedly partisan – statements of the controversy over how to understand the impact of Barth's 'correction' of election is provided by Hunsinger, who concludes that both 'the traditionalists and the revisionists ... would agree that for Barth, God determines himself in pre-temporal election, and that when God does so, it has far-reaching consequences not only for humankind but also for God himself'. George Hunsinger, *Reading Barth with Charity: A Hermeneutical Proposal* (Grand Rapids: Baker Academic, 2015), 137–8.

starts with heaven is sensitive to those who live in the hell of this earth; whereas the one who begins with earth is blind to the situation of exploitation upon which the earth is built.'[54] Barth's treatment of discipleship has the potential to contribute to the contemporary discipleship conversation precisely *because* it is so resolutely theological – and only in that way practical. More concretely, it is resolutely christological. As Barth sees it, the call to discipleship is primarily about Jesus Christ – and only in that way is it also subsequently about the church and Christian living. To put it in Webster's terms, there is a 'coinherence of theology and ethics' in Barth's mature thought, which provides the key to appreciating the potential of Barth's treatment of discipleship. The presence of this 'coinherence' alerts us to an important theological intuition latent in the way Barth seeks to integrate the traditional, magisterial Reformation emphasis on sanctification in Christ with the more contemporary, Anabaptist-inspired focus on the active life of discipleship. That intuition is that at the centre of both, joining them together, is the determinative, directing and humanizing presence of Christ, the risen and living Lord of his people. Discipleship – and sanctification as a whole – is about Christ. He is its living centre and must always remain so. This means that it is only insofar as discipleship is about Christ that it is about those who are awakened by the Spirit to 'correspond' to him in their identity and activity. All of this throws into a markedly different light the typical concerns of the contemporary discipleship conversation – such as the relation between church and world, the distinctiveness of Christian community or behaviour and the formation of Christian character.

---

54. Gustavo Gutiérrez, 'Theology from the Underside of History', in *The Power of the Poor in History*, trans. Robert R. Barr (New York: Orbis Books, 1983), 203.

Chapter 2

BARTH AND HIS CRITICS ON DISCIPLESHIP

In this chapter, I provide the necessary orientation for my investigation of discipleship in Barth's theology of sanctification. I do this in three ways. First, I locate Barth's 'turn' to discipleship in the context of the distinctive theology of sanctification he articulates in *Church Dogmatics* IV/2 §66. Second, I establish the need to further examine this 'turn' by surveying the most influential treatments of Barth on sanctification. I show that no major critic – whether sympathetic or hostile towards Barth's thinking on sanctification – has given adequate attention to the presence in and positive significance of discipleship in this context. Third, emerging from this, I review some important arguments for and against listening to Barth's voice on discipleship, considering both the fact that his contribution appears to be overshadowed by Bonhoeffer's and the difficulties posed by his own problematic discipleship, both politically and interpersonally.

2.1 Discipleship in Barth's theology of sanctification?

At the midpoint of his treatment of sanctification in §66, Barth picks up and extensively develops the New Testament language and concept of discipleship. This is a sudden and in some ways unexpected turn on Barth's part, for it appears to involve a departure from the magisterial Reformation sources that inform his approach up until this point. However, the theology of sanctification Barth articulates in §66 has already been reworking and revising the doctrine derived from these sources – even before the motif of discipleship gains prominence within it. Nevertheless, it remains recognizably attuned to the Reformed accent on the Christian's participation in the reconciling work of Christ, even as it also continues to draw on distinctively Lutheran concepts and expressions. Before I proceed, therefore, it is worth providing a brief outline of §66.

Barth begins in §66.1 with the question of the appropriate relationship between sanctification and justification. As such, he directly addresses the equivocation that Protestant theology has frequently displayed with respect to sanctification. Should justification be given precedence in order to safeguard the divine initiative in salvation or should sanctification be given precedence to foreground the divinely wrought transformation of human life that results from salvation? Significantly,

Barth takes the unusual order in which Calvin treated the two doctrines within the *Institutes* as inspiration for a proposed dialectical, dynamic approach to coordinating the two doctrines. He insists that justification and sanctification are both united by being grounded in Christ and the reconciliation of the world effected in him (501–3), although they name 'two different aspects of the one event of salvation' (503) – neither of which can be reduced to or explained in terms of the other. Drawing on the language of Chalcedon, Barth argues that 'justification and sanctification must be distinguished, but they cannot be divided or separated' (505). This reflects the overarching emphasis of *CD* IV/2 on the exaltation of humanity in Christ, which corresponds to the humiliation of God that dominates IV/1 (505):

> As God turns to sinful man, the conversion of the latter to God cannot be lacking. And the conversion of man to God presupposes at every point and in every form that God turns to him in free grace. That the two are inseparable means that the doctrine of justification has to be described already as the way from sin to the right of God and man, and therefore as the way from death to life, which *God* goes with him. And it means for the doctrine of sanctification that it has to show that it is really with *man* that God is on this way as He reconciles the world with Himself in Jesus Christ (emphasis in original).

At this point, Barth again invokes Calvin in order to offer a twofold answer to the question of the relation between justification and sanctification, in which the relative precedence of each doctrine depends on the perspective adopted (507–11).

In §66.2, Barth explores how it is possible to speak – as the Bible does – of God's 'saints' or 'holy ones', given the Bible's equally firm insistence that there is only one 'holy one' and that even Christians are 'not yet this by a long way' (513). In this context, Barth invokes his famous doctrine of election, arguing that it is Christ's status as the electing God and the elect human being that ensures the singular holiness displayed in his personal history also represents and includes human beings. Sanctification is thus concentrated in Christ, and therefore entirely relative to him at the same time as it becomes a reality as an event in the reconciliation achieved in his person and work (514–15): 'Sanctification, the action of the God who is always holy in His mercy, the activity in which He crosses this gulf, does indeed involve the creation of a new form of existence for man in which he can live as the loyal covenant-partner of God who is well-pleasing to and blessed by Him.' Here, Barth develops the basis of sanctification in Christ by working carefully with Calvin's doctrine of the *participatio Christi*, the fountainhead of both justification and sanctification in *Institutes* III. Without letting go of Luther's insight that the holiness of Christians is always 'alien' (*aliena sanctitate*) and never their 'proper' (*propria*) possession, he follows Calvin's lead in turning to Pneumatology at this point (522):

> The Holy Spirit is [Christ] Himself in the action in which He reveals and makes Himself known to other men as the One He is, placing them under

His direction, claiming them as His own, as the witnesses of His holiness. The Holy Spirit is the living Lord Jesus Christ Himself in the work of the sanctification of His particular people in the world, of His community and all its members.

Specifically, he portrays the experience of sanctification in terms of the Spirit's work of rousing or 'disturbing' the slumber of sinners (524–30), drawing on the portrayal of sin in terms of sloth, misery and inertia in §65. This disturbance is not only negative, an interruption and limitation of the sin and sinful tendency all humans are captive to; it is also positive, taking shape in a new capacity and permission to lift themselves up and walk in freedom (530–3).

In §66.3 Barth decisively takes up the theme of discipleship, which he had mentioned fleetingly in §66.1 and §66.2. As he does this, he exchanges Calvin for Bonhoeffer as his chief dialogue partner, labouring to emphasize the dynamism and personal implication of Christ in our sanctification: '"Follow me" is the substance of the call in the power of which Jesus makes men His saints' (533). The final three subsections examine different aspects of the existential realization in human life of the call to discipleship by which Christ sanctifies his people – the awakening to conversion it effects (§66.4), the active life of good works it sponsors (§66.5) and the crowning glory Christ's holy ones are privileged to share in as those who take up and bear the cross (§66.6). Such is Barth's theology of sanctification in broad outline.

For all that Barth scholarship is comfortable to acknowledge the novelty of this theology of sanctification, the prominence of discipleship within it is only occasionally acknowledged and even less frequently treated with seriousness as an integral aspect of it. Yet it must not be overlooked; for Barth's approach to the theme of discipleship labours to display its conceptual and practical unity with his innovative account of sanctification. In this, Barth avoids the danger of allowing the discipleship theme to eclipse or swallow all others. As Webster observes, 'the motif of discipleship is not the only motif in the theology of the Christian life, and should not be extracted from its place in the wider scope of God's dealings with humankind as creator, reconciler and perfecter.[1] Discipleship, like all theological language – including the biblical imagery about the church and Christian life – is not automatically transparent to the reality of the divine work of which it speaks or to its concrete and personal point of focus in Jesus Christ. It requires 'evangelization.'[2] As we will see, a certain self-consciousness about this on Barth's part is crucial to his careful integration of the discipleship motif with a more Pauline or Johannine approach to sanctification in terms of union with or participation in Christ.

---

1. Webster, 'Discipleship and Calling', 135.
2. I borrow the notion of 'evangelizing' theological language from Robert W. Jenson, *Systematic Theology Volume 1: The Triune God* (Oxford: Oxford University Press, 1997), Chapter 6.

2.2 The critics on discipleship in Barth

It is possible to overstate the significance of Barth's 'turn' to discipleship within his revision of sanctification. Some have posited a 'Free Church turn' in Barth's late theology, treating his emphasis on discipleship in §66 as reflective of radical new developments in his Christology, ethics and ecclesiology.[3] However, George Hunsinger has rightly drawn attention to the substantial continuity within Barth's theological vision of politics, arguing with reference to Barth's political theology in particular that 'there is nothing even in tendency in Barth's later writings in which he approaches a sectarian Protestant doctrine of the state and that, in fact, the tendency of his thought runs very much in the opposite direction'.[4] With regard to those who read Barth's turn to discipleship as indicative of a movement from a symbolic Christology to a more fully human rendering of Jesus,[5] Hunsinger admits that CD IV sees the full flowering of the 'general tendency for Barth to move in the direction of a narrative Christology, or at least a Christology with strong narrative aspects'. But he disputes the characterization of Barth's earlier Christology as symbolic, identifying elements of a 'narrative turn' as early as II/2 and concluding that moments like §66.3 are 'a special instance and consequence of the narrative turn in his Christology rather than something fundamentally new in its own right'.[6] Nevertheless, this 'special instance and consequence' of Barth's narrative turn calls for closer examination.

In his fuller examination of Barth's treatment of sanctification, Hunsinger strongly accents the debt Barth owes to the thinking of the Magisterial Reformers, Luther and Calvin, on this topic. He highlights Barth's reliance on their emphasis on union with Christ.[7] For Hunsinger, Barth's chief innovation lies in how he brings together themes traditionally associated with one or the other of the Lutheran and Reformed approaches, coordinating them in relation to Christ. Specifically, Hunsinger sees in §66 an attempt to bring together Luther's emphasis on the Christian's identity in Christ as *simil iustus et peccator* with Calvin's emphasis on the simultaneity of justification and sanctification as 'benefits' that together flow from our basic *participatio Christi*.[8] In Hunsinger's judgement, this attempt is unsuccessful. This is because it results in an apparent inability on Barth's part

---

3. See, for example, John Howard Yoder, 'The Basis of Barth's Social Ethics' (1978) in Yoder, *Karl Barth and the Problem of War, and Other Essays on Barth*, ed. Mark Thiessen Nation (Eugene: Cascade, 2003), 133–48.

4. George Hunsinger, 'Karl Barth and the Politics of Sectarian Protestantism: A Dialogue with John Howard Yoder', in *Disruptive Grace: Studies in the Theology of Karl Barth* (Grand Rapids: Eerdmans, 2000), 119.

5. Yoder, 'The Basis of Barth's Social Ethics', 140–1.

6. Hunsinger, 'Karl Barth and the Politics of Sectarian Protestantism', 120n19.

7. George Hunsinger, 'A Tale of Two Simultaneities: Justification and Sanctification in Calvin and Barth', *Zeitschrift für dialektische Theologie* 37 (2001): 316–38.

8. Hunsinger, 'A Tale of Two Simultaneities', 325.

to take seriously the possibility of gradual, progressive growth in grace. Indeed, even if Barth were to explicitly allow for such growth and progress, Hunsinger contends, it would be inconsistent on the terms he establishes within §66.[9]

Curiously, Hunsinger's explanation of how Barth strives to hold together the Lutheran and Calvinian emphases by appeal to the personal presence of Christ looks away from §66 at the decisive point.[10] Instead of attending to Barth's turn to the motif of discipleship, Hunsinger appeals to a broader consideration of how Christ's 'yesterday, today, and forever' (Heb. 13.8) are united with and relate to one another. This is illuminating as far as it goes. And Hunsinger's summation expresses concisely the reservations of many with regard to the supposed eclipse of ethics (and ecclesiology) by soteriology in Barth:

> That there is only one work of salvation, that it has been accomplished by Jesus Christ, that it is identical with his person, and that being perfect it needs no supplementation but only acknowledgement, reception, participation, anticipation, and proclamation for what it is – these are the great themes of Barth's soteriology. We have been made to participate in Christ by grace, Barth maintains, before we ever do so actively by faith. … His prior and total inclusion of us in himself and in his work by grace is precisely what we actively and properly acknowledge when he then dwells in us by faith.[11]

For Hunsinger, this represents the theological *cul de sac* of the Magisterial Reformation approach to sanctification in terms of participation in Christ's finished work – raised to a new level of consistency. Hunsinger contends that this leaves the Christians with nowhere to go and no progress to make. Following Luther, the existential reception of sanctification in Barth's thinking is not a 'more and more' – some kind of 'process of gradual growth' – rather it is an 'again and again' – something that comes to us 'continually from without, and ever anew'.[12] Although he admits that Barth could and occasionally does speak of the holy life as a matter of growth (he cites IV/2, 566), Hunsinger contends that 'Barth left a large logical space at this point'.[13]

Hunsinger is right to highlight the determinative status of Christ when it comes to Barth's vision of sanctified moral agency and activity. This is crucial to Barth's revision of sanctification. It is a christological revision before it is anything else. But this characterization is incomplete. The rest of the story needs to be told on the basis of closer attention to §66 in its context in *Church Dogmatics* IV/2. Telling this fuller story is the substantial burden of the coming chapters. To anticipate: in *CD* IV/2, Barth describes this determinative presence of Christ in terms of his

---

9. Hunsinger, 'A Tale of Two Simultaneities', 337–8.
10. Hunsinger, 'A Tale of Two Simultaneities', 330–4.
11. Hunsinger, 'A Tale of Two Simultaneities', 333.
12. Hunsinger, 'A Tale of Two Simultaneities', 334.
13. Hunsinger, 'A Tale of Two Simultaneities', 337.

living 'direction' (*Weisung*) of his people. *Weisung* usually means 'instruction' or 'direction', and it is frequently employed in a military context. But Barth uses it to mean both Christ's (objective) movement towards his people on the basis of his resurrection as well as the corresponding (subjective) movement in which he mobilizes, energizes and directs them in the power of the Spirit. Barth discusses this 'direction' in §64.4 and then unfolds its consequences in §66. I will demonstrate that Barth's appropriation of the idiom of discipleship (e.g. call, following) is the capstone of this depiction of Christ's moral 'direction'. Contrary to his own insights into Barth's narrative turn, Hunsinger fails to reckon with the specific narrative of Christology that Barth draws on to coordinate the Lutheran and the Calvinian themes in §66. Symptomatic of this, he overlooks the prominence of discipleship in Barth's treatment of sanctification. He subsequently neglects the way in which Barth's vision of discipleship – and therefore of the active life of genuine, free, human agency elevated to covenant partnership with God – belies any construction of participation in Christ that leaves no room for human activity. Without doubt, God's grace in Christ circumscribes and shapes human agency and activity as Barth envisages it. But grace does not obliterate human agency and activity. Rather, it calls forth this agency and activity. This, I will argue, is one of the chief contributions of Barth's integration of discipleship and sanctification.[14]

A very different conclusion from that drawn by Hunsinger is advanced by Daniel Migliore. Earlier in the same edition of *Zeitschrift fur Dialektische Theologie* as Hunsinger's paper, Migliore argues that the motif of participation is the central theme of Barth's doctrine of sanctification.[15] He argues this in response to the very question that looms over the reading of §66.3 that I develop in this book: 'In what sense and to what extent is this paragraph a coherent whole? What is its unifying theme?'[16] Unlike Hunsinger, however, Migliore explicitly addresses the theme of discipleship. He notes that '§66.3 is the only section of the paragraph on sanctification that does not explicitly mention the theme of *participatio Christi*'. Nevertheless, Migliore goes on to claim, 'it is precisely this section … that sets the distinctive course of Barth's understanding of participation in Christ.[17] Far from undermining human agency and the possibility of the ethical, Migliore underscores the way in which Barth's emphasis on discipleship actually wards off possible misconceptions about sanctification and establishes its ethical character:

---

14. In addition, this integration of discipleship and sanctification provides further specification to and grounding for the kinds of claims advanced by Michael Bartolomaeus about Barth's cheerful use of the language of growth seen through the lens of the Christian life as an ongoing encounter with Christ in §67.2; Michael Bartholomaeus, 'The Place of Growth in the Theology of Karl Barth', *International Journal of Systematic Theology* 21.2 (2019): 157–81.

15. Daniel L. Migliore, '*Participatio Christi*: the Central Theme of Barth's Doctrine of Sanctification', *Zeitschrift für dialektische Theologie* 37 (2001): 286–307.

16. Migliore, '*Participatio Christi*', 288.

17. Migliore, '*Participatio Christi*', 291.

> By moving directly from his initial discussion of sanctification as *participatio Christi* in §66.2 to the theme of the 'call to discipleship' in §66.3, Barth deliberately steers away from all speculative, privatistic, or quietistic interpretations of sanctification. Thus §66.3 serves to underscore the ethical aspect of participation in Christ, speaking of it in terms of the call of Jesus to the new freedom, new obedience, and new service of discipleship. In brief, Barth chooses not to define the Christian life as determined primarily by sacramental rites, mystical practices, or moral codes. Instead, he defines participation in Christ in terms of being personally addressed by the living Lord and being called to free, responsible, and mature discipleship.[18]

Migliore is right to point out that in §66 discipleship defines participation in a manner that is personal and ethical rather than sacramental, mystical or moralistic. When the role of discipleship in Barth's vision of sanctification is taken seriously, it is possible to understand his emphasis on participation as securing, delimiting and ultimately liberating human agency and activity.

Despite appreciating the positive attention Migliore gives Barth's turn to discipleship in §66.3, my proposal differs from his in four ways. First, discipleship is even more integral to Barth's theology of sanctification than Migliore allows. This is the converse of his point that discipleship speaks of participation. If discipleship is the form of participation – itself a unifying thread running through Barth's entire account of sanctification – then sanctification is already implicitly discipleship-shaped. This is not just a matter of semantics. As I show in Chapter 3, Barth's turn to discipleship takes us to the heart of how Barth sees himself to be revising sanctification, deploying both Calvin and Luther's insights in a way that is faithful to – yet moves beyond – either Reformer's theology of sanctification. Second, discipleship provides the positive substance of Barth's vision of the free and active 'direction' Christ gives his disciples and their correspondence to him in freedom. According to Migliore, the theological significance of discipleship in Barth's account is primarily polemical. It functions to ward off possible misunderstandings, but it has little positive content of its own. In contrast to this, I demonstrate in Chapter 4 that discipleship has positive as well as polemical significance for Barth. Third, as I establish in Chapter 5, the logic of discipleship has structural significance for Barth's vision of human agency, action and suffering as analogous to Christ's. Migliore moves on too rapidly from identifying how Barth's stress on discipleship establishes the ethical character of sanctification over the alternatives. The bulk of his discussion of discipleship is devoted to Barth's treatment of the 'awakening to conversion' in §66.4. What is more, while he admits that discipleship gives decisive form to participation, Migliore hardly mentions it outside of his discussion of §66.3. In particular, he fails to develop its role in Barth's exploration of 'the dignity of the cross' in §66.6. There is far more at stake, theologically, in discipleship than Migliore appears to realize. Fourth, discipleship

---

18. Migliore, '*Participatio Christi*', 292.

has more far-reaching implications for Barth's vision of the church and Christian living – both in §66 and in IV/2 more widely – than Migliore recognizes. In keeping with its structuring role with regard to the correspondence between divine and human freedom, discipleship looms large in the account of moral agency underpinning Barth's treatment of conversion in §66.4 (as we will see in Chapter 7) as well as in Barth's vision of moral activity in §66.5 (see Chapter 8) and his dynamic evaluation of moral suffering in §66.6 (see Chapter 9).

In arguing for a higher view of the significance of discipleship in §66, my proposal also diverges from two major attempts to identify the positive import of this turn within Barth's theology of sanctification – those of Katherine Sonderegger and Bruce McCormack, respectively.[19] Specifically, my thesis differs from what is explicit in Sonderegger's reading of Barth on sanctification and implicit in McCormack's. In different ways, both see Barth equivocating between an emphasis on the reality of human freedom and an emphasis on its alienness and relativity to Christ. They both also propose that Barth's view be revised or supplemented in order to do justice to human freedom and the integrity of human agency. And they both do this in ways that strive to respect what they regard as the foundational Christocentric insight Barth develops. For Sonderegger, this insight must be supplemented by a robust vision of sanctified freedom sponsored by Pneumatology. Although, this pneumatological supplement need not displace Christology: 'the work and Lordship of the Holy Spirit within us – our sanctification – [is] the Almighty God claiming and ruling us in a "second time in a very different way"'.[20] Similarly, McCormack's claims about a possible rapprochement with Wesleyanism (albeit a Wesleyanism stripped of metaphysics) insist on their consistency with his christocentricity. Characteristically, McCormack performs his revision *within* his reading of Barth rather than subsequent to it.

I now turn to a closer examination of Sonderegger's treatment. Sonderegger attends to the partially submerged and only fleetingly visible language of 'impartation' (*die Mitteilung*) in Barth's theology of sanctification. According to Sonderegger, *die Mitteilung* is the verbal and conceptual link between the Christology and the implied theological anthropology of IV/2:

> Indeed, it may be too small a thing to say that 'impartation' bears the load of the doctrine of sanctification. More justly, we might dare to say that 'impartation' bears the load, in Barth's doctrine, of the very Reality, the *Sache* of Christ, His Holy Presence and His direction, His Radiance, His revelation, His Spirit and outstretched arm.[21]

---

19. Katherine Sonderegger, 'Sanctification as Impartation in the Doctrine of Karl Barth', *Zeitschrift für dialektische Theologie* 37 (2001): 308–15. Bruce L. McCormack, 'Sanctification after Metaphysics: Karl Barth in Conversation with John Wesley's Conception of "Christian Perfection"', in *Sanctification: Explorations in Theology and Practice*, ed. Kelly M. Kapic (Downers Grove: InterVarsity Press, 2014), 103–24.

20. Sonderegger, 'Sanctification as Impartation', 315.

21. Sonderegger, 'Sanctification as Impartation', 309.

Sonderegger reads §66 attentively. While the language of discipleship remains out of focus in her treatment, the image could be said to sponsor her entire proposal. The vision of the human agent for which she contends – responding and corresponding to Christ, authoritatively called by him and authentically following after him – closely aligns with the figure of the disciple. She argues that 'to understand impartation is to grasp ... the presence, history, and outworking of Christ with his own'.[22] According to Sonderegger, *die Metteilung* speaks in one breath of two things. On the one hand, it speaks of the sovereign and determinative reality and agency of Christ – the true human being, unique in his holiness. On the other, it speaks of the accompanying reality and agency of the people he chooses not to be without, those who are included with, participate in and actively respond to him. Consequently, *die Mitteilung* appears to be but another way to talk about the reality named in discipleship.

Importantly, Sonderegger contends that 'we must be struck by the radical departure Barth takes from his Reformed household'.[23] As evidence for this 'departure', she highlights the strong statements that can be found in both past and present Reformed theologies about the reality of holiness, gradually developed by human effort with the assistance of the Spirit. She goes on to discern a methodological proximity to Schleiermacher in the possibility that in his doctrine of sanctification, Barth may ultimately 'use and echo Reformed doctrine while reshaping or evacuating [its] meaning'.[24] In doing this, she countenances the possibility that far from a Reformed vision par excellence, Barth's discipleship-shaped account of sanctification effects a decisive turn away from the Reformed vision – under cover of perpetuating it!

Developing this insight, Sonderegger connects the conceptual weight-bearing role of impartation in Barth's account of salvation to Barth's dialectical understanding of the doctrine. This, she contends, is the significance of his commendation of Bonhoeffer and his theme of discipleship, especially when considered in conjunction with his programmatic treatment of 'The Direction [*die Weisung*] of the Son' in §64.4: 'To be sanctified ... is to have an action imparted to us: we are commanded to obey a directive, and we rise up from our sloth and misery to begin carrying it out'.[25] Barth's vision of sanctification stands at the intersection of actualism, indirectness and passivity. For Barth, human agency cannot compete with the utterly sovereign divine agency operative in Christ. He calls and directs. We follow – with the concreteness, directness and activity that discipleship demands. Nevertheless, Sonderegger detects irresolution and equivocation here, which she traces to a neglect on Barth's part of the work of the Spirit.[26] Ultimately, rather than being upheld, Sonderegger suggests that

22. Sonderegger, 'Sanctification as Impartation', 309.
23. Sonderegger, 'Sanctification as Impartation', 310.
24. Sonderegger, 'Sanctification as Impartation', 310.
25. Sonderegger, 'Sanctification as Impartation', 312.
26. Sonderegger, 'Sanctification as Impartation', 312–15.

human agency is qualified and threatened by Barth's relentless insistence on the alienness of sanctification: 'Our sanctification is not a repetition, or appropriation, or disposition towards holiness, but rather only a following, an acknowledgment, a correspondence by sinners, standing under the Word in alien sanctification'.[27] I would say that this qualification and relativization of human agency with respect to the alien sanctification embodied in Christ is not an undervaluing of human agency in the power of the Spirit; instead, it bestows on human beings the proper dignity and value we have as covenant partners following after their Master.

A second positive assessment of Barth's turn to discipleship – and apparent turn away from a more traditional Reformed understanding of sanctification – is provided by Bruce McCormack in his essay, 'Sanctification After Metaphysics'. McCormack suggests that Barth's revision of sanctification moves him close to John Wesley. Specifically, McCormack argues that Barth approximates Wesley's notion of 'entire sanctification' – albeit in a post-metaphysical way. Granting full play to the dialectical character of Barth's account of sanctification, he acknowledges its contrast with Wesley's vision of sanctification as a kind of divine surgery, a work of God in the individual, in which the soul is cleansed of the contagion of original sin and liberated from its power. McCormack demonstrates that sanctification for Barth is far more Christocentric:

> For him, the 'new creation' of which Paul speaks is something that happens in Christ. It does not first need to be 'applied' to us before it can be effective. It is already effective in that it takes place in him. We need only be awakened to its truth and efficacy, so that we can begin to live from and to it.[28]

Like Sonderegger, McCormack concedes that Barth's view raises questions: if sanctification is already effective in Christ rather than by virtue of its application to us, does not the human agent (and the distinctive work of the Spirit) disappear, submerged completely in Christology? McCormack forcefully puts the problem of how to square Barth's strongly objectivist and Christocentric approach – grounded as it is in God's decisive, unilateral and all-embracing decision in election – with the value and reality of Christian living and agency: 'Now, such an answer does raise questions about the significance of the Christian life. Why should it matter that we be awakened to faith and obedience in this life if, as those so awakened, we have no future? If it is only as those raised in Christ that we have a future?'[29] Although McCormack does not particularly develop the connection, the prominence of the language and imagery of following Christ, with its clear active character and implicit recognition of the disciple's own real (albeit responsive) agency, could be read as further evidence of a convergence between Barth and Wesleyanism.

---

27. Sonderegger, 'Sanctification as Impartation', 314.
28. McCormack, 'Sanctification after Metaphysics', 104.
29. McCormack, 'Sanctification after Metaphysics', 116.

Curiously, for all McCormack's seriousness about the Christocentric constitution of identity – Christian identity in this essay, divine identity in his work on the significance of Barth's 'correction' of the doctrine of election in II/2[30] – he comes close to conflating the Christian's new self with Christ:

> Psychologically considered, the person awakened to faith by the power of the Holy Spirit is no longer 'in control' of his life; he has surrendered control to Another. He is now made a witness to his true self in Christ. Ontologically, his true being, his new being, exists outside of himself. His being and existence is, henceforth, 'eccentric'.[31]

The Christian's (new) self threatens to displace Christ in this formulation. To be sure, there is an appropriate dialectic between the relativity of Christian sanctification to Christ and its reality in the human reflection it finds in Spirit-awakened persons. Left unqualified, however, McCormack threatens to purchase the integrity of the human agent at the expense of the divine. Ultimately, without further attention to the prominence of discipleship in Barth's theology of sanctification, McCormack has no consistent means to insist on the reality of human freedom while upholding its relativity to Christ. It is hard to see, for example, how Christ's act remains his own and does not 'become ours' (as Sonderegger observes of Schleiermacher's vision)[32] when McCormack formulates the significance of Christian living in this way: 'Every time a Christian achieves, by the grace of God and in faith, victory over temptation, a signpost is erected in this world of the world to come.'[33] Notwithstanding the equivocation built into the image of a 'signpost', this vision of Christian living suggests a very strong rendering of the extent to which human action can anticipate the eschaton. Even if McCormack does not intend this, a direct identity rather than an indirect analogy between divine and human holiness haunts such an unguarded formulation.

I do not dissent from either Sonderegger or McCormack in seeing Barth's approach to sanctification as dialectical. Indeed, as Webster has shown, the dialectical tension between divine and human agency or action is an enduring preoccupation of Barth's moral theology.[34] It is evident from *Der Römerbrief* to *The Christian Life*. However, I will demonstrate that the image and logic of discipleship plays a stabilizing role in Barth's theology of sanctification – explicitly so in §66.6 but implicitly before this. The dialectic here is not animated by an outright contradiction that calls for supplementing – whether by an account of human freedom or of the work of the Spirit developed at a remove from Christ.

---

30. See, for example, McCormack, 'Grace and Being', 183–200.
31. McCormack, 'Sanctification After Metaphysics', 117.
32. Sonderegger, 'Sanctification as Impartation', 313.
33. McCormack, 'Sanctification after Metaphysics', 122.
34. John Webster, *Barth's Earlier Theology: Four Studies* (London: T&T Clark, 2005), vii–viii.

Instead, it is Barth's appropriation of the motif of discipleship that allows him to embrace the paradox of sanctification. Holiness belongs (*propria*) to Christ uniquely and decisively. At the same time, it belongs (*aliena*) to Christians insofar as our identity and activity are relative to him, depending upon and receiving their reality in him – not only as we passively participate in the true human who represents and includes us *de iure*, but also as we are awoken to this and come to actively participate in him *de facto*. Christ's disciples are one with him – they are the people he freely chooses and calls to accompany him. Yet they always follow after him – responding to his lordly direction and corresponding to his freedom.

Whatever our assessment of the merits of these various proposals for and against Barth's turn to discipleship in §66.3, its significance evidently demands closer examination. As surprising as Barth's turn to discipleship appears on the surface, I will argue that it is thoroughly integrated with sanctification as he understands it. Both sanctification and discipleship are defined and shaped in relation to Christ in carefully specified ways. In fact, I will show that Barth's revision of sanctification in the early subsections of §66 provides the conceptual scaffolding for his deployment of the discipleship motif in §66.3. What is more, Barth's intensive and explicit engagement with Calvin and other Reformed sources in §66.1 and §66.2 does not simply precede this moment only be set aside when it arrives. Rather, it provides the impetus and raw materials for his turn to discipleship. Barth's revision of sanctification, it turns out, is already discipleship-shaped – well before discipleship is explicitly mentioned. A corollary to this is that Barth's turn to discipleship is not an alien addition to or turn away from Reformed thinking about sanctification. Rather, it is a heightening of what he saw as its distinctively *Reformed* seriousness about the ethical implications of the Reformation emphasis on divine initiative and action. Barth makes this point directly in *The Theology of John Calvin*. There, he characterizes the specifically Reformed branch of the Reformation as an 'ethical reformation'. In that context, he describes Calvin's contribution in particular as an intensive effort to answer the Renaissance question of human life and ethical action on Reformation premises about sovereignty and divine action: 'Just because Calvin was so much an ethicist, he had to be such a strong dogmatician. His own Reformed, ethical reformation had to raise the question what we are to actually think of that which actually takes place in time, in the world, in life. His concept of God ... was Calvin's own answer.'[35] If this is so, then it is hardly surprising that Barth does not leave discipleship behind as he continues to develop his theology of sanctification in §66.4, §66.5 and §66.6. Discipleship decisively shapes what he says in those subsections about conversion, work and 'bearing the cross'.

---

35. Karl Barth, *The Theology of John Calvin*, trans. Geoffrey W. Bromiley (Grand Rapids: Eerdmans, 1995), 118.

2.3 Bonhoeffer and Barth's 'turn' to discipleship

At this point, it is worth stating the significance of my thesis against the backdrop of the contemporary enthusiasm for discipleship and its relative neglect in the literature on Barth's theology of sanctification. This will lead to a consideration of two objections – the first in this section, the second in the next.

Three potential contributions of Barth's turn to the language and imagery of discipleship can be identified. First, in seeking to take following Jesus seriously Barth strives to shape his theology of sanctification in a way that is explicitly biblical. Barth is committed to taking his cues from the way the New Testament uses the language of discipleship. In fact, he is so committed to this that at the beginning of §66.3 he resists the specific term 'discipleship' – as indicating a status or nature that might allow the being of disciples to be understood apart from an active relationship to Christ, the living, dynamic and personal centre of their being (534): 'We are dealing with what is obviously on the New Testament view an event that cannot be enclosed in a general concept'. Instead, Barth prefers to speak of the call, instruction or 'direction' (*Weisung*), and sending out of Christ's disciples. In doing so, he emphasizes its character as an event and encounter. As a result, Barth refuses to allow being a disciple or responding to Christ's call to become something invisible or intangible – a pietistic matter of mere private and inward devotion, for example.[36] Barth insists that the response of disciples to Christ's call must manifest itself in visible, active obedience to Christ, self-denial and resistance to idolatry and ideology. This biblical, and typically Barthian, emphasis on active relationships rather than metaphysical states or natures both feeds into his turn to discipleship and highlights the value of his seriousness about this theme. Barth is not interested in discipleship because it is a watchword of a contemporary trend in theology. If anything, he anticipates this trend – and, in an indirect way, influences it. Barth sees in the language and imagery of discipleship the potential to help theology and ethics to grapple with the concrete, dynamic and determinative reality of Jesus Christ – as a person rather than a principle – and to follow this into an equally concrete, dynamic and christologically determined rendering of the church and Christian life in terms of active response and correspondence to God's free action in Christ.

---

36. On Barth's critique of pietism in his *Romans* period, see Eberhard Busch, *Karl Barth and the Pietists: The Young Karl Barth's Critique of Pietism and Its Response*, trans. Daniel W. Bloesch (Downers Grove: InterVarsity Press, 2004). Acknowledging the presence and force of this critique, Christian Collins Winn argues for an underlying continuity that reflects the overall positive influence of pietism on Barth's thought; see, Christian T. Collins Winn, *'Jesus Is Victor!': The Significance of the Blumhardts for the Theology of Karl Barth* (Eugene: Pickwick, 2009), especially chapter 5. Certainly, in his later theology – and particularly in his treatment of sanctification – Barth appears to be involved with 'taking up the pietists' concern' but speaking of it 'in a *different* way', as Busch remarks in his article on 'Pietism' in *The Westminster Handbook of Karl Barth*, 163.

Second, Barth's approach to discipleship is unapologetically theological. Discipleship takes its place within a broader theology of sanctification for Barth. For all its prominence, discipleship does not displace other important themes and images in Barth's handling of sanctification. In this, he shows himself alert to the danger of so magnifying discipleship as to eclipse the properly theological character of ecclesiology and ethics. That is to say, in pursuing an integration of his theology of sanctification with his treatment of discipleship, rather than simply shearing off sanctification – or its traditional dominant images of union with Christ and life in Christ – he sets discipleship in dynamic relation to them. As a result, Barth's discipleship-shaped theology of sanctification shows itself alert to the caution sounded by Webster: 'the motif of discipleship is not the only motif in the theology of the Christian life, and should not be extracted from its place in the wider scope of God's dealings with humankind as creator, reconciler and perfecter'.[37]

Put positively, Barth's placement of discipleship in its wider theological context also enables it to do its proper work. Specifically, the way Barth deploys the discipleship motif brings his revision of sanctification to its climax and gives it its distinctive shape. As I show in Chapter 5, the logic of discipleship – the unity of, distinction between, and irreversible relationship of Master and disciples – structures the way Barth understands the divine-human correspondence in which God's sanctification of all *de iure* in Christ finds its Spirit-awakened echo in the *de facto* holiness of Christians. This holiness never becomes a possession of Christians but always remains alien to them. Belonging properly to Christ, it encounters them as a gift they embrace as the Spirit enables them to respond to him. Disciples therefore correspond to Christ as they encounter him, manifesting rather than forging their sanctification in him as they actively heed his call, receive his direction and are sent out by him as his witnesses in the world. Discipleship cannot displace sanctification because it is the (provisional) evidence and visible form taken in human existence by God's sanctifying action in Christ. As Webster puts it, 'Sanctification is not only the holiness that the gospel *declares* but also the holiness that the gospel *commands*, to which the creaturely counterpart is *action*.'[38] Discipleship is the form of obedient and creaturely – that is to say, responsive – action. As such, it attests the sanctifying grace of God, becoming its human form or 'echo'.

Third, Barth's turn to discipleship is not only thoroughly biblical and theological; it is also intensely practical. His discipleship-shaped revision of sanctification bristles with ethical and ecclesiological implications. As developed in Chapters 7, 8 and 9, the vision of moral agency, moral activity and moral passivity contained within this discipleship-shaped theology of sanctification speaks eloquently into a number of contemporary debates. For example, I will argue in Chapter 7 that it has implications for how the church understands its

---

37. Webster, 'Discipleship and Calling', 137.
38. John Webster, *Holiness* (London: SCM, 2003), 87.

difference from others – irrespective of the cultural context in which it finds itself. To anticipate: the church cannot regard itself as an independent agent, standing over against the world as a culture in its own right. Christ stands over both the church and the world in his singular holiness. Therefore, the church's distinctiveness is only ever provisional.

The resulting fundamentally missiological vision of Christian existence is the practical significance of the 'permanent dislocation' of which discipleship speaks. Disciples are called out because they are called to Christ. But in being called to Christ and instructed by him, they do not become an exclusive or elitist community – much less one that should withdraw into a fantasy of sociological purity. Rather, they are sent out by him to bear witness to him and his significance for all. Following after Christ, disciples are not turned inward but outward, towards others. Discipleship is not a matter of the church's self-regard. Within Barth's discipleship-shaped account of sanctification, the church must understand its difference from the world in fundamentally missionary terms. It therefore cannot adopt a militant or combative stance – whether the primary strategy is one of cultural attack or withdrawal. Nor can it attempt to minimize its (provisional) difference from the world – positioning the church as a mere chaplaincy to or belated echo of some aspect of the culture. Discipleship refuses to either demonize the culture (in part or whole) or idolize it.

Notwithstanding the constructive contribution Barth's discipleship-shaped account of sanctification makes, two major preliminary objections need to be addressed. The first is the objection that Barth's account of discipleship is overshadowed by Bonhoeffer's, which the latter articulated and lived with a force that Barth himself acknowledged. The second is that Barth's own discipleship is so questionable – ambiguous where it needed to be clear (in public) and compromised at a crucial point (in his personal relationships) – as to render whatever he might say about it is profoundly problematic.

With regard to the objection that Bonhoeffer rather than Barth would appear to provide a more suitable resource for developing the potential of the language and imagery of discipleship, I perhaps need only observe the enormous existing literature engaging with Bonhoeffer's treatment of the theme. Bonhoeffer is frequently invoked in the contemporary discipleship conversation. He is claimed as a precedent by many contributors to the conversation, including some with whom he would no doubt be uncomfortable.[39] Compared with this, the presence and impact of the discipleship motif in Barth's theology of sanctification is rarely treated with seriousness. I have shown that Barth's treatment of discipleship within his theology of sanctification is relatively neglected. When discipleship is touched on in contemporary Barth studies, it is usually only tangentially so – and even then,

---

39. While Bonhoeffer's attempted cooption by political conservatives is well known, Barth himself may be subject to increasing attempts to appropriate him for a more conservative constituency. See, for example, Mark Galli, *Karl Barth: An Introductory Biography for Evangelicals* (Grand Rapids: Eerdmans, 2017).

it is rarely ever developed with any detail. With regard to sanctification, many of the most significant studies of Barth's approach fail to mention discipleship or mention it and then promptly move on or look elsewhere to account for the distinctiveness of his view. What is more, Stanley Hauerwas has articulated some very powerful and enduring objections to the supposedly 'episodic' character of Barth's approach to sanctification, which either deter interest in investigating Barth's theology of sanctification or reflect the already-existing lack of interest (presumably based on Barth's reputation for downplaying or undermining human agency or action in other spheres).[40] Rather than lacking depth or theological significance, Barth's discipleship-shaped view of sanctification is an under-appreciated aspect of his theology, as we have already glimpsed.

Potentially more seriously, Barth himself indicates at the commencement of §66.3 that his account of discipleship owes much to Bonhoeffer. Indeed, he goes so far as to suggest that he should merely reproduce Bonhoeffer's masterful treatment in an extended quotation! Surely, this is not only a high-profile example of the 'reciprocal indebtedness' some critics claim to detect between Bonhoeffer and Barth – in which the younger theologian influenced the older, and not simply the other way around[41] – but also prima facie evidence of the value of preferring Bonhoeffer's formulation (from Barth's own mouth no less)?

Three things need to be taken into account in response. First, Barth develops the content of his appropriation of the discipleship motif in a distinctive way. This is particularly evident in the way he pursues its integration with his Christocentric revision of sanctification. Second, while there is undoubtedly a 'reciprocal indebtedness' between Barth and Bonhoeffer, this is a significantly more complicated matter than merely finding moments where one theologian cites or alludes to the other. In Bonhoeffer's case, for example, much of his theological project is indebted to Barth – for all its distinctively Lutheran provenance and explicit criticisms of Barth at points. As Charles Marsh observes, 'Bonhoeffer's theology is possible only in view of Barth's revolution in theological method'.[42] If

---

40. See, for example, Stanley Hauerwas, *Character and the Christian Life: A Study in Theological Ethics* (Notre Dame: University of Notre Dame Press 1994).

41. Matthew Puffer produces evidence for such 'reciprocal indebtedness' between Bonhoeffer and Barth. Puffer, 'Dietrich Bonhoeffer in the Theology of Karl Barth', in *Karl Barth in Conversation*, ed. W. Travis McMaken and D. W. Congdon (Eugene: Pickwick, 2014), 46–62. Tom Greggs likewise highlights numerous moments of Bonhoeffer's influence upon Barth in 'The Influence of Dietrich Bonhoeffer on Karl Barth', in *Engaging Bonhoeffer: The Impact and Influence of Bonhoeffer's Life and Thought*, ed. Matthew D. Kirkpatrick (Minneapolis: Fortress Press, 2016), 45–64.

42. Charles Marsh, *Reclaiming Dietrich Bonhoeffer: The Promise of His Theology* (Oxford: Oxford University Press, 1994), ix. Andreas Pangritz establishes the pervasive influence on and presence of Barth in Bonhoeffer's theology. Pangritz, *Karl Barth in the Theology of Dietrich Bonhoeffer*, trans. Barbara and Martin Rumscheidt (Grand Rapids: Eerdmans, 2000).

Bonhoeffer's emphasis on discipleship came to be significant for Barth at this point of his own project, this is hardly an instance of Barth's adoption of something entirely alien to his own thought. Third, in his *Ethics* Bonhoeffer himself expressed dissatisfaction with the approach adopted in his *Nachfolge* – as Barth almost certainly knew. Bonhoeffer cites the counter-cultural vision of *Nachfolge* in the same breath as he proposes a more robust vision of Christian engagement with and responsibility for the world: 'For the Christian there is nowhere to retreat from the world, neither externally nor into the inner life. Every attempt to evade the world will have to be paid for sooner or later with a sinful surrender to the world'.[43] Bonhoeffer apparently saw a need for the discipleship theme to be more consistently theologized and approached within a broader framework – which is exactly what Barth does.

2.4 Discipleship in Barth and Barth's discipleship

A second objection to invoking Barth in the contemporary discipleship conversation is his own questionable discipleship – both in public and in his interpersonal relationships.

The questions surrounding Barth's public witness to the lordship of Jesus, come into sharp focus in light of his lifelong socialist sympathies. Regarding his apparent equivocations about Communist policies after 1945, Reinhold Niebuhr famously reproached Barth for articulating a theology that was only relevant in times of acute crisis – 'it can fight the devil if he shows both horns and both cloven feet' – but not for making 'discriminating judgments about good and evil if the evil shows only one horn or the half of a cloven foot'.[44] This was hardly an isolated criticism, or merely an optical illusion arising from Niebuhr's transatlantic perspective. Frank Jehle and more recently Christiane Tietz have both charted the fraught course of Barth's perceived rapprochement with Communism after the Second World War.[45] For many, this equivocation detracts dramatically from the clarity of Barth's stand against National Socialism – not only in being the chief architect of the *Barmen*

---

43. Dietrich Bonhoeffer, *Ethics*, Dietrich Bonhoeffer Works (English edition), volume 6 (Minneapolis: Fortress Press, 2005), 61. In highlighting this moment, I do not mean to endorse the 'Niebuhrian misinterpretation' of Bonhoeffer's development in terms of a shift from pacifism to a more mature 'realistic' view that embraces the need to get dirty hands. See Nation, Siegrist and Umbell, *Bonhoeffer the Assassin? Challenging the Myth, Recovering His Call to Peacemaking* (Grand Rapids: Baker Academic, 2013).

44. Reinhold Niebuhr, 'We Are Men and Not God', in *Essays in Applied Christianity*, ed. D. B. Robertson (New York: Meriden Books, 1959), 172.

45. Frank Jehle, *Ever against the Stream: The Politics of Karl Barth, 1906–1968*, trans. Richard and Martha Burnett (Grand Rapids: Eerdmans, 2002), chapter 10. Christiane Tietz, *Karl Barth: A Life in Conflict*, trans. Victoria J. Barnett (Oxford: Oxford University Press, 2021), chapter 12.

Declaration but also in his letters, lectures and other public statements that were critical of Hitler. But such a sharp contrast between the unequivocal Barth of the 1930s and 1940s and the equivocal post-War Barth is overdrawn. In particular, it underestimates the continuity in his political ethics. Barth's approach to politics was far more consistent – and, at the same time, far more consistently equivocal in its appearance – than this picture allows.[46]

Regarding the consistency of Barth's socialist sympathies, Helmut Gollwitzer's description of how Barth conducted himself during his first pastorate in Safenwil bears repeating:

> He treated his pastoral office in the way that many church officials today fear left-wing theology students will do: He combined the Sunday sermon with weekday political agitation. He did not feel that being a pastor obligated him to political restraint. On the contrary, precisely *because* he was a pastor, he had to be at the forefront of the class struggle.[47]

Upon taking up his appointment at Göttingen, however, things seemed to change. Suddenly, instead of advocating socialism, Barth was cautioning against identifying the action of God with human action – even revolutionary human action. For a variety of reasons – some of which Gollwitzer teases out – Barth appears to approach the task of politics with a different focus: 'To find and lay a solid foundation for Christian thought and action – that was why he now had to become a professor of theology, that was his political task'.[48]

The difference here should not be overplayed. It appears that Barth had adopted a different perspective on the 'social question'. Yet in reality, it was more of a change in emphasis. In highlighting the analogy between God's action and the promotion of more just social arrangements, Barth consistently refused to endorse an ideological absolutization of the socialist cause. At best, it was a parable of the kingdom rather than the kingdom itself, as he affirmed so memorably in his famous Tambach lecture, 'The Christian in Society' (1919). There, he called on Christians to 'take an open-hearted, broad-minded and honest attitude toward *social democracy*' not merely as onlookers but as 'hope-sharing and guilt-bearing players and comrades *within* it'.[49] But he also warned that 'we have to protect

---

46. Discussing the same public statement that attracted Niebuhr's censure, Jehle points out that if 'the *entire* passage which contains the unfortunate expression "a man of the stature of Joseph Stalin" [is] read', a very different picture emerges: 'If one reads this text slowly and carefully, it is clear that this was *not*, of course, about justifying Stalinism (much less its horrors). Barth spoke emphatically about the "very dirty and bloody hands" of the Communist regime. But … [in] Marxism (not in Joseph Stalin) there were at least high ideals at the beginning'. Jehle, *Ever against the Stream*, 88–9.

47. Gollwitzer, 'Kingdom of God and Socialism', 51.

48. Gollwitzer, 'Kingdom of God and Socialism', 54.

49. Karl Barth, 'The Christian in Society (1919)', in *The Word of God and Theology*, trans. Amy Marga (New York: T&T Clark, 2011), 64.

ourselves from expecting that our criticizing, protesting, reforming, organizing, democratizing, socializing, and revolutionizing can achieve a standard sufficient for the kingdom of God, *however fundamental and comprehensive they may be*'.[50] For, even the 'parables, in which we think, speak, and act' exhaust themselves – and us – teaching us to 'yearn for *another thing*, not just *any* other thing but the *wholly other* thing of the kingdom, the kingdom of *God*'.[51]

Consonant with this, in the second edition of his *Epistle to the Romans*, Barth sounds a sustained warning against identifying human action with the action of God. This is no doubt why he appeals to the language of a 'demonstration' (*Demonstration*) in rendering Paul's 'turn' to ethics in Romans 12. Specifically, he employs this language in the context of drawing an analogy to the difference between the Labour Movement itself and a May Day procession. The latter is a 'necessary and obligatory' demonstration of the former. Indeed, it manifests and belongs to it. But it must not be identified with it. The same, Barth maintains, goes for God's action and human action – the latter may be the necessary manifestation of the former, but they are not to be identified.[52] This invites being read as a direct riposte to a danger lurking in the language of the first edition. There, he treated the 'movement' (*Bewegung*) under the heading of *DER WILLE GOTTES: Das Eine Notwendige* ('The Will of God: The One Necessity').[53] To be sure, Barth insisted on the secondary status of Christian moral exhortation in relation to the new creation in Christ. But the way he developed the thought that the kingdom renews the world through its own 'movement' (*Bewegung*) – its exhortations retaining their own 'quiet, original dynamism' (*ihrer stillen, originellen Dynamik*) – resulted in talk of 'taking sides with God' (*für Gott Partei zu ergreifen*), which was open to misunderstanding.[54] By contrast, his emphasis at the equivalent point in the second edition, falls overwhelmingly on the impossibility of identifying God's action and human action. Here, Barth declares that 'the mercies of God ... define the world as this world without being themselves in any way depressed into the things of this world'. Or again: 'When ... the mercies of God form a subject of exhortation, they advance to this side, whilst belonging wholly to the other'.[55] Correcting the

---

50. Barth, 'The Christian in Society', 64.

51. Barth, 'The Christian in Society', 65.

52. Karl Barth, *The Epistle to the Romans*, 6th edn, trans. Edwyn C. Hoskyns (London: Oxford University Press, 1968), 431.

53. Karl Barth, *Der Römerbrief*, 1st edn (Zürich: Theologischer Verlag Zürich, 1919), 462.

54. Barth, *Der Römerbrief*, 464–6. Michael O'Neil draws attention to the way in which Barth's use of predominantly organic metaphors in the first edition of *Der Römerbrief* functioned to subvert his intent. Although he wanted to highlight God's action, which breaks through into human life in surprising, hidden and unexpected ways, he opened the door to identifying the divine and human and reversing the direction of dependence between them. Michael D. O'Neil, *Church as Moral Community: Karl Barth's Vision of Christian Life, 1915–1922* (Milton Keynes: Paternoster, 2013), 116.

55. Barth, *The Epistle to the Romans*, 427.

possible misreading of the first edition, Barth insists on the sharpest of distinctions, especially where treating of the movement from God into human life and history.

Barth appears to turn away from political and social action in drawing such sharp distinctions, distinctions which he doggedly pursues in his theological work from the 1920s onwards.[56] As Gollwitzer notes, after 1945, Barth opposed the politics of the Cold War but seldom resorted to the word 'socialism' as a term that 'could no longer be used as a shorthand formula for that toward which God's activity was directed and for the new human activity which it initiates'.[57] Barth never forsook an analogy between divine and human action, seeing Christian living and community as caught up and carried along, participant in God's work to bend social arrangements parabolically towards justice. Yet his accent changed. Socialism – not as an ideology but as a description of more just social arrangements – went from being a parable of *God's kingdom* to being a *parable* of God's kingdom. As a result, Barth 'assumed the appearance of having changed from a socialist bent on destroying the present system of exploitative power relationship to a Social Democrat whose resigned pragmatism stuck within the system and sought only isolated improvements'.[58]

A similar story unfolds with respect to Barth's involvement in the German Church struggle. His leading role in producing the *Barmen Declaration*, which served as a rallying cry for the Confessing Church in its refusal to endorse or

---

56. To take one example salient to the argument of this book, Webster highlights the relative prominence of human agency in *The Christian Life*, but concedes that Barth still goes to great lengths to relativize it with respect to the sovereign and decisive agency of God. In describing the Christian life as one of 'revolt' – some of the strongest language Barth uses in his entire corpus to depict human action – Webster notes that Barth heavily qualifies this. To begin with, he embeds his entire consideration of the Christian's invocation of God in §76.3 within a discussion of the Father's mysterious working and the children's miraculous response. He then prefaces it with an exclamation of wonder that God's children might claim to invoke and converse with their Father:

> Only with great surprise, profound amazement, and even consternation and fright can one speak of the fact that there may and should be this calling upon God by Christians as his children. We stand before the mystery of the covenant – in its way no less a mystery than that of the incarnation and resurrection of the Lord – when we reckon with it that this is so. (Webster, 'The Christian in Revolt', 89).

Further, as Webster notes with regard to the material in §77 dealing directly with the Christian's 'revolt', 'Barth ranges "here" over some of the ways in which the Christian's deeds and decisions are limited, fragmentary, lacking in the finality and absoluteness which can be predicated only of God's perfect act'. Webster, 'The Christian in Revolt', 133. Barth is rarely more alert to the danger of confusing or equating divine and human action than when seeking to grant human action proper solidity and significance.

57. Gollwitzer, 'Kingdom of God and Socialism', 55.

58. Gollwitzer, 'Kingdom of God and Socialism', 55.

cooperate with Hitler, appears relatively uncomplicated. Although, even here, many have objected to his famous declaration in the June 1933 pamphlet *Christian Existence Today* that the contemporary challenge for Christians is 'to do theology, and nothing but theology, as if nothing had happened'.[59] Eberhard Busch enumerates the various misunderstandings this declaration attracted at the time and shortly after the war.[60] One misunderstanding focused on Barth's apparent endorsement of a principled apolitical stance – as if Barth was indicating that theology is entirely self-referential and can have no stake in the political questions of the day. According to this view, Barth offered a theological reason for refusing to engage in politics. As Busch summarizes this (mistaken) view, 'Barth offered Hitler the church's abstinence from politics in exchange for the freedom to preach and to study theology'.[61] Another misunderstanding took Barth to a temporary and tactical suspension of the relationship between theology and politics. According to this view, 'the position taken by Barth in the pamphlet [was] entirely bound to the time and one he soon moved away from in order to be free to do theology with a constant political reference'.[62] Busch highlights Barth's later expression of frustration about both of these misunderstandings: 'In 1956 he warned against the "Scylla of a *theology* before which politics fades into insignificance" and the "Charybdis of a *politics* in and around which one has no energy left for theology"'.[63]

Gollwitzer, Jehle and Tietz all underline the complexity of Barth's situation as a Swiss national in Germany before the outbreak of war. In this context, the same theological convictions that would lead him to oppose the tendencies that he saw taking hold among the German Christians and later in the broadening threat of National Socialism, contributed to a reluctance about raising his voice too loudly. The rise of Hitler in the mid-1930s was, as Barth saw it, a matter to which the German people needed to respond. As a result, Busch contends that 'Barth's ... statements from 1933 to 1938 offer a confusing array of contradictions which are difficult to reconcile. Some resist bringing theology and politics together while others urge precisely that'.[64] Tietz highlights the many and varied pressures Barth was under in this period to help account for the shifts in footing that can be witnessed in letters and public statements.[65] After making allowances for the different contexts in which Barth produced such statements, Busch notes that

---

59. Karl Barth, *Theological Existence Today: A Plea for Theological Freedom*, trans. R. Birch Hoyle (London: Hodder & Stoughton, 1933), 9.

60. Eberhard Busch, '"Doing Theology as if Nothing Had Happened"—The Freedom of Theology and the Question of Its Involvement in Politics', trans. Martin Rumscheidt, *Studies in Religion* 16.4 (1987): 459–71, especially 459–61.

61. Busch, 'Doing Theology as if Nothing Had Happened', 460.

62. Busch, 'Doing Theology as if Nothing Had Happened', 460–1.

63. Busch, 'Doing Theology as if Nothing Had Happened', 461 – citing from Busch, *Karl Barth*, 411.

64. Busch, 'Doing Theology as if Nothing Had Happened', 461.

65. Tietz, *Karl Barth*, 206–30.

Barth was ever the contrarian. Shoulder to shoulder with the biblical prophets and apostles, Barth 'always said exactly that which *went against the grain* of [people's] own situation and that of their contemporaries'.[66] But more significantly, he points out that Barth's apparently apolitical declaration – in its context – is nothing of the sort. Rather, in the face of Hitler's rise to power, and to the subsequent enthusiasm in German church circles to shape their lives in response to this 'new hour of God', Barth's infamous statement is profoundly political:

> In *that* situation to say 'as if nothing had happened' was the most direct *counter-*statement imaginable to that 'command'. The seemingly harmless statement became a biting affront for it replied to the question, What does this hour signify for Christianity? with a radical, Nothing! That hour has nothing at all to tell us about what we as Christians must or must not do.[67]

Despite appearances, then, this statement of Barth's is provocative and daringly political – precisely because of its claim to theological independence. It embodies Barth's principled, theologically-driven deabsolutization of politics. Barth, as Werpehowski emphasizes, 'makes clear that Jesus Christ calls out disciples from the dominion of the orders or forces of the old aeon to which God's Kingdom stands in "indissoluble antithesis"'.[68] Consequently, ideology – especially the openly totalitarian ideology of National Socialism, but also the insistence on the rightness of Western capitalist democracies after 1945 – must be exposed, and its idolatrous pretensions unmasked.

In this respect, the stance expressed in Barth's much-misunderstood statement of 1933 is the very same stance expressed in the *Barmen Declaration*: supreme allegiance is owed to Christ alone – even and especially if this involves the church in defying other claimants to that allegiance. 'One fails to understand him when one does not see that he meant theology to be done *always* as if nothing had happened, comparable *always* to the chanting of the hours which did, in fact, go on uninterrupted in the Third Reich'.[69] And this, Jehle argues, contains the ultimate rejoinder to the criticisms levelled at Barth for his apparent equivocations over Communism. Jehle notes that 'in Switzerland', during the War, 'Barth was one of the most decisive champions of an uncompromising resistance against National Socialism'. At the same time, he was far from an uncritical advocate of resistance in the name of Swiss nationalism. According to Jehle, Barth 'mocked every Swiss "folk ideology" and every Swiss national "myth"'.[70] This same duality is evident in his post-War statements as well – albeit with new targets: 'After the war, Barth

---

66. Busch, 'Doing Theology as if Nothing Had Happened', 462.
67. Busch, 'Doing Theology as if Nothing Had Happened', 464.
68. William Werpehowski, 'Karl Barth and Politics', in *The Cambridge Companion to Karl Barth*, ed. John Webster (Cambridge: Cambridge University Press, 2000), 240.
69. Busch, 'Doing Theology as if Nothing Had Happened', 464.
70. Jehle, *Ever against the Stream*, 102–3.

was against an ideological anti-Communism and at the same time against a Christian glorification of Communism in the East'.[71] Barth was opposed to the absolutization of politics whether it occurred before, during or after the war, on the right or the left, in the Eastern Bloc or the capitalist West. He disdained the horrors wrought in the name of Communism, by men of such 'stature' as Stalin. He did this while acknowledging *both* that compared to National Socialism, the Communist project was animated by a very real and important question – namely, the social question of justice and equitable economic arrangements – *and* that the Communists were not the only ones vulnerable to reifying their politics into an idolatrous and ideological project.[72]

More difficult than the ambiguity of Barth's statements when it comes to politics are the questions that cannot be avoided with regard to his interpersonal ethics – specifically as pertains to the impact on his marriage and household of his troubled and troubling relationship with Charlotte von Kirschbaum. These questions are being engaged with renewed vigour since Christiane Tietz rendered into English parts of the extensive correspondence between von Kirschbaum and Barth dating from 1925 to 1935 (which was published in German in 2008).[73] Although the fact and difficulty of this relationship was relatively well established in Barth studies before this, Tietz has provided further detail.[74] Notwithstanding her insistence on avoiding both voyeurism and moralism, the portrait that emerges from Tietz's account is tragic, disturbing and reveals the problematic status not only of Barth's conduct but also of the extent to which his theological formulations played a role in his self-justifying and at times manipulative attempts to interpret it.[75] Moreover,

71. Jehle, *Ever against the Stream*, 103.
72. Jehle, *Ever against the Stream*, chapters 10 and 11.
73. Tietz, 'Karl Barth and Charlotte von Kirschbaum', 86–111. Tietz acknowledges that for all the new material we now have, between 1926 and 1932 we are still chiefly in possession of Barth's letters to Charlotte and not hers to Barth (presumably because he destroyed the evidence of their correspondence, but she did not).
74. Important earlier studies include Selinger, *Charlotte von Kirschbaum and Karl Barth* and Renate Köbler, *In the Shadow of Karl Barth: Charlotte von Kirschbaum*, trans. Keith Crim (Eugene: Wipf & Stock, 2013).
75. Tietz, 'Karl Barth and Charlotte von Kirschbaum', 89. At the end of her article, Tietz offers some explicit reflection about the 'theological dimension' of this correspondence; 107–11. She highlights, first, the burden Barth, Charlotte and Nelly all bore when it came to Barth's 'responsibility' for theology and the church at the time. This informed their initial attempts to avoid divorce while keeping Charlotte involved in Barth's work as well as their later (grudging and painful) acceptance of Charlotte's disruptive presence in Barth's household under the guise of her being 'his secretary'. Second, Tietz observes that Barth is explicit about the impact of his experience with Charlotte on his theology. Perhaps further evidence for this is the way in which a number of Barth's own signature terms and concepts ('impossible possibility', tension, a non-equilateral triangle, etc) are invoked in the ongoing attempt to interpret the 'necessity' of Charlotte's presence and partnership. At times, Barth appears alert to the danger of self-justification in this. Even if these are apt descriptions of

the emergence of these details into public scrutiny roughly coincides with the broader cultural phenomenon in the late-modern West, uncovering the extent to which powerful men – within the church as well as outside it – have tended to exploit and abuse their position. This cultural phenomenon heightens the impact of Sonderegger's observation about the problematic status and implications of Barth's interpersonal conduct: 'Barth's own intimacies with women do not make an alliance with feminism appear too promising'.[76]

The problematic status of Barth's own discipleship at this level cannot be explained away or protected from difficult questions. While we must avoid the 'genetic fallacy' – disregarding Barth's ideas because he failed to live them out – Barth's compromised discipleship should alert us to potential imbalances in his account of discipleship. Specifically, it should prompt us to enquire whether and to what extent it opens itself to the same kind of misappropriation he evidently engaged in with other theological concepts and formulations. At the same time, I suggest that Barth's own account of discipleship can supply a set of criteria against which to measure his failures in discipleship. Anticipating my findings in subsequent chapters, Barth's vision of discipleship itself poses at least four questions to Barth at this point:

(1) How is his secrecy with regard to the nature of his relationship with Charlotte compatible with the requirement that the call to discipleship demands tangible and concrete steps of obedience in the open?
(2) How does Barth's selfish behaviour – not only in indulging his wrongdoing but also in seeking to justify it to himself (struggle as he evidently did with this) – manifest the central demand of discipleship to mortify the self?
(3) Insofar as Christ's call to participate in his program of liberating human life enables suffering and less-than-ideal circumstances to be received as gifts – even if they lack positive value in themselves – why did Barth refuse to accept his marriage to Nelly as it was?
(4) To what extent does Barth's insistence that Charlotte and Nelly – along with the rest of their household – endure such a confusing, painful and damaging arrangement, fail again when measured against discipleship's summons

the '*Notgemeinschaft zu dritt*' between Barth, Nelly and Charlotte, this does not absolve it of guilt. Third, and less fully, Tietz hints at the possible implications of the way in which Barth (and to a lesser extent also Charlotte) strives to understand their situation as not disordered but an imperfect attempt to align themselves with God's order. Their words to each other are sometimes resonant and sometimes strike dissonant notes with the theology of marriage he articulates in *CD* III/4 §54.1 as 'life-partnership' as well as with his emphasis on the imperfect alignment between human political and social ordering and God's kingdom. These implications would no doubt be worth examining more closely, though they depart from the present focus on Barth's explicit treatment of the theme of discipleship.

76. Katherine Sonderegger, 'Barth and Feminism,' in *The Cambridge Companion to Karl Barth* (Cambridge: Cambridge University Press, 2000), 259.

to humanize others by refusing to treat others as means for one's own self-assertion?

I return to such questions when I take up the constructive task of venturing beyond Barth on discipleship in Chapter 10. Ultimately, Barth's discipleship-shaped vision can and must be read against him in order to be read with and beyond him. To do this, however, we must examine this vision more closely. Such is the task to which we now turn.

Chapter 3

THE PROBLEM AND PROMISE OF DISCIPLESHIP IN *CD* IV/2 §66

Whatever we may have to say ... about the sloth and sanctification of man, and the edification of the Church, and love, is wholly included and enclosed already in the being and action of the Son of Man, and at bottom it can be understood and represented only as a development and explanation of it. (*Church Dogmatics*, IV/2 §64.4, 265)

3.1 Christology and the context of discipleship in Barth

In this chapter, I set Barth's treatment of discipleship in the context of his mature vision of sanctification. My main contention is that while Barth's Christocentrism plays a decisive role in his revision of sanctification in *CD* IV/2, his appropriation – and extended exposition – of the New Testament discipleship motif provides the most distinctive feature of §66. In the context of his account of sanctification, Barth insists that the centrality of Jesus Christ is concrete and personal rather than a merely abstract principle. It is concrete and personal because it entails his living direction given form in the call to discipleship (533):

> 'Follow me' is the substance of the call in the power of which Jesus makes men His saints. ... The lifting up of themselves for which He gives them freedom is not a movement which is formless, or to which they themselves have to give the necessary form. It takes place in a definite form and direction. Similarly, their looking to Jesus as their Lord is not an idle gaping. It is a vision which stimulates those to whom it is given to a definite action. The call issued by Jesus is a call to discipleship.

The centrality of Christ in sanctification and the call to follow him mutually condition and imply one another. As I will develop more fully in the next chapter, discipleship is the distinctive form of Christian holiness for Barth. What this means is that even where discipleship is not explicitly mentioned, sanctification is discipleship-shaped. Far from being an alien, free church intrusion on – or departure from – a fundamentally Reformed vision of sanctification, Barth's treatment of the call to discipleship in §66.3 is its natural and obvious culmination. In fact, the sudden prominence of discipleship in Barth's account is prepared for by the way Barth's locates it in its context in §66 – as well as in relation to §64.4 and §65. Looking to Jesus as living Lord and centre of all reality – and of Christian existence – is the occasion and motivation for the Christian's active response to his call to discipleship. Consequently, this chapter will focus on the context of Barth's treatment of discipleship here.

In the contemporary discipleship conversation, church and world are frequently treated in ways that mutually implicate one another, resulting in a failure to give due attention to Christ himself. Church and world are often envisaged as locked in a bitter and intractable struggle, relentlessly opposed and hostile to one another. Alternatively, they are pictured as dealing with each other directly and without mediation. The church (a supposedly self-contained and distinct actor) is seen to consciously appropriate from the world or act upon it in the manner it chooses and deems relevant. Either way, each is incapable of doing without the other – whether negatively or positively. Arguably, this sense of opposition and mutual dependence is a significant factor contributing to the embattled mentality characterizing much of the contemporary discipleship conversation in post-Christian contexts. While talk of discipleship often promises to carry Christians beyond such a mentality, without due attention to Christ it simply reinforces the presumption of a permanent and necessary conflict between church and world.[1]

In contrast, the way Barth sets his treatment of discipleship in context – ensuring it remains governed by its centre in the living and active Lord Jesus Christ – opens the way to a less oppositional and more dynamic, 'world positive' development of Christian distinctiveness.[2] For Barth, discipleship is *not* everything. Indeed, it has no meaning apart from its living connection with Christ. Jesus is the decisive personal centre of both sanctification and discipleship. Christian holiness – whether of the community or the individual within it – is 'actualized' in him. This means that its reality is accomplished and completed in him. As such, it always remains his possession. Even when it is shared with us in the power of the Spirit, it

---

1. It is not entirely wrong to detect conflict and opposition here. The question is: where should the conflict and opposition be located, and is it absolute and insoluble or relative and provisional?

2. In a sense, I m revising and relativizing H. Richard Niebuhr's framework from *Christ and Culture* by refusing to collapse 'Christ' into any one of the various Christian stances towards the culture that Niebuhr arrays on his typology. Niebuhr's approach has been variously (and rightly) criticized. See Justin Lewis-Anthony, *If You Meet George Herbert on the Road, Kill Him: Radically Rethinking Priestly Ministry* (London: Mowbray, 2009); and Volf, 'Theology, Meaning and Power: A Conversation with George Lindbeck on Theology and the Nature of Christian Difference', in *The Nature of Confession: Evangelicals and Postliberals in Conversation*, ed. T. R. Philips and D. L. Okholm (Downers Grove: InterVarsity Press, 1996), 45–66.

remains properly alien to us. Our sanctification is entirely relative to and dependent upon him. Crucially, this includes the distinctiveness of which discipleship speaks.

At least three things follow from Barth's location of sanctification and discipleship with respect to Christ, each of which I will deal with in turn in this chapter.

First, the Christ-centredness of Barth's account of sanctification and discipleship is 'world positive' because it dynamically coordinates Christian distinctiveness from and solidarity with the world. Barth affirms that Christians are included together with all others within the ambit of Christ's reconciling work. Along with all others, Christians are mired in the sloth and misery of sin in need of Christ's reconciling work. And equally, Christians are beneficiaries of and participants in that work which, as a result of election, is universal in scope. Hence, the distinctiveness of Christian disciples is a by-product of the way in which they provide a 'creaturely reflection' of God's own holiness, disclosing in advance the *telos* of all humanity and creation. Solidarity and distinctiveness are woven together in Barth's vision. This gives Barth's entire theology a missionary caste, as various scholars have recognized.[3] In particular, it makes his account of sanctification resistant to the tendency to imagine (or attempt to manufacture) a sharp ontological distinction between Christians and others.[4] Deprived of any absolute distinction, Christian distinctiveness cannot be spatial or social. Christians cannot stand apart from or over against others as if they possessed or were the sole beneficiaries of Christ's work. At most, they are awakened – or 'disturbed from their slumber' – by the Spirit, who makes them aware of the changed eschatological situation that has resulted from Christ's work of reconciliation. As such, Christian distinctiveness consists in the witness Christians offer not to themselves but to Christ.

In the next part of this chapter (3.2), I will show how Barth arrives at this 'world positive' vision of sanctification in conversation with Calvin. Barth recognizes the revisionary nature of his engagement with Calvin, but also sees himself as carrying forward Calvin's intention and best insights rather than setting off in an entirely new direction. Fundamentally, Barth's discipleship-shaped vision takes its bearings from the Lord, whose objective, universally effective and unrepeatable work establishes Christian holiness. Just as for Calvin, it is participation with Christ that grounds sanctification for Barth. But Barth differs from Calvin with respect to the scope and implications of this participation. Nevertheless, his revision of Calvin employs the resources and answers to the overarching rationale of Calvin's vision rather than importing material foreign to it – whether from Roman Catholic or more Anabaptist sources.

---

3. See, for example, John G. Flett, *The Witness of God: The Trinity, 'Missio Dei', Karl Barth, and the Nature of Christian Community* (Grand Rapids: Eerdmans, 2010) and Mark Lindsay, 'The Abandonment of Inauthentic Humanity: Barth's Theology of Baptism as the Ground and Goal of Mission', *Pacifica* 26.3 (2013): 229–45.

4. Flett, *The Witness of God*, 190–4 and 231–5.

Second, the Christ-centredness of Barth's vision makes the nonconformity of Christian disciples with their culture real but also relative and provisional. I argue that Barth characterizes Christian nonconformity as real but relative because he regards it as a by-product of their unity with and witness to Christ rather than the substance of that unity. Christ rather than their nonconformity is at the centre. Hence, it is relative – relative to Christ. But it is not unreal, a merely notional, spiritual or inward matter. It is real and tangible. It presses for active expression as, enabled by the Spirit, we respond to Christ's call to follow him. One outcome of simultaneously relativizing and establishing the reality of Christian nonconformity like this is that it is dynamic and flexible. It is not solid, inappropriately reifying some aspect of Christian cultural nonconformity and treating it as the timeless and essential core of Christian holiness.[5] Nor is it entirely liquid, as though it were slippery and lacking in any kind of substance or cultural astringency. Rather, we might say that it is plastic. Substantial and viscous but also flexible and adaptable.

To substantiate this claim I must specify the character of Barth's Christocentrism and its role in relation to his appropriation of the discipleship motif. I do this in the third part of this chapter (3.3), which detours through the finer points of the secondary literature as it bears on how Barth's Christocentric approach to sanctification relates to Calvin's. This discussion is necessary because the character and role of Barth's Christocentrism differ in important ways from those which both his champions and his critics typically assert. In particular, rather than representing a step away from the concrete and pastoral realities that dominated Calvin's account of the Christian life, I find that Barth's Christocentristic revision of Calvin's doctrine of sanctification is thoroughly 'Calvinian' (although we will also see that it owes much to Luther). It follows and develops Calvin's own programme, but radicalizes its Christocentrism in order to underwrite a profoundly concrete, pastorally oriented and joyful vision of Christian holiness. For Barth, holiness is a reality in Christ that is joyfully apprehended and experienced by believers in the power of the Spirit. It is a gift given by Christ himself, given in and with himself as the goal and outcome of his reconciling work. It is neither a matter of arduous duty nor something that spontaneously and unexpectedly ambushes Christians. 'The human does not add to the completed event of reconciliation, but in its completion, the human community lives as it is active in its corresponding movement to the world.'[6]

Finally, the Christ-centredness of Barth's account yields a conception of discipleship with a particular vision of Christ in 'threefold form' at its heart. This 'lively Christology', which borrows more strongly from Luther than Calvin, has three aspects:

---

5. Pete Ward rightly warns against this danger when it comes to ecclesiology in *Liquid Ecclesiology: The Gospel and the Church* (Leiden: Brill, 2017), 5–11.
6. Flett, *The Witness of God*, 192.

3. *The Problem and Promise of Discipleship*

- Christ is the director and 'captain' of Christian holiness, personally present to it;
- Christ is the definitive source of holiness secured in his objective work of reconciliation and
- Christ is the perfect standard of holiness, embodied in his holy life as well as the judgement he will render when he brings Christian holiness to completion.

Although this lively Christology is largely implicit – and the relationships between its three 'forms' never fully systematized – it can be seen clearly in Barth's account of the 'direction' (*Weisung*) of Christ in §64.4. I draw the connections between this account and §66 in the final part of this chapter (3.4). Specifically, I argue that the Christ-centred revision of sanctification that Barth carries out in §66.1-2, which provides the conceptual scaffold for his turn to discipleship in §66.3, assumes a Christology in something like this threefold form. Put differently, I propose that the lively Christology of §66.2 establishes the conceptual reference points and basic notions (call, following, etc.) that eventually become explicit in Barth's turn to discipleship.

3.2 Sanctification as Christ-centred discipleship

In order to begin investigating Barth's Christ-centred revision of sanctification which takes the form of discipleship, it is worth pausing to pinpoint two coordinates from John 17, which establish the lines within which Barth's account unfolds. The first coordinate is an embrace of a 'world positive' approach to Christian distinctiveness, in which the opposition Christ's disciples are taught to expect in the world is reframed such that they are prevented from defining themselves over against a demonized world. The second coordinate derived from John 17 is the need to identify and unmask the different forms of idolatry besetting different cultures and contexts – including the church's own culture. It is in light of the basic affirmation of the world's goodness that the true horror of its idolatries can be appreciated. Orientated by these two coordinates, Barth's Christ-centred approach to discipleship distinguishes Christians from the world in a manner that answers to, and is tempered by, their overarching affirmation of it.

In John 17, Jesus spends the evening before his betrayal impressing upon his disciples the significance of his imminent death and resurrection. At the heart of this significance is the unity and witness of the disciples. He sees his death and resurrection – his 'lifting up' in the language of John's Gospel – as fundamentally aimed at securing their oneness, a oneness which will itself advertise and draw others into the renewed people of God. This reflects an emphasis on the missional distinctiveness of Christ's renewed and unified people that can be detected throughout the Fourth Gospel. Such missional distinctiveness is a major burden of Jesus' so-called High Priestly prayer in John 17, for example. But this theme is always intimately bound to the governing motif of John's Christology – namely, 'the singularity, the uniqueness of Jesus, the one shepherd, the one man who dies for the people'.[7] Jesus wants his disciples to know that their unity is entailed by his uniqueness.

The connection between the uniqueness of Jesus and the unity of God's people – as represented by his disciples – is stitched into Barth's theological vision. This is seldom more evident than when he speaks of election. At least as early as his 1937–38 Gifford Lectures, he could declare: 'To know Jesus Christ is to know God, the one and only God, majestic and personal, the Creator and Lord of the world and man.'[8] At the same time, 'To know Jesus Christ means not only to know God but also to know the *election* of man … and thus to know Jesus Christ means to know a new man, the elect *man*.[9] As his extended treatment of this connection in II/2 *CD* indicates, this vision of election has massive pastoral, ecumenical, inter-religious (extending to Israel as those on the 'shadow side' of election) and missiological implications. Significantly, in that context he summarizes these implications in terms of discipleship: '*election is the divine ordination to discipleship*, to the apostolate, to the community' (*CD* II/2, 16; emphasis added). This connection receives further exposition in *CD* IV/2 §66, where Barth takes the additional step of linking the themes of election and community to the disciple's distinctiveness with respect to the world.

In linking the disciples' election in Christ with their distinctiveness over against the world, Barth could easily claim the farewell discourse and High Priestly prayer from John 14–17 as his precedent. There, Jesus repeatedly points to the enmity and opposition directed towards him by the world. He does this to prepare his disciples to face much the same hostility and opposition he did. This appears to vindicate the church-world opposition we have observed in the contemporary discipleship conversation. Jesus' disciples *are* drawn into the opposition and hostility that was directed towards him. As Stanley Hauerwas provocatively puts it, 'Christianity is unintelligible without enemies.'[10] However, reifying the world's opposition to Christianity and conflating Christ and Christianity like this is problematic. To begin with, it yields a dualistic sense of the purity of the church – as a place free of enmity and hostility towards Christ's rule – over against an imagined monolithic hostility and enmity apart from them. In addition, tying the *intelligibility* of Christianity to the existence of its 'enemies' suggests that there is no need to engage with others with anything deeper than the occasional (verbal) skirmish.

---

7. Richard Bauckham, *The Gospel of Glory: Major Themes in Johanine Theology* (Grand Rapids: Baker Academic, 2015), 32.

8. Karl Barth, *The Knowledge of God and the Service of God according to the Teaching of the Reformation: Recalling the Scottish Confession of 1560*. Trans. J. L. M. Haire and Ian Henderson (London: Hodder & Stoughton, 1938), 71.

9. Barth, *The Knowledge of God and the Service of God*, 74.

10. Stanley Hauerwas, 'Preaching as though We Had Enemies', *First Things*, May 1995. Accessed 5 January 2016, http://www.firstthings.com/article/1995/05/003-preaching-as-though-we-had-enemies.

3. The Problem and Promise of Discipleship 49

In reality, however, Jesus subverts this dualism not by denying the reality of the opposition and hostility but by relocating it. According to Jesus, the opposition properly belongs between himself and the world. The church and the world are opposed to one another in a merely derivative and, ultimately, provisional way. That is to say, the world's enmity towards the church is a refraction of the light of Christ through the distorted lens of its constitutive idolatries. In fact, the church itself is not free of enmity towards Christ. Rather than promoting some false ideal of purity in which there is no room to admit the enmity within the church – and within each and every disciple – the world's hostility to Christ and his church sits alongside the disciples' need for sanctification, and holds up a mirror to it. Furthermore, Jesus teaches his disciples to expect that their unified witness will overcome the merely provisional opposition of the world, drawing others into the ever-widening circle of God's life and love.

There is no scope in all this for either dismissing the enmity between church and world nor for demonizing the enemies 'out there'. The enmity is real. Even Christ's own people need reconciling and unifying. Indeed, Jesus' own inner circle included one 'destined to be lost' (Jn 17.12). But the enmity between the church and the world is also relative. It is relative because the hostility and opposition belongs not primarily between the church and the world, but between Christ and those forces that have invaded and distorted his good world. In this, the goodness of the world is positively affirmed prior to and in a way that frames any hostility towards Christ experienced from it – or shared in by the church.

Barth develops exactly this kind of dynamic and world-positive vision of discipleship in the course of his Christocentric reworking of the doctrine of sanctification in *CD* IV/2 §66. Here, what Hunsinger observes of Barth more generally proves true in the detail: 'For Barth nonconformity takes place for, and only for, the sake of solidarity ... It is only because the church is for the world that it must also be against it.'[11] My contention is that Barth's explicit and extensive development of the New Testament discipleship motif in §66.3 exemplifies this dynamic vision of Christian distinctiveness from the world for the sake of the world. While his development of the discipleship motif is the most distinctive feature of his account of sanctification, it is thoroughly 'christologically determined'.[12] The doctrine of sanctification is fundamentally discipleship-shaped, for Barth, because the it is decisively reshaped in light of election, and 'election is the divine ordination to discipleship' (*CD* II/2, 16). As such, discipleship is the capstone of Barth's theology of sanctification not a foreign intrusion into it.

Underwriting Barth's discipleship-shaped account of sanctification is a Christocentric reworking of the doctrine of sanctification. This reworking is undertaken in particularly close conversation with Calvin's understanding.[13] The

---

11. George Hunsinger, *Disruptive Grace: Studies in the Theology of Karl Barth* (Grand Rapids: Eerdmans, 2000), 122.
12. Bender, *Barth's Christological Ecclesiology*, 2–10.
13. Richard Muller, *The Unaccommodated Calvin: Studies in the Foundation of a Theological Tradition* (New York: OUP, 2000), 187, sounds fair warning about the dangers

position Barth arrives at has been described as 'ground-breaking' for it constitutes nothing short of a full-scale revision of Calvin.[14] Throughout §66 Barth is engaged in a sustained and often explicit conversation with Calvin. §66.1 opens with a discussion of the problem of the relation between justification and sanctification. Here, Barth appreciatively – though also critically and constructively – appropriates Calvin's insights. Indeed, he mostly uses Calvin's own raw materials to construct his position. For instance, Barth draws upon the insight embodied in the order in which Calvin treated justification and sanctification in the *Institutes* (510–11):

> We can and should learn from the classical example of [Calvin's] mode of treatment that we can give only a twofold answer to the question of priority in the relationship between these two moments and aspects. Calvin was quite in earnest when he gave sanctification a strategic precedence over justification. He was also quite in earnest when he gave the latter a tactical precedence. Why could he be so free, and yet so bound, in relation to the two? Because he started at the place which is superior to both because it embraces both, so that in the light of it we can and must give the primacy, now to the one and now to the other, according to the different standpoints from which we look. The basic act in which they are a whole, in which they are united and yet different, and in which – without any contradiction – they have different functions according to which they must each be given the primacy, is as Calvin sees it … the *participatio Christi* given to man by the Holy Spirit.

Barth regards Calvin's reticence to present justification as the foundation – as the objective and punctiliar commencement of the Christian life – upon which

---

of comparing Barth with others: 'Projects that compare Calvin and Barth or Calvin and Schleiermacher will not enlighten us particularly about Calvin – nor probably about Barth or Schleiermacher, for that matter.' As David Gibson remarks, it is likely that Muller is intent on preventing any kind of Barthian distortion of Calvin (*Reading the Decree: Exegesis, Election and Christology in Calvin and Barth* [New York: T&T Clark, 2009], 17). However, it is not clear why a moratorium on comparison best serves that aim. Gibson is surely right to contend that 'the examination of connections and motifs internal to Barth's own thought is not, in the final analysis, truly penetrating apart from consideration of his debt to the Reformed tradition, and notably to Calvin himself'. This is especially true in this instance. For, as we will see, Barth explicitly maintains an ongoing and close conversation with Calvin throughout this section, with the notable exception of §66.3.

14. George Hunsinger, 'Sanctification', in *The Westminster Handbook to Karl Barth*, ed. R. E. Burnett (Louisville: Westminster John Knox Press, 2013), 139, articulates the first, claiming that compared with 'familiar received traditions, whether Protestant or otherwise, there is nothing quite like it'. Bruce L. McCormack, 'Sanctification after Metaphysics: Karl Barth in Conversation with John Wesley's Conception of Christian Perfection' in *Sanctification: Explorations in Theology and Practice* (Downers Grove: IVP, 2014), 114, makes the second, slightly stronger claim.

sanctification is progressively built as his foundational insight. Calvin envisages justification and sanctification as two distinct but inseparable aspects of the one work of reconciliation which are dynamically interrelated. Justification has the primacy from one perspective, sanctification from another. Behind this, Barth highlights Calvin's emphasis on the *participatio Christi*. Participation in Christ paves the way for both justification and sanctification, soteriology and ethics. Calvin saw that union with Christ is both the grounds for the believers' righteous status (which powers their holy living) and the content and power of their holy life (which is the goal and purpose of their altered status). Christ himself is the objective basis for both.

Barth develops Calvin's insight here in terms of his distinctive 'actualistic ontology'. He does this when he construes the *participatio Christi* not as a metaphysical state but as an event, a history, a divine action. Being and action belong together for Barth, and cannot be rightly conceived apart from each other. According to Paul Nimmo, this entails rigorously following through the (post-metaphysical) insistence that 'The true identity of God is revealed in the works of God.'[15] In contrast to the more or less classical and therefore substantialist character of Calvin's thinking,[16] Barth insists that participation in Christ – along with the justification and sanctification that are bound up with it – is a gift rather than a given, something to be ever renewed and received afresh in the power of the Spirit. Barth does not conceive of the *participatio* as an impersonal 'sphere' into which humans may enter, but as a deeply personal encounter between God

---

15. Paul T. Nimmo, *Being in Action: The Theological Shape of Barth's Ethical Vision* (London: T&T Clark, 2007), 6–7.

16. The traditional metaphysical character of Calvin's thinking is easily detected when it comes to the infamous *extra calvinisticum* – Calvin's insistence that the divine nature of the Son could not be totally bounded by the human nature of the incarnate Jesus: 'Although the boundless essence of the Word was united with human nature into one person, we have no idea of any enclosing. The Son of God descended miraculously from heaven, yet without abandoning heaven; was pleased to be conceived miraculously in the Virgin's womb, to live on the earth, and hang upon the cross, and yet always filled the world as from the beginning' (*Inst.* II.xiii.4). While potentially underestimating the role of counter-Lutheran polemic in this formulation, E. David Willis has established that this was not an innovation but a feature of catholic tradition stretching at least as far back as church fathers like Augustine and Athanasius. E. David Willis, *Calvin's Catholic Christology: The Function of the So-Called Extra Calvinisticum in Calvin's Theology* (Leiden: Brill, 1966). Nevertheless, the distinction between Calvin and Barth at this level ought not be overplayed. Even Bruce McCormack – who champions the post-metaphysical reading of Barth – can concede that 'we ought not to get overly excited by the substitution of actualistic ontology for a substantialist one'. McCormack, 'Sanctification after Metaphysics', 105. Both approaches begin with the same insights and press towards the same goal.

and human persons.[17] This emphasis on personal encounter, and the covenant partnership it enacts, reflects the overarching perspective adopted by Barth in this second part of the doctrine of reconciliation. *CD* IV/2 is governed by Barth's integration of Christ's royal office and the state of exaltation under the heading of 'The Exaltation of the Son of Man'. The exaltation of Christ as the true and representative human being is the exaltation or 'lifting up' of humanity to dynamic and intimate fellowship with God. This is the goal of the entire covenant history, itself the 'internal basis' of creation. Therefore, while Barth claims to be building on Calvin's foundation with raw materials derived from Calvin, here (as elsewhere) he is appropriating and putting them to work according to his own blueprint.

The way Barth draws on Calvin in §66.1 – building on his foundational insights and appropriating his raw materials in his own distinctive way – prepares for his distinctive account of sainthood (or holiness) in §66.2. This subsection is almost a textbook case of the way Barth explicates his subject matter by deploying the six organizing motifs that George Hunsinger has identified as characteristic of Barth's thinking – actualism, particularism, objectivism, personalism, realism and rationalism.[18] It is possible in 'expounding Barth in terms of motifs' to unintentionally turn 'away from the material dogmatic matters with which Barth's work is centrally concerned'.[19] If identifying motifs becomes an end in itself, it can become a distraction from the task of understanding Barth's theology. Worse, it can detach the criteria of assessment from the substance of his theology. Alert to this danger, I will employ Hunsinger's motifs in the following paragraphs not simply to trace the distinctive contours of Barth's thinking about sanctification but also to direct attention to its substance, pausing along the way to highlight its connections with Calvin's account.

In §66.2, Barth insists that God's sovereign and gracious activity in the concrete person of Jesus Christ is the true locus of holiness. In doing so, he displays what Hunsinger calls actualism and particularism. Actualism 'is the motif which governs

---

17. See Migliore, '*Participatio Christi*', 292–4, and also, more recently, Bartholomaeus, *Karl Barth's Doctrine of Sanctification: An Exploration of Church Dogmatics §66* (Lanham: Lexington Books, 2021).

18. See George Hunsinger, *How to Read Karl Barth: The Shape of His Theology* (Oxford: OUP, 1991), 4–5. According to John Mark Capper ('*Karl Barth's Theology of Joy*' [PhD diss., University of Cambridge, 1998], 69), the motifs Hunsinger has identified 'shape the doctrinal content of Barth's mature theology as a whole', but they do not determine that content. Instead, they arise from it – and from reflection on it – in important ways. Two implications follow from this. First, Hunsinger's motifs have more power for explication and conceptual clarification than as heuristic devices. As Capper puts it, 'Once a theme … has been discerned, however, they provide a simple and powerful set of tools for analysis.' Second, as Capper also emphasizes, the true power of Hunsinger's motifs comes less from isolating different strands of Barth's thought than from sensitizing us to their interplay as he deals with his subject matter.

19. Yocum, *Ecclesial Mediation in Karl Barth*, xvi.

3. The Problem and Promise of Discipleship

Barth's complex conception of being and time. Being is always an event and often an act (always an act whenever an agent capable of decision is concerned).[20] Reflecting patterns of thought he finds over and over again in the Bible, Barth insists that creaturely realities – like holiness – must never be treated as givens that we somehow possess apart from or over against God. They can only ever be gifts, actively and miraculously given by their Giver, who is and always remains the active subject, giving himself ever anew in his gifts. Paired with actualism, particularism is the motif that insists on the uniqueness and decisiveness of Jesus Christ and his history for the methods as well as subject matter of theology. Instead of moving from generalities – about God or what is real or possible – to the particularities of salvation and the Bible, 'Barth strove to take his bearings strictly from the particularities of … the events of grace as attested in scripture and centred on Jesus Christ.'[21]

The actualism and particularism of Barth's conception of holiness is evident in the way he relates the holiness of God's people to the decisive holiness of Jesus at the very start of subsection two. While noting the biblical description of God's people as his 'saints' or 'holy ones' (511–13), he insists that properly speaking there is only one Holy One, and that all other holiness is merely a refraction of his self-sanctification (514–15):

> In the existence of this One, in Jesus Christ … it really came about, and is and will be, that God Himself became man, that the Son of God became also the Son of Man, in order to accomplish in His own person the conversion of man to Himself, his exaltation from the depth of his transgression and consequent misery, his liberation from his unholy being for service in the covenant, and therefore his sanctification. This is the divine act of sanctification in its original and proper, because direct, form; in its once-for-all uniqueness. All its other forms, the sanctification of Israel and the community with the distant goal of that of the whole of the human race and the world, are included in this form, by which they are all conditioned.

Barth refuses to regard the holiness of God's people as some quality or predicate that may be ascribed to them independently. Nor can it be a substance they may come possess (e.g. by infusion). Rather, it is entirely relative to the Holy One who stands in their midst, actively sharing his holiness with them in reflection of the fact that he has included them in the unique and unrepeatable history of his own sanctifying work. Few are clearer on the implications of this than John Webster, who remarks in his own constructive theological work on the significance of making 'the miracle of election central to the Church's existence and nature'.[22] The emphasis both Webster and Barth put on election in generating the actualism

---

20. Hunsinger, *How to Read Karl Barth*, 4.
21. Hunsinger, *How to Read Karl Barth*, 33.
22. Webster, *Holiness*, 52.

and particularism at work in sanctification serves to underscore grace: it 'draws attention to the way in which the Church has its being in the ever-fresh work of divine grace. The Church is what it is in the ceaseless gift of its being through the risen Christ and the Holy Spirit who accomplish the will of the Father in gathering a holy people to himself.'[23]

Despite the novelty of this actualistic and particularist approach to holiness, Barth once again claims Calvin as his precedent for making God's active sovereignty in Jesus Christ the locus of holiness (522):

> We cannot overlook ... the exemplary determination and power with which, in the first chapter of the third book [Calvin] asserted the Christ-created participation of the saints in the sanctity of Jesus Christ, and therefore their membership in Him as their Lord, as the basis of all soteriology. It is because of this, as the result of his thinking from this centre, that he has the clear insight into the relation between justification and sanctification which we had cause to admire in our first sub-section.

The way Barth grounds sanctification (and justification) in participation in Christ is explicitly derived from the place of the *participatio* as the cornerstone of *Institutes* III – and apex of the entire *Institutes*.[24]

However, Barth radicalizes this Calvinian insight, maintaining that the holiness secured by Christ's sanctifying work is objectively real and universally effective. Unlike for Calvin, it does not await some additional 'application' to become real and effective. According to Calvin, 'as long as Christ remains outside of us, and we are separated from him, all that he has suffered and done for the salvation of the human race remains useless and of no value for us'.[25] It is the work of the Spirit to apply what was accomplished in Christ's saving work: 'he unites himself to us by the Spirit alone'.[26] But Barth rejects this and the later Protestant notion of the *ordo salutis* that built upon this (*CD* IV/2, 502–3). Instead, he sees the subjective application and appropriation of Christ's work as included within his objective accomplishment of reconciliation. Indeed, its application to human beings is the goal of Christ's reconciling work. Ultimately, Christ's sanctification includes all in its ambit by virtue of their election in him. This is Barth's signature 'objectivism'. Holiness, like every other aspect of revelation and salvation, is 'real, valid, and effective – whether it is acknowledged and received by the creature or not'.[27]

Barth explains his divergence from Calvin in these terms (520):

---

23. Webster, *Holiness*, 52.

24. See Robert C. Doyle's work on the architectonics of the *Institutes* in *The Context of Moral Decision-Making in the Writings of John Calvin: The Christological Ethics of Eschatological Order* (PhD diss., University of Aberdeen, 1981).

25. Calvin, *Inst.* III.i.1.

26. Calvin, *Inst.* III.i.3.

27. Hunsinger, *How to Read Karl Barth*, 5.

3. The Problem and Promise of Discipleship

Calvin's doctrine of the *participatio Christi* has one weakness which we can never too greatly deplore and which we can never forget in all his thoughtful and instructive presentation of justification and sanctification. This consists in the fact that he found no place – and in view of his distinctive doctrine of predestination he could not do so – for a recognition of the universal relevance of the existence of the man Jesus, of the sanctification of all men as it has been achieved in Him.

Barth locates the source of the inadequacy in Calvin's account in a failure to allow Christ to decisively determine his vision of God. Calvin is not Christocentric enough because the 'objective presupposition of the participation of the saints in the sanctity of Jesus' lies in 'the abyss of the absolute decree of a God who is absolutely hidden and anonymous' (520). For Barth, by contrast, Christ reveals that all participate in sanctification in Christ *de iure*. Sanctification is objective and universally effective. However, Barth also maintains that people only experience and live in this holiness insofar as the Spirit awakens them to it. To the event of universal sanctification in Christ there corresponds a personal encounter which the Spirit dynamically mediates and in which we are sanctified *de facto*. This is Barth's 'personalism'. As Hunsinger puts it, 'God's objective self-manifestation in revelation and salvation comes to the creature in the form of personal address' – freeing us for fellowship with God and others. Here, Barth again 'rejoins' Calvin (522) since the dynamic, personal rule of Christ by the agency of the Holy Spirit is a well-known emphasis of Calvin's theology – so much so, in fact, that his doctrines of the Christian life and the church have been memorably described as 'pneumatocratic'.[28]

Barth develops this 'pneumatocratic' personalism in the context of his revision of sanctification in terms of the 'direction' (*Weisung*) Christ gives by the Spirit. Indeed, the entirety of *CD* IV/2 §65-§68 is presented as the exposition of the theme of 'direction', which Barth introduced in §64.4. I will develop the connections between §64.4 and §66 more fully in the final section of this chapter (3.4). For the moment, however, it is worth noting the twofold structure of Christ's 'direction' as it is presented there. In the first instance, the 'direction of the Son of Man' is the movement of the risen Christ to us, 'present-ing' himself as the living Lord in the power of the Spirit. Barth could well be directly refuting Calvin when he declares: 'The New Testament does not know of a Jesus Christ who is what He is exclusively for Himself' (280). Christ closes the distance between him and us, achieving the transition from his own history for us to his ongoing history with us. His 'direction' therefore describes how Christ is present with us. At the same time and on this basis, Christ's 'direction' speaks of the concrete guidance he provides us, ensuring we are not alone or left to our own resources: 'Nor does [the New Testament] know of a self-enclosed human being confronting this man

---

28. See Willem Balke, *Calvin and the Anabaptist Radicals*, trans. William Heynen (Grand Rapids: Eerdmans, 1981).

Jesus' (280–1). As Barth emphasizes in §66, this 'direction' reorients people's whole existence as he claims and constitutes them as his holy ones (522–3): 'the "saints" are those whose existence is affected and radically altered and re-determined by the fact that they receive direction in a particular address of the One who alone is holy. He creates saints by giving them direction.'

Barth is at pains to stress that this 'direction' operates in a manner consistent with the authority the Lord Jesus exercises in the gospel. Specifically, it is liberating (not coercive), life-giving (not crushing) and partnership-creating (not mechanical, magical or unilateral). This insistence is in keeping with Barth's objectivist emphasis on God's having achieved our sanctification in Christ and his personalist emphasis on the existential encounter and covenant relationship this draws us into. The divine agency is not, as John Webster emphasizes, 'omnicausal', leaving no room for any other genuine agency. Rather, it summons and calls forth genuine agency in response to its sovereign initiative.[29]

The actualism, particularism, objectivism and personalism of Barth's account of sanctification undergirds its 'realism' when it comes to Christian holiness. This realism can be glimpsed when Barth speaks of Christ sharing his holiness with his people such that they come to participate in a 'new form of existence as the true covenant-partner of God'. As with other areas of his thought, Barth's realistic vision of human holiness needs to be distinguished from a literalistic view on the one side and mythological or purely symbolic view on the other.[30] That is to say, when Barth maintains that Jesus shares his holiness with his people 'in supreme realism', he means that we genuinely share in the holiness that is a reality in Christ even though it remains his. That is, it does not mean that we come to possess it somehow (the literalistic view), as if holiness comes to inhere in or to be infused into us. Nor that it is merely metaphorical. It is not the conceptual analogue of the sort of 'legal fiction' that Protestant approaches to justification often appear to involve. It is not something distant from us and which we might admire or strive to imitate but that we do not genuinely share in. Christian holiness subsists entirely in its living source, template and active Giver – the Holy One, incarnate, crucified, risen and present.

The resulting relative but still real holiness of Christians takes a particular shape. Defined and called forth by God's decisive action in Christ, it is objectively and universally effective in liberating us for covenant partnership under the personal 'direction' of the Lord Jesus. As such, Christian holiness is stretched between distinction from and solidarity with the world. Christ's holy people are 'marked off from the race, from others, in order that [they] may make a provisional offering of the thankfulness for which the whole world is ordained by the act of the love of God' (511). For Barth, Christian holiness is essentially a matter of worship – offering the very worship, praise and thanksgiving here and now that all of creation

---

29. See, for example, John Webster, 'The Christian in Revolt: Some Reflections on *The Christian Life*' in *Reckoning with Barth*, 119–44.

30. See Hunsinger, *How to Read Karl Barth*, 43–9.

is destined to offer when Christ returns. Christians and Christian communities are holy insofar as they are broken open, finding their centre in Christ rather than in themselves – whether directly or indirectly in affirming or rejecting the world or some aspect of it.

In this way, Barth's vision of the holy, sanctified people is fundamentally world-positive rather than negative or hostile towards the world – although it does preserve a provisional distinction from it. By virtue of Christ's status as the Electing God and elect human being, Christians participate in Christ in solidarity with the world. All stand in need of his reconciling work to lift them out of the misery and sloth of sin (in the terms of §65). All are *de iure* beneficiaries of Christ's omnipotent sanctifying work in reality and can anticipate enjoying it in the eschaton. All are 'passive participants' in the holiness of Christ. However, it is only those whom the Spirit awakens who become 'active participants' in his holiness, recognizing and embracing the sanctification achieved in him.[31]

World-positivity is expressed here firstly in terms of the witness God's holy people give to God's love for the world exerted unreservedly and for all in Christ. It is Christ's positivity towards the world – his love for it – that proves definitive here. Indeed, it is the motive force of the 'provisional task' of mission, broadly conceived: 'In all its particularity their sanctification speaks of the universal action of God, which has as its purpose and goal the reconciliation of the world, and therefore not merely this group of individuals in the world' (518–19).[32] In other words, Christian existence – and flowing from it all the tasks of speaking and showing forth the holy love and freedom of God in Christ – is distinctive insofar as it provides a concrete preview of God's ultimate intention for humanity and the world. But world-positivity is also expressed in both the reality and the relativity of Christian distinctiveness. Both the reality and relativity of this distinctiveness – the concrete differentiation and separation of the holy people from others – consists in Christians providing a 'creaturely reflection' of Christ's active holiness (511). The reality of Christian distinctiveness is constituted by its relativity to Christ. Conversely, the relativity of Christian distinctiveness reflects its reality in Christ. Christian holiness is the echo and reflection of 'the holiness in which God confronts ... both [Christians] and the world' (511) rather than an abstract or self-contained truth.

Christian distinctiveness is primarily relative to God's holy distinctiveness. But it is also relative – secondarily and derivatively – to the world and the rest of humanity. Christians stand in solidarity with the world and others. God confronts all in his singular holiness (and electing love). There is no sharp ontological distinction between Christians and others.[33] This is evident in the first instance

---

31. G. Hunsinger, 'Sanctification', in *The Westminster Handbook to Karl Barth*, ed. R. E. Burnett (Louisville: Westminster John Knox, 2013), 193–8.

32. Flett's discussion of the terminology Barth employs to describe mission across his developing corpus is worth consulting; Flett, *The Witness of God*, ix–xiii.

33. Flett expounds this at length in *The Witness of God*, 180–95.

in the fact that Christians remain entangled with sin: 'He, the Holy One, being revealed to them as such and not hidden, present as their living Lord, has laid His hand on their creaturely and sinful being and thinking and action and inaction, claiming it for Himself as such, making them witnesses of His sanctity, and therefore and to that extent fellow-saints with him, *even as the sinful creatures they are*' (522, emphasis added). In other words, the real holiness of Christians is relative not only to *the* Holy One but also to the others with whom they stand shoulder to shoulder in sin. As a result, Christians are only ever provisionally distinct from those who do not yet experience the sanctification that is objectively theirs in Christ. At the conclusion of §66.2, Barth teases out what may be said on the basis of Scripture about this provisional distinction of Christians from others. In particular, he describes this provisional distinction in terms of their being both disturbed – because contradicted, limited and compromised by God's direction – and also called to conformity with Christ – as those corrected, instructed, lifted up and liberated by him (524–33).[34] Characteristically, Barth's emphasis falls on the second, more positive term (533): 'It is all provisional, for the saints are still captives. But it is all very real, for they are already liberated. If it is true that they are still prisoners, it does not count. The captivity is behind them, freedom before them. And all this is in their fellowship with with the Holy One. All this in virtue of the fact that they are called by Him.'

Finally, Barth's 'rationalism' – the last of Hunsinger's motifs – finds expression in his account of discipleship in §66.3, although it is foreshadowed in §66.2. This 'rationalism' is encapsulated in the Anselmian formula *fides quaerens intellectum* (faith seeking understanding). While potentially a misleading term, 'rationalism' according to Hunsinger describes the way Barth fleshes out doctrines in terms of their cognitive content. Within the limits set by his attentive 'post-critical' biblical exegesis,[35] Barth conceptually elaborates the cognitive content of doctrines

---

34. The provisionality of the distinction of Christians from others is also reflected in Barth's frequently expressed expectation that Christian growth will be neither neat and straightforward nor simply occasionalist and episodic. Webster's description of the impression that emerges from reading *The Christian Life* captures the way Barth presses beyond the merely episodic: 'As one reads through *The Christian Life*, it soon becomes evident that Barth, too, is immersed in a search for categories to describe the self as a weighty reality, continuous between its moments of choice and formed not simply in the instant of decision but by its convictions about the realities outside itself to which it must give assent'; Webster, 'The Christian in Revolt', 120. At the same time, Webster points out that in *The Christian Life*, 'Barth ranges over some of the ways in which the Christian's deeds and decisions are limited, fragmentary, lacking in the finality and absoluteness which can be predicated only of God's perfect act', Webster, 'The Christian in Revolt', 133.

35. A fuller account of Barth's 'post-critical' approach to exegesis is given by Hans W. Frei, 'Scripture as Realistic Narrative: Karl Barth as Critic of Historical Criticism' in *Thy Word Is Truth: Barth on Scripture*, ed. George Hunsinger (Grand Rapids & Cambridge: Eerdmans, 2012), 49–59.

'beyond the surface content of scripture as a way of understanding scripture's deeper conceptual implications and underlying unity'.[36] Put in contemporary terms, Barth's rationalism is a matter of theological interpretation of Scripture. In the context of his revision of Calvin on sanctification, this motif appears in his exegesis of the relevant texts concerning the call and commitment of discipleship.

Here in §66.2, the 'rationalism' of Barth's theological attention to Scripture can be glimpsed as he fleshes out the relative realism of Christian holiness. Barth picks up the terminology he developed at length when treating 'the sloth and misery of man' (§65) – about the slumbering insensitivity of self-enclosed and imprisoned humanity under sin – in order to concatenate a number of New Testament texts he mentions but does not pause to exegete (2 Cor. 3.17, 5.6 and 17; Lk. 21.28, Heb. 12.2, Jn 12.32 and 15.3; Gal. 4.25–5.1) as well as others to which he only alludes (e.g. Eph. 4–5). Almost all of these texts speak, in one way or another, of the new reality of those who are in Christ. They typically contrast it with the past reality that nonetheless still exerts its influence on the situation and behaviour of Christians in the present. A picture of the experience of sanctification under the direction of the Lord Jesus emerges in which Christian holiness is a struggle to overcome sleep, stupor and brutishness in order to stand tall as the clear-eyed, free and fully human children of God Christ reconciles people to be. For Barth, Christian sanctification is the present and active (and provisional) experience of the exaltation of humanity to truly humanizing covenant-partnership with God in Christ. This emerges into sharp relief against the backdrop of §65, which Webster characterizes well as 'a long meditation on human sloth' that 'is grounded in sober observation of human habit and of the sheer mediocrity to which men and women can condemn themselves'.[37] This, in turn, provides the conceptual scaffolding for Barth's turn to discipleship in §66.3, which we will examine more fully in the next chapter.

I have stressed the simultaneous presence of the motifs Hunsinger identifies – which mark out the distinctiveness of Barth's approach – as well as the profound and ongoing debt to Calvin here for two closely related reasons. First, the conjunction of the Barthian 'thought form' with the obvious debt to Calvin here illustrates the 'Calvinian' character of Barth's revision sanctification. Barth builds on Calvin's foundation, uses much of Calvin's own raw materials and when he parts ways with Calvin – as he does most dramatically in §66.2 – he seeks to develop Calvin's best insights within a new context. Barth builds on Calvin's Christocentrism with respect to sanctification, even as he revises it in light of his 'correction' of election. He appropriates Calvin's emphasis on the simultaneity of sanctification along with justification, its objectivity in Christ and the role of the Spirit in bringing us to participate in it. As Hunsinger remarks, when Barth 'forcibly shifts the whole axis of salvation (justification and sanctification) away from what takes place in us existentially (*in nobis*) to what has taken place apart

---

36. Hunsinger, *How to Read Karl Barth*, 5.
37. Webster, 'The Christian in Revolt', 133.

from us pertinently in Christ (*extra nos*)', he does so in 'logical fulfilment of a general though still somewhat unsteady move in this direction by Reformation soteriology'.[38] However, Barth takes this one step further, making sanctification even more concrete. We must look to Christ as the defining centre and active agent of both our definitive sanctification and our continual (although not automatic or effortless) experience of it. As we do so, we come under his 'direction' as the royal Son of Man, setting out on the way of the 'pneumatocratic' community and Christian life of which Calvin was such a well-known exponent. This 'way' is what Barth will describe in detail in terms of discipleship.

The second reason I have stressed the distinctively Barthian as well as thoroughly Calvinian character of Barth's revision of sanctification in §66.2 is to emphasize how Christocentrism and discipleship imply and interpret each other. Although Barth does not decisively turn to the language of discipleship until §66.3, everything we have so far seen paves the way for it. Likewise, when I come to analyse Barth's argument in the remainder of §66 (the task of Chapters 7–9), I will show that the concept of discipleship continues to shape and determine everything Barth goes on to say there about conversion, good works and bearing the cross. Barth's vision of sanctified community and Christian living is already discipleship-shaped, even before he explicitly and extensively deploys the language of discipleship. Ultimately, it is discipleship-shaped because it is relentlessly Christ-centred – and because of the way Barth understands Christ to be the living, ruling, active and personal Lord, directing his holy people in living towards their (already real and effective) sanctification.

To summarize, I have established that in his revision of Calvin, Barth's commitment to Christ-centredness leads him to a distinctively discipleship-shaped vision of sanctification – even before he explicitly picks up the language of discipleship. This goes well beyond Calvin. It brings Barth closer to the 'practical Christocentrism' of the Anabaptist vision, which itself harks back to the medieval monastic tradition (as the early Reformers recognized). Yet Barth understands himself as following Calvin's lead in taking this step beyond Calvin. He builds on the foundation of the *participatio Christi*, draws extensively and appreciatively on Calvin's treatment of sanctification (especially in terms of its relationship to justification) and attempts to resolve some of the most troubling inconsistencies in

---

38. Hunsinger, 'A Tale of Two Simultaneities', 316–38. My emphasis on the Calvinian character of Barth's revision of sanctification appears to run counter to Hunsinger's insistence that Barth incorporated Calvin's emphasis on the *simul* of justification and sanctification within the fundamentally Lutheran framework of *simul justus et peccator*. According to Hunsinger, Luther's 'again and again' edges out Calvin's 'more and more' in Barth. However, Hunsinger's thesis needs nuancing with respect to the history of Reformed engagement with these questions that Willem van Vlaustin, for example, has unearthed in 'Personal Renewal between Heidelberg and Westminster', *Journal of Reformed Theology* 5 (2011): 49–67. By the time Barth takes up the tension between Calvin's 'more and more' and Luther's 'again and again', it is well and truly located *within* the Reformed tradition.

Calvin's approach not by importing alien materials but by using what already lies 'to hand' in the Reformer's thinking. Barth's approach can therefore be considered an appreciative and creative 'Calvinian' revision of Calvin's doctrine of sanctification.

3.3 Which Christocentrism? Whose discipleship?

So far I have argued that the decisive Christ-centredness of Barth's theology of sanctification yields it distinctive shape as discipleship. I established the distinctiveness of Barth's discipleship-shaped account in relation to Calvin's approach. Specifically, I demonstrated that this involves a 'Calvinian' revision of Calvin. This departs in some important ways from the scholarly consensus on Barth, Calvin and the contrast between their approaches to sanctification. In this section, I develop a more fine-grained account of Barth's vision of the sanctified Christian life as Christ-centred and discipleship-shaped. I do this by examining the chief theological sources of Barth's account. This examination involves comparing and contrasting Barth's account not only with Calvin but also Luther. While it is Christocentrism that proves decisive for Barth's theology of sanctification, this is not enough in itself to fully characterize it – for many can lay claim to being Christocentric.[39] The question that must be addressed is therefore: which Christocentrism? And, following on from this, whose discipleship?

3.3.1 Barth and Calvin on sanctification

The current consensus on the relation between Barth's vision of sanctification and its source in Calvin is articulated by scholars like Hunsinger and McCormack. These scholars maintain that Barth's Christocentrism is the distinguishing feature of his account of sanctification vis a vis Calvin. In what follows, I dissent from this consensus. As such, my specification of the character and function of Barth's Christocentrism in the context of sanctification will require a moderately technical engagement with their arguments.

To begin with, the character and function of Christocentrism in Barth's vision of sanctification with respect to Calvin needs to be specified with greater precision.

---

39. The appropriateness of such a characterization in Calvin's case is, of course, disputed – especially as it tends to be invoked in pitting Calvin against later post-Reformation Reformed thinkers. What is more, even if it is an apt characterization at some level, further clarification is required (this applies to Barth too). Richard A. Muller, 'A Note on "Christocentrism" and the Imprudent Use of Such Terminology', *Westminster Theological Journal* 68 (2006): 253–60, identifies three types of christocentrism: soteriological, prototypical and principial. David Gibson, *Reading the Decree: Exegesis, Election, and Christology in Calvin and Barth* (London: T&T Clark, 2009), chapter 1, suggests that to this should be added a distinction between 'extensive' and 'intensive' versions of christocentrism, specifically as this describes the function of centring on Christ with regard to other doctrines.

As I have said, the current consensus distinguishes Barth's approach from Calvin by recourse to his Christocentrism. Having declared that 'familiar received traditions, whether Protestant or otherwise, there is nothing quite like' Barth's treatment of sanctification, Hunsinger contrasts it explicitly with Calvin's approach:[40]

> The main reason for Barth's innovative approach was the priority he assigned to the idea of sanctification 'in Christ' ... Because sanctification, like justification, took place first of all apart from us in Christ, the grammar or logical structure of both doctrines was much the same. It was not as though justification was something 'instantaneous' in the life of faith while sanctification was in turn something 'continual'. On the contrary, each of them was instantaneous and continual in its own way. Justification and sanctification were each seen as a unitary, two-phased event involving a necessary transition from the 'objective' aspect in Christ there and then to the 'subjective' or 'existential' aspect, taking place in us, or among us, here and now.[41]

Hunsinger claims that Calvin failed to adequately insist on the objectivity of justification and sanctification apart from us in Christ. He compares this unfavourably with Barth's innovation in making sanctification 'objective and passive by grace before it became active and subjective in faith working by love'. As he does this, Hunsinger strongly implies that Calvin regarded sanctification as the subjective sequel to justification.[42]

McCormack takes this further, arguing that Barth revises Calvin on sanctification as part of his post-metaphysical overhaul of all the doctrines of grace – justification, sanctification and regeneration.[43] As for Hunsinger, McCormack maintains that Christocentrism is the distinctive feature of Barth's account, marking it off from the 'classical view' he ascribes to Calvin. According to this view, sanctification proceeds progressively and continually on the basis of a punctiliar and definitive justification.

For McCormack, Barth advances on this in two ways. First, Barth successfully answers the accusation typically levelled against forensic views of justification (like Calvin's) – namely, that it makes God's declaration of our innocence rest on a legal fiction. Barth answers this charge, according to McCormack, by treating justification as ontologically real in Christ: 'justification is complete in Christ because we are already in him when he does what he does'.[44] This contrasts with what McCormack sees in Calvin: 'Basic to Calvin's answer to this charge was the

---

40. George Hunsinger, 'Sanctification', in *The Westminster Handbook to Karl Barth*, ed. Richard E. Burnett (Louisville: Westminster John Knox Press, 2013), 193.

41. Hunsinger, 'Sanctification', 193.

42. Hunsinger, 'Sanctification', 193.

43. Bruce L. McCormack, 'Sanctification after Metaphysics: Karl Barth in Conversation with John Wesley's Concept of "Christian Perfection"', in *Sanctification: Explorations in Theology and Practice*, ed. Kelly M. Kapic (Downers Grove, IL: IVP, 2014), 103–24.

44. McCormack, 'Sanctification after Metaphysics', 115.

claim that justification is never without regeneration as the initiating moment in the process of sanctification.'[45] On this reading, Calvin fails to be sufficiently Christocentric at the decisive point: he 'looks away from the ground of justification in the alien righteousness of Christ and directs our attention instead to what God is doing in us'.[46] Barth, by contrast, emphasized the radical objectivity and effectiveness of our justification in Christ. By virtue of Christ's identity as both the Electing God and the elect human being, he is ontologically one with all of humanity. This succeeds where Calvin fails, according to McCormack, because there is no legal fiction; instead, as those who have died (facing judgement for our sin) and been raised (as new creatures no longer beholden to sin) in and with Christ, 'we are rightly judged innocent'.[47] The second way in which McCormack sees Barth's view as an advance on Calvin's is in its movement away from a substantive to a more personal and existential understanding of sanctification. As McCormack renders Calvin, sanctification becomes the way God makes real and actual the righteousness believers are declared to have in their justification: 'God does not merely impute Christ's righteousness to us; God makes us to be in ourselves what he declares us to be in justification: upright and holy persons.'[48] This appears to be yet another variation on the 'classical view' of sanctification: 'Sanctification [is] … understood as a process, a movement from the lesser to the greater, from the provisional to the more complete, from a minimal to a greater acquisition of "grace".'[49] In contrast to this, Barth is reluctant to admit any substantive 'more and more'. The believer's sanctification is whole and complete in Christ – not as a metaphysical substance that must be somehow transferred to individuals but as 'the history of Jesus' lived faith and obedience', which includes all and in which believers come to participate as they correspond to it in the power of the Spirit.[50] While there is a 'more and more' to Christian sanctification for Barth, it is not substantive but personal, existential and actual.

There are several problems with this consensus about how Christocentrism distinguishes Barth's view from Calvin's. For one thing, *both* Calvin and Barth's views can be characterized as Christocentric. To describe Barth's view of sanctification as Christocentric can only be the beginning rather than the end of an attempt to compare and contrast him with Calvin. McCormack himself makes this observation in another context:

> 'Christocentrism' means different things to different people. Formally, it simply means that a Christology stands at the approximate centre of a particular theology, giving it its characteristic shape and content. That much is true of all

---

45. McCormack, 'Sanctification after Metaphysics', 114.
46. McCormack, 'Sanctification after Metaphysics', 114.
47. McCormack, 'Sanctification after Metaphysics', 116.
48. McCormack, 'Sanctification after Metaphysics', 114.
49. McCormack, 'Sanctification after Metaphysics', 117.
50. McCormack, 'Sanctification after Metaphysics', 117–18.

so-called 'christocentric theologies'. Materially, however, the meaning of the term can differ widely for the simple reason that the doctrine of Christ which is placed at the centre of theology differs from one 'christocentric' theologian to the next.[51]

Without denying the very real differences between Barth and Calvin when it comes to justification and sanctification, Alister McGrath's careful description of Calvin's position places it much closer to Barth than Hunsinger and especially McCormack appear to allow: 'Calvin understands both justification and sanctification to be the chief *beneficia Christi*, bestowed simultaneously and inseparably upon the believer as a consequence of his *insitio in Christum*.'[52] To be sure, Calvin differs from Barth in making this union with Christ depend on the believer being 'grafted in' by faith, rather than being itself a definitive achievement of Christ in his ontological unity with humanity as the elect human being. But the objectivity of justification and sanctification as based in what, quite apart from us, God has achieved in Christ, is *a* – if not *the* – hallmark of Calvin's account.[53] Indeed, Barth's own most intensively Christocentric material in relation to sanctification – his treatment of 'The Holy One and his saints' in §66.2 – bears the unmistakable Calvinian provenance we have already established.

Barth's debt to Calvin is evident even when it comes to a fuller specification of the character and function of Christocentrism in their respective theologies. David Gibson has carefully examined the differing shape and function of Christocentrism in Calvin and Barth with particular reference to the doctrine of election. Gibson deploys a pair of distinctions to pick out the key differences. It is worth taking the time to understand and evaluate these distinctions.[54]

The first distinction Gibson (following Muller) deploys to distinguish between Calvin and Barth's versions of Christocentrism is that between 'soteriological' and 'principial' Christocentrism. The soteriological–principial distinction picks out an apparent difference in terms of the content and focus of their respective Christologies. According to Gibson, Calvin's Christocentrism primarily concerns soteriology. Even when it comes to election, Calvin focuses on the role of Christ within the divine economy of (creation and) salvation rather than its eternal 'background' in the immanent or essential Trinity. Hence, Barth's allegation that Calvin so emphasized Christ's role as the 'mirror' of election – the first and pre-eminent elect human – that he neglected to attend to the fact that Jesus is

---

51. Bruce L. McCormack, *Karl Barth's Critically Realistic Dialectical Theology: Its Genesis and Development 1909–1936* (Oxford: Clarendon Press, 1995), 453. See also Marc Cortez, 'What Does It Mean to Call Karl Barth a "Christocentric" Theologian?', *Scottish Journal of Theology* 60.2 (2007): 127–43.

52. Alister E. McGrath, *Iustitia Dei: A History of the Christian Doctrine of Justification*, 2nd edn (Cambridge: Cambridge University Press), 224.

53. McGrath, *Iustitia Dei*, 225.

54. Gibson, *Reading the Decree*, 6–16.

himself also and primarily the electing God (see *CD* II/2 §32). Undoubtedly, Calvin hesitated to pursue Christ's election and mediation of the Father's will into eternity – in keeping with the anti-speculative thrust of much Reformation theology.

Indeed, even when he does speak of Christ as both the author and the Mediator of election, Calvin tends to present this primarily in terms of how it bears on us in time (rather than any implications it might have for God in eternity). Richard Muller's judicious conclusions are apposite:

> From the divine side to which Calvin, in his desire to avoid speculation, only points indirectly, from the vantage of eternity and transcendence, the decree and the Christ, considered as God, are inseparable. For Christ is one with the Father, is the author of salvation, and claims with the Father the right to choose. Christ is more than 'election itself' and more than the 'index' or 'mirror' of election. In the depth of the triune God, to whom both the person of the mediator and the work of salvation point, Christ is the electing God. In terms of the trinitarian ground of theology, Christ can never be reduced to a mere means. [But …] Calvin never sought to develop this more speculative side of his doctrine, never meditated in detail upon the trinitarian ground of theology as the point at which the lines of christological and predestinarian doctrine converge.[55]

Barth's Christocentrism appears to work very different from this. Instead of focusing primarily on the temporal, soteriological aspect of Christ's person and work – as Calvin did – he reads it back into pre-temporal eternity. Consequently, it becomes the governing 'principle' or 'interpretive key to understanding and elucidating all doctrinal topics.'[56] Hence, 'principial Christocentrism'. Barth famously locates his treatment of election within the doctrine of God itself in *CD* II/2: Christ as the electing God and the elect human being is the 'eternal presupposing' of all God's works and ways *ad extra*. As such, not only election but every doctrine – including the doctrine of the Trinity – is christolologically determined in a more far-reaching way than in Calvin.[57]

It is possible to overplay the difference between the Christocentrisms of Calvin and Barth at this point. Calvin's soteriological emphasis clearly answers to his pastoral and anti-speculative bias. His instinct is to direct attention to what God has done in history for humanity rather than allowing people to wander off into a 'labyrinth' – his favourite image for the obscurity and confusion to which speculation could lead. But Barth's desire to theologize in response to the concrete revelation of God in Christ – even or especially when it comes to election and

---

55. Muller, *Christ and the Decree*, 38.

56. Muller, 'A Note on "Christocentrism"', 256.

57. This holds whether or not we can sustain Bruce McCormack's contention that, for Barth, election 'constitutes' the Trinity since God is lord even over his own being as Father, Son and Spirit.

the wild hinterland of pre-temporal eternity within God's triune 'inner life' – is governed by a very similar pastoral impulse. Indeed, Barth's desire to direct his readers towards Christ is something he learnt from Calvin. For the function of his speculative seeming principial Christocentrism is anti-speculative in intent. In keeping with Calvin's intention, Barth seeks to rule out abstraction and speculation at every point, especially when it comes to the disastrous and assurance-destroying *syllogismus practicus* that frequently came to be deployed in the Reformed tradition for discerning whether someone is elect (see *CD* II/2, 333–40). As a result, the soteriological–principial distinction needs to be set within a charitable reading of the stated aims of each theologian in following through their Christocentric convictions.

Parallelling the soteriological–principial distinction, Gibson deploys a second distinction, this time between extensive and intensive varieties of Christocentrism. Here the emphasis falls on the differing hermeneutics through which the Calvin's soteriological and Barth's principial christocentrism are expressed. Gibson incisively describes the difference:

> To describe a hermeneutic as christologically extensive means that Christology clearly defines the hermeneutical approach, but the centre of Christology points outwards to other doctrinal loci which have space and scope to exist in themselves at a measure of distance from Christology and from each other … Conversely, to describe a hermeneutic as christologically intensive means that the christological centre defines all else within its circumference. Within this circle, Christology draws everything else to itself so that all other doctrinal loci cannot be read in Scripture apart from explicit christological reference.[58]

The implications of this difference become tangible in the diverging ways Barth and Calvin handle various doctrines. It is clearly evident, for example, when it comes to their doctrines of sanctification. As we have seen, Calvin's approach to sanctification is closer to Barth than Hunsinger and especially McCormack seem to realize.[59] But it does differ in that Calvin makes the union from which the benefits flow to us from Christ's saving work, subsequent to rather than itself part of the definitive accomplishment of reconciliation. Pneumatology – and behind it election – touches Christology but it is not included within its circumference in Calvin. Hence, the decisiveness and universality of Christ's person and work stand alongside the particularity of election, leaving a cesura in which the Spirit must work to create faith. Sanctification (along with justification) is therefore the Spirit's application of Christ's work. This application either cuts across the intention of Christ,

---

58. Gibson, *Reading the Decree*, 15.
59. McGrath, *Iustitia Dei*, 224–5.

narrowing in its limited application that which was intended for all, or faithfully carries through the already particular intent of Christ.

Not so for Barth. He integrates Christology and election, displaying an intensive Christocentrism in treating them as mutually constitutive. In the context of sanctification, the result is that the Spirit's work of evoking faith and particularizing Christ's reconciling work to make us holy comes in at a different point: it is not coextensive with sanctification, but merely the means of our present subjective and existential realization of the objective reality of sanctification forged in Christ. In being this present means, the Spirit draws the anticipated future of all into the present experience of Christians. What is more, this is itself the active work of Christ, ingredient with and based upon his objective history as the risen Lord.[60]

This analysis of how Barth's Christocentrism plays out differently from Calvin's in the context of sanctification underlines how radical Barth is in grounding sanctification in what God has achieved objectively and for all in Christ. Taking up Hunsinger's terms again, it is the radical actualism, particularism, objectivism and personalism of sanctification that pave the way for the (relative) realism and (scripturally attentive) rationalism of his discipleship-shaped vision of Christian holiness. Holiness is always a gift of the eternally active and generous Giver and never a given that can be possessed or presumed upon. It is something that looks unwaveringly to the Lord, never to ourselves or other so-called lords. It is entirely an objective work of God for us – something that stands over against us, and in which we are included by his grace in election, rather than by means of some intrinsic entitlement or meritorious performance. And it aims at drawing us into personal, Spirit-governed fellowship with God – fulfilling and perfecting rather than overturning or undermining our humanity and freedom. In short, for Barth Christian holiness is a reality forged in Christ, which by the power of the Spirit we joyfully receive as a gift freeing us to anticipate and announce the fellowship with God for which all humanity is created.

3.3.2 Barth and Luther on sanctification

Although I have given close attention to the relationship between Barth and Calvin on sanctification – understandably enough given Barth's self-conscious place within the Reformed tradition – Barth's relation to Luther also bears examination at this point. As Amy Marga points out, 'the thought of Martin Luther ... casts a long shadow over Barth's theology'.[61] No doubt, the circumstances of Barth's initial encounters with Luther during the so-called Luther renaissance left its stamp

---

60. Again, Barth may actually be able to claim Calvin as his precedent here. If the details of Calvin's language at the beginning of *Inst.* III.i are pressed, he too would seem to envisage the Spirit's role in effectually uniting us with Christ as Christ's active work.

61. Amy E. Marga, 'Jesus Christ and the Modern Sinner: Karl Barth's Retrieval of Luther's Substantive Christology', *Currents in Theology and Mission* 34.4 (2007): 260.

on his appropriation of the Reformer.[62] This raises questions about the extent to which the Luther who is encountered and casts such a shadow in Barth's writings corresponds with the historical Luther. Nevertheless, attention to Lutheran sources and themes – even those that are submerged as they frequently are by this point in the Church Dogmatics – promises to bear fruit. This is especially the case with respect to the current topic: Barth's Christocentrism. It has long been established that Barth owes a particular and substantive debt to Luther with regard to the content of his Christocentrism.[63] A number of the choices we have seen Barth make as he brings this Christocentrism to bear on sanctification could be said to display Luther's influence in parting from or radicalizing Calvin's Christocentrism.[64] In particular, Hunsinger's summary of Luther's Christocentrism could well read as a description of the dynamic, personal realism we have seen Barth ascribe to sanctification in §66:

> Luther's christocentrism is ... not merely formal but also and eminently substantive. Jesus Christ is not seen as the source of a salvation other than himself. He is uniquely and irreplaceably our salvation. His saving significance is not located abstractly in his predicates or in his spirituality, but in the concrete events of his incarnation, death, and resurrection for our sakes. He is inseparable from his saving predicates, because he is finally identical with them. He himself and he alone ... is our righteousness and our life.[65]

This Lutheran Christocentrism leaves a stamp on Barth's theology of sanctification materially, formally and methodologically.

Materially, the significance of Luther's Christocentrism is evident in the matter which occupies Hunsinger – namely, the extent to which three key aspects of sanctification receive due attention and are properly integrated in Barth's interpretation of Luther's dictum, *simul iustus et peccator*: once for all, again and again and more and more. Luther's thinking on sanctification makes reference to all three, although with a strong emphasis on the once-for-all

---

62. See, for instance, Heinrich Assel, 'Luther Renaissance and Dialectical Theology – A tour d'horizon 1906–1935', in Heirich Assel and Bruce L. McCormack, eds, *Luther, Barth, and Movements of Theological Renewal (1918–1933)*, Berlin, Boston: De Gruyter, 2020.

63. See, for example, Gerhard Ebeling, *Lutherstudien*, vol. 3 (Tübingen: Mohr Siebeck, 1985), 495–506 and Karin Bornkamm, 'Die reformatorische Lehre vom Amt Christi und ihre Umformung durch Karl Barth', in Joachim Heubach, ed., *Luther und Barth* (Erlangen: Martin-Luther-Verlag, 1989), 127–59.

64. As Hunsinger contends, 'this is [a] place where it can be argued, remarkably, that Barth stands with Luther against Calvin, or at least against Calvin's ambiguities. It might even be said here that Barth stands with Luther against much of the Lutheran theological tradition as well'. George Hunsinger, 'What Karl Barth Learned from Martin Luther', in *Disruptive Grace*, 295.

65. Hunsinger, 'What Karl Barth Learned from Martin Luther', 284–5.

aspect of Christ's achievement, less emphasis on the again-and-again and less still on the more-and-more.[66] Marga draws attention to this feature of the Christocentrism of Luther's *Galatians* commentary: according to Luther, 'the ongoing event' of 'Christ's *presence* to the reconciled sinner' dynamically holds together the once-for-all and the more-and-more of sanctification. In this, the again and again has tremendous significance even if it does not receive quite the same emphasis as the once for all: 'Luther's Christ is the One who comes, who is coming.'[67] Commenting on Galatians 2.20, Luther declares: 'We may now understand how spiritual life originates. It enters the heart by faith. Christ reigns in the heart with His Holy Spirit, who sees, hears, speaks, works, suffers, and does all things in and through us over the protest and the resistance of the flesh.'[68] Luther, of course, is acutely aware that this does not remove sin instantly or automatically from the life believers continue to live in the flesh. Indeed, Luther insists that considered apart from Christ we remain mired in sin and stand condemned: 'When we look at ourselves we find plenty of sin. But when we look at Christ, we have no sin. Whenever we separate the person of Christ from our own person, we live under the Law and not in Christ; we are condemned by the Law, dead before God.'[69]

In contrast to Luther, Calvin emphasizes the more-and-more (along with the once-for-all), allowing a gravitation pull towards gradualism to displace the again-and-again. As he puts it in *Institutes* III, 'through continual and sometimes even slow advances God wipes out in his elect the corruptions of the flesh, cleanses them of guilt, consecrates them to himself as temples renewing all their minds to true purity that they may practice repentance throughout their lives and know that this warfare will end only at death.'[70] The again and again of the warfare with the flesh that will end only at the believer's death is mentioned, but only as an afterthought. Much greater is Calvin's desire to create conceptual space for growth and progress to unfold.

Against Calvin, Barth reemphasizes Luther's again and again in thematizing the ongoing need to encounter Christ. Indeed, he emphasizes this so strongly that, in Hunsinger's view, no consistent place remains for growth or progress in sanctification.[71] Hunsinger is certainly not alone in regarding Barth's approach in this way; nor is he alone in finding it deficient as a result. Barth himself may even appear to give support to the view that he has no coherent way to give place to moral growth or progress. As a case in point, he frequently and categorically sweeps aside any gradualist or partial notions of sanctification, typically appealing

---

66. See Hunsinger, 'What Karl Barth Learned from Martin Luther', 299–300.
67. Marga, 'Jesus Christ and the Modern Sinner', 263.
68. Martin Luther, *Commentary on the Epistle to the Galatians (1535)*, trans. Theodore Graebner (Grand Rapids: Zondervan, 1949), 82.
69. Luther, *Commentary on the Epistle to the Galatians*, 81.
70. Calvin, *Inst.* III.iii.9
71. Hunsinger, 'What Karl Barth Learned from Martin Luther', 300–1n.30.

to Luther as he does so. This is certainly the case in his discussion of conversion in §66.4 (572):

> Static and quantitative terms may seem to help, but they are not adequate to describe the true situation. They involve a separation into constituent elements. It is true that the situation seems to cry out for this separation. It seems much more illuminating if, instead of saying that the whole man is still the old and yet already the new, in complete and utter antithesis, we say that he is still partially the old and already partially the new. But if we put it this way we mistake the matter. For the new man is the whole man; and so too is the old. And conversion is the transition, the movement, in which man is still, in fact, wholly the old and already wholly the new.

The reason Barth gives for preferring Luther's *totus-totus* approach to the *simul* is that this actually proves more faithful to the lived reality of Christian experience than the triumphalism implicit in a more partial, gradualist approach. He argues that a *partim-partim* resolution of the dialectic takes us out of 'the sphere of the *vita christiana* as it is actually lived for a psychological myth which has no real substance' (572). In contrast to this, Barth portrays the Christian life in terms of Christ's continual summons to conversion answered by his disciples' growth and progress, conceived in terms of receiving afresh the gift of holiness in Christ: 'each new step on the path from good to better can only ever be a matter of once again humbly and unassumingly offering obedience much in need of forgiveness to the one who bears us ever upwards'.[72] Formally, the debt Barth's theology of sanctification owes to Luther stems from their shared recognition of the priority of encounter with the person of Jesus Christ in the present. As Brian Brock points out, 'both thinkers take' this 'encounter with Jesus Christ ... to be the essence of theological ethics'.[73] This formal principle leads to Barth's reluctance about and difficulty giving consistent conceptual space to growth and progress in sanctification. This reluctance and difficulty has been widely recognized by those who disdain Barth's moral theology as well as those who would defend it. At the same time, as Michael Bartholomaeus has shown in the context of his most sustained explicit discussion of growth in §67.2, Barth interprets growth through the lens of encounter – which, I would add, takes the form of discipleship – rather than marginalizing growth altogether: 'Barth disciplines the concept of growth by the reality of the gospel made known to us in Jesus Christ through the Holy Spirit.'[74] Helpfully, Bartholomaeus emphasizes the richness and everyday resonance of this gospel-disciplined account of growth and progress, noting its seriousness and joy in particular.[75] In order to illustrate this

---

72. Michael Bartholomaeus, 'The Place of Growth in the Theology of Karl Barth', 177.
73. Brian Brock, 'Living in the Wake of God's Acts: Luther's Mary as Key to Barth's Command', in Brian Brock and Michael Mawson, eds, *The Freedom of a Christian Ethicist: The Future of a Reformation Legacy* (London: Bloomsbury T&T Clark, 2016), 65.
74. Bartholomaeus, 'The Place of Growth in the Theology of Karl Barth', 163.
75. Bartolomaeus, 'The Place of Growth in the Theology of Karl Barth', 170–1.

richness, Bartholomaeus looks away from the *Church Dogmatics* itself to Barth's account of wonder in *Evangelical Theology*. This is perfectly valid and illuminating. However, the immediate backdrop to Barth's insistence on viewing growth in sanctification through the lens of encounter with Christ is found in his account of Christ's lively and lordly 'direction' (*Weisung*) of his people in §64.4. I interrogate the connections between that subsection and Barth's vision of sanctification in the final part of this chapter, where I establish how it sponsors his turn towards discipleship (3.4). It is a Christology *for* discipleship. For the moment, though, it is worth registering how profoundly indebted to Luther such a Christology is.

Finally, it is worth noting the methodological evidence of the stamp Luther has left on Barth's thinking about sanctification here. According to Brock, Luther's characteristic approach to ethics – of which the biblical figure of Mary is the model – is oriented towards training 'Christians to pay attention, to provoke them to a deeper responsivity to God's care for others by weaning them from the desire to either live by "applying moral norms" or to "form themselves" into better people.'[76] The task of theological ethics, for Luther, is not so much to discriminate between cases or make authoritative moral pronouncements as it is to prepare Christians for and lead them to the necessary encounter with Christ. Christian theological ethics is about inculcating greater responsivity to God. As I will show at some length later in this book, Barth's theological ethics of encounter in general and his discipleship-shaped theology of sanctification in particular is conceived and expected to function very much along these lines. In this, once again, Barth sides unequivocally with Luther.[77]

3.3.3 The dogmatic location of discipleship

Another matter must be dealt with before giving fuller attention to Barth's 'turn' to discipleship in §66.3. If Barth's decisively and radically Christ-centred approach to sanctification does in fact yield an account of the Christian life that is distinctively discipleship-shaped, what does this Christ-centred framework suggest about how discipleship should be conceived? In particular, what does it say about the Christian distinctiveness and nonconformity discipleship entails? John Webster's notion of 'dogmatic location' is illuminating in this regard. According to Webster, the 'location' of any doctrine will dramatically impact its shape and significance. In the context of the doctrine of Scripture, for example, the post-Reformation relocation of the doctrine of revelation to the prolegomena to dogmatics results in a 'mislocation' with disastrous effects. As Webster puts it, revelation 'is transplanted out of its proper soil – essentially the saving economy of the triune God – and is made to do duty as a foundational doctrine'.[78] This not only gives the doctrine of

---

76. Brock, 'Living the Wake of God's Acts', 77.

77. Although, as Brock contends, Barth appears to finds the thought of God evoking our responsivity through creaturely means and occurrence less congenial than Luther does.

78. John Wesbter, 'The Dogmatic Location of the Canon' in *Word and Church: Essays in Christian Dogmatics* (Edinburgh & New York: T&T Clark, 2001), 9–10.

Scripture an independent significance that it cannot finally bear, it also materially affects its content. We see something similar with the 'dogmatic location' in which Barth embeds his sustained treatment of sanctified nonconformity. Barth locates his treatment of sanctification within the context not only of Pneumatology but of what may be called a 'christologized Pneumatology'.[79] Christian nonconformity is fundamentally Jesus-shaped as well as Christ-centred, reflecting the Spirit's role in anticipating the life of the eschaton. Like its Lord and primary reference point, sanctified nonconformity takes a servant and missional form. It freely and joyfully affirms the world it stands in solidarity with as it witnesses to what Christ has achieved and promises to unveil in giving himself for it. Barth puts it well in *CD* IV/4 (150):

> Since Jesus Christ is a Servant, looking to Him cannot mean looking away from the world, from men, from life, or, as is often said, from oneself. It cannot mean looking away into some distance or height. To look to Him is to see Him at the very centre, to see Him and the history which, accomplished in Him heals everything and all things, as the mystery, reality, origin and goal of the whole world, all men, all life. To look to Him is to cleave to Him as the One who bears away the sin of the world. It is to be bound and liberated, claimed, consoled, cheered and ruled by Him.

So what do we learn from the doctrinal location of Barth's account of Christian nonconformity with the world? We learn that again Calvin is Barth's precedent. Calvin treated sanctification under the heading of Pneumatology – and a decisively 'christologized' Pneumatology at that. Barth imitates this, correcting what he saw to be the deficiencies in Calvin's view with recourse to a more lively Christocentrism that echoes Luther's. For Barth, the Christian's sanctified distinction from the world is centred on Jesus. It is a matter of joyfully and freely responding to his direction. Moreover, it follows Jesus in extending itself in mission and service, anticipating and announcing God's vision for all.

But Barth moves even further beyond Calvin here. In particular, Barth much more clearly renders the universal basis for and horizon of sanctified distinctiveness and nonconformity. For Calvin, sanctification is essentially the plucking out of the elect from the world by grace. To be sure, the graciousness of election does mitigate against prideful elitism, and the unknown number of the elect holds open the need for mission. For all this, however, particularity trumps universality. Calvin's approach to nonconformity is grounded in universal solidarity looking backwards – along with all others, Christians are entirely dependent on God for their sanctification as both creatures and sinners. But looking forwards, there is murkiness and even anticipation of ultimate separation rather than solidarity in

---

79. Christopher R. J. Holmes, 'On Becoming Aligned with the Way Things Really Are', in *Apocalyptic and the Future of Theology: With and Beyond J. Louis Martyn*, ed. Joshua B. Davis and Douglas Harink (Eugene: Cascade, 2012), 219–35.

the eschaton. In contrast, Barth more decisively renders sanctification not only as provisional against its backdrop in common creatureliness and sin but also in terms of its eschatological prospect. In §66 the nonconformity of discipleship is missional and proleptic – a temporary distinction of this peculiar people for the sake of the world, announcing and anticipating the telos of humankind in general. As he put it in a programmatic statement in §64 (329), 'For all its peculiarity', Christian existence 'is not a particular one, but that of a universal mission'. Particularity and universality are thus dynamically interwoven in Barth. Sanctified nonconformity does not eclipse but expresses solidarity with others in service and mission.

Barth's Christ-centred approach to sanctification also corrects some less obvious, latent difficulties in Calvin's account – such as the lack of joy that can be traced to the way Calvin's approach to election produces uncertainty about who God wills to sanctify. Consistent with the pastoral and soteriological emphasis of Calvin's Christocentrism, Barth resists the tendency of either abstract speculation or the *syllogismus practicus* ('practical syllogism') to rush into the void of unknowing when it came to God's will in election. That is, Calvin wanted people to look to Christ rather than the fruitfulness of their own lives as proof that they belong to God. In *CD* II/2, Barth claims that this pastoral concern is the key to the *utilitas* of the doctrine of election as Calvin sees it (37).[80] He emphasizes how Calvin's exposition of election is framed by his conviction about its beneficial functions: to inculcate confidence in God's mercy, to demonstrate the glory of God and to teach humility. Nevertheless, as Barth shows, after Calvin these beneficial functions took on a life of their own, distorting the doctrine in the process (37–8). Joy became the ceaseless efforts of Weber's 'Protestant ethic', confidence in God's mercy became presumption of assurance (or an anxious attempt to secure it), humility that gave glory to God became fatalistic resignation before a divine tyrant. Barth's 'corrected' doctrine of election, however – which he invokes explicitly in §66.2 – allows him to restore to sanctified nonconformity its proper joy, manifested in confidence in and worship of the true God.

In the context of his theology of sanctification, therefore, Barth's specification of Christocentrism underwrites and energizes a thoroughly concrete, practical, missional, pastorally sensitive and joyful vision of Christian holiness. This vision is a long way from the pastorally destructive abstraction and speculation Gibson alleges it leads to. By 'locating' sanctified nonconformity in this way, Barth presents it as a divinely enacted, living reality in Christ, rather than a more or less tenuous human achievement cobbled together from the stolen fruit of God's gift along with all-too-human denial and self-delusion. What is more, he also presents it as something to be joyfully received and experienced by believers in the power of the

---

80. Of course, Calvin is concerned with the *utilitas* of all doctrine, setting a trajectory for Reformed theology as a whole. See, for example, Richard A. Muller, *After Calvin: Studies in the Development of a Theological Tradition* (Oxford: Oxford University Press, 2003), chapter 6.

Spirit without closing them off from the world in a spiritual elitism. In Christian sanctification, nonconformity and distinctiveness serve a larger solidarity, sending its recipients out to anticipate and announce the beauty of God's achievement for all.

3.4 A 'Lively Christology' for discipleship

In concluding this chapter, I will interrogate what about Barth's Christology makes his turn to discipleship in §66.3 not only possible but also necessary. What does Barth see about Christ and his sanctifying work that means that discipleship is the natural and obvious form for the provisional and world-positive distinctiveness of the Christian community and church? In brief: Barth develops a Christology for discipleship in §64.4, which he draws upon in §66 – and especially §66.2. It is a Christology for discipleship in that it provides the conceptual framework for his extensive development of the discipleship motif in §66.3. It establishes the points of reference for and the necessity of Barth's invocation of notions such as call, following, instruction and sending. In addition, it brings into focus important questions around the definiteness of the divine command that emerge whenever Barth engages with ethics.

To demonstrate that Barth develops and then draws upon a theology for discipleship here, I must engage some modest reconstruction. Barth indicates that his presentation of Christ in §64.4 includes and controls what needs to be said here (265): 'Whatever we may have to say later about the sloth and sanctification of man, and the edification of the Church, and love, is wholly included and enclosed already in the being and action of the Son of Man, and at bottom it can be understood and represented only as a development and explanation of it.' Yet neither §64.4 nor §66 provides a systematic statement tying up all the loose ends. Both are examples of Barth's 'narrative Christology'. We may develop a true picture of Christ from this narrative – although this picture will always be just that, a picture, liable to all the distortions of being a picture and lacking the dynamism of a narrative.

The picture of Christ that emerges in §64.4 aligns in important respects with Hunsinger's description of the threefold form of Christology in Barth as *Christus adventus*, *Christus praesens* and *Christus futurus* – the Christ who has come, the Christ who is present and the Christ who will come: 'For Barth, Christ's presence to faith cannot be considered apart from its profound interconnection with his life history in the past and also his future glorious manifestation.'[81] Hunsinger explains the 'unity-in-distinction' of these three forms of Christ in terms of mutual

---

81. Hunsinger, 'A Tale of Two Simultaneities', 330. This also coheres with Ian McFarland's contention that 'presence' rather than 'freedom' is the primary category in Barth's mature vision of God. See Ian A. McFarland, 'Present in Love: Rethinking Barth on the Divine Perfections', *Modern Theology* 33.2 (2017): 243–58.

3. *The Problem and Promise of Discipleship*

coinherence 'without separation or division, and without confusion or change'. Yet he insists that there is also an 'asymmetrical ordering' to them. 'It is the *Christus adventus* – the Jesus Christ who in his life history has perfectly accomplished our salvation – who defines and constitutes the identity of his other two forms.'[82] Barth certainly takes the accomplished work of reconciliation as his reference point in §64.4. He opens his investigation of how Christ is present with his people to give them his lordly direction by saying (265),

> Jesus Christ is in fact our Lord, and power flows from Him. The way from the one to the other, from Him to us, is wide open, and He Himself already treads it. We are not speaking, then, of a power of His existence which is merely possible or hypothetical or contingent, but of the power which is operative and effective. His being as the Son of Man is *per definitionem* His being with us, and His action is as such His action for us. For it to be His being with us or action for us no addition or completion is needed.

The representative and inclusive nature of Christ's accomplishment of reconciliation already contains within itself its presence and determining power for his people. It does this because the resurrection crowns Christ's accomplished work. Christ lives. As such, he is able to be present with his people – the people who are awakened to the fact that they are present with and participate in him in what he has done for them. He is neither still enclosed in the tomb nor ensconced in a sealed heaven. Although he is absent in the body – or rather, following the logic of Jesus' own teaching in John 14–17, because he is absent in the body – he is present in and through his Spirit. In this way the 'direction' (*Weisung*) of the royal Son of Man speaks first of him (and us in him) and only then and on that basis of us (as with him). 'We are the ones who are reached and affected by the existence of the Son of Man Jesus Christ' and 'we are the recipients of the direction of this Lord' because 'we are the ones to whom He is already on the way as the Resurrected' (266).

Because of its objective basis and reality in the risen Lord and his achievement, Barth goes on to speak at length about us as the recipients of this 'direction' in §64.4. Significantly, in doing so he indicates that he is speaking about Christians in particular and not all people in general or humanity in the abstract. What is more, he invokes the imagery of discipleship in the process – although he does not dwell on or develop it here: 'we are those who belong to this man, to Jesus, who have in Him their Master' (266). The Christ who in his living freedom is with and lays claim to his people – along with all others – sets us free in doing so. In the language he uses in §66 and will eventually come to use towards the end of §64.4, the Spirit awakens us to the reality of our participation in Christ. But at this point, Barth insists that this liberation is transformative and not simply epistemic: 'We come to a serious and transforming realization of this enclosing and controlling of our

---

82. Hunsinger, 'A Tale of Two Simultaneities', 330.

anthropological sphere by the royal man Jesus, and ... we achieve this knowledge of ourselves in which we know and confess that we are Christians' (266). The freedom Christ freely brings his people is practical (not merely notional), concrete (not abstract or general) and 'self-involving'. As Hunsinger observes elsewhere, 'the truth of the gospel, as Barth understood it' is 'the event whereby God [has] so fully entered into the depths of human distress that the very heart of God was present in the death of Jesus for the sake of the world'.[83] The gospel announces the accomplishment of reconciliation by God in Christ, involving God's own self in it. Moreover, it is also self-involving from the human side in that 'the Word of the cross, as mediated by Scripture and proclaimed by the church, [is] so actualized in the present that' those who receive it are 'transformed from the heart'.[84]

Barth does offer two qualifications about this transformative freedom. First, in liberating his people, Christ himself remains free. He does not compromise his freedom or allow us to bind him to ourselves in freeing us. He claims us; we do not claim him. In the terms of discipleship, he is the Master, we mere followers. In §64.4, Barth emphasizes that our understanding and living of this freedom – imperfect as it will no doubt be – does not call into question the decisiveness and potency of Christ's achievement: 'The power and lordship of the Son of Man, which as such reach and affect all men ... and therefore concretely ourselves as individuals' is 'not merely as an offer and possibility, but ... a reality, an event, which in its scope is actually determinative of all human existence' (267). Barth underlines the freedom of Jesus in this matter by speaking of him as the judge (*Christus adventus!*). It is his judgement, determination and decision that counts even when it comes to human self-examination with regard to the genuine transformation his 'direction' effects in freeing people to live a new way (267–9).

The second qualification Barth makes about Christ's transforming liberation of his people follows from recognizing the lordly freedom Christ retains – and that is that this transformation is truly questionable on the human side. Even as the recipients of his direction, his people must ask and answer the question of their active participation in Christ. And the answer given can only ever be indirect rather than direct. It can only be indirect because the reality of the transformation and freedom that Christ achieves for his people, remains relative to him (271):

> A true knowledge of ourselves as such, and therefore of our Christian actuality, stands or falls for all of us with our knowledge of Jesus Christ. In Him we are hidden from ourselves. Only in Him can we be revealed. We cannot, therefore, be revealed to ourselves or know ourselves directly, but only indirectly, in relation to the One who for us too is the Mediator between God and men.

---

83. George Hunsinger, 'Truth as Self-Involving: Barth and Lindbeck on the Cognitive and Performative Aspects of Truth in Theological Discourse', *Journal of the American Academy of Religion* 61.1 (1993): 41. Hunsinger treats the 'self-involvement' of God's reconciling work at length in *How to Read Karl Barth*, chapter 6.

84. Hunsinger, 'Truth as Self-Involving', 41.

Nevertheless, Barth does not fail to specify the reality of what this means for human existence in Christ and together with him. As those who are directed by him, our brother and captain, who is alive and present among us, his people actually experience the transformation and liberation of their humanity – that is, its elevation to covenant partnership with God. Barth is clear and emphatic on this (271–2):

> We, too, are directly elevated and exalted in the elevation and exaltation of the humiliated Servant of God to be the Lord and King. Apart from Him we are still below, but in Him we are already above. Without Him we are turned from God and disobedient, but with Him we are turned to God and obedient. Outside Christ, looking abstractly and subjectively at ourselves, we are not Christians. But as we look at Him we are Christians indeed.

For all the exultation and triumph in this vision of human inclusion in the representative humanity of Christ, and the freedom and transformation that result, Barth insists that the pattern of Christ's own life testifies to the costliness of this victory, and gives form to the freedom to which Christians are called in its power. The cross, he stresses, is the 'dominating characteristic' of Christ's royal office (292). Teasing this out over a number of densely argued pages (292–9), Barth shows that the cross defines and in a sense conceals Christ's lordship and freedom from us – even his own people. He goes to the cross but they do not. He does it for them, and in their place. Therefore, he is absent from them in an essential sense: Jesus is 'the Crucified who as such closes Himself off from us' (299). But Barth immediately adds that in this absence Christ is present to his people. He is also 'the Resurrected who as such discloses Himself to us' (299). As such, the priority Barth relentlessly insists on ascribing to Jesus – which he sees as grounded in the decisiveness of his all-inclusive accomplishment of salvation – ultimately functions to secure and uphold the agency of Christ's people (not undermine it) and fill their lives with significance (not empty them). 'The power of the resurrection of Jesus Christ may be known by the fact that it snatches man upwards' (316). The exaltation his people experience as they receive Christ's 'direction' is holistic, tangible and active rather than merely spiritual, interior or passive. It reorients their whole existence just as Barth says the Holy One does for us as his holy ones in §62.2. In doing so, this exaltation humanizes us. And this humanization ultimately means the conformity of human existence and action to the humanity of Christ in the power of his Spirit. This is the eschatological horizon of the Christology Barth develops here.

Before concluding my analysis of this Christology of Christ's lordly, directing presence-in-absence, it is worth pausing to notice how it implicitly takes up and advances some less-than-fully-resolved aspects of Barth's treatment of the divine command in his programmatic general ethics (especially in *CD* II/2 §38.2) and his special ethics of creation (*CD* III/4 §52).[85] It is fairly said that 'Barth's ethic most nearly approximates an intuitive act-deontology in which, through prayerful

---

85. Barth's insistence on the definiteness of the divine command has been the subject of serious criticism, particularly by theological ethicist Oliver O'Donovan. See, for

exegesis and reflection, individuals seek to enact an obedience that corresponds to the obedience of Jesus Christ.'[86] It resembles an act-deontology because of its emphasis on the divine command, which Barth insists must be concrete, definite and direct rather than abstract or general (*CD* II/2, 662–5). To be sure, some Barth interpreters have tried to rescue him from what they regard as the problematic implications of this.[87] Many see in his unwavering insistence on the definiteness of the command, which must be given ever afresh in encounter with God, an open door to arbitrariness and unrestrained subjectivity in ethics. As one critic provocatively asks, 'when did *you* last hear an absolutely definite command of God?'[88] This leads to the 'intuitive' aspect of Barth's ethic; for while the command of God is absolutely definite from the divine side, Barth also recognizes an inescapable indeterminacy when it comes to our reception of the command. Human apprehension of the divine command is a matter of *kennen* ('to be acquainted with') rather than *wissen* ('to be fully conversant with')(667; *KD* II/2, 744):

> If it is a question of the imperative itself, the detailed and concrete determination of what is required of us is none of our business. The command is intrinsically concrete. It is already interpreted and applied to myself and my circumstances, to my position at the moment. There is nothing that I myself can add to it. I am asked only concerning my obedience or disobedience. I am not asked concerning my interpretation, but only my perception (*Erkenntnis*) and the consequent practical recognition of the form in which it is given me.[89]

---

example, O'Donovan, 'How Can Theology Be Moral?', *Journal of Religious Ethics* 17.2 (1989): 87–9; and, more recently, O'Donovan, *Finding and Seeking: Ethics as Theology 2* (Grand Rapids: Eerdmans, 2014), chapter 8. McKenny subjects it to extensive analysis in *The Analogy of Grace*, chapter 7, vindicating it against many of the charges levelled against it (including O'Donovan's), although he concludes that it still leaves some matters unresolved.

86. Matthew Puffer, 'Taking Exception to the *Grenzfall*'s Reception: Revisiting Karl Barth's Ethics of War,' *Modern Theology* 28.3 (2012): 496.

87. Nigel Biggar, for example, proposes to exploit the semantic range of *Gebot*, Barth's preferred term for command, so as to construe God's command in more of a legislative than a military fashion. He suggests this in order to 'tame … the notion that God's will is entirely unpredictable, that it cannot be articulated in terms of principles or rules, that it cannot be reflected upon and interpreted rationally, and that it expresses itself in such a way that leaves no room for the responsible exercise of creaturely discretion'. Biggar, 'Karl Barth's Ethics Revisited', in *Commanding Grace: Studies in Karl Barth's Ethics*, ed. Daniel L. Migliore (Grand Rapids: Eerdmans, 2010), 31. Against this, Nimmo suggests that 'Biggar's desire to find fixed "moral principles" in Barth's ethics … hints at an unnecessary will to systematization which Barth stubbornly resists, and undervalues Barth's profound appreciation of the constancy of God.' Nimmo, *Being in Action*, 36.

88. Biggar, 'Karl Barth's Ethics Revisited', 30.

89. John E. Hare, *God's Commands* (Oxford: Oxford University Press, 2015), 177.

Because God's decision and judgement remain decisive, the best that theological ethics can hope to offer is help arriving at an approximation of the definite command, which it also cannot relieve us of responsibility to hear and obey.[90] 'The discipline of ethics supplies neither exceptional rules nor certainty in perceiving God's command, but rather guidance in discerning how this command may give rise to acts that are congruent with, or correspond to, God's self-revelation in Jesus Christ.'[91]

The continuity between this account of ethics and the Christology that Barth develops in §64.4 and draws upon in §66 is clear even from such a brief examination of his approach to the divine command. To take but one example: the combination of directness and indirectness that characterizes how Christ supplies 'direction' to his people in §64.4 aligns closely with the definiteness-indeterminacy of the divine command. Just as in his treatment of the command, Barth insists that the transforming and liberating 'direction' of Christ does not fall under our control. Christ remains free and sovereign in giving it, and never becomes our possession or sponsors self-confidence in the face of his supreme judgement. At the heart of both his approach to the divine command and the Christology he develops here, Barth obviously seeks to honour and recognize the reality that Christ remains free and sovereign; at the same time, he is striving to do justice to the relative but still real nature of human moral agency, discernment and action. This twofold attempt is not without its residual problems, of course. And I will address some of these more fully in the next chapter when I analyse Barth's treatment of discipleship as providing 'formed reference'. At this point, however, it is worth observing three ways in which the Christology of Christ's (discipleship-shaped) presence-in-absence helps mitigate some of the potential issues with his theological ethics.

First, Barth's treatment of the 'direction' of Christ here 'evangelizes' it. Interpreters have often recognized that this is Barth's intention in his most direct discussions of the command. For example, one interpreter observes: 'In accordance with Barth's insistence that every word we use to speak of God gains its proper meaning from the identity and activity of God rather than from our common usage or assumed meanings of the word, the command of God is not to be subsumed under what we generally mean by "command".'[92] Rather, 'the command of God is the command of the gracious God made known in Jesus Christ.'[93] Such an 'evangelization' is manifestly Barth's intention in locating his initial discussion of the ethics of command within his treatment of the doctrine of God, and

---

90. Nimmo and McKenny both highlight Barth's careful discussion of the preparatory function of ethical reflection, pointing out that it nevertheless cannot take the place of the encounter with the commanding God for which it sensitizes us. See Nimmo, *Being in Action*, 52–61, and McKenny, *The Analogy of Grace*, chapter 7.

91. Puffer, 'Taking Exception to the *Grenzfall*'s Reception', 496.

92. Daniel Migliore, 'Commanding Grace: Karl Barth's Theological Ethics', in *Commanding Grace*, 10.

93. Migliore, 'Commanding Grace', 10.

(importantly) subsequent to his treatment of election in the first part of II/2. In §64.4, however, this is made even clearer. Here, as I have shown, Barth construes Christ's 'direction' in terms that speak of freedom, life and the exaltation of the human covenant partner in Christ. Relative as it is to Christ, and as destructive of presumption it is as a result, Barth sees that it will produce 'genuinely happy Christians who can and even should know and confess that they are such' (272). What is more, in 'evangelizing' the command as Barth does here, he also implicitly provides more clarity and concrete indication about how to recognize Christ's 'direction' as a work of God's Spirit rather than something demonic. The closing pages of §64.4 flesh this out in terms of the constancy of God as it is displayed in the narrative of Jesus' life, death and resurrection.

Second, Barth's treatment in §64.4 implicitly extends and specifies what is involved in receiving definite 'direction' beyond the relatively thin conceptuality of an intuitive leap taken in prayerful Bible reading. It is possible, of course, to reconstruct a more-or-less plausible phenomenology of the reception of the command from Barth's remarks in *CD* II/2 and III/4. At least one interpreter has attempted this.[94] But in the context of narrating Christ's 'direction' – and even more so in the way he employs this in §66, and especially §66.2 – Barth provides further resources for characterizing and recognizing the appropriate reception of Christ's 'direction'. I have already established that Barth's account of sanctification results in world-positivity and a dynamic coordination of nonconformity with missional solidarity. In subsequent chapters I will show that by means of the turn to discipleship that draws the threads together, Barth attends to the implications of these aspects of sanctification for the church, the Christian life and Christian suffering. In doing this, these *locii* provide additional reference points for establishing and testing appropriate reception of Christ's 'direction'.

Third, the Christology Barth develops in §64.4, which Christ is present with his people, actively directing and tranformatively liberating them, upholds the reality and genuine significance of human moral action. It does this, furthermore, while insisting that this reality remains relative to Christ, who retains his sovereign priority. It cannot reverse the trajectory of the 'direction' or claim to put itself on par with Jesus. He always goes ahead; we follow. Barth may still equivocate about human reason and allow little to no space for processes of moral deliberation and interpretation. Nevertheless, he is straining – even within the 'form' of his Christology that most clearly accents the presence and lordship of Jesus to his people – to do justice to human agency and action. Barth was never as full-throated as Wesley in uplifting the transformed capacity of the human moral agent directed by Christ. But as I will establish when examining his appropriation of the Reformed motif of *mortificatio* and *vivificatio* in §66.4, he expresses cautious optimism with regard to the reality of moral transformation – while continuing to insist on its relativity to Christ. Either way, the accusation that Barth dismisses

---

94. See Hare, *God's Commands*, 176–83.

human moral agency or undermines the logical possibility of obedience flies in the face of what he does affirm on the basis of this (discipleship-shaped) Christology.

I have now established the conceptual reference points and basic necessity for Barth's turn to discipleship in §66.3. In the next chapter, I provide a close reading of that section, exposing its inner logic and thematization of the dialectics of freedom.

Chapter 4

THE DIALECTICS OF DISCIPLESHIP

Discipleship of the Crucified leads necessarily to resistance to idolatry on every front. This resistance is and must be the most important mark of Christian Freedom.

—Ernst Käsemann, 'The Freedom to Resist Idolatry'.[1]

In the previous chapter, we saw that Barth develops the discipleship theme in §66.3 as the logical and organic expression of his Christocentric revision of sanctification. Far from standing in tension with his vision of sanctification, I demonstrated that Barth's turn to discipleship is demanded by it. Barth revises Calvin's account of sanctification, drawing on its most important aspects – specifically its grounding (together with justification) in the *participatio Christi* – to radicalize it in light of the emphasis on the presence of Jesus that he shares with Luther. This results in a vision of sanctification that is more inclusive than Calvin's. It is more inclusive because all are passive participants in Christ's holiness by virtue of his status as Electing God and elect human, and thus his representation of all in his reconciling work. At the same time, it is more concrete than Calvin's in demanding more than a merely 'theoretical Christocentrism'. In keeping with the 'form' of his Christology that comes to the fore in §64.4, those whom the Spirit awakens to their participation in Christ are enabled not only to passively look to Jesus but also to actively follow after him, responding to his present and lordly 'direction' (*Weisung*). Consequently, insofar as Christocentrism proves decisive for Barth's vision of sanctification, discipleship is its distinctive form.

An earlier version of the analysis underpinning this chapter can be found in Chris Swann, 'Discipleship on the Level of Thought: the Case of Karl Barth's Critique of the Religion of Revelation', in *Revelation and Reason in Christian Theology: Proceedings of the Theology Connect Conference*, ed. Christopher C. Green and David I. Starling (Bellingham: Lexham Press, 2018): 166–81.

1. Ernst Käsemann, 'The Freedom to Resist Idolatry', in *Theologians in Their Own Words*, ed. Derek R. Nelson, Moritz and Peters (Minneapolis: Fortress Press, 2013), 111.

In this chapter, I expose the inner logic of Barth's distinctive presentation of discipleship in §66.3, which crowns his account of sanctification. There are two key aspects to Barth's presentation, both of which display the catalytic role Bonhoeffer plays for Barth at this point. First, for Barth discipleship fundamentally speaks of freedom: Christ's freedom and the concomitant freedom of his people. In the first part of this chapter (4.1), I highlight the liberative aspect of Barth's vision of discipleship. I demonstrate how Barth follows both Bonhoeffer's cues and develops the younger theologian's insights in terms of his own emphasis on the freedom entailed by sanctification in Christ. I dwell particularly on what is implied by Barth's transposition of the language of costliness into that of freedom.

The second key aspect of Barth's presentation of discipleship complements the first. Barth emphasizes that discipleship is something with tangible form. Discipleship gives form to sanctification and the freedom it entails. I interrogate this formative aspect of Barth's vision of discipleship in the second part of this chapter (4.2), highlighting its emergence from the way §66.3 thematizes the presence and activity of Christ in calling people to follow him, giving them definite moral direction in the process. Christ calls his disciples to take a concrete step, breaking with their old selves and joining in his assault upon the idolatrous and imprisoning 'given factors' of the present age. The form of discipleship emerges as Christ directs his people into freedom. To establish this, I focus on how Barth treats the New Testament texts that portray Jesus calling people to and instructing them in discipleship. I demonstrate that Barth envisages such texts providing a 'formed reference' for Christian living, preparing and provoking Christ's disciples to heed his call to live with maximal (albeit costly) freedom in every circumstance.

4.1 Discipleship and freedom

Barth's turn to discipleship is the outcome of a more fundamental and decisive turn to Christ. His revision of sanctification – resulting in the theoretical Christocentrism of his 'actualized' version of the doctrine (*CD* IV/2 §66.2) – primes it for completion in the 'practical Christocentrism' of his programmatic focus on discipleship (§66.3). Barth relentlessly insists on maintaining Christ's centrality for sanctification, accenting his living presence and activity in directing Christians on their way. This insistence underwrites and energizes a vision of the human covenant partner as active in response to Christ's living direction and call – although not self-contained or standing on a par with Christ. The characteristic 'actualism' of the resulting focus on 'the event of following after Christ rather than a steady state of being a disciple' is frequently regarded as hampering Barth's ability to do justice to the concrete continuity of agency required to affirm the experience of moral progress and growth.[2] Yet it actually turns out to be crucial to it. The

---

2. Kirk J. Nolan, *Reformed Virtue after Barth: Developing Moral Virtue Ethics in the Reformed Tradition* (Louisville: Westminster John Knox, 2014), 78.

vision of human agency implicit in Barth's account of discipleship is fundamentally realistic. Discipleship concerns both the defining reality of Christ and the realities of the arena of human moral action. As such it is direct and concrete. Its attention to the living centrality of Christ attunes it to the lived realities of human moral life, rather than desensitizing it to them. The dynamism and event-character of the resulting vision of discipleship enables it to do justice to experiences not only of moral progress and growth but also of struggle and failure. In doing this, it outdoes the 'blueprint ecclesiologies' that loom so large in the contemporary discipleship conversation.[3]

Barth's vision of sanctified Christian community and Christian living, developed in the chapters to follow, displays both 'actualistic concreteness' and 'indirect directness'. His discipleship-shaped ecclesiology is actualistic because it is framed in terms of the dynamism and event-character of following Jesus. It is concrete because it is not thereby rendered insubstantial, abstract or episodic. Instead, it is affirmed in its creaturely reality and integrity. Likewise, his discipleship-shaped vision of Christian living is indirect because the decisive ethical action is the action God has already taken in Christ's incarnation, earthly ministry, death, resurrection and ascension. Relative to this decisive action, it is direct because that action includes the ongoing, lordly presence of Christ in the Spirit.

Actualistic concreteness – and indirect directness – proves its value in the process of forming materially Christian moral agents and not only in aiding the performance of moral discernment and resolving dilemmas in moments of crisis. Materially Christian agents have a moral vision aligned with the moral ontology of God's world – as that is disclosed in the economy of creation, reconciliation and redemption. Central to this, they have their ears opened and their hearts tuned by the Spirit to Christ's free, living and gracious 'direction'. Because Barth's revision of sanctification is Christ-centred and therefore discipleship-shaped, its vision of Christian community and living is attuned to the Spirit's work in commandeering the ordinary happenings, processes, continuities and discontinuities of life (behind the scenes of the dilemmas as it were) in order to awaken Christians to the freedom of their identity in Christ.

The location of Barth's discipleship-shaped vision of sanctification within the second part of his treatment of the doctrine of reconciliation is significant. Under the heading of 'the exaltation of the Son of Man', Barth historicizes the representative humanity of Christ. Here, Barth continues his reinterpretation of two-natures Christology in terms of two-states Christology and vice versa.[4] In IV/1 he treats the divinity of Christ in terms of his state of humiliation under the controlling perspective of his priestly office. In IV/2, however, he treats the humanity of

---

3. 'Blueprint ecclesiology' is Nicholas Healy's phrase for approaches to the church that eclipse its lived reality by appeal to some doctrinally pure or otherwise idealized vision. See, Nicholas M. Healy, *Church, World, and the Christian Life: Practical-Prophetic Ecclesiology* (Cambridge: Cambridge University Press, 2000), 37.

4. Barth explicitly discusses his method in these terms in *CD* IV/1 §58.4.

Christ in terms of his state of glorification, viewing it from the perspective of his kingly office. Barth's presentation of sanctification – and discipleship – is therefore determined by the narrative of Christ's human history culminating in his ascension and subsequent sending of the Spirit. Because of this controlling perspective and interest, the emphasis of the narration of Christ's humanity falls on his freedom, presence and authoritative activity – rather than simply on his finiteness, limitation and dependence as might be expected. Although, as we will see, these are not excluded. Barth has been accused of retaining an 'idealist residue' at this point in presenting the humanity of Jesus in such a way as to smooth out the angularities and irregularities of his earthly life. Barth supposedly focuses on the risen and ascended humanity of Christ, failing to attend to his humility and humiliation. Arguably, the result of this is an inability to relate our inescapably angular and messy human histories to Christ's humanity in anything but a generic and abstract way.[5] However, this criticism misses the mark; for Barth gives sustained attention to the humility and humiliation of Christ in IV/1, drawing out its implications for Christian living. What is more, this account dovetails significantly with Barth's Christology of sanctification in IV/2 §66, especially as it takes concrete shape in the need for self-denial in response to Christ's call to discipleship. As Barth presents it, self-denial is the distinctive glory of human life as it recognizes in Christ its living Lord and centre.

In the context of the Christology that proves decisive at this point in the *Church Dogmatics*, sanctification is not something that the Spirit does subsequent to or independently of Christ's decisive saving action. Rather, it is the present and lordly action of Christ in the power of the Spirit – who is, as Holmes argues, best seen in this light as thoroughly 'christologized'. The risen and ascended Christ does not stand at a distance from us but takes our human lives to himself in all their messiness, angularity and ordinariness. He triumphantly commandeers our lives, making us his own special possession and liberating us to be fully human in the midst of our struggles, sloth and misery (see IV/2 §65). This aligns with the recognition articulated by T. F. Torrance that in Barth's theological vision, God is free 'in the sheer majesty of his divine nature and in his absolutely unique existence and power, while man, disenchanted of his pretended divinity, [is] free at last to be truly and genuinely human'.[6]

This emphasis on freedom is again evident in the way Barth handles the doctrine of sanctification in §66. After discussing the simultaneity of justification and sanctification on the basis of their equal grounding in participation in Christ (§66.1), Barth effects a characteristic 'actualization' of sanctification (§66.2). What this 'actualization' amounts to is an insistence that sanctification finds its truest and most natural referent in Christ alone. He is *the* Holy One, uniquely so over against

---

5. Kerr makes this criticism, following Richard Roberts, in *Christ, History, and Apocalyptic*, 84–8.

6. T. F. Torrance, 'The Problem of Natural Theology in the Thought of Karl Barth', *Religious Studies* 6 (1970): 121.

4. The Dialectics of Discipleship

all other contenders – including those who come to share in his sanctification as 'creaturely reflections' of his holiness. At the same time, all are sanctified in him. He sanctifies all humanity *de iure*, for all are included as passive participants in his holiness by virtue of his status as the Electing God and elect human being. Nevertheless, it is only those whom he awakens to this reality by the work of the Spirit who come to actively participate in this universal sanctification, experiencing *de facto* what is true of all *de iure* in Christ. This distinction between *de iure* and *de facto* sanctification is not to be characterized as that between a principle and its instantiation, a potentiality and its realization or even an accomplishment and its application. Rather, it is a distinction between the objective reality of holiness in Christ's reconciling work and the subjective realization of that experience, which is itself enclosed within its objective reality. As a result, Christians experience their sanctification as the ever-renewed gift of their new identity in Christ. Their sanctification is derived from and therefore entirely dependent on and relative to Christ's singular holiness. It is the free gift of their free and living Lord.

The motif of 'realism' that Hunsinger has identified, must be considered further to see how the relative reality of Barth's vision of sanctification demands discipleship. I have established that Christian sanctification is both relative and real for Barth. It is relative in the sense that it depends entirely and derives completely from Christ. Sanctification is a free gift, which Christ gives as he gives himself. As such, it can never be presumed upon. Christ always remains free in making himself present and sharing his holiness with his people. Sanctification therefore cannot be detached for Christ, *the* Holy One, like some kind of independent substance. It subsists wholly in him. (In this sense, Barth does not have a theology so much as a Christology of sanctification.) The reality of sanctification is upheld by this, rather than being rendered unreal. Those whom the Spirit awakens to active participation in their holiness in Christ are really sanctified. They are elevated to the freedom of full covenant partnership with God, fulfilling the design and destiny of humanity in the process. They are no longer bound to sin; they are bound to God in Christ. This God is their God, and they are this God's people. As such they are free.

Barth's christologically determined vision of sanctification does not so much render Christian holiness unnecessary or unreal as give it a distinctive shape – the shape of discipleship. As John Webster puts it, 'Sanctification is not only the holiness that the gospel *declares* but also the holiness that the gospel *commands*, to which the creaturely counterpart is *action*'.[7] Barth develops a similar insight in §66.3, where he explicitly mobilizes the New Testament discipleship language.

> 'Follow me' is the substance of the call in the power of which Jesus makes men his saints … The lifting up of themselves for which He gives them freedom is not a movement which is formless, or to which they themselves have to give the necessary form. It takes place in a definite form and direction. Similarly, their looking to Jesus as their Lord is not an idle gaping. It is a vision which stimulates

---

7. John Webster, *Holiness* (London: SCM, 2003), 87.

those to whom it is given to a definite action. The call issued by Jesus is a call to discipleship. (533)

Barth relinquishes Calvin and adopts Bonhoeffer as his chief conversation partner at this crucial turning point in §66. Barth does not disguise his admiration for Bonhoeffer's handling – and living – of the theme of discipleship, suggesting that he cannot surpass the way Bonhoeffer treats this theme in the opening sections of his *Nachfolge* (1937): 'In these the matter is handled with such depth and precision that I am almost tempted simply to reproduce them in an extended quotation' (533). Here Bonhoeffer's work proves catalytic for Barth. One scholar sees in this evidence for a 'reciprocal indebtedness' between Barth and Bonhoeffer.[8] Another argues that 'even in those areas where Barth is not uncritical, there is nevertheless a sense of shared discourse around certain themes, particularly relating to the Christian life'.[9] This sense of shared discourse and common labour in seeking to rightly characterize the Christian life is palpable at the start of §66.3. This is why Barth acknowledges that Bonhoeffer's treatment of discipleship provides the occasion for him to draw out and make explicit what is latent in his own thinking on sanctification – if not to modify his essential position. The substance of Barth's treatment, structured around four features of the call to discipleship, likewise mirrors and develops Bonhoeffer's *Nachfolge* (534–46), as does his ultimate recasting of the costliness of discipleship in terms of freedom (546–53).

The first feature of the call of discipleship that Barth singles out is that it manifests the sovereign freedom and authority of Christ: 'The call to discipleship is the particular form of the summons by which Jesus discloses and reveals Himself ... in order to claim and sanctify [someone] as his own, and as His witness in the world' (534). Summarizing the call narratives of the Gospels as instances of Christ's commanding grace, Barth observes that Christ's call to discipleship is issued to those he has chosen. In this way, it attests his freedom and lordship in election. Webster observes the same thing in relation to the first call narrative in Mark's Gospel – Mark 1.14-20. According to Webster, the otherwise mysterious responsiveness of the first disciples to Christ's summons is explained by the emphasis of the preceding narrative on the identity and mission of Jesus: 'The one who calls is Jesus, the Father's beloved Son; his call is supremely authoritative and lawful because it is the call of the one who is in person the saving rule of God and who brings help and blessing to sinners'.[10] This is the deepest reason why discipleship is the normative New Testament way in which people become 'active participants' in their *de iure* sanctification in Christ. The call points back to the

---

8. Matthew Puffer, 'Dietrich Bonhoeffer in the Theology of Karl Barth', in *Karl Barth in Conversation*, ed. W. Travis McMaken and David W. Congdon (Eugene: Pickwick, 2014), 46–62.

9. Greggs, 'The Influence of Dietrich Bonhoeffer on Karl Barth', 63.

10. John Webster, 'Discipleship and Calling', *Scottish Bulletin of Evangelical Theology* 23.2 (2005), 135–6.

4. The Dialectics of Discipleship

one who issues it. And it sets people free because it manifests the royal Son of Man in whom humanity itself is representatively exalted to the freedom of covenant partnership with God.

The second feature of the call of discipleship to which Barth attends is its function as the concrete instance and expression of the gospel's demand for faith. Barth insists that the call is the personal, active and authoritative means by which Christ binds people to himself, sanctifying them. As such, it is always concrete and never general or abstract. It always enacts a person's union with and allegiance to Jesus: 'In practice the command to follow Jesus is identical with the command to believe in Him' (536). The New Testament call of discipleship is for Barth the full flowering of a theme he traces throughout biblical ethics – namely, that the Law is the form of the Gospel. As Joseph Mangina puts it, 'Christian ethics coincides with the believer's relation to Jesus Christ; Christ is the content of God's commandment, and knowing what to do in a given situation is a matter of hearing what God, in Christ, has to say'.[11] At the climactic moment in the covenantal history narrated in Scripture, Jesus calls people to discipleship. This call encounters people in freedom, cutting through all prior determinations. And in binding these people to Jesus himself, it thereby sets them free. The restoration of the demoniac in Mark 5 is emblematic of this dynamic: once Jesus has driven the legion of demons out of the man, his humanity is restored and his freedom finds expression not only in his gratitude to Jesus but in an intense urge to 'go with' him. In this way, discipleship unites faith and obedience as the active form of trusting attentiveness to the living Lord.

A third aspect of call to discipleship is its demand for a two-fold turning – turning from oneself in self-denial and turning to Jesus in active, definite and specific 'simple obedience' (538–40). Discipleship cannot remain hanging in midair as a matter of private attitude change or inner reform, with no visible concrete manifestation in obedience. Barth clearly envisages something much more radical than gradualist step-wise progress in sanctification here. Viewed in terms of the call, discipleship is always a matter of changing sides, making a clean break and dying to the old self in order to live to God in Christ. As Barth goes on to say in §66.4, the biblical vision of sanctification involves a 'falling out with oneself'(563) – in that the old self, condemned in Christ, is pitted against the new, called by and to Christ. As I have already explored, this emphasis on the total rather than the partial in sanctification displays Barth's affinity with Luther thinking about the Christian life.[12] However, the intense conflict between the disciples' new identity in Christ and their old identity is the necessary outworking of their Spirit-bestowed experience of Christ's victory rather than a pessimistic concession to the persistence of sin. Although offered as a criticism

---

11. Joseph L. Mangina, *Karl Barth: Theologian of Christian Witness* (Burlington: Ashgate, 2004), 147.

12. Hunsinger, 'A Tale of Two Simultaneities: Justification and Sanctification in Calvin and Barth', *Zeitschrift für dialektiche Theologie*, 18 (2002), 316–38.

of Barth, G. C. Berkouwer provides an apt description of this discipleship-shaped view of sanctification: 'The intensified struggle is indissolubly associated with the victory'.[13] Discipleship is the struggle to live out the sanctified freedom Christ has decisively secured.

The fourth and final aspect of the call of discipleship Barth singles out follows directly from this picture of struggle as participation in Christ's victory. Discipleship means freedom. According to Barth, the call to discipleship is nothing short of the unveiling of God's kingdom, which confronts and opposes all other kingdoms, unmasking their false claims, disarming them and triumphing over them so that people – and ultimately all of God's world – can be set free. In this light, the call of discipleship is the summons to an existence that witnesses to and corresponds with the prior and determinative 'onslaught' of God's liberating kingdom in Christ (543):

> In this onslaught it is a matter of God's destruction, accomplished in the existence of the Son of Man, of all the so-called 'given factors', all the supposed natural orders, all the historical forces, which with the claim of absolute validity and worth have obtruded themselves as authorities—mythologically but very realistically described as 'gods'—between God and man, but also between man and his fellows; or rather which inventive man has himself obtruded between God and himself and himself and his fellows.

These idolatrous forces – themselves merely projections of self-deluded humanity – distort human life and relationships as they lay perverse claim to human worship and allegiance. But Christ's call exposes and liberates people from these forces. As a result, the freedom granted disciples of Jesus with respect to these 'given factors' becomes a tangible sign and public attestation of the triumph of God's kingdom, and a foretaste of the *telos* of creation. Discipleship unifies resistance to idolatry with the freedom for which humanity is restored.

Each of these four features of Barth's account of discipleship speaks of freedom – Christ's in the first instance and, echoing this, his people's. Discipleship speaks of freedom in attesting Christ's sovereign freedom, and in his free and liberating encounter with people – announcing the gospel in the form of law, grace in and as God's ever-fresh command. Discipleship equally speaks of freedom in summoning disciples to break with their past selves to embrace Christ's gift of freedom, just as it does in its invitation to join God's eschatological onslaught against every imprisoning idolatry. The call of discipleship is issued in the name of freedom. It is therefore entirely unsurprising that Barth closes §66.3 by again explicitly interacting with Bonhoeffer, translating the younger theologian's signature emphasis on the costliness of discipleship into the language of freedom (553):

---

13. G. C. Berkouwer, *The Triumph of Grace in the Theology of Karl Barth* (London; Paternoster, 1956), 238.

4. The Dialectics of Discipleship

Grace ... cannot have become more cheap today (to use another expression of Bonhoeffer's). It may well have become even more costly. Or, to put it another way, it may well be that the freedom given in and with obedience to the call to discipleship has not become less but greater.

Every act of translation involves both gains and losses. So it is worth pausing to consider what is gained and what is lost when Barth here 'translates' Bonhoeffer's language of costly grace into the register of freedom. What is gained is coherence with Barth's insistence that the call to discipleship cannot mean slavery or oppression for us when it meant freedom 'in and with obedience' for those the New Testament depicts as called by Jesus. Consistent with Bonhoeffer's distinction between costly and cheap grace, Barth emphasizes the intrinsic connection between the free gift of justification and the transformed life of the justified.[14] Christ's call leads to freedom. Disciples may live in a way that breaks with the slavery of their old ways and participates in the liberating newness of the kingdom. Developing Bonhoeffer, Barth's language keeps this liberative aspect in focus. Conversely, what is lost – or at least overshadowed – in Barth's preference for the language of freedom, is a frank recognition that breaking with the old and participating in the new does not come naturally, automatically or even easily. Christ calls disciples to the path of freedom. But walking that path will not always feel like freedom; indeed, it will often feel burdensome and costly – a lot like bearing a cross.

Barth is critically constructive as well as appreciative in following Bonhoeffer's cues and developing his insights here. It speaks volumes that Barth turns repeatedly to Bonhoeffer in §66.3, follows the sequence and progression of the *Nachfolge* and makes frequent reference to the younger theologian's language as well as explicitly praising him. In its immediate context in the *Church Dogmatics*, such extensive, sympathetic and yet not uncritical interaction compares with Barth's engagement with Calvin in §66.2. The fact that Calvin disappears from view and is replaced by Bonhoeffer as Barth's chief interlocutor here is significant. Yet there is a difference. As he is with Calvin, Barth is both critical and constructive when he appropriates Bonhoeffer's insights. Yet he is evidently less burdened to show himself faithful to Bonhoeffer's intention in doing so. Indeed, his references to Bonhoeffer in §66.3 tend to draw the younger theologian's formulations into the conceptual orbit of the 'lively Christology' that dominates his revision of sanctification. This is not entirely foreign to Bonhoeffer's presentation. For Bonhoeffer, discipleship demands that Christian living must take a tangible form, and this form correlates with a proper orientation towards Christ: 'Disciples live completely out of the bond connecting them with Jesus Christ'.[15] Likewise for Barth. Discipleship bestows form on the Christian life. However, in Barth's hands, the form discipleship bestows on Christian living is more transparently 'evangelical' in that it speaks of Christ's freedom and the corresponding freedom of his disciples. There is, therefore, a

---

14. Bonhoeffer, *Discipleship*, 43–56.
15. Bonhoeffer, *Discipleship*, 170.

backhanded criticism in the way Barth appropriates and constructively 'translates' Bonhoeffer's language here. The younger theologian's emphasis on 'costly' rather than 'cheap' grace is necessary. But it must also be set within a wider and more positive framework to allow the reality of Christ and his living presence to shine through.[16]

Bonhoeffer's material is adapted to serve the more basic emphasis on freedom in Barth's vision of discipleship. This vision displays the pattern of 'paradoxical identity' that can be discerned in his mature thought.[17] Some commentators see a basic 'Chalcedonian pattern' in Barth's thought.[18] Others dispute this, especially given Barth's self-conscious revisionism with respect to the metaphysics of Chalcedon.[19] Sidestepping the terminological aspect of this dispute for the moment, I submit that W. Travis McMaken's concept of 'paradoxical identity' best accounts for how Barth envisages the historicized, 'narrative unity' of divine and human agencies in Christ – and elsewhere by analogy. In the case of the call of discipleship, Barth insists on the identity of Christ's lordly and free activity with the active human response of freedom. At the same time, he paradoxically refuses to compromise the integrity of either by thinking of them as somehow reversible or interchangeable – indeed, they remain asymmetrical with Christ standing in irreversible priority with respect to the disciples. Christ remains free in calling people to himself. And the freedom disciples experience in breaking with the old and being swept up in the liberating onslaught of the new is entirely determined by Christ, attesting to his freedom and lordship in its 'correspondence' to him.

4.2 Discipleship as formed reference

A criticism that may be made of Barth's emphasis on freedom here is that its focus on Christ turns it away from the concrete details of the church and the Christian life.[20] Along similar lines, a number of theologians and ethicists have found

---

16. This constructive use of Bonhoeffer is consistent with the reservations Barth regularly expressed with regard to the younger theologian's work. Famously, Barth suggested that systematics may not have been Bonhoeffer's strength. See Puffer, 'Dietrich Bonhoeffer in the Theology of Karl Barth', 46.

17. W. Travis McMaken, 'Definitive, Defective or Deft? Reassessing Barth's Doctrine of Baptism in Church Dogmatics IV/4', *International Journal of Systematic Theology* 17.1 (2015): 98–107.

18. Hunsinger, *How to Read Karl Barth*, chapter 7. See also George Hunsinger, 'Karl Barth's Christology: Its Basic Chalcedonian Character', in *The Cambridge Companion to Karl Barth*, ed. John Webster (Cambridge: Cambridge University Press, 2000), 127–42.

19. Bruce McCormack, 'Karl Barth's Historicized Christology: Just How "Chalcedonian" Is It?' in *Orthodox and Modern*, 201–34; Paul Nimmo, 'Karl Barth and the *Concursus Dei* – A Chalcedonianism Too Far?' *International Journal of Systematic Theology* 9 (2007): 58–72.

20. This is the substance of the criticism of Barth in Richard H. Roberts, *A Theology on Its Way? Essays on Karl Barth* (London: T&T Clark, 1992). According to Roberts, Barth

Barth's account inadequately attuned to the positive role that may be played by rational processes of moral deliberation and discernment – which have classically attended to the concrete particulars of human life by means of casuistry – as well as a failure to allow adequate scope for gradual moral growth and progress.[21] With such criticisms in view, I will devote the remainder of this chapter to showing that for Barth discipleship thematizes the liberating presence of Christ in such a way as to give more than adequate attention to the lived realities of church and the Christian life. Crucial to this is the way Barth views the New Testament discipleship texts as providing 'formed reference' for the inescapable and decisive personal encounter with the living Lord Jesus Christ that lies at the heart of his vision of Christian living. As Barth sees it, Christ frees his disciples to centre attentively upon him by listening and responding to his present direction in the power of the Spirit. This direction cannot be preempted and is always able to surprise – as befits the fact that Christ is Lord and Master and his disciples follow after him. Nevertheless, we may expect it to be consistent with his moral direction in the past. More than this, the posture of listening, attentive responsiveness that characterizes following Christ itself forms and prepares Christ's disciples for a freedom that echoes his in ever-new circumstances. In this way, the freedom of discipleship responds to the living direction of Christ, the exalted Son of Man, and corresponds to his free self-giving for the sake of others – becoming increasingly human in doing so.

I have already shown that Barth transposes Bonhoeffer's stress on the 'cost' of discipleship into the key of freedom at the conclusion of §66.3. This reflects the way Christ determines Barth's vision of discipleship. In the closing sentences of this subsection, Barth draws together everything he has said about the freedom of the living Lord who calls his disciples – today as much as in the New Testament – and the freedom that results from their sanctification in and

---

escapes from Schleiermacher into an idealism, in which eternity exerts an inexorable monistic pull that swallows up time – and the concreteness of human life with it. Roberts's landmark criticism is largely followed by Kerr in *Christ, History, and Apocalyptic*, when he accuses Barth of perpetrating a 'twofold metaphysical abstraction' by making God's eternal decision in the election of Christ determinative for his history and ours. Kerr argues that Barth fails to give consistent attention to the concreteness either of Christ's own human life or of the church and Christian living. Roberts's verdict is more cautiously endorsed by Nathan Hitchcock with specific reference to Barth's vision of God being all in all at the eschaton. Nathan Hitchcock, *Karl Barth and the Resurrection of the Flesh: The Loss of the Body in Participatory Eschatology* (Eugene: Pickwick, 2013), 166–8.

21. Examples of the former category of criticism include Nigel Biggar, 'Hearing God's Commands and Thinking about What's Right: With and Beyond Barth', in *Reckoning With Barth*, 101–18, and 'Karl Barth's Ethics Revisited', and Oliver O'Donovan, *Self, World, and Time: Ethics as Theology 1* (Grand Rapids: Eerdmans, 2013). Examples of the latter include Stanley Hauerwas, *Character and the Christian Life*, and George Hunsinger, 'A Tale of Two Simultaneities'.

through that call. For Barth, the freedom of discipleship takes tangible form. Christ's yoke may be easy and his burden light (Mt. 11.30), but a yoke and burden they still are, which New Testament scholarship suggests are metaphors for the instruction or moral direction Jesus provides. Barth is worth quoting at length at this point (553):

> As we have to remember in relation to every 'rule', we might try to copy everything that Jesus demanded and that these men did, and yet completely fail to be disciples, because we do not do it, as they did, at His particular call and command to us. There is, of course, no reason why He should not ask exactly the same of us as He did of them. But again—along the same lines—He may just as well command something different, possibly much more, or the same thing in a very different application and concretion. In these circumstances it might well be disobedience to be content to imitate them, for if we are to render simple obedience it must be to the One who, as He called them then, calls us to-day. It is now our affair to render obedience without discussion or reserve, quite literally, in the same unity of the inward and the outward, and in exact correspondence to the New Testament witness to His encounter with them. There can certainly be no question of a deviation from these main lines. What we find along these lines can never be a mere *consilium evangelicum* [counsel of the gospel]. It is always a binding *mandatum evangelicum* [mandate of the gospel] which demands the response of a corresponding decision and action. And there will always be reason for distrust against ourselves if we think that what may be required of us along these lines will be something less, or easier, or more comfortable than what was required of them. Grace – and we again recall that in the call to discipleship it is a matter of grace, of the salvation of the world, and therefore of our own salvation – cannot have become more cheap to-day (to use another expression of Bonhoeffer's). It may well have become even more costly. Or, to put it another way, it may well be that the freedom given in and with obedience to the call to discipleship has not become less but greater. But however that may be, the freedom given in this way was then, and still is, our sanctification.

Crucially, Bonhoeffer's polemic against cheap grace is subsumed under Barth's theme of freedom here at the culmination of his presentation of the way the New Testament discipleship texts provide a 'formed reference' (*geformter Hinweis*) for Christian living in any context. Barth develops the notion of a 'formed reference' in *CD* III/2 §52, but draws on the conceptuality (although not the explicit phrase) again here in this final discursive section of §66.3. As Nimmo explains, the concept of 'formed reference' is Barth's way of allowing 'greater material specification to the discipline of theological ethics' by positing at the heart of ethics a horizontal dimension 'alongside the vertical dimension of the command of God as a unique, concrete, particular event'. This horizontal dimension places the always discontinuous and new command of God – the form of his grace – into its context in 'the history of encounter in the covenant of grace', thus supplying a continuity correlated with the constancy of God in freely electing and acting to have a human covenant partner.[22]

In §66.3, Barth draws on the conceptuality named 'formed reference' to do three things, which he holds in dynamic tension.[23] Holding together these three things yields the distinctive discipleship-shaped approach to moral discernment that I will outline in the final part of this chapter (4.3).

First, Barth draws on the notion of 'formed reference' to maintain that discipleship is given form by reference to the concrete ways in which Christ 'directed' and people responded (or failed to respond) in faith and obedience in the Gospels. That is to say, it directs would-be followers of Jesus to the discipleship texts in the New Testament to discern in them 'certain prominent lines along which the concrete commanding of Jesus, with its demand for concrete obedience, always moved in relation to individuals, characterizing it as His commanding in distinction from that of all other lords' (547). Discipleship cannot go around these texts that depict Jesus Christ encountering people he calls and 'directs' or 'instructs' (the semantic range of *Weisung* is broad enough to accommodate both renderings, although it would have been familiar to Barth from military contexts where the 'instruction' inevitably bore the same authoritative note of 'direction').[24] As a result, these texts – in all their concreteness – indicate the 'main lines along which [discipleship] takes concrete shape' in the present, for 'the call of discipleship as it comes to us will always be shaped also by this correlated picture' (552). Barth emphasizes the concreteness of these texts. Discipleship always has a definite form. The freedom it speaks of consists in correspondence to Christ's rather than in invention or even in the creative application of abstract principles.

Treating the encounters with Jesus depicted in the Gospels as a 'formed reference' is thus vastly different from treating them as examples of deeper patterns or instantiations of abiding principles. At the centre of these texts is the living Lord. They primarily attest to him in his freedom. Therefore, they cannot implicitly bind him to a principle or ideal he is taken to more or less adequately embody. At the same time, they consistently display the liberative thrust of his call. The Jesus who appears in the Gospel accounts consistently sets people free from their imprisonment to their old ways and the power of idolatry and ideology. For example, in discussing Christ's challenge to the imprisonment that so often accompanies wealth and possessions, Barth points out that 'Jesus, according to

---

22. Nimmo, *Being in Action*, 44.

23. These three aspects of 'formed reference' here essentially cohere with what A. Katherine Grieb observes with regard to Barth's handling of the Decalogue and the Sermon on the Mount in *CD* II/2. Grieb, '"Living Righteousness": Karl Barth and the Sermon on the Mount', in *Thy Word Is Truth: Barth on Scripture*, 86–110.

24. McKenny highlights the authoritative note the divine *Weisung* bears for Barth, drawing attention at the same time to the explicitly ethical and personal (rather than natural, mechanical or impersonal) nature Barth insists it bears as the work of the Holy Spirit. McKenny, *The Analogy of Grace*, 214.

the Gospel tradition, obviously commanded many men, as the concrete form of their obedient discipleship, to renounce their general attachment to the authority, validity and confidence of possessions, not merely inwardly but outwardly, in the venture and commitment of a definite act' (547–8). In the background here is the concrete call issued in Jesus' encounter with the rich young ruler (Lk. 18.18-25), his instruction about the spiritual gravitational pull of wealth in the Sermon on the Mount (Mt. 6.19-24) and numerous other texts. Nevertheless, Barth insists that this is not a general pattern from which we are invited to read off a self-evident principle (548): 'We do not have here the realization of an ideal or principle of poverty as it was later assumed into the monastic rule. Nor do we have the basis of a new society freed from the principle of private property'. Instead, it is a matter of 'the specific summons to specific men', which 'cannot be reduced to a normative technical rule for dealing with possessions'. To anticipate, the 'formed reference' provided by these texts functions to provoke and prepare the imagination – or, better, attune the ear – of contemporary disciples to hear Christ's concrete call to them, expecting it to be consistent with his challenge to 'the self-evident attachment to that which we possess' but not bound or limited by the forms that challenge takes in the New Testament. Such is the concrete form the New Testament texts give to discipleship as they attest to both the liberating ways of the Lord with his people and the freedom of the Lord that underwrites them.

Second, and emerging from his emphasis on their attestation to the freedom of Christ, Barth treats the New Testament discipleship texts as a 'formed reference' for discipleship today in the sense that they prepare us to expect Christ to act with that same freedom in calling and 'directing' us here and now. In giving us a 'formed reference' rather than exemplifications of a principle or ideal, they warn us against trying to determine ahead of time what Christ will call us to today. Discipleship for Barth – like his approach to ethical reflection and instruction in general – centres upon the necessity of a personal encounter with Christ and refuses to short-circuit this. It directs us to and prepares us for this encounter. But it does take the place of this encounter. On the one hand, it eschews replacing the encounter with general principles that we deliberate on with an eye to our context. On the other hand, it refuses to allow us to so identify ourselves with one or other of the discipleship narratives in the New Testament that Christ's word in the past becomes a direct word to us today. Just as it is depicted in the Gospels, the call to follow Jesus today is the utterly concrete and definite form of Christ's free and lordly 'direction' of his people (552):

> The picture of these men and the way in which they were concretely ordered and concretely obeyed is one which ought to impress itself upon us. In this respect it forms, with the call issued by Jesus, the content of the New Testament kerygma. The reason why we have to bring out these main lines along which it takes concrete shape is that the call to discipleship as it comes to us will always be shaped also by this correlated picture. Yet as it was for them, it will be a call which here to-day is addressed directly and particularly to each one of us, so that its specific content is not fixed by the specific content of His call there and

4. The Dialectics of Discipleship 97

then as we have learned it from the Gospels. To be sure, the call of Jesus will be along the lines of the encounter between the kingdom of God and the kingdoms of the world. And it will have to be accepted in this form. But this does not mean that the living Son of Man is confined as it were to the sequence of His previous encounters, or that His commanding moves only in the circle of His previous commanding and the obedience which it received.

This vision of discipleship respects both Christ's freedom and the concrete particularity of our historical circumstances. In fact, it is precisely by respecting the freedom of Christ – as attested to in the New Testament discipleship texts – that it also takes seriously the particular realities of the church and Christian life today. As Barth goes on to explain of the pictures provided in these texts (552): 'It is not for us simply to reproduce those pictures. That is to say, it is not for us to identify ourselves directly with those who were called then, and therefore to learn directly from what they were commanded what we are necessarily commanded, or from their obedience what our own obedience must be'. Discipleship is not a matter of forcing the contemporary situation to 'fit' the texts, so that it is identified without remainder with one or other situation of encounter found there. Such a procedure can be carried out in a fundamentalist manner – either by 'finding' some aspect of the present world directly in the text or by declaring it invalid, illusory or not morally significant if it does not find it. It can also be carried out in a more postliberal mode, where the story of Scripture is said to 'absorb' the world. Here again, the risk is that troublesome details of the present situation are trimmed to make the situation 'fit' the overarching story, leaving aspects of the present reality aside in order to avoid the risk inherent in the more typically 'liberal' hermeneutic task. Either way, Barth insists that the impulse behind such approaches is mistaken. The texts are not scripts to be woodenly acted whenever a vague similarity is discerned between our situation and theirs. Nor are they a mere 'renarration' of all present situations which translates everything into dogmatic categories and passes over anything that does not fit.[25] Instead, they are testimonies to Christ, from which we may learn to recognize his voice and the freedom to which he calls us (552): 'We will always know that it is His voice which calls us from the fact that in what is demanded of us we shall always have to do with a break with the great self-evident factors of our environment, and therefore of the world as a whole'. In this way, the 'formed reference' provided by the New Testament discipleship texts allows us to do justice to the particularity of present

---

25. This is a common way of understanding Barth's theological method. And it is true enough at one level, as Ingolf U. Dalferth points out, 'Karl Barth's Eschatological Realism', in *Karl Barth: Centenary Essays*, ed. Stephen Sykes (Cambridge: Cambridge University Press, 1989), 14–45. But Dalferth also highlights the secondary, 'hermeneutical' strategy that is evident in the *Church Dogmatics*. While not always adequately executed, this secondary strategy nevertheless seeks to do justice to the variety of common experience within the framework of Barth's dogmatic 'renarration' of reality with reference to Christ.

circumstances while straining to hear Christ's consistent call to freedom in the midst of them.

Third, Barth insists that the preceding two aspects point towards the way in which the New Testament picture of discipleship speaks to us today and summons us to freedom. The concreteness of the encounters depicted in Scripture and the concreteness of the encounter demanded of disciples today work together, rather than contradicting each other: 'From what the New Testament tells us of [Christ's] commanding, and of the obedience demanded from these particular men and rendered by them, we have to hear His voice as He speaks to us, calling us in the particular situation of obedience determined by His Word' (553). The key to the contemporary significance of the New Testament narratives of Christ calling and directing his first disciples lies in their concrete witness to him – and his consistent ways with his people. According to this witness, Christ is not a figure locked in the past or some Platonized realm of abstract 'accomplishment' awaiting a more or less pneumatologically assisted 'application' by human agents. Nor does he offer us a mere example or vague inspiration – an impressionistic portrait of the kinds of freedom we can creatively pursue and freely improvise for ourselves. Nor does he embody a principle that once again we must draw down upon and apply by the interpretive effort of our own agency detached from his determining agency (his direction and call). Rather, Christ's living reality encompasses our present reality.[26] This side of the resurrection, the living Lord Jesus Christ is the most decisive context for moral discernment and action. What is more, he is alive and present to his people rather than dead or hidden from them. At one level, this demands that we attend closely to the Jesus attested to in Scripture; for the Jesus who is the determinative context for moral action today is also the one who issued the call to discipleship that we read about in all its concreteness in the New Testament. The way in which he directed his people then is therefore replete with significance for us today. At another level, recognizing the living reality of Jesus turns us towards our present situations. It summons us to attend to how the risen Jesus speaks the most decisive word about us and our contexts. In attending to this – informed by the New Testament witness – we are taught to expect his surprising and liberating presence and activity here and now. In this present activity, Christ acts consistently with the precedent provided in the New Testament. At the same time, he demands more costly and demanding correspondence with himself (not less).

4.3 Discipleship, sanctification and moral discernment

The dynamic interplay between these three features of the call of discipleship – namely, the concreteness and specificity of Christ's 'direction' as we see it in the

---

26. Christopher Holmes emphasizes this strongly in his *Ethics in the Presence of Christ* (London: T&T Clark, 2012).

New Testament, the dynamism of this direction in present circumstances and his consistent work to bring freedom from the idolatries and spiritual slaveries we are subject to – yields a distinctive approach to moral discernment. Discipleship-shaped moral discernment operates in the space of 'disciplined imagination'. It operates in this space because it engages with the imaginative, hermeneutical work of attending to Scripture and our situation in order to discern Christ's present 'direction' for us. At the same time, it is disciplined by and answerable ultimately to Christ. The situation and even Scripture recede in importance compared with the present reality and activity of Jesus. Whatever the outcome of the creative and imaginative work of interpretation – and however rationally it is carried out – it remains subordinate to Christ. It can neither displace nor stand side-by-side with him as an equally ultimate factor in moral evaluation. Attending to the Bible and the situation is always the work of a follower of Jesus. Following after him is the crucial thing, which cuts across the apparent demands of the present context – as is so memorably depicted in Jesus' summons to those who would put familial, social or economic obligations ahead of discipleship (Lk. 9.57-62). Likewise, following Jesus demands a re-examination of present understandings of Scripture – if not Scripture itself – as Jesus' repeated formula in the Sermon on the Mount highlights: 'You have heard that it was said … But I say to you' (Mt. 5.21-22, 27-28, 31-32, 33-34, 38-39 and 43-44). The hermeneutical labour of moral deliberation and discernment is inescapable – indeed, it is occasioned by the call of Christ. And yet it is the call itself, the concrete and present form of his authoritative 'direction', that disciplines and judges our hermeneutical labour and our action on its basis.

Whether or not it is appropriate to describe this hermeneutical work in terms of moral deliberation is debatable. Barth himself appears to exclude deliberation from a properly dogmatic and materially Christian approach to ethics in *CD* II/2 §38. There, he contends that the present command of God is so concrete, contemporaneous and definite that it 'does not need any interpretation, for even to the smallest details it is self-interpreting' (665). Certainly, this seems hard to reconcile with what theological ethicists like Oliver O'Donovan envisage when it comes to deliberation. According to O'Donovan, deliberation is the search in the present moment for God's direction and the purpose or agenda for action that we must form in correspondence with it:

> Time passes, ordering the goods of the world in their sequence, commanding their coming-to-be and ceasing-to-be, and about this passing world-time we may reflect, and perhaps even become wise. But time does not merely pass; it comes to us, opens before us, and demands that we step into the future to meet it. Deliberation is the response of thought to this opening, thought reaching forward to the immediate future.[27]

---

27. O'Donovan, *Finding and Seeking*, 179–80.

For O'Donovan, moral deliberation is a human activity that unfolds within the framework of divine action and responds to the proclamation of that action.[28] While O'Donovan acknowledges that there must always be an excess of divine action, commanding our worship and recognition, he also insists that there must be 'something like an excess' of human action. Citing the first Christian sermon in Acts, he argues that the response made by the crowd to the announcement of God's mighty act of raising Jesus – 'What shall we do'? (Acts 2.37) – is the paradigmatic ethical question. According to O'Donovan, it is the question of moral deliberation. The human hermeneutical labour of determining how to respond to God's action has its own integrity and necessity when it comes to theological ethics – although it remains circumscribed by divine action. What is more, it is a labour that invites evaluation in terms of the rationality of its process and product, drawing on a range of factors that appear to be explicitly excluded by Barth when he sidelines moral deliberation in favour of direct encounter with God in §38. As O'Donovan sees it, Barth's account leaves human 'decision … isolated and absolute, answerable only to the immediacy of the divine, unapproachable by thought, and refusing every attempt to give it form'.[29] In particular, Barth appears to rule out the generic. For Barth, God's commands are always concrete and definite, given in the present by the living Lord, rather than occurrences in the past that provide patterns and principles we must discover and apply to present circumstances: 'Barth claims so much for the definite command that no work is left to the generic, and so no work for our thoughtful interpretation. This has the troubling effect of representing human decision as an exact mirror-image of the sovereign decision of God.'[30]

O'Donovan argues elsewhere that 'obedience' that is automatic and unthinking hardly counts as obedience since it bypasses the human response altogether, becoming a mere transcription of divine action in human life. In proposing 'an ideal relation of text to action which, in the name of obedience to scriptural authority, effectively abolished thinking, it would abolish morality, and thereby abolish itself'.[31] When considered in terms of Barth's account of discipleship, the question of the role of Scripture in ethics is critical – and intimately connected with his invocation of the conceptuality of 'formed reference' that I have been developing. On the one hand, Barth's account of discipleship upholds (against O'Donovan) the present authority and agency of Christ. It is his call that gives decisive direction to those he encounters – as we see so clearly in the New Testament accounts. This is consistent with his emphasis on the definiteness of the divine command in §38. On the other hand, Barth's account of discipleship appears to allow (subordinate)

---

28. O'Donovan summarizes this vision, in the process of distinguishing theological ethics from dogmatics on the one side and practical theology on the other, in *Self, World, and Time*, chapter 4.

29. O'Donovan, *Finding and Seeking*, 188.

30. O'Donovan, *Finding and Seeking*, 190.

31. O'Donovan, *Self, World, and Time*, 77.

space for the kind of 'necessary indeterminacy' that O'Donovan insists must be a feature of 'the obedient action required by the faithful reading of the text'.[32]

The several worked examples Barth provides of the hermeneutical labour of moral discernment display this mix of definiteness and indeterminacy. As he scrutinizes the New Testament records of encounter with Christ, Barth highlights both the consistent 'form' the call to discipleship takes – specifically, as a personal encounter demanding the disciple turn from whatever idolatry imprisons them in order to entrust themselves to Jesus as the one who grants them a new freedom – and the 'reference' that provides for our own response to Christ's concrete direction in the present. In this, the Bible provides more than either a mere transcript for action or a pattern or principle we may freely appropriate and creatively apply. As O'Donovan admits, we do not obey Scripture *per se* but '*the realities which the Scripture attests:*' 'Obedience to Scripture can only be an exercise of faith— not, that is to say, faith in Scripture, but faith in the creating and redeeming work of God, to which Scripture bears authoritative witness'.[33] Barth would no doubt modify that formulation to personalize it: 'to which' would become 'to whom'. Disciples exercise faith in reading Scripture by trusting the God who creates and redeems, to whom Scripture bears authoritative witness. Of course, this God self-identifies in the story of the divine work of creating and redeeming. Knowledge of God cannot be had apart from that story and work. This is the basic contribution of the notion of 'formed reference', anchoring the fundamental personal encounter with God within the wider history of the covenant: 'As the command of God encounters the ethical agent vertically, in all its varied particularity, it also does so in a horizontal context, as part of a history of encounter in the covenant of grace. And thus each individual encounter in this history is always part of something larger.'[34] A more Barthian and disciple-shaped way of framing the obedient reading of Scripture would draw attention to the presence of the Christ to whom the Bible witnesses, inculcating the expectation that he remains free and active, calling his people today to follow him with the same liberating authority as he displayed in those encounters recorded in the Gospels. In the power of his resurrection, Christ is *both* the most decisive reality for every moral situation *and* personally and authoritatively present to direct his people in his way here and now. Moral discernment is therefore a work of correspondence with Christ, whose direction is truly decisive because he is the most decisive reality in any context.[35]

The resulting vision of moral discernment contrasts with fundamentalist and post-liberal approaches as well as with the liberal or liberationist approach. The literalistic hermeneutic shared by fundamentalist and post-liberal approaches views Christ's call to discipleship as straightforwardly contemporary. In this case, the world is absorbed by the text – the direct and concrete claims with which

---

32. O'Donovan, *Self, World, and Time*, 77.
33. O'Donovan, *Self, World, and Time*, 80 (emphasis in original).
34. Nimmo, *Being in Action*, 45.
35. Holmes develops this thought at length in *Ethics in the Presence of Christ*, chapter 5.

Jesus confronted everyone he called to discipleship in the Gospels, are taken as immediately binding in the present. On this view, the readers of Matthew 19.22-26 – no matter their situation – simply are the rich young ruler. What Christ said to him then he says to us today, with no hermeneutical cesura. To be sure, Barth displays sympathy with this view, especially in its uncompromising insistence on the ethical contemporaneity of Christ. Nevertheless, he does not settle here. This is because his handling of the New Testament discipleship texts upholds both the present freedom of Jesus and the non-interchangeable concrete specificity and moral significance of our historical circumstances. Seen against the backdrop of his presentation of Jesus as the royal man in *CD* IV/2 – that is, the Son of Man exalted to the right hand of the Father in and through his history of Spirit-enabled obedience – Barth renders the identity and moral authority of Jesus in a deeply historicized way that follows the Gospel narrative through to the ascension and sending of the Spirit. Consequently, Barth emphasizes the concreteness and specificity of Christ's call now as then, without directly identifying us with those called to discipleship in the first century.

Equally, however, Barth's view stands in opposition to a tendency to treat Christ's summons to discipleship along merely exemplarist lines. Taking such an approach, what happened in the past functions primarily to provide as an example or inspiration for present improvisation in the name of freedom. Lessing's ditch is decisive here, corresponding closely with the expressivist tendency George Lindbeck observes in classical liberalism to view the content of Christian beliefs – whether in Scripture or the creeds and confessions – as merely symbolic.[36] Advocates of such a view operate with a hermeneutic that maximizes the distance between now and then. The New Testament discipleship texts have currency only insofar as they can be absorbed by the contemporary world. That is to say, it is only as they are made to speak in present terms about currently pressing problems that they have value. In contrast to this, Barth maintains that the New Testament discipleship texts witness to Christ's living presence and lordly direction. As such, they relate to Christian living today in a much more decisive, specific and binding way. They indicate the 'main lines along which [discipleship] takes concrete shape;' for 'the call of discipleship as it comes to us will always be shaped also by this correlated picture' (552).

Ultimately, Barth's discipleship-shaped approach to moral discernment is not only more freeing than the fundamentalist or post-liberal approach and more concrete than the liberal, it is more humanizing. At the centre of Barth's vision of discipleship stands the royal Son of Man, in whom humanity is representatively exalted to its true destiny of perfect covenant-partnership with God. He is living, present and active in determining the moral agency and action of Christians. As such, he is the determinative reality for the lives of his disciples. More than this, he also directs them in sovereign freedom. As a result, in allowing him to determine

---

36. George A. Lindbeck, *The Nature of Doctrine: Religion and Theology in a Post-Liberal Age* (Louisville: Westminster John Knox Press, 2009), 17–18.

their moral agency and action as they respond to his direction, Christians find their own humanity increasingly restored in correspondence to his. This is because they not only come to embrace their own creaturely status in response to Christ's sovereign freedom rather than seeking an illegitimate (and illusory) sovereignty for themselves. They also learn to relate to others in ways that recognize and uphold their humanity.

Chapter 5

DISCIPLESHIP AND THE ANALOGY OF GRACE IN *CD* IV/2 §66

George Hunsinger declares: 'The promise of Barth's theology, for me, has largely been one of combining doctrine with justice and peace. Those who think they can have Barth's doctrine without his radical politics show they have yet to understand him'.[1] In an important sense, this chapter will take this as a given – although later chapters will in a sense take it up and flesh it out. Here, however, I will argue the converse of Hunsinger's declaration – namely that those who think they can have Barth's radical politics without his doctrine have equally misunderstood him. Barth's emphasis on discipleship and 'practical Christocentrism' depends upon his corresponding 'theoretical Christocentrism'. The language and conceptuality of correspondence (*Entsprechung*) has long been recognized as enormously important for understanding the divine–human relation in Barth's mature theology.[2] And here it is the key term. The burden of this chapter is to establish that Barth draws upon the account of discipleship he gives in §66.3 to structure the concept of correspondence. This is evident in all the subsections that follow §66.3 to the end of the paragraph. But Barth makes this move most explicitly in §66.6, the focus of this chapter.

The key claim of this chapter is that the explicitly discipleship-shaped structuring of correspondence enables Barth to anchor the ethically and politically charged concept theologically. The interplay between the concepts of discipleship

---

1. Hunsinger, preface to *Karl Barth and Radical Politics*, 2nd edn, xii.
2. Kimlyn Bender highlights the significance of 'correspondence' in the context of Barth's ecclesiology in *Karl Barth's Christological Ecclesiology*. Equally, in the realm of ethics, John Webster draws attention to its importance – and Barth's innovative use of the conceptuality – in his examination of the 'ethics of reconciliation' as it appears in the lecture fragments now published as *The Christian Life*. David Neville anatomises the most important aspects of its significance in David Neville, 'Grace Elicits Correspondences: The Theologian as Peacemaker', in *Embracing Grace: The Theologian's Task*, ed. Heather Thomson (Canberra: Barton Books, 2009), 119–33. And, of course, Eberhard Jüngel's exploration of the theme is masterful. Eberhard Jüngel, 'Humanity in Correspondence to God: Remarks on the image of God as a Basic Concept in Theological Anthropology', in *Theological Essays, Volume 1*, trans. John Webster (London: T&T Clark, 2014), 124–53.

and correspondence takes us to the heart of my theological investigation – and to the theological significance of discipleship in Barth's doctrine of sanctification. In the first part of this chapter (5.1), I will establish the connections Barth makes between correspondence and discipleship in §66.6. In the second part (5.2), I will draw attention to three aspects of this move that must be recognized. First, I will highlight the way in which Barth's discipleship-shaped vision of correspondence displays the 'eschatological realism' of his theological method in order to lay the groundwork for his ethics of reconciliation. Second, I will trace the dynamic, concrete, and explicitly biblical way in which discipleship functions to bestow form on the 'paradoxical identity' that has been discerned in Barth's understanding of the relation between divine and human action. Third, I will show how these two factors together obey the logic of Barth's 'christologized pneumatology' in the context of sanctification. It is this 'christologized Pneumatology' that provides the material theological principle that establishes the dialectic governing Barth's treatment of sanctified moral agency, moral action, and moral passion in §66.4–6.

In the next chapter, I extend this analysis by considering the connection Barth makes here between discipleship and correspondence diachronically in terms of his analogical approach to ethics and ecclesiology from *Romans* II to *The Christian Life*. Once I have established the theological significance of the shape that the language and logic of discipleship gives to the crucial notion of correspondence, I will be able to assess the resources Barth's account of discipleship provides for Christian living in our current context. Specifically, I will trace its consequences for Barth's vision of the church, the Christian life, and suffering (Chapters 7, 8 and 9). Before I do this, I will pause at the conclusion of this chapter (5.3) to identify some ways in which recognizing that correspondence is discipleship-shaped moves forward debates about Barth's theological ethics and the historicization of his Christology.

5.1 Discipleship and the shape of correspondence[3]

§66.6 brings Barth's sustained exposition of sanctification to a climax under the heading of 'The Dignity of the Cross'. Here, Barth presents participation in the sufferings of Christ as the fulfilment of Christian sanctification. Barth had already indicated this in his treatment of discipleship in §66.3: 'In many of the New Testament records the call to discipleship closes with the demand that the disciple should take up his cross. This final order crowns, as it were, the whole call, just as the cross of Jesus crowns the life of the Son of Man' (552). Now Barth teases out

---

3. Key parts of my analysis in the following section appear in Chris Swann, 'Karl Barth on the Dignity and Crown of Suffering: Reimagining the Fourth Age for Discipleship', in *Embracing Life and Gathering Wisdom: Theological, Pastoral, and Clinical Insights into Human Flourishing at the End of Life*, ed. Stephen Smith, Edwina Blair and Catherine Kleeman (Macquarie Park: SCD Press, 2020), 145–70.

the 'just as' in the Christian's taking up the cross. To anticipate: Barth proposes a particular discipleship-shaped way of relating the various sufferings that Christians experience – and ultimately the suffering of death – to Christ's suffering. What emerges from this is a carefully specified vision of Christian correspondence with Christ within which the logic of discipleship unifies the various ways in which Barth employs the notion of correspondence.[4] Webster highlights Barth's 'conviction that the narration of God's mighty deeds cannot proceed without the narration of the corresponding deeds of God's fellow-workers, for grace evokes correspondence'. My proposal advances this by anchoring the gracious evocation of the human correspondence in the logic of discipleship—that is, in terms of the disciples' following after the pattern provided by the unrepeatable work of Jesus as the Master rather than in some kind of ontologically equivalent attempt at imitation or improvisation inspired by his work, in which the Christian response has the priority.

To begin with, Barth argues that the cross Christians bear 'fulfils' their sanctification as the 'indispensable' concluding (and conclusive) 'element in any Christian doctrine of sanctification'(598). The Christian's cross concludes and proves conclusive for sanctification in two ways: First, Barth says, it is the 'limit' (*die Grenze*) of sanctification. By 'limit' Barth means the point at which discussion of active, Spirit-awoken participation in Christ's holiness ceases to concern sanctification per se and 'reaches out beyond itself' to its eschatological completion. If sanctification is the necessary outworking of the exaltation of humanity in Christ – that is, 'the raising up of slothful man in the power of the resurrection of Jesus Christ' – it is nevertheless only provisionally so. It is merely (albeit truly) a step along the path towards the glorious prospect of humanity, at the head of all creation, exalted to the unbroken experience of joyful covenant partnership with God for which we were made. As a result, the cross further relativizes Christian sanctification. The sanctification that Christians experience on the basis of their participation in Christ is only ever penultimate. The ultimate outcome of their participation awaits the eschaton for its unveiling: 'The resurrection of the flesh and the last judgment, when the saints will be revealed as such, the contradiction will be ended between what they still are and what they are already, and they will enter into the eternal life, the light, to which as the people of God they are now moving with the whole cosmos' (598).

Second, and closely tied to this, Barth claims that 'it is with reference to the cross' that human sanctification in all the aspects dealt with to this point – participation, discipleship, conversion and good works – is set and seen to belong within the grand 'movement' (*Bewegung*) towards its eschatological destiny. That is to say, apart from the limit drawn by the cross Christians must bear, participation in Christ, the call to discipleship, the existential activation of these as the Spirit awakens us to conversion and enables us to do works that God praises and that

---

4. According to David Neville, five distinct senses of the notion of 'correspondence' are identifiable in Barth's corpus; Neville, 'Grace Elicits Correspondences', 121–2.

bring God praise – all of these are emptied of significance. This is because their significance is tied to the goal towards which they strain, and emerges only 'in the light of the great Christian hope' (598). As such, the Christian's cross binds together the eschatological unveiling of participation in glory and its anticipation in the church and the Christian life here and now. The cross is the place from which the light of the eschaton breaks into the present. From the cross, sanctification is filled to overflowing with eschatological significance. The cross a Christian bears is therefore a real and tangible signpost of the ultimate exaltation of humanity in Christ, a foretaste and preview of this in the present.

The cross, according to Barth, does more than bestow eschatological significance on sanctification. It also circumscribes our expectations about the traction the eschaton might gain in our present experience. Barth underlines this by prefacing his exposition of the dignity and nature of the Christian's cross with an extended treatment of the uniqueness and unrepeatability of Christ's cross (599–606). At most, Barth asserts, Christians 'exist only … in the echo of His sentence, the shadow of His judgment, the after-pains of His rejection. In their cross they have only a small subsequent taste of what the world and they themselves deserved at the hand of God, and Jesus endured in all its frightfulness as their Head and in their place' (604). In addition, Barth treats under the heading of the Christian's cross such weighty matters as persecution and social dislocation alongside the suffering of 'an ordinary toothache' (607). Barth amplifies this almost comically prosaic example, saying that things like toothaches can provide tangible indicators of 'the limited nature' of Christian existence, including the 'frailty and pettiness' of Christians. As such, they function to chasten our all-too-human tendency to take ourselves and our achievements – including our spiritual achievements – 'with a seriousness which has no place for criticism or humour' (607).

These rhetorical flourishes receive substantial conceptual undergirding in §66.6. As his account of sanctification reaches its existential apex in the Christian's conformity to Christ in bearing their cross, Barth carefully specifies the relation between the Christian's cross and Christ's. The disciple's cruciformity is 'the most concrete form of the fellowship between Christ and the Christian' (599). In this, Christ and his disciples are one. And yet this concrete fellowship and oneness is not direct or unqualified: 'We must be very clear at the outset that the connexion between the cross of Jesus Christ and that of the Christian, for all its direct necessity, is not a direct but only an indirect connexion' (599). In this way, Barth resists presenting 'participation' by itself as the key to sanctification.[5] In its place, the asymmetry and even paradox that characterizes the oneness between Christ and his disciples once again thrusts itself into the spotlight. Discipleship

---

5. Migliore displays appropriate caution when he observes that for Barth 'the *participatio Christi* is … marked by a differentiated co-agency of Jesus Christ and the saints in which Jesus Christ is the living Lord and the saints act as his servants whose works neither augment nor complete, let alone replace, his saving work, but simply attest and correspond to it.' Migliore, '*Participatio Christi*', 295.

shapes Christian cross-bearing as the fulfilment of sanctification just as it shapes sanctification as the active and practical form of its Christocentrism.

I will examine the most important implications of this discipleship-shaped vision of sanctification for the moral appropriation of suffering in Chapter 9. For the moment, I want to focus on the way Barth explicitly specifies the 'correspondence' between Christians and Christ in terms of discipleship. As he draws together discipleship and suffering – and particularly as he specifies the 'indirect directness' of fellowship between disciples and their Master in suffering – the discipleship-shaped character of the correspondence between Christians and Christ emerges with clarity. For example, Barth offers this programmatic statement of the basis for the parallel between Christ's cross and the Christians in their 'material, historical connexion' (599):

Without the cross of Christ the Master there is no cross of the disciples, Christians. It is by the fact that He bore and suffered His cross that they are sanctified and called to discipleship and set in conversion and freed for the doing of good works. And it is by the same fact that they also come to bear and suffer their cross. It is on the basis of His exaltation in His death on the cross as the One who was rejected in our place that there takes place their elevation with its limit and goal in the fact that they too come to bear and suffer their cross.

Note the presence of discipleship language here. It occurs not only in the sequence rehearsing the content of §66 – sanctification, the call to discipleship, conversion and good works – but more significantly at their head. Discipleship provides both content and structure for the Christian's sanctified correspondence with Christ as it reaches its apex in their cruciformity.

The prominence of the discipleship motif at this point is not accidental. What this quote reveals – and what is developed in more detail throughout §66.6 – is the importance of the imagery of discipleship for generating both sides of the 'paradoxical identity' between Christ's suffering and that of Christians. McMaken's account of 'paradoxical identity' (introduced in 4.1) foregrounds this way of specifying the Christological determination of the relationship between divine and human agency in Barth – sometimes described in terms of its Chalcedonian pattern. 'Paradoxical identity' moves beyond the binary opposition between parallel and instrumental (or causal) constructions of how divine and human agencies relate. In the parallel construction, human action and divine action occur alongside each other. As McMaken puts it, 'They occur together, but they remain clearly distinct.'[6] In the instrumental construction, that distinction is blurred in so far as it 'understands the relation between divine and human action to involve causal interpenetration.'[7] God acts in and through human action.

6. W. Travis McMaken, 'Definitive, Defective or Deft? Reassessing Barth's Doctrine of Baptism in *Church Dogmatics* IV/4', *International Journal of Systematic Theology* 17.1 (2015): 92.
7. McMaken, 'Reassessing Barth's Doctrine of Baptism', 92.

Despite its clear basis in the Bible's testimony to Christians suffering *as* Christ suffered – that is, in a similar or parallel way – Barth refuses to make the parallel construction primary. At most, he allows that Christian suffering echoes or shadows Christ's in a decidedly secondary manner. Barth appears to recognize that emphasizing the similarity between Christ's sufferings and those of Christians risks suggesting that they somehow belong on the same level. And he will allow no ontological parity between the two. As one reader of Barth notes, the correspondence Christian action displays to God's action in Christ – which Barth can speak of as a 'repetition' or 'reiteration' – does not 'imply that in the human sphere people can somehow replicate God's initiative on our behalf'.[8] Correspondence is asymmetrical and irreversible. Significantly, it is the asymmetrical and irreversible relation between Master and disciple that safeguards this. Barth fleshes out his qualification of the connection between Christ and Christians by explicitly invoking the language of following (599–600): 'Those who take up their cross only follow Him in this ... They do not accompany Him in an equality of their cross with His. And they certainly do not precede Him in the sense that His cross acquires reality and significance only as they take up their cross.' Barth insists on construing correspondence according to the structure of discipleship, with the peculiar combination of oneness and asymmetry that goes with the relation between Master and disciple. He does this, moreover, to combat the tendency of the parallel construction to imply an ontological parity or interchangeability between Christ's cross and the Christian's.

The dialectics of discipleship shape the Christian's correspondence to Christ. This explains Barth's hostility to the traditional language of imitation in §66.3. As already noted, Christian correspondence to Christ must be understood in terms of discipleship in part to prevent it from becoming merely a matter of repeating Christ's suffering. At the same time, the instrumental or causal construction by itself is an equally inadequate way of specifying the relation between the Master and his disciples. While the instrumental construction does speak truly of the dissimilarity between them, the biblical testimony is that Christ suffers as our representative and ultimately our substitute – that is, in place of us. Indeed, representation necessarily includes a substitutionary 'moment'. The representative must not only stand as one of us but also in our place, doing for us something we cannot.[9] Elsewhere, McMaken traces the profound connections between Barth's treatment of election – the ontological basis of Christ's representation as both the Electing God and the elect human being – and the substitutionary 'pattern of exchange' that lies at the heart of his account of the atonement.[10] This aspect of the achievement of Christ is evident in the programmatic statement from page 599: it

8. Neville, 'Grace Elicits Correspondences', 123.
9. See Oliver O'Donovan, *Desire of the Nations: Rediscovering the Roots of Political Theology* (Cambridge: Cambridge University Press, 1996), 120–57, especially 125–8.
10. W. Travis McMaken, 'Election and the Pattern of Exchange in Karl Barth's Doctrine of the Atonement', *Journal of Reformed Theology* 3 (2009): 202–18.

5. Discipleship and the Analogy of Grace

is the cross of 'the One who was rejected in our place'. Moreover, Barth explicitly highlights the substitutionary nature of Christ's suffering: 'He suffers this rejection not merely as a rejection by men but, fulfilled by men, as a rejection by God – the rejection which all others deserved and ought to have suffered, but which He bore in order that it should no more fall on them' (600). In this fundamental sense, then, Christ's cross displaces Christian suffering rather than causing it: 'God's rejection … has been suffered already by Him (as their rejection). It can no longer be borne by them.' It is evident that Barth will not construe the relation between Christ and Christians in primarily causal or instrumental terms.

Barth does admit that Christ's suffering occasions the suffering of Christians – although in a secondary rather than the primary sense implied in the causal construction. Christ's cross is the occasion of our cross, which corresponds to his. Barth makes this explicit in what follows, which is worth quoting at length (600):

> The exaltation accomplished in His crucifixion and therefore in the suffering of that rejection is His and not that of His disciples or the world above which He was exalted as the Lord in His death. To His exaltation there corresponds that of His elect and called, the elevation which now comes to Christians and is promised to all men, their awakening from the mortal sleep of the slothfulness of sin. And we have seen already that this upraising of man has its basis and thrust in Him, in His exaltation to the right hand of the Father as effected in His death; that it becomes and is a fact wholly and utterly in virtue of this exaltation. Yet their elevation is not identical with His exaltation. It is only thanks to His exaltation, and in the strength of it, that it takes place at all.

In the exaltation – and therefore the suffering – of the cross, Master and disciple are united but not equated. As Barth immediately adds, 'the relationship between the two is irreversible'. The Master's suffering is the cause and occasion of the disciple's. But as is the case with the parallel construction, no suggestion of parity of interchangeability can be allowed to creep in. Barth is uncompromising. Again, this correspondence is explicitly construed in terms of the relation between disciples and their Master (600, emphasis added):

> If their elevation consists ultimately in the fact that they have to take up and carry their cross, this is not a re-enactment of His crucifixion. It takes place in correspondence to it; *with the similarity proper to a disciple following his Master*; but not in any sense in likeness, let alone identity.

The standard English translation obscures the point here. Upholding the genuine 'similarity' (*Ähnlichkeit*) Christians display to Christ in bearing their cross, the image of discipleship here enables Barth to insist that this cross-bearing is 'not in equality [*Gleichheit*], let alone identity [*Identität*] with Christ's. According to Barth, the Christian's cross has its basis and origin in Christ's – indeed, it corresponds to it. In establishing this, Barth effectively defines the important but elusive notion of correspondence in the terms supplied by the image, concept and reality of discipleship. The Christian's correspondence with Christ is a matter of following after him, not repeating or otherwise rising to the level of ontological equality or identity with him.

Barth immediately employs this discipleship-shaped construction of correspondence to establish the relationship and distinction between the 'dignity' of bearing the cross like Christ and the 'crown' disciples anticipate receiving from Christ (600):

> His own crown and the dignity which comes to the disciple in discipleship are two distinct things. The crown of life, which the disciple is promised that he will receive at the hand of the King (Rev. 2.10), is the goal of the way which he may go here and now as the bearer of this dignity.

The distinction between 'dignity' and 'crown' illustrates how discipleship structures and gives content to the Christian's correspondence with Christ in suffering. In an important sense, this is the ramification of the 'limit' the Christian's cross sets for their sanctification. Barth maintains that the cross Christians bear does not crown them in the way Christ's cross crowns him. Nor is it identical with the crown they anticipate at the eschatological consummation of their sanctification. It is not identical with their exaltation (as it is with his); for that crown – the Christian's ultimate exaltation to the joy of unhindered covenant fellowship with God – awaits the eschaton, when it will be given as the final gift from their risen King, the perfection of their union with him. Nevertheless, while they await this crown, the cross Christians bear does bestow dignity on them as Christ's disciples. As such, it gives form and structure to their relationship.

The cross Christians bear in discipleship characterizes *how* they correspond to Christ for Barth. They are (indirectly) one with him, participating in him and therefore sharing in his sufferings. He is their Master. As it went for him, so it must go for those he has chosen and called. At the same time, they must not be confused or interchanged with him. He remains the Master and they his disciples. Consequently, they do not re-enact or repeat his crucifixion. Nor do they directly experience what he experienced. They follow after him. And what they experience only ever echoes, shadows and follows what he experienced as 'a small subsequent taste' of it (604). In this way, the New Testament image of discipleship – in the same way but even more clearly than that of head and body – becomes the preeminent biblically sanctioned way of extending the 'paradoxical identity' between Christ's divinity and humanity so that it structures the correspondence between Christ and his people.

In sum: the key Barthian notion of correspondence is given shape and structure according to the logic of discipleship. For Barth, correspondence is discipleship. In bearing their cross, Christians correspond to Christ in the way the call of discipleship demands – by following after him. His cross displaces theirs before it occasions it. Their cross is not primarily parallel to his (this further explains why Barth rejects the traditional language of imitation at the start of §66.3).

Although, Barth does think that Christians should be like Christ. In fact, they should correspond to him, which they do as they hear his call and follow after him. Equally, the cross of Christians is not a purely mechanical effect of his – as though their suffering was irrelevant or insignificant. Christ's representation of and substitution for Christians does not primarily cause their suffering. His agency and action is primary. But it does occasion their suffering as it draws their agency and action after him – spurring them into motion as his followers. As Webster puts it, 'grace establishes a community of agency between God and his human covenant partners'.[11] Christians genuinely and actively *follow* after Christ, even as they follow *after* him.

5.2 Correspondence as discipleship?

The theological significance of discipleship emerges with greater clarity when we appreciate its role in structuring the 'correspondence' (*Entsprechung*) between Christ and his people, which extends the 'paradoxical identity' of Christ's divinity and humanity.

The concept and language of correspondence is well established in Barth studies. Webster, for example, has demonstrated its significance in Barth's mature ethics. He observes that 'Barth chooses the rubric of "invocation" (*Anrufung*) as the term to describe the Christian life as creaturely response to divine grace' in *The Christian Life* precisely because of its basis in the Christian's correspondence to the grace of God:

> To say that the Christian invokes the gracious God is certainly to envisage human persons as *subsequent*, since invocation is 'the normal action corresponding to the fulfilment of the covenant in Jesus Christ' and in invocation the Christian 'acts as one who is referred wholly to God and has absolute need of Him' ... Yet the gracious God so invoked is not the inhibition of action or the removal of its necessity, for 'God has turned to [the Christian] and summoned him to this venture,' so that in invoking God 'man in his whole humanity takes his proper place over against God' (emphasis in original).[12]

In *The Christian Life*, Barth daringly speaks of God's activity as itself responding and corresponding to Christian invocation. In doing so, Barth rules out any notion of 'divine sole causality' – as Webster points out.[13] What results is a carefully specified vision of divine freedom. The God revealed in Jesus Christ is free *for* genuine covenant partnership with free human agents rather than free *from* it: 'To

---

11. Webster, 'The Christian in Revolt', 123–4.
12. Webster, 'The Christian in Revolt', 124.
13. Webster, 'The Christian in Revolt', 129.

affirm the reciprocity of human and divine agency is not a limitation of divine freedom, but rather its specification.'[14]

Given the prominence of correspondence in Barth's moral theology, the shaping role of discipleship has consequences across the breadth of his theology of sanctification. Crucially, it impacts his construal of human moral agency, moral activity and moral passivity. I will return to each of these in Chapters 7–9, but here I will interrogate the overarching methodological, formal and material aspects of this correspondence-shaping role of discipleship. As I have just shown, the logic of discipleship structures correspondence. In doing this, it specifies and safeguards Barth's careful configuration of the relation between divine and human freedom. This appeal to the structuring logic of discipleship enables Barth to configure divine and human freedom methodologically in terms of 'eschatological realism', formally in terms of his invocation of Chalcedonian Christology as the model of their 'paradoxical identity', and materially in terms of the 'christologized Pneumatology' governing his vision of sanctification. I will examine each of these aspects in turn.

5.2.1 Discipleship, correspondence and 'eschatological realism'

Methodologically, the fact that correspondence is structured by the logic of discipleship instantiates Barth's 'eschatological realism'.[15] 'Eschatological realism' names the way Barth's theological method is more like science than philosophy. It begins with what *is* rather than what could be, and it explores how it is so.[16] As 'the true reality' (*die washer Wirklichkeit*), as Barth puts it in the first edition of *Der Romerbrief*, Christ is the necessary starting point. For Barth, the reality of the risen Jesus determines all other reality *de iure*, a determination that will be disclosed *de facto* at the eschaton. Hence, 'eschatological realism'. This method remains in force in Barth's insistence that the theological decisions he makes in *CD* IV are foundational for and translate directly into the ethics they imply. Commenting on Barth's preface to IV/1, Alexander Massmann observes: 'Barth suggests ... that the one right fundamental decision makes everything else fall more or less into place.'[17] To the degree that this is accurate, Barth's discipleship-shaped rendering of correspondence establishes the decisive trajectory for his ethics of sanctification. From one perspective, it binds the disciples' sanctification to Christ – and to

---

14. Webster, 'The Christian in Revolt', 130.

15. Dalferth, 'Karl Barth's Eschatological Realism', 14–45.

16. As Dalferth puts it, 'in theology, we have to start from what is and try to understand how it can be as it is, and not from a transcendental analysis of what for us can be. It is the methodological procedures of scientific inquiry, not of philosophical reflection, which Barth accepts as his model for theological method.' Dalferth, 'Karl Barth's Eschatological Realism', 19.

17. Alexander Massmann, *Citizenship in Heaven and on Earth: Karl Barth's Ethics* (Minneapolis: Fortress Press, 2015), 341.

God's commanding grace in him. From another perspective, the discipleship-shaped correspondence between Christians and Christ leaves their sanctification underdetermined or 'open-ended'.[18]

These two perspectives on the sanctification of Christian disciples conform to the dialectic of Barth's eschatological realism. Barth attends to the complex realities of the world and human life, but does this by providing a thoroughgoing redescription of these according to the theological categories derived from the reality of the risen Christ. In this, the reality of Christ has the clear priority. As one scholar puts it, 'the reality to which theology refers is the eschatological reality of the risen Christ and the new life into which we are drawn by the Spirit.'[19] This reality generates and establishes the criteria for all of theology – including sanctification – which then unfolds as a more or less thick description with reference to these criteria.[20] In this sense, Barth's theology retains an 'idealist residue', even after it moves away from the idealist language and conceptual vocabulary of *Der Römerbrief*.[21] As in Hegel's idealism, the world of sense experience is neither self-evident nor sufficient of itself to lay claim to our recognition as reality. 'What we take to be concrete, [Barth] calls abstract, and what to us looks at best highly improbable, to him is the surest of all realities.'[22] Unlike Hegel, however, 'Barth does not arrive at these conclusions from a philosophical analysis. On the contrary, this divine prototype of our concreteness and historicity cannot be made tangible and concrete to us except in the historicity of Jesus Christ.'[23] Methodologically, then, there is a resemblance to idealism. Dialectic *is* required for rightly apprehending reality, both the foundational reality of Christ and the rest of reality as illuminated by Christ. However, it is more apt to characterize the idealist legacy within which Barth works in Kantian terms.[24]

Barth's commitment to the determinative reality of the risen Jesus yields realism that resembles idealism at the level of method because it is critical in the Kantian sense. In terms of method, Barth is decidedly modern.[25] At the same time, he is also resolutely theological in a sense that would have been inimical to Kant. This is because Barth's primary turn is towards God rather than to the human

---

18. William Stacey Johnson, *The Mystery of God: Karl Barth and the Postmodern Foundations of Theology* (Louisville: Westminster John Knox Press, 1997), 153–75, makes this case more fully.

19. Dalferth, 'Karl Barth's Eschatological Realism', 21.

20. Dalferth, 'Karl Barth's Eschatological Realism', 22.

21. Hans Urs von Balthasar, *The Theology of Karl Barth: Exposition and Interpretation*, trans. Edward T. Oakes (San Francisco: Ignatius Press, 1992), 220–50, especially 233–50.

22. Dalferth, 'Karl Barth's Eschatological Realism', 28.

23. Balthasar, *The Theology of Karl Barth*, 234.

24. McCormack, *Karl Barth's Critically Realist Dialectical Theology*, 464–8, makes this case, highlighting the way in which Barth's Kantianism was inflected by that of Wilhelm Herrmann.

25. McCormack, *Karl Barth's Critically Realist Dialectical Theology*, 466.

subject. Yet this primary turn to God in Barth's theological method does not mean a turn away from the world, because the God to whom he turns has already turned decisively to the world.

Barth remains interested in the complexities of shared human experience. As Balthasar admits, Barth is 'as open to the world as any theologian could be.'[26] Indeed, Barth's thoroughgoing theological reinterpretation of the world, beginning with the reality of Christ, seeks to render ordinary experience with greater attentiveness than was possible under the reigning paradigm of his theological education. The world and our experience of it is granted the integrity to be itself. The creation depends upon God and finding its 'internal basis' in the covenant that culminates in Christ. This contrasts with both idealist and historicist approaches. Idealism effectively empties the world and our experience of meaning by privileging transcendent reality over it, whereas historicism dispenses with transcendence so the world and human experience can be everything.[27] Barth's eschatologically-oriented critical realism, however, finds expression in the task of 'describing the new world and new form of life which corresponds to the action of God in Christ', as one scholar puts it.[28] This does not mean that it has no other task. Indeed, in a manner analogous with the correspondence-shaping logic of discipleship, attention to Christ as the methodological centre and starting point of theology calls for a rich and full account of human agency, activity and passivity. Barth consistently attempts to take these matters seriously, gathering up and explaining our observations and intuitions about the world and human life by relating them decisively to Christ. Barth employs the dogmatic categories generated by attentiveness to Christ as the interpretive matrix 'to elucidate our experience of natural reality in the light of faith.'[29] Dalferth's depiction of this twofold method is worth quoting at length:

> Barth does not exclude but includes the variety and plurality of our worldly experience within the theological perspective: he does not attempt, as his critics have complained, 'to preserve Christian theology from the indifference and hostility of a secular world' through 'a profound ontological exclusiveness'. Rather he unfolds in a painstaking and detailed way a theological perspective of universal inclusiveness which incorporates and reconstructs the shared and public reality of our world within theology; and he achieves this by interpreting it theologically within the frame of reference provided by the christological exposition of the eschatological reality described.[30]

---

26. Balthasar, *The Theology of Karl Barth*, 157.

27. Regarding historicism see Kerr, *Christ, History, and Apocalyptic*, especially chapter 2, and Oliver O'Donovan, *Resurrection and Moral Order: An Outline for Evangelical Ethics*, 2nd ed. (Leicester: Apollos, 1994), chapter 3.

28. Michael Banner, *Christian Ethics and Contemporary Moral Problems* (Cambridge: Cambridge UP, 1999), 27.

29. Dalferth, 'Karl Barth's Eschatological Realism', 36.

30. Dalferth, 'Karl Barth's Eschatological Realism', 30.

This work of redescription is realized far more imperfectly in Barth's thought – even his mature thought – than Dalferth suggests. However, the attempt to do justice to human agency and reality in the light of the sovereign priority of God's grace is an enduring preoccupation for Barth. It is for good reason that Barth's theological method could be characterized as 'discipleship at the level of thought'.[31] The grace of God calls forth its human correspondence – not least in the work of theology. As such, this work displays the logic of discipleship in its method.

5.2.2 Discipleship, correspondence and the 'Chalcedonian pattern'

Christology not only anchors but also provides the pattern for Barth's open-ended redescription of all of life, within which his account of sanctification sits. There is, in other words, a unifying form or 'grammar' to Barth's theological project – including his theology of sanctification. This form or grammar is supplied by Chalcedonian Christology, interpreted in terms of the enhypostasis–anhypostasis theologoumenon. To elaborate on the formal 'grammar' of Barth's thinking, it is worth dwelling on how Christology unifies the twofold theological method I've just described. Dalferth puts it like this:

> It is the task of dogmatic discourse proper to work out the world of meaning that the presence of Christ carries with it; and because of the centrality of the resurrection, everything it states is to be determined christologically. This amounts to nothing less than a sustained hermeneutical process of redefining virtually every dogmatic concept in christological terms: 'God', 'power', 'freedom', 'person', 'man and woman', 'predestination', 'history', 'time', 'law', 'being', and everything else is – in sometimes quite complicated and twisted ways – derived from the central eschatological reality of the risen Christ ... He then reapplies these categories by the rule of analogy to interpret critically both traditional theological discourse, and non-theological discourse alike.[32]

Here the discipleship-shaped method of 'eschatological realism' takes shape in the christological form of both the theological and the hermeneutic tasks. The theological task, which is primary, is that of 'redefining ... every dogmatic concept' with reference to Christ. The secondary, hermeneutical task then follows this by analogically reinterpreting these dogmatic concepts again with reference to Christ, now oriented towards a richly textured, open-ended redescription of all of life within which theological ethics sits. Barth deploys the conceptual tools of Christology at both levels of his project – anchoring them in Christ dogmatically as well as patterning them after Christ hermeneutically.

---

31. Eberhard Busch, *The Great Passion: An Introduction to Karl Barth's Theology*, trans. G. Bromiley (Grand Rapids: Eerdmans, 2010), 27.

32. Dalferth, 38.

The way Barth employs Christology to give concrete form to both aspects of his theological method bears a Chalcedonian stamp – albeit of a historicized variety that is better characterized in terms of 'paradoxical identity'. While Barth dispenses with its metaphysics,[33] Chalcedon nevertheless provides him a definite pattern. This follows inexorably from the way Barth historicizes Christology such that the 'natures' of Christ are interpreted in terms of the history of Jesus of Nazareth. The event of the incarnation is not about a generic divine nature coming into conjunction with a generic human nature. Rather, in Christ, the one living, active and electing God becomes also the elect human covenant partner of God. In this unique event, the entire history of humanity – as it is focused in the history of the covenant – is taken up and reconciled by God in Christ. One result of this is the actualization of sanctification along with justification (as described in Chapter 3). The unique, objective and unrepeatable Christ-event includes and necessarily presses towards its subjective manifestation, establishing the pattern for divine–human relations.

Barth tends to avoid explicit references to Chalcedon in describing the relation between divine and human actions more broadly, as this relation is shaped by the representative inclusion of all humanity in Christ. He is perhaps more alert than many of his subsequent interpreters to the risks involved with employing Chalcedonian language and concepts outside the bounds of Christology proper. As Paul Nimmo rightly observes, Chalcedon 'is concerned with the unique history of Jesus Christ, and not with the history of the Christian in general.'[34] Therefore, we must attend to the danger that 'to describe the relationship between divine action and human action in the *Church Dogmatics* ... by means of a "Chalcedonian" pattern runs precisely [the] risk of violating the particularity of the mystery and miracle' of the broader relation in assimilating it to the unique history of Jesus Christ.[35]

I contend that the description of Barth's vision of the relation between divine action and human in terms of their 'paradoxical identity' is the most persuasive clarification of this matter to date. My thesis builds on this clarification by drawing attention to how the logic contained in the image of discipleship can safeguard the oneness ('identity') as well as the irreversible asymmetry ('paradox') between Christ and Christians. Discipleship speaks of Christ's freedom and the concomitant freedom of the Christian in a way that exhibits this 'paradoxical identity'. At the same time, the logic of discipleship itself structures the correspondence between Christ and Christians (see 5.1). In this way, an emphasis on discipleship allows us to heed the warning sounded by Nimmo. Specifically, it preserves the uniqueness of the Christ event – he is the Master, in whom God uniquely acts in

---

33. He does this explicitly in his discussion of how the Symbol points to the reality with which theology must continue to wrestle in his discussion of it in *CD* IV/1.

34. Paul T. Nimmo, 'Karl Barth and the *concursus Dei* – a Chalcedonianism Too Far?', *International Journal of Systematic Theology* 9.1 (2007): 72.

35. Nimmo, 'Karl Barth and the *concursus Dei*', 72.

5. Discipleship and the Analogy of Grace 119

his representative humanity – while also suggesting the aptness of an analogical extension of its pattern to divine–human relations more broadly, and Christian lives in particular, which both resemble and find their basis in the unique history of Christ as they follow after him.

The correspondence-structuring logic of discipleship sponsors a cautious borrowing of the Chalcedonian pattern – and the conceptual tools it entails, specifically the anhypostatic–enhypostatic pairing. It may be borrowed to describe the form not only of the relation between Christ and his people, but also of their sanctified existence as disciples. One North American analytic theologian, who examines this pairing carefully, defines it like this: 'the human nature assumed by the second person of the Trinity, though never a person as such (independent of the Word), exists "in" the hypostasis or person of the Word and is thereby "personalized" (that is, hypostasized) by the Word'.[36] Christ's humanity is 'impersonal' (*anhypostatic*) apart from its union with the divine person of the Son, who 'personalizes' it such that it becomes *enhypostasia*. Rendered in more historicist terms, we may say that Christ's human history is powerless – lacking in personal agency and potency (*anhypostasia*) – apart from its assumption into the history of God's own inner life by virtue of its unique union with God the Son. But in this union it attains potency as the representative, inclusive and truly human history (*enhypostasis*), in and through which God sums up the entire history of the covenant and humanity and reconciles it to Godself. By an analogical extension that is implied in its historicist recasting, the anhypostatic–enhypostatic pairing describes the form of the relation between Christ and his people in their sanctified existence as disciples. Apart from Christ, his people are nothing – specifically, they are not holy. As we have seen, their holiness is entirely relative to Christ. But in fellowship with Christ they are holy, sharing in his holiness with supreme realism. The result in Barth's vision of discipleship is that Christian freedom is 'ec-centric'. The disciples' moral agency, activity and suffering find their centre in the free and living Lord Jesus – he is the Master, uniquely and unrepeatably forging the path of true humanity that his disciples may walk. In walking this path, Christ's disciples correspond to him, responding to his present call, instruction and sending of them as those who follow after him.

In three subsequent chapters of this book (Chapters 7, 8 and 9), I interrogate how the 'ec-centric' freedom of disciples in their correspondence to Christ plays out in relation to their moral agency, moral activity and moral suffering or passivity. I will uncover the presence and working of the 'paradoxical identity' between divine freedom and human freedom that utilizes the Chalcedonian conceptuality – analogically extending the anhypostasis–enhypostasis pairing – to describe (1) the mysterious oneness of Christ and his people, (2) the relativizing priority of Christ as the Master and (3) the graced reality and integrity of the

---

36. Oliver D. Crisp, 'The Anhypostasia–Enhypostasia Distinction', in *Divinity and Humanity: The Incarnation Reconsidered* (Cambridge: Cambridge University Press, 2007), 72–3.

resultant agency, activity and passivity of the disciples of Christ. Importantly, this task of analogical redescription is itself discipleship-shaped, for it follows after and does not displace attentiveness to the free, living and present Lord as the foundation and ever-new starting point for this task. Instead, it thematizes this at every point. As a result, Barth's discipleship-shaped account of sanctified moral agency, activity and suffering must be evaluated in terms of how well it corresponds to his lively Christology before it is evaluated in other terms. This is how I assess it – drawing on some important critics of Barth insofar as they illuminate the success of this project.

As an example of this kind of assessment, consider Massmann's charge that Barth gives an inadequately christological form to male–female relations in IV/1. Massmann demonstrates that Barth's treatment of male–female relations on analogy with the Son's unilateral 'obedience' to the Father in CD IV/1 is lopsided.[37] Barth attempts to leverage his christological insight that 'humiliation and exaltation coincide' in the unique history of Jesus Christ to redescribe gender relations. But Massmann argues that in this case its analogical application reveals a one-sided focus on the submission of wives to husbands without attending to the complementary call to husbands to sacrificially love their wives – as Christ loved the church – or the foundational insistence on mutual submission (Ephesians 5.21). It is not wrong that Barth engages in the secondary task of redescribing human experience on the basis of the primary task of attending to Christ. However, for whatever reason – and given what we have noted about Barth's tragic and complicated relationships with women, we must register the possibility of self-justification here – Barth gives an inadequately christological form to male–female relations in IV/1. He needed more Christology not less. Massmann's criticism of Barth's analogical redescription of male–female relations establishes that it fails on its own terms. In doing so, it illustrates how to respect the 'eschatological realism' of Barth's method by contesting his analogical extension of Christology at this point and offering an alternative construction of the christological redescription of gender relations.

Barth's discipleship-shaped method and the christological form it bestows on human experience invites precisely these kinds of discriminating judgements. The twofold task of theology as he construes it – consisting of the primary dogmatic derivation of theological categories from Christ and the secondary hermeneutic redescription of experience in analogous terms – is an exercise in and aid to discipleship. Failure in this task (including Barth's own failure) summons us to do better than Barth rather than to discard his contribution. In this vein, I will articulate my contribution to the contemporary discipleship conversation in a way that works with Barth, but goes against and beyond Barth at important points. In order to secure the tangible and practical definition of Christian living that it seeks, the contemporary discipleship conversation must learn from Barth to be more theological – and to more resolutely prioritize the

---

37. Massmann, *Citizenship in Heaven and on Earth*, 359–68.

living presence of Christ, attending to and corresponding to him. In doing so, it must acknowledge where Barth himself fails on his own terms. At the same time, it must move beyond him at those points as well as in those areas that remain underdeveloped.

5.2.3 Discipleship, correspondence and 'christologized pneumatology'

Barth's vision of sanctification is governed materially by a 'christologized pneumatology'. This christologized Pneumatology complements and grounds the methodological and formal aspects of the relationship between divine and human freedom as these operate in Barth's discipleship-shaped presentation of the Christian's correspondence to Christ. It does this by anchoring and animating the dialectical relation between divine and human freedom as it pertains to Christian living. The Spirit enables the emergence of human freedom in discipleship-shaped correspondence with Christ. Through the Spirit, Christ, though absent in the body, is present to authoritatively interpret the moral context and direct his people into the path of discipleship, in which they realize their freedom and humanity.[38] This freedom remains subsequent to and follows after Christ, attesting his own lordly freedom as its centre and basis at the same time as it corresponds to him in a manner structured and safeguarded by the logic of discipleship. The freedom of discipleship is determined by Christ's Spirit-filled humanity, in which he represents, exemplifies and makes himself present to his people. His active lordship as the exalted human being galvanizes the active life of discipleship. Christian freedom is realized as the Spirit awakens disciples to follow after Christ.

Barth's christologized pneumatology functions primarily to explain Christ's lordly freedom and presence in the context of his actualization of sanctification. In doing so, it sponsors the 'lively Christology' that is primed for and demands the turn to discipleship at §66.3. This is because the holiness that is objectively real and effective in Christ becomes existentially real and transformative for Christians by the power of the Spirit. It is the Spirit's work to awaken people to their sanctification in Christ. The Spirit enables them to enter into covenant partnership with and joyful service of God – that is, into a discipleship-shaped correspondence with God in Christ. But this enabling work does not unfold 'in the name of a Jesus who is not present' because 'Jesus Christ is present through the Spirit', as Christopher Holmes emphasizes.[39] Barth speaks of sanctification in a way that draws Christ and the Spirit together. Holiness is objectively real *de iure* in Christ, but becomes real *de facto* in the existential encounter with Christ effected by the Spirit. In deploying pneumatology to close the 'gap' between objective reality and existential encounter, Barth 'christologizes' the Spirit. The Spirit's activity is identified with

---

38. Holmes develops this perspective more fully in *Ethics in the Presence of Christ*, chapter 1.

39. Holmes, *Ethics in the Presence of Christ*, 9.

Christ's freedom, agency and personal presence – exercised in this case to claim and 'direct' Christians.

Barth's christologized pneumatology also enables the emergence of genuine human freedom for Christians, the freedom of which discipleship speaks. It does this as a result of its vindication of Christ's freedom. So it upholds and follows after the authority of Christ rather than displacing it. In Barth's discipleship-shaped vision of sanctification, human freedom is shaped by the priority of God's action in Christ. This is one implication of the way Barth refers to the Spirit in §64.4. Although its deployment is deliberately delayed (see 3.3), pneumatological material is extraordinarily prominent there – especially in comparison to other sections where it might have been expected (such as §38). Noting this, Massmann contends that 'Barth's characterization of the work of the Spirit in *CD* IV/2 suggests that ethics should be a process in which Christians also take part according to standards open to rational communication and discursive evaluation.'[40] But Massmann surely oversteps here. He himself admits that §64 displays a 'surprisingly strong' emphasis on the authority of Christ, harking back to earlier treatments.[41] What is more, the chief statement from §64.4 that Massmann relies upon to support his reading exhibits just such an emphasis, framing the Spirit's operation in enacting Christ's 'direction' in terms of the 'only reality' rather than 'one possibility among many' or even 'the norm' (361–2). Massmann is correct to see a link between Barth's emphasis on the Spirit in *CD* IV/2 and a robust vision of human freedom alongside and in partnership with God. This is entirely in keeping with Barth's overarching emphasis on the exaltation of humanity in Christ, and especially with its polemical thrust.[42] Yet Massmann is wrong to imagine that a robust account of human freedom requires the limitation of the lordly claim made by Christ. For Barth, human correspondence with Christ – with the vision of free human moral agency, moral activity and moral passivity that this entails – does not require God to lessen or surrender his sovereign freedom and authority. As Webster says, it specifies rather than limits it. In doing so, it allows human freedom to emerge as itself – created and human. In discipleship, human freedom takes its proper place in response to the grace of God in Christ.

---

40. Massmann, *Citizenship in Heaven and on Earth*, 425. Curiously, Massmann himself registers the militaristic resonance of Barth's preferred metaphors in this context – 'direction' (*Weisung*), 'field' or better 'battlefield' (*Feld*), 'orders' (*Ordnung*) – but argues that they somehow point to a pneumatological softening of Christ's unilateral commanding.

41. Massmann, *Citizenship in Heaven and on Earth*, 420.

42. Barth comments in the preface to *CD* IV/2 that much of his energy here is invested in providing 'an attempted Evangelical answer to the Marian dogma of Romanism' – with its elevation of the human factor in salvation – achieved by showing 'that it is made superfluous by the "Exaltation of the Son of Man" and its anthropological implications' (ix).

5.3 Discipleship, correspondence and theological ethics

Barth's use of the New Testament motif of discipleship therefore establishes a decisive trajectory for his theology of sanctification and for the vision of Christian living it entails. Specifically, Barth's turn to discipleship effects a christological determination of his vision of Christian living. This is both a determination 'from above' in relation to Christ's direction and call as the Master, and a determination 'from below' in relation to the Christian correspondence to Christ as his disciples.

'From above', Barth's construal of correspondence as discipleship grounds and energizes the dialectic between Christ's representation and exemplarity as it impinges upon human freedom in his vision of sanctification. In describing the 'essentially unfinished nature of his theology' as evident in *The Christian Life*, John Webster notes that Barth's 'theological instincts were various, and he remained deeply suspicious of moves to suppress one or other of them by according preponderant significance to one fact alone'.[43] Connected with this, Webster argues that apparently competing representative and exemplary constructions of Christ's ongoing significance testify to 'the unsettled character of his Christology, which has still not crystallized into a single theological principle, in the face of which all other theological work is a matter of mere corollaries'.[44] I believe that for Barth both the representative and exemplary images are anchored in the christologized Pneumatology that governs his vision of sanctification and finds fragmentary expression in *The Christian Life*. At root, it is the presence of Christ in the Spirit issuing his call to discipleship with both urgent contemporaneity and settled 'formed reference' – because it is the living Christ who calls and instructs his disciples today as he always has – that grounds and energizes Barth's in-principle endless variations on these themes.

'From below', Barth's construal of correspondence in terms of discipleship establishes the dialectic operative with regard to Christ's human covenant partners. The life of discipleship-shaped correspondence to Christ moves between two poles. At one pole, it follows after Christ. It is receptive, subsequent to and attentive to him as its Lord and Master. Listening is the fundamental posture of God's human covenant partners as they are disturbed and awakened by the Spirit of Christ. Christ retains the precedence and his present direction is decisive for them. No emphasis on human discernment or activity can be allowed to displace that. As one scholar puts it, Christian living according to Barth 'demands ... an openness, a constant readiness to hear something new, something different, something arresting, something that takes by surprise, something that provokes change, something that converts'. The result is explicitly a matter of discipleship: 'It is our proper role to correspond, not to predict. We follow; we do not precede.'[45]

---

43. Webster, 'The Christian in Revolt', 130.
44. Webster, 'The Christian in Revolt', 130.
45. Biggar, 'Hearing God's Command', 106.

At the other pole, Barth's ethics of sanctification is 'open ended'.[46] Christian correspondence with Christ is patterned on him and his self-giving relation to others. Barth develops this vision of the Christian's self-giving love for others – premised and patterned on Christ's – most fully in §68, admitting of the pluriform nature of its expression given the ever-shifting character of human history, experience and context. This vision is underdetermined as a matter of principle (801–2):

> When obedient action consists in the establishment of the rigid counterpart of a compact Christianity, it loses its significance as an imitation of God's own love. For God, and therefore its original, is not a fixed and static and rigidly determined figure which is dead for all the majesty ascribed to it. He is a living and acting person, who for all His faithfulness to Himself is continually electing and willing and creatively producing new things, and thus speaking and commanding and ordering new things. Obedience to Him can consist only in a continual readiness and willingness to follow His action, to do justice in a continual subjection to His electing and willing and producing, and therefore to His speaking and commanding and ordering, and thus to correspond with the greatest possible loosening of one's own rigidity.

The principled underdetermination of Barth's vision of Christian living is already evident in the ways he presents the call of discipleship in §66.3. Following Christ is active and concrete, entails self-denial and enlists us in the 'kingdom onslaught' against idolatry and ideology. But it does not repeat exactly the way in which any other disciple was called to follow Christ – in the New Testament or elsewhere. It is 'formed' by reference to them, to be sure; but Barth transposes Bonhoeffer's language of the costliness of discipleship into that of the 'greater freedom' Christ summons his people to in every new context.

Recognizing this twofold way discipleship reflects Christ's determination of ethics, allows me to employ the conceptual tool of the anhypostatic–enhypostatic pair that Barth develops in his historicization of Chalcedon. Both anhypostatic and enhypostatic aspects belong together in describing Christian freedom in discipleship-shaped correspondence to Christ, for they establish the moral ontology for human freedom. It is a creaturely reality, 'anhypostatic' in the sense that it is not self-contained or autonomous. It finds its centre in Christ, remaining relative to him. In doing this, it proves 'enhypostatic'. It is real in its dependence upon and determination by Christ. As the one who is personally present in the Spirit, he is the 'true reality' – the Master – who underwrites and actively directs his people into the freedom of following after him.

Beyond establishing the moral ontology for human freedom, Barth's discipleship-shaped vision of the christological determination of human freedom also contains a particular vision of moral agency, moral activity and moral passivity. In this vision, human freedom in its responsiveness to Christ is

---

46. Johnson, *The Mystery of God*, chapter 7.

5. Discipleship and the Analogy of Grace 125

patterned on and follows after Christ's freedom. Human freedom corresponds to Christ in a way structured by the logic of discipleship. Consequently, human agency is not characterized by unlimited or unconstrained choice – like Hercules at the crossroads. Such a vision would set human agency proudly alongside or even above that of God. Yet neither is human agency characterized by freedom from choice or the need for action – the fantasy nurtured by many in their sloth. Barth puts it evocatively in §65 (495–6):

> To be sure, the slothful man chooses – in that dreadful negation of true choosing – as he always did. But he chooses only on the path that he has entered. And on this path, however he may choose, he cannot choose as a true man (for he has turned aside from this genuine possibility), but in all his choices, having yielded to corruption, he can only act corruptly. His starting-point is the repudiation of his freedom. He cannot, therefore, do that which corresponds to his freedom. He necessarily does that which he could not do in the exercise of it. This is the bondage of the human will which is the bitterest characteristic of human misery.

Theological construction must work with Barth and move beyond Barth here. The situation is the mirror-image of that which can be identified in the *Romans* II. There Barth does not appear to be consistent in applying his conceptual framework.[47] For example, he speaks far more – and more positively – about the church than the rhetoric of the 'infinite qualitative distinction' appears to allow (whether because it is the rhetorical clothing rather than the true substance of his thought, or because Barth is pursuing biblical faithfulness rather than metaphysical consistency).[48] In terms of the moral formation of the community, Barth must presuppose a vision of moral agency that flies in the face of the dominant rhetorical and conceptual tone of his commentary. This vision requires not only 'extensive theological instruction and exhortation, as well as substantial reflection upon the daily realities of human life and society' but also a grasping of the 'imperative of grace' by each member of the church.[49]

In the context of Barth's early reflections on moral agency, his best insights into the reality and integrity of human agency demand he be read against himself. What he had to say about human agency and formation in *Romans* II was typically implicit and contrary to its characteristically antithetical, uncompromising conceptual vocabulary. Doing justice to his ethics in *Romans* II is a matter of explicating what is implicit even if it contradicts what is explicit. By contrast, in Barth's mature thought – and especially in the context of his vision of sanctification in §66 and its unfinished ethical counterpart in *The Christian Life* – Barth is everywhere insistent on the clear implications of his foundational theological commitments. He sees, for example, that the unity of God's freedom *from* and

---

47. O'Neil, *The Church as Moral Community*, 116.
48. Hunsinger, *Reading Barth with Charity*, xiv–xvi.
49. O'Neil, *The Church as Moral Community*, 249.

for humanity calls for a robust account of the covenant partner corresponding to God in Christ, with genuine agency and integrity – although not full-blown autonomy. However, for a variety of reasons (not least the fact that his project remained incomplete), Barth never fully developed these into a complete and concretely specified ethics of sanctification. To do justice to his vision of Christian living therefore requires following the trajectory beyond what is explicit. This movement *beyond* Barth must continue to work *with* Barth – attending to the insights contained in its trajectory-setting foundation in IV/2 as well as taking cues from the fragmentary *The Christian Life*, especially when it comes to the necessarily unsettled and unsettling character of his discipleship-shaped vision of sanctified freedom in correspondence to Christ.

The concept of correspondence as it is structured by the logic of discipleship recommends itself as a decisive feature of his vision of Christian living. It does this because (not in spite of) that fact that it is underdetermined and lacks a detailed agenda for action. Correspondence is more like a compass than an itemized and inflexible set of directions. It demands the alignment of Christians with their Lord, manifested in attentiveness to his living direction. His direction provides the decisive word by which to interpret any context. At the same time, it leaves the specifics of that interpretation underdetermined. As such, they are open to moral argument and reflection, especially at the secondary, hermeneutical level of the analogical redescription of experience.

Before following through on the ramifications of Barth's use of the motif of discipleship to structure the analogy upon which his theological ethics rests, I will underscore its significance by a diachronic analysis of Barth's approach to this by taking some 'core samples' from Barth's early and late thought on moral agency and action.

Chapter 6

DISCIPLESHIP AND ANALOGY FROM *ROMANS* II TO *THE CHRISTIAN LIFE*

In this chapter I will take up a question implicitly posed by the previous one. If Christian correspondence to Christ in freedom constitutes the essential aspect of discipleship (Chapter 4) and if, more radically, Barth's crucial ethical notion of correspondence is itself structured by the logic of discipleship (Chapter 5), is §66 the only place these concepts connect with each other? In other words, when Barth declares here that correspondence consists in the analogy between master and disciple, is this a fleeting moment of alignment – embraced and then laid aside as part of the ever-shifting kaleidoscope of Barth's dynamic theology? Or is it a glimpse into enduring substructure of Barth's theological ethics?

In this chapter, I will evaluate the extent to which bringing together discipleship and analogy uncovers the way in which Barth's mature theology comes to 'push beyond the neat confines of the instrumentalist and parallelist' constructions of the relation between divine and human agency.[1] I show that the truth is more complex than an either – or framing of the question suggests. As Balthasar famously points out, Barth's theological project – from *Romans* II to *Church Dogmatics* (and, I would add, beyond to *The Christian Life*) – is not simply the steady unfolding of an unvarying insight. Balthasar sharply articulates the problem with this approach:

> Any attempt to explain the *Church Dogmatics* (and Barth's later writings in general) solely in terms of *The Epistle to the Romans* is an outright absurdity; in fact, it is an insult to the author. For more than once Barth has distanced himself from his Romans commentary, as he had already made clear in the foreword to the fifth edition (1926); moreover, he has from time to time warned his readers not to take literally what he wrote there. Indeed, he has given up the whole conceptuality determining the early work.[2]

Neither is Barth's project the polar opposite – namely, a sequence of more or less inadequate attempts to arrive at the dazzling synthesis achieved late in the *Church Dogmatics*. Such a position is immediately called into question by the

---

1. McMaken, 'Definitive, Defective, or Deft?', 97.
2. Balthasar, *The Theology of Karl Barth*, 70.

obviously unfinished but also necessarily incomplete and fragmentary nature of the material published as *The Christian Life*. Moreover,

> the other approach – the one that simply puts Barth's early work in the shadows and sees it as a thing of the past, wanting only to concentrate on the fruit of his mature years – can only lead to a very imperfect understanding of the very works on which it wishes to concentrate. There can be no doubt that Barth's latest works are, in a very real if hidden sense, his earliest works as well: the intense explosion into the *Church Dogmatics* is ultimately but the unleashing of an intellectual power that was there from the very beginning.[3]

In contrast to both of these inadequate approaches to Barth's project, I adopt Webster's proposal that it is best conceived as a matter of a lifelong wrestling with some basic enduring preoccupations. Further, I endorse Webster's claim that Barth's fundamental preoccupation was to give a satisfactory answer to the Renaissance question of the reality, integrity and dignity of human moral agency in Reformation terms – terms that emphasize the reality, freedom and priority of the divine agency and activity centred in Christ.[4] In wrestling with these preoccupations, moreover, Barth draws on different conceptual vocabulary at different points in his career. In this, he shows himself less interested in conceptual clarity and consistency at a terminological or philosophical level than in faithfulness to the generative and criteriological biblical narrative of God and God's world.[5]

Notwithstanding the consistency of Barth's enduring preoccupations, he also appears to gain increasing clarity at crucial points – not least of which is the decisive recognition, articulated with such force in Barth's treatment of election in *CD* II/2, that if there is 'no God behind the back of Jesus Christ', as T. F. Torrance frequently put it, then God's freedom *from* the world and his freedom *for* it are bound together. Divine freedom and divine grace are united in election. In election, Christ is both the electing God and the elect human being. Christ is God in sovereign freedom and love determining not to be without the human creature and covenant partner. Layered on top of this, the contexts in which Barth writes also vary across his career. He has different polemical targets and conversation partners in the *Romans* era than he does late in the *Church Dogmatics*. As Bender

---

3. Balthasar, *The Theology of Karl Barth*, 71.

4. See Webster, *Barth's Earlier Theology*.

5. As Bruce McCormack concedes, 'we ought not to get overly excited by the substitution of an actualistic ontology for a substantialist one. In truth, Barth did not adopt his actualistic mode of thinking about questions of "being" in the final analysis because he thought that Kant had demolished classical metaphysics or because Hermann Cohen had treated the human "self" as task or because Hegel had inscribed "becoming" into the very being of God. He adopted it finally because he believed that the earliest Christian confession was that "Jesus is Lord" and that this conviction was set forth in the New Testament in the form of a narrated *history*.' McCormack, 'Sanctification After Metaphysics', 105.

notes in the case of Barth's ecclesiology, he shifts from a predominantly 'critical' stance in *Romans* II to something more 'constructive' by the time he has begun *The Church* Dogmatics – and, I would argue, shifts even further to something more 'exploratory' in *The Christian Life*.[6] Recognizing the polemical and occasional character of Barth's theology has a number of advantages. First, it 'reinforces a picture of Barth as an eminently *churchly* theologian, concerned about the integrity of the life and witness of the Church'.[7] Second, it 'can allow one to avoid an all-or-nothing approach to Barth, that is, a stark choice between accepting or rejecting Barth's theology wholesale'.[8] Third, in inviting attentiveness not only to what Barth says but also what he refuses to say, and why he does both of these things, it offers to shed 'light on some of the tensions, antinomies and even reversals within the *Dogmatics* itself'.[9]

While Barth picks up and then discards different conceptual vocabularies, varies his emphasis, exchanges his polemical targets and conversation partners and shifts from a 'critical' to a more 'constructive' stance, his preoccupations remain remarkably stable. Consequently, even at the end of his lifelong *agonia* with these preoccupations – and notwithstanding his real gains and breakthroughs in terms of increased clarity – Webster is right to note that Barth's guiding 'theological instincts were various, and he remained deeply suspicious of moves to suppress one or other of them by according preponderant significance to one fact alone'.[10] In *The Christian Life*, this plays out in a dialectic as sharp and abrupt as anything in *Romans* II: a representative Christology – including an emphasis on Christ as the moral example and pattern for Christians – exists alongside a more soteriological and substitutionary Christology jostling with one another. As Webster puts it, this aspect of *The Christian Life* 'shows something of the unsettled character of his Christology, which has still not crystallized into a single theological principle, in the face of which all other theological work is a matter of mere corollaries'.[11] Indeed, the fact that these varying Christological configurations continue to coexist – dialectically correcting and contesting but never overshadowing or displacing each other – evidences a deeper consistency across Barth's theological project: the living Lord Jesus Christ meets us again and again, striking us in fresh ways, generating new language as we respond to him and seek to grapple with his reality, and disciplining all this as he summons us to follow after him.[12]

---

6. Bender, *Karl Barth's Christological Ecclesiology*, 59–65.
7. Yocum, *Ecclesial Mediation*, xix.
8. Yocum, *Ecclesial Mediation*, xix.
9. Yocum, *Ecclesial Mediation*, xx.
10. Webster, 'The Christian in Revolt', 130.
11. Webster, 'The Christian in Revolt', 130.
12. As Dalferth among others has argued, Barth's theology is consistently orientated towards the 'true reality' of the risen and living Christ, who generates the very theological formulations that he then unsettles. This is the deep, discipleship-shaped reason Barth's theology is always beginning ever again at the beginning.

If it is right to conceive of Barth's project in this way, it becomes less pressing to establish whether discipleship is an interesting but short-lived mutation in the concept of correspondence or the fundamental and invariant DNA that is the secret of its identity. Rather – and this is the burden of this chapter – it appears as a pre-eminently biblical means of bestowing a degree of stability and resolution to Barth's ongoing attempt to employ notions of correspondence and analogy to do justice to his enduring preoccupation with the relationship between divine and human freedom. The language and logic of discipleship does not only reflect this enduring preoccupation. It significantly advances his project of adequately specifying human moral agency and activity without diluting the actualism, indirectness and passivity ingredient in ensuring the centrality of Christ. The discipleship motif therefore provides a platform upon which Barth builds after §66, enabling him to deploy correspondence in a more constructive and even daring and exploratory mode in his ecclesiology and ethics. To change the metaphor, the logic of discipleship establishes the fundamental chord progression over which Barth improvises to generate new configurations of divine–human correspondence. In this way, the turn to discipleship makes a decisive contribution to Barth's lifelong project of specifying the shape of divine–human correspondence in terms that answer to the history and living reality of Jesus Christ. I will establish the correspondence-shaping contribution discipleship functions to provide in Barth's moral theology by means of some 'core samples' from the *Romans* II, *Church Dogmatics* and *The Christian Life*. In particular, I will examine these 'core samples' with a view to Barth's vision of human agency (6.1) – considering ecclesial agency in particular – and human moral activity (6.2).

6.1 The identity and agency of the church in *Romans II* and *Church Dogmatics IV*

6.1.1 The cruciform and repentant church in *Romans II*

We begin with Barth's articulation of ecclesial agency in the second edition of his Romans' commentary. Beginning here establishes that one of Barth's enduring concerns is to adequately specify the concrete identity and agency of the church. This is hardly a novel or controversial point. Many have recognized that this is an enduring preoccupation for Barth – whether or not they judge him to have achieved satisfactory concreteness in doing so. Beyond this, therefore, my examination of Barth's early account of ecclesial agency is oriented towards establishing the decisiveness of Barth's integration of discipleship with sanctification in *CD* IV/2 §66. Barth's integration of discipleship with sanctification offers an explicitly biblical and robustly theological anchor to enable the dialectical coordination of ecclesial actualism – with its resulting relativization of churchly agency – and concreteness – in upholding its (creaturely) reality and integrity – that Barth was already seeking in *Romans* II.

6. Discipleship and Analogy from Romans II

To this end, three things are worth noticing in Barth's rendering of ecclesial identity and agency in *Romans* II. First, Barth's images for the church in *Romans* II are relentlessly negative. This is evident already in the *locus classicus* of Barth's 'actualistic' ecclesiology in the first chapter (36):

> To the proclamation and receiving of this Gospel, the whole activity of the Christian community – its teaching, ethics and worship – is strictly related. But the activity of the community is related to the Gospel only in so far as it is no more than a crater formed by the explosion of a shell and seeks to be no more than a void in which the Gospel reveals itself. The people of Christ, His community, know that no sacred word or work or thing exists in its own right: they know only those words and works and things which by their negation are sign-posts to the Holy One.

The radical and far-reaching nature of this description ought not to be missed. When Barth speaks negatively about the shell crater, void and signpost 'by negation', he is speaking explicitly of the Christian community (*Gemeinde*) and not merely the institutional church. It is the invisible and true Church of Jacob and not simply the visible and corrupt Church of Esau (to use the language he introduces in discussing Romans 9) that answers to this negative description.

Therefore, it is hardly a shock that when he turns to address the guilt of the church, following the argument of Romans 10, Barth deploys negative and even ugly images. For instance, he describes the KRISIS of the church's self-knowledge is an 'open wound' (366). That is to say, the church is aware – painfully so – of its inescapable humanness. Because it is merely the channel within which grace and revelation of God have flowed in human history, the church lacks any power or right to claim God's grace or revelation for itself, as its possession. Of course, it is often tempted to lay claim to such a possession – either by setting itself against the world by 'accusing [it] of sinful hardness of heart, and ... launching an offensive against it' (364), or by turning inwards to sacralize its own activity, becoming preoccupied with its institutions, community and sophistication in stewarding religious experience (365–6). But all such claims are illegitimate (366):

> The Church can, and presumably should, mount guard over the course down which the sacred stream may flow when the Hour of God be come. But it has no power of compulsions; and it is important that it should not forget its incompetence. This unforgetfulness – this open wound – is the supreme advantage of the Church. Religion is not the Kingdom of God, even if it be the Kingdom-of-God-Religion of Blumhart's decadent successors. Religion is a human work.

In using this gruesome and startlingly negative language for the church, Barth utterly relativizes the church – along with all human religiosity. It is nothing compared with the revelation and grace of God itself. Barth seldom appears more creative than in coining new metaphors to express this truth. Commenting on the combined effect of all this negativity, Michael O'Neil observes that 'If Barth were to apply his theological framework in *Romans* II with utter consistency there would be no possibility of Christian and ecclesial existence, no possibility of a life of faith, of progress in sanctification, of moral community.'[13] Barth's relentlessness in prioritizing divine freedom and agency appears to obliterate anything positive we might be drawn to say about the human – especially as that applies to the church, the site of the cosmic impact 'vertically, from above'. However, it is worth registering that Barth is commenting on Romans 9–11. He is therefore understandably focused on election – that is, on 'the divine order, whereby God chooses us and not we Him' (370). In this context, a negativity about human choice and agency is at least comprehensible as he strives to magnify God's grace in election. (Of course, Barth would come to see the importance of finding other ways to do this.)

The second point to observe is that alongside and within this relentless negativity, Barth stresses the positive possibility of the church – although he is at pains to underline that it is an impossible possibility. According to O'Neil (and in this he is following McCormack and Smart), Barth does not appear to be consistent in applying his theological framework to the agency of the church.[14] Happily, he speaks much more – and more positively – about the church than the rhetoric of the 'infinite qualitative distinction' would appear to allow. In one sense, Bender is right to opine that in *Romans* II 'the church seems to be a community of sin that precedes and opposes the resurrection more than a new community that is established in the light of and through the resurrection.'[15] But, in another sense, this is not the full story. For Barth continually insists on seeing positive significance in the midst of all this negativity. Take this statement for example (370):

> Were the Church to appear before men as a Church under judgement; did it know of no other justification save that which is in judgement; did it believe in the stone of stumbling and rock of offence, instead of being offended and scandalized at it; then, with all its failings and offences – and certainly one day purified of some of them – it would be the Church of God.

Paradoxically, Barth sees the church anticipating its eschatological perfection and purification in its willingness to embrace, own and confess its lack of perfection and purity and consequently its deservingness of judgement. For all Barth's searing realism about the church here (in the same context he notes but discounts as finally telling a litany of contemporary criticisms of the church), he is confident that in confessing its sin, the church genuinely becomes the Church of God. As such, it anticipates in its present justification, its ultimate and ultimately certain, eschatological reality.

13. O'Neil, *Church as Moral Community*, 241.
14. O'Neil, *Church as Moral Community*, 210–21.
15. Bender, *Karl Barth's Christological Ecclesiology*, 36.

6. Discipleship and Analogy from Romans II

Barth's confidence about the eschatological status of the church stands in marked tension – even paradox and contradiction – with a rigorous and logical application of his relativization of ecclesial being and agency. This tension resonates with what O'Neil has uncovered in Barth's stress on the moral formation of the community. In Barth's treatment of Romans 6, Barth's vision of ecclesial agency requires not only 'extensive theological instruction and exhortation, as well as substantial reflection upon the daily realities of human life and society' but also a grasping of the 'imperative of grace' by each member of the church.[16] In order to exist as the church 'under judgement', the church must seek no other justification for itself than that which is to be found in God's judgement upon it (and the world along with it). To do this, it must be taught, reminded and have this reality continually impressed upon it. And for this to take place, it must have a kind of identity and agency to be the object of such formation. Indeed, the fact that Barth takes the trouble to say these negative and critical things, rather than simply giving up and walking away, is itself an example of the kind of moral formation he appears to envisage as necessary and right for the church. In such a way, the church is enabled to be itself, fulfilling its calling and mission in the world to witness to Christ.

Third, and as the upshot of the first two points, Barth envisages ecclesial agency here in an obviously dialectical way. The criticism – even outright relativization – that God's judgement brings, stands alongside a joyful affirmation of the church, albeit on the other side of its KRISIS. Here in *Romans* II, the marks of the church are repentance, renunciation and a refusal to pretend it has anything of itself to offer. This is so, Barth insists, because the essence of the church's being is its tribulation and guilt.

Barth teases out the theme of the church's tribulation and guilt across his examination of Romans 10, and it is worth attending closely to the dynamics of this. He begins by distancing himself from those 'who are accustomed to make hasty and direct attacks upon the Church' (362). Rather than joining the chorus of the church's critics – either inside or outside the church – Barth insists that he has been 'compelled hitherto to speak of [the church's] tribulation, of that tribulation imposed upon it by the knowledge of God, which is its proper theme, and gift, and task'. Sharing in the misery of sin with all others, the church must recognize the 'infinite qualitative distinction' between humanity and God. The weight of sin, the terrible sentence of death, the ontological clouds and darkness that obscure our view of the living God, the source of our life, lie heavy upon humanity. Barth insists that the church knows this (362):

> In the Church humanity becomes conscious of itself and is manifested as religious. And then it suffers, because God is God. Humanity does not suffer from this pain and from that pain, not here and there, not more and less. It suffers because every concrete and temporal thing is confronted, not, it must be

---

16. O'Neil, *Church as Moral Community*, 249.

remembered, by some second thing, but by nonexistence, by Primal Origin, by the Creator of all things visible and invisible.

'God-sickness' afflicts the church because, along with all humanity, it *is* guilty, sharing in the sin of Adam. 'Creatureliness', Barth declares, 'is a curse ... in virtue of our sin'. That is to say, the ontological distance between human beings as creatures and God their Creator becomes toxic and deadly as the Adamic shadow falls upon it. One way to picture this would be to imagine a goldfish lying beside its bowl, flapping about in its death throes as its gills – the very organs of its creaturely life and well-being when it inhabits the environment it is made for – inexorably suffocate it. In the same way, human beings are defined by our difference from and drawn to our Creator as the source of life and flourishing. Yet we are destroyed by that very difference when we are thrust out of relationship with God by our own fault.

According to Barth, the church confronts the true horror of humanity's misery, suffering and tribulation – namely, the fact that we are to blame for it – in recognizing our guilt and complicity in our sin and judgement. This recognition is something that is only possible by God's self-revelation. Possibly invoking psychoanalytic categories, Barth describes it this way (363): 'The misery of men is occasioned by the fact that their knowledge of God is itself embarrassed, troubled, under KRISIS, and by their inability to escape from a sense of guilt and responsibility for this whole situation.' Put differently, a 'knowing unknowing' or half-suppressed sense of our complicity in our own subjection to sin and death – and all the complications these bring to human life – itself occasions our misery.

In contrast to this 'knowing unknowing', the church is characterized by repentance and self-renunciation – and even by iconoclasm directed against its own human 'byproducts'. This phenomenon might best be characterized as an unguarded confession of our complicity in the general tribulation and misery of humanity. This is the church's 'unknowing knowing', so to speak. As Barth evocatively puts it, 'The Church – if it be aware of itself and is serious – sets fire to a charge which blows up every sacred edifice which men have ever erected or can ever erect in its vicinity' (375). For all its rhetorical force, Barth's understanding of the dynamics of repentance and self-renunciation is difficult to pinpoint. He speaks about it with the utmost indirectness. This indirectness may be a function of the particular conceptual vocabulary he is deploying across the commentary. Alternatively, it may stem from an intuitive awareness of the danger of turning this self-criticism into a virtue in which dialectical theologians and preachers might sit in self-satisfied splendour.[17]

Either way, it is clear that repentance is the essential form of ecclesial agency as Barth construes it. Central to his account of repentance is a dialectical affirmation

---

17. Barth shows his awareness of this possibility in 'The Word of God as the Task of Theology, 1922' in Karl Barth, *The Word of God and Theology*, trans. Amy Marga (New York: T&T Clark, 2011), 171–98.

of both the relativization of the church and the insistence that its God-given being and agency are nevertheless real. The church stands under the divine 'No'. It is utterly exposed in its sin and compromise. At the same time, it hears a divine 'Yes' enclosed within this 'No'. The church is upheld not in spite of but because of and through its subjection to judgement.

Ultimately, we may say that the church in *Romans* II has a cruciform ontology. It is, as Bender and others have observed of Barth's ecclesiology, more generally 'ec-centric' or anhypostatic: 'Ecclesiology, while itself a pneumatological doctrine, is thus grounded in … Christology and shares its inherent logic and patterns.'[18] For the church is centred not upon itself but on Christ. Hence, its relativization. Yet in being so centred, it genuinely participates in the Christ event via its grace-wrought correspondence to it. This is the significance Barth recognizes in calling it the 'Church of Jacob' as distinct from the 'Church of Esau'. When introducing this distinction, Barth acknowledges that we only ever see and speak of the Church of Esau – the church that is not identified with Christ, constituted by its antithesis to the gospel and dispossession of grace (342). But in the same breath he affirms that 'we cannot speak of it without recollecting that its theme is the Church of Jacob'. For, he continues, 'The very life of Esau, questionable as it is, depends upon Jacob; and he is Esau only because he is not-Jacob.' Governed by this dialectic, the negativity of Barth's depiction of the church proves the secret to his positive affirmation of it, not as a kind of ecclesiological *via negativa* but through a *theologia crucis* in which we are confident that the true face of God is revealed in its opposite, as God's true glory was displayed in the suffering and monstrosity of the cross.

Practically, what this amounts to in *Romans* II is the frank recognition of guilt and failure characteristic of repentance. This repentance moreover does not lead to despair so much as to seeking from God his promised but undeserved blessing: 'our duty is to take seriously to heart the known tribulation of the Church, and to wrestle with God, the God of Jacob: I will not let thee go, except though bless me' (342).

6.1.2 Christ, church and context in Church Dogmatics IV/1-3

Across the first three-part volumes of *Church Dogmatics* IV, there emerges a distinctive vision of the church as the human product of and privileged participant in Christ's reconciling work. Viewed from each of the perspectives of Christ's threefold office (*munus triplex*) – as priest, king and prophet – Barth consistently emphasizes and dialectically holds together the two poles of this vision of the church. Significantly, he also consistently locates his focused treatments of the church here within the theological context of Pneumatology. In *CD* IV/1 §62, where the church is treated from the perspective of Christ's priestly work in his humiliation as the Son of God, the heading is 'The Holy Spirit and the Gathering of the Christian Community'. In *CD* IV/2 §67, it is 'The Holy Spirit and the

---

18. Bender, *Karl Barth's Christological Ecclesiology*, 160.

Upbuilding of the Christian Community'. And in *CD* IV/3 §72, it is 'The Holy Spirit and the Sending of the Christian Community'. As ever for Barth, the Spirit's working is decisively 'christologized'. The christological determination of each of the key verbs in these sections of *CD* IV is obvious. Christ's priestly representation and self-substitution for all frames the church's 'gathering', his kingly exaltation of humanity underwrites its 'building up' and his prophetic self-attestation entails the 'sending' of the church as a commissioned and empowered community. Perhaps less obvious, but no less important, is the correspondence between each of these verbs and the defining moments of Christ's call to discipleship as the New Testament depicts it – namely, his calling of people to be with and follow after him (actualizing their election), his teaching and instructing of them in a variety of ways and his sending of them as his witnesses empowered by his living presence and promise.

At one level, these connections between discipleship and the gathering, upbuilding and sending of the church should hardly be surprising. As Webster has shown in his two important essays on discipleship, in the New Testament discipleship reconfigures the grand theological themes of Scripture such as election and covenant, divine self-revelation and personal presence, attentive listening and active obedience.[19] Barth is less explicit about this role of the discipleship material with regard to the overall movement and thematic motifs of the Bible. But his treatments of the church in *CD* IV/1-3 consistently strike the same notes as his treatment of discipleship in §66 – specifically the all-relativizing sovereign freedom and living presence of Christ alongside the (appropriately circumscribed) reality of the responsive attention and obedience of his people.

For example, in Barth's treatment of the Spirit's 'gathering' (or calling) of the church as the community of discipleship in *CD* IV/1 §62, he makes much of the fact that the church *is* the 'earthly-historical form' of Christ risen and ascended. Explicating the biblical image of the church as Christ's body, the analogy with the overarching christological theme of *CD* IV/1 is palpable. Mangina puts this well:

> In IV/1 … the accent falls on Christ's being *as God*, the divine Lord who humbled himself and became a servant for our sake. Just so, the ecclesiology of this volume stresses the divine action of calling the community into being, along with, as a corollary to this, the radically contingent character of the church's existence.[20]

The church in its being and agency echoes Christ. Indeed, Barth employs the language of identity: the church *is* the 'earthly-historical form' of Christ's existence. Consequently, as 'fragile' as the church may be – with 'no resources of its own

---

19. See Webster, 'Discipleship and Calling', 133–47, and John Webster, 'Discipleship and Obedience', *Scottish Bulletin of Evangelical Theology* 24.1 (2006): 4–18.
20. Mangina, 'Bearing the Marks', 273.

that would make it worthy of its mission' – it is 'strong because its hidden essence consists in its identity as Christ's very body.'[21]

This statement of identity is not without qualification, of course. Barth staunchly resists moving away from 'the christological subject-matter of the doctrine of reconciliation' – even here as he focuses on its 'subjective realization' (645): 'The history which we consider when we speak of the Christian community and Christian faith is enclosed and exemplified in the history of Jesus Christ.' No space here for the Roman Catholic doctrine of the *Christus prolongatus*, the church as an extension of the incarnation. Christ is not absent, leaving the church – somehow raised to ontological parity with Jesus – to stand in vicariously for him. Instead, Jesus is present as the context and environment of the church. The church's agency is thus relativized with respect to Christ. Barth further relativizes the church by emphasizing the cosmic scope and eschatological horizon of Christ's work of reconciliation (645):

> In a way which is still hidden, the history of Jesus Christ is the history of the reconciliation of the world with God. It is not exhausted in the history of the Christian community and Christian faith. But in this history – as the proclamation of the meaning of world history which has yet to be revealed – we do have to do with the history of Jesus Christ.

This twofold relativization of ecclesial identity is the ground on which Barth willingly builds when he risks speaking of an identity between Christ and his church. In its proleptic and prophetic anticipation of the eschaton, the church is transparent to the history of Jesus Christ. Context is everything here. As Bender underscores, 'Barth's concern is to provide a "thick description" of human action that sees it … as a free and true response to the complete and sufficient salvation of God effected in the history of the person of Jesus Christ.'[22] Bender helpfully foregrounds the polemics in which Barth is engaged here, noting that Barth flags them explicitly in the prefaces of *CD* IV/1 and 2. On the one side, Barth set himself against the project of Protestant liberalism with its tendency to wrest space for human agency at the expense of God. For the liberal, God must decrease so that the church may increase. On the other side, Barth stands against the Roman Catholic emphasis on a synergy or cooperation between the divine and human, which finds its apotheosis in the Marian dogma.

In this polemical context, Barth labours to emphasize the living *presence* of Jesus on earth and in human history. Unlike the notion of *Christus prolongatus*, which depends on Christ's absence and distance from the church in the present, Barth insists on the earthly presence of Christ in and through (and over against) the church. The language of the 'earthly-historical form' stresses the fact that Christ and his church do not stand at a distance from each other; rather, they

---

21. Mangina, 'Bearing the Marks', 273.
22. Bender, *Karl Barth's Christological Ecclesiology*, 136.

already embrace one another – for Christ is present in the Spirit, gathering the church to himself in faith. He is its Head, it his body. As such, when the church is acting, Christ is acting. In this theology of church – which is strictly speaking a *Christology* of church – Christ is the true agent, implicitly relativizing the church's own agency.

Importantly, this relativization upholds the church's agency rather than abolishing it. Far from being hollowed out and left with nothing to do, Barth's Christology of the church in §62 sets the church into motion as God's real and active covenant partner. In this partnership, the church's humanity is not diminished or set aside. The partnership the church enjoys with God is 'a partnership of service, in which [it] does not cooperate in salvation but "responds" [*antworten*] and "corresponds" [*entsprechen*] to what is "simply the work of God." '[23] Such is the identity and reality of the church. It responds to God as a 'creature of the Word' and corresponds to Christ in its identity and agency. As a result, Barth stresses the church's concrete human history (652): 'The Church *is* when it takes place, and it takes place in the form of a sequence and nexus of definite human activities.' There is no hint here that these human activities are irrelevant or unreal. Yet Barth emphasizes that the church's reality in its substantial history has a definite shape and form, and set within definite limits given to it by Christ.

Both sides of this are important. In §62.2, Barth first stresses the limits that give shape and definiteness to the real history and agency of the church. This is the force of his extended exposition of the creedal designation of the church as one, holy, catholic and apostolic (668–725). In Barth's hands, each of these aspects of the church's identity are true only in Christ, turning the church over and again towards its living source and head. None of these distinguishing features of the church is readily observable with the naked eye. But they are visible to the eye of faith. Faith must see through the evident pluriformity – and even conflict and schism – in which the church exists in history to its spiritual oneness which can only ever be *believed* this side of the eschaton (685):

> Above all ... we must not be afraid to enter the way of the *credo unam ecclesiam* at its very beginning, at the acknowledged centre of every Christian community, and therefore at the lordship of the One to whom the Church belongs, whose body it is, who is Himself its true unity. As we look from Him, the actual unity of the Church will certainly be visible at a greater or lesser distance.

It is the sovereign presence of Christ in his churches – gathering each of them to himself by the power of the Spirit, directing and calling them to correspond to him in discipleship, to be the body in unity and integrity because he is its head – that grounds our confession of the church's oneness. The same goes for the church's holiness, catholicity and apostolicity. The church's agency and identity are real, but they are chastened insofar as they are always relative to Christ. In this, as Bender

---

23. Bender, *Karl Barth's Christological Ecclesiology*, 137.

explains, we glimpse the 'Chalcedonian pattern to Barth's understanding of the nature of the church as event and institution, as invisible and visible, along with an asymmetrical relation between them rooted in an anhypostatic–enhypostatic Christological paradigm'.[24]

In §62.3 then Barth finally turns more positively the reality of ecclesial agency in 'the time between the first *parousia* of Jesus Christ and the second' (725). He explains that the church's history unfolds in the gap between two occurrences of 'the immediate visible presence and action of the living Jesus Christ Himself' – that is, between the forty days after Easter and the promised return of Christ. On the surface, this appears to contradict the overwhelming emphasis of the first two subsections of §62. For rather than the presence of Christ, it is his (temporary) absence that appears to grant the church its 'time', the time in which its history unfolds and its agency takes shape. However, what is really at stake is the *mode* of Christ's presence. In each *parousia* bracketing of the history of the church, Christ is immediately and visibly present. In the time of the church, however, his presence is 'mediated' and invisible.

Barth spells out the significance of this in terms of the result in history of the ongoing working of God in Christ on the basis of and wholly determined by his definite work of reconciliation – the *Christus praesens* on the basis of the *Christus adventus* (736–7):

> What does it mean that God still has a time for humanity, for us? In the first instance, of course, it means that even after He has done and spoken that supreme and final thing, even after He has set and revealed – in that penultimate form – its goal and end, His activity in and with the world and humanity created by Him has not in fact ended. That the world is still there and that this new and further time has begun carries with it as a final presupposition the fact that God is still at work as its Lord. Strangely enough, for what more can God will and work when everything has already been accomplished? But that is how it is. And if that is how it is, it is obvious that He still has a goal and goals, that He still expects something in the world and humanity created and preserved by Him. He has spoken His final Word, but He has not yet finished speaking it. The last hour has struck, but it is still striking. And this means that there is still space for humanity, and in that space it can still exist – surplus space, and a surplus existence, but still a possibility of being, and actual being. It can still develop. There is still a history. A history which is a postscript, but a real history, and therefore more generations, more opportunities for human existence from God and before God and to God, more opportunities of fellowship, of psychophysical life, more spans of life – and all within the great and astonishing span which has still been allotted to the world as a whole. It has to have this great span, this end-time.

---

24. Bender, *Karl Barth's Christological Ecclesiology*, 193.

The decisive presence of Christ who was declared with power to be Lord in his resurrection is not yet universally manifest and realized. Consequently, there is a real (albeit relative) time and space for human history and agency. Yet in this time and space, Christ does not surrender his lordship but remains sovereignly at work. Furthermore, this sovereign working aims to elicit human responsiveness and correspondence to it in active covenant partnership. By God's grace, the church in its time and space between the first *parousia* of Christ and the second acquires an exalted reality and significance relative to the Lord who remains sovereignly at work in, through and despite it.

Barth's dialectical coordination of the relativity and reality of the church throughout §62 reaches its climax in his account of the church's mission. This is, finally, what it means for the church to be the 'earthly historical form' of Christ's existence. It means that the active, lordly presence of Jesus is currently concealed in the church. This is where he is still speaking the word he decisively spoke in achieving reconciliation. This is where by the power of the Spirit he is gathering to himself the world he has decisively claimed, which he represented and bore down to death in his priestly work of self-substitution. This is where the church expresses its real covenant partnership, in the power of the resurrection and in anticipation of the eschaton, as it renders its service. Its service is to receive and respond to God's grace in faith and repentance. As it does this, it may in turn become the occasion for others to similarly receive and respond to God's grace through its praise and proclamation. 'There is still time even though the last hour has struck: time for the work of the Holy Spirit and for the prayer for Him; time for faith and repentance; time for preaching the Gospel throughout the world; time for the Christian community, and in this sense the time of grace' (739).

Barth's account of ecclesial agency in *CD* IV/1 takes shape under the impress of his polemically sharpened insistence on (1) the absolute priority and sovereign freedom of the Christ who calls people to himself on the one hand and (2) the genuine responsive and corresponding freedom in covenant partnership of those so called. Much the same can be said for *CD* IV/2 and IV/3, albeit from the varying Christological perspectives of each part volume and with increasing conceptual refinement – especially as Barth's treatment of discipleship in §66 opens this up. For example, part way through his treatment of the 'upbuilding' (or instruction) of the church as the community of discipleship in §67, Barth asserts the Spirit-effected identity of Christ as the Holy One, the kingdom he established and 'the communion of saints on earth, which as such is also a communion of sinners' (656). This strong statement of the identity of Christ, the kingdom and the Christian community paves the way for Barth to clarify his understanding of the church as Christ's body by recourse to the logic of *totus Christus*. The effect of this clarification emerges when he declares (657):

> He, Jesus Christ, must increase (Jn 3.30), and He does in fact increase. The kingdom of God grows like the seed. It is for this reason that the community also grows – the fellowship of men who with open eyes and ears and hearts come from Jesus Christ, from the kingdom of God, and move towards Him. It grows

as it gives Him room to grow, and to the extent that it 'decreases', as the Baptist said of himself. It lives because and as its Lord lives. It lives wholly and utterly as His people.

Once again, the church's identity, holiness and activity are decisively located and enclosed in Christ. Much as in *CD* IV/1, the church is relativized with respect to Christ. Yet now Barth even more clearly underscores the connection between this relativization and the establishment of community's reality and significance in correspondence to Christ.

As Mangina points out, 'the ecclesiology of this volume stresses the character of the church as a community that is "built up" through definite human actions'.[25] In this way it echoes the Christological accent of IV/2 on Christ's *human* work in glorifying and being glorified (or exalted) by God. This is evident in the quote given earlier where Christ – the focal point and kingly substance of the kingdom – is the secret of the church's growth: 'It grows as it gives Him room to grow, and to the extent that it "decreases"' (657). Hence, following Origen and Tertullian, Barth expounds the various New Testament kingdom sayings as referring primarily to Christ. He is the presence of God's kingdom in its full and eschatologically real sense. But then derivatively, Barth also reads these sayings in an Augustinian sense as 'also a reference to [the community] in its wonderful but genuine existence as the provisional form of the kingdom in the world' (657). Hence the 'definite human actions' that build up the church do so in a dynamic and internally complex correspondence to Christ's all-inclusive work of glorifying God in his human agency. Ecclesial agency is thereby underwritten by Christ in the power of the Spirit. The Spirit securing the genuineness and integrity of the church's christologically determined agency is evident in its growth via ongoing encounter with Christ.[26]

The resulting interplay between the relativity and reality of ecclesial agency has important implications for churches, especially as they seek to relate to each other across their differences. In a very significant discursive section, Barth considers what happens when churches with very different orders and constitutions confront each other. Here, Barth carries forward his thinking about the oneness of the church from §62.2. Specifically, he paints a picture of a kind of ecumenical interaction that does not turn away from or bypass particularity but embraces it – without thereby embracing relativism. He insists that when we confront others whose loyalty to Christ takes a different ecclesial shape from ours, 'the only possibility is the open question whether the Lord has not spoken and been heard on the other side' (718). At the same time, he stresses that asking this question 'cannot alter the loyalty of obedience on our own side'. We must pursue loyalty to Christ in our own particular circumstances and leave others the freedom to do the same in theirs. No church can claim to be the exclusive venue of encounter with

---

25. Mangina, 'Bearing the Marks', 273.
26. See Bartholomaeus, 'The Place of Growth in Karl Barth's Theology', 157–81.

Christ on the basis of its moral or doctrinal perfection. Rather, different churches are venues of encounter with Christ – in spite of their imperfections: 'No Church order is perfect, for none has fallen directly from heaven and none is identical with the basic law of the Christian community' (718).

Barth presses this point home powerfully in his evocative conclusion (718–19):

> It is always perfectionism which makes Church law sterile, as it does also the life of the individual Christian, and theology. What is needed is openness and readiness to learn in the comparison of different forms. What is needed is a sincere ecumenical encounter – which will lead to integration as well as debate. Where there is this, the law of the community, like its theology and preaching, will always be fruitful in its particular forms. For these forms will not act as a restraint on any Church, but stir them, at the transitional point which they have reached, to seek and find afresh, and with fresh seriousness, their living and therefore their true law.

Such 'openness and readiness to learn', which is the presupposition of the kind of 'ecumenical encounter' that Barth believes to be fruitful, is the intensely pastoral and practical manifestation of his vision of the church's real but relative agency in response to Christ's call and instruction.

Something similar can be said about Barth's treatment of 'the ministry of the community' *CD* IV/3 §72.4.[27] Located in the context of his discussion of the 'sending' (or commissioning) of the church as the community of discipleship, Barth's account of the forms of ministry unfolds as an extensive description of the concrete reality and activity of the church. Bender's general observation about this subsection is astute: 'What is significant and indeed fascinating regarding Barth's approach is that he grounds the concrete forms of the community's current practices in the concrete life of Jesus as presented in Scripture.'[28] To be sure, Barth significantly declines to specify all the endless complexity and pluriformity that the church's ministry has displayed, currently displays and may one day display. There are important reasons for this, to which we will return. But right from the start he insists that the church's 'ministry ... is very definite, and therefore limited, but also full of promise' (830). As a result, his description of the historically stable core of the reality, nature and forms of the church's ministry is remarkably concrete – surprisingly so for those accustomed to think of Barth as given to thin rather than thick description of human activity.

Ultimately, Barth's description of ministry is concrete insofar as it takes the concrete human witness of Christ as paradigmatic. Barth's opening statement of

---

27. For the neglect of this section, see especially Joseph L. Mangina, 'The Stranger as Sacrament: Karl Barth and the Ethics of Ecclesial Practice', *International Journal of Systematic Theology* 1.3 (1999), 322–39, but also Bender's rejoinders to Healy, Hütter and Yocum in *Karl Barth's Christological Ecclesiology*, 270–87.

28. Bender, *Karl Barth's Christological Ecclesiology*, 255.

the christological determination of the church's ministry is programmatic in this regard (830–1):

> As the living Word of God in the calling, enlightening and awakening power of the Holy Spirit, He marches through the history of humanity which hastens to its goal and end, continually moving from our yesterday, through our to-day into our to-morrow. Yet He does not do so alone. He is accompanied by the community gathered, built up and sent by His attestation. He is surrounded by the people established and characterized by the ministry laid upon it. Thus the ministry of this people also takes place in the course, in the constantly changing stages and situations, of ongoing human history. And its ministry of witness, ordered in relation to that of Jesus Christ, is also both a ministry to God and a ministry to man: a ministry to God in which it may serve man; and a ministry to man in which it may serve God; and therefore a ministry to the God who speaks to man in His Word, and to the man who is already called and now summoned to hear, perceive and accept the Word of God.

Here Barth emphasizes the living, present and determinative agency of Christ in the ministry of witness. As he does so, he leans upon the discipleship-shaped logic of *totus Christus* in order to ensure that this emphasis highlights rather than downgrades the accompanying ministry of the community as his covenant partner.

As the work of discipleship, Barth explains the church's ministry of witness is always 'ordered in relation to that of Jesus Christ' – it never graduates to mastery or otherwise displaces him. Nevertheless, it does echo and align with Christ's work, repeating it in 'the constantly changing stages and situations, of ongoing human history'. This, significantly, is why he declines to venture an account of ecclesial ministry in all its historical pluriformity. For throughout these ever-changing circumstances, the church's ministry and witness display an irreducible diversity and contextually appropriate concreteness. Bender is entirely right, therefore, to suggest that 'we can imagine Barth' responding to critics who attack his supposed lack of concreteness by pointing out 'that such critics themselves are not thinking concretely enough'. For, Bender goes on, 'it is precisely the variation of specific circumstances across time and space that make a complete description of church order and forms of ministry impossible'.[29] Such complete description lies beyond the bounds of dogmatic theology – and would take us far into the realm of Christian freedom. Instead, Barth concentrates on the enduring realities governing the correspondence of the church's ministry of witness to Christ's own ministry of witness – in both word and deed.

The concrete reality of ecclesial agency is the result of Barth's relentless prioritization of Christ's agency here in §72.4 therefore – perhaps even more clearly than in §62 and §67. It is no impairment for disciples to see their Master and Teacher exalted. He is the Servant making space and time for the service for

---

29. Bender, *Karl Barth's Christological Ecclesiology*, 276.

which he calls and gathers them. He is the Lord directing and instructing them in the work of building up the body of which he is the Head. He is the True Witness prophetically revealing himself in the words and actions he commissions for them as those privileged to witness him.

6.2 Ethics and the analogy of grace in Romans II and The Christian Life

Having considered human agency in the form of ecclesial agency, I now turn to establish the background for the ethics entailed by Barth's discipleship-shaped theology of sanctification. This background is Barth's enduring preoccupation with doing justice to the Renaissance question of human moral activity on the basis of the Reformation insight into the radical priority of God's grace. Within this vision, human moral activity takes shape as the human analogy of the divine working of grace, responding and corresponding to the decisive action of God in Christ. As in the previous part my aim is twofold: to outline some key features of Barth's ethics as they reflect the enduring preoccupations to which the language and logic of discipleship provide a decisive contribution, and to prepare the ground for the fuller treatment of human moral activity (and passivity) under the banner of discipleship in Chapters 7, 8 and 9. The following 'core samples' from the ethical material of *Romans* II as well as Barth's incomplete sketches for the ethics of reconciliation in *The Christian Life* bear this out, each in its own more or less satisfactory register and conceptual articulation.

6.2.1 Demonstration, difference and disgust in the ethics of Romans II

The dominant note sounded in Barth's exposition of ethics or 'Christian exhortation' in *Romans* II is that of the relativization of human freedom by revelation. For Barth, the 'problem of ethics' is but another perspective on 'The Great Disturbance' or breaking of thought itself by the event of God's movement towards humanity – to which dialectic corresponds (426): 'As the thought about God disturbs all human being and having and doing, so the problem of ethics disturbs our conversation about God, in order to remind us of its proper theme; dissolves it, in order to give it its proper direction; kills it, in order to make it alive.' This is why, for Barth, Paul's turn to *paraenesis* in Romans 12–15 proceeds in essential continuity with the foregoing chapters of the Epistle. Dogmatics and ethics are one because it is the same Lord who is the true and living subject of both, anchoring our knowing and directing our living. 'We are not now starting a new book or even a new chapter of the same book', Barth insists. 'Paul is not here turning his attention to practical religion, as though it were a second thing side by side with the theory of religion' (426).

As Barth sees it, Paul's eleven-chapter-long exploration of the indicatives of the gospel is entirely practical. It is addressed from first to last to the concrete historical and existential situation of the church in Rome. Barth therefore emphasizes what contemporary commentators call the Epistle's occasional character. No timeless compendium of abstract doctrine – all 'coherence' with no 'contingency' – Romans for Barth is thoroughly occasional and contingent. But rather than eclipsing its coherence, this contingency is the key to it. Barth detects in the thoroughly timely and situation-specific address of Paul to the Romans an echo of the divine disruption of human thinking and living by the revelation of God, which is always specific and contingent – for the Romans in the first century as much as for Abraham so many centuries before, and today as much as for those Barth addressed in the 1920s.[30] The timeliness of God's revelation 'commandeers' Paul's Epistle as we read it, just as it commandeered Paul in writing it.

Within this approach to Romans, ethics must take its bearings from the priority and decisiveness of God's self-revealing action in Christ. 'All human doing or not-doing is simply an occasion or opportunity of pointing to that which alone is worthy of being called "action", namely, the action of God' (432). Revelation utterly relativizes human action. This is the 'infinite qualitative distinction' as Barth expounds it. As we saw in relation to ecclesial agency, human action embraces its relativization by God's revelation most characteristically in repentance. This is the meaning Barth detects behind the summons of Romans 12.1 to offer our bodies as a 'living sacrifice' in response to God's mercies. 'Repentance', Barth declares, 'is the "primary" ethical action upon which all "secondary" ethical conduct depends and by which it is illuminated' (436). Repentance is the most fitting activity for the moral community of the church because it is a negative, self-critical movement of self-overcoming in order to glorify God. Repentance is the echo Christians sound in their action of the decisive relativization of the church and humanity as a whole by God's self-revelation.

Crucially, however, this self-overcoming does not obliterate human agency. Rather, it upholds it. In, with and under all the signature negativity of *Romans* II, Barth does in fact countenance the positive possibility of genuine moral action. In the context of framing the ethical material in Romans 12–15, for example, Barth develops the image of a 'demonstration' (*Demonstration*). This image, while consistent with the 'negativity' of craters, voids and 'mere' signposts, also admits of a more substantial fleshing out (431):

> Sacrifice is … a 'demonstration' demanded by God for His glory. The act of sacrifice is in itself simply a human act as good or bad as any other human act. God remains God even when confronted by the greatest sacrifice; and after the

---

30. Importantly, Barth recapitulates the hermeneutical process governing his exegesis in *Romans* II in his Göttingen lectures: 'Historical distance and conceptual abstraction are overcome. The witness becomes for me a Word, a Word for the hour. Even as I do this, Romans, which I investigate and reflect on, becomes a letter to me and a letter which I must write to the people of Göttingen and to anyone who will listen.' Barth, *The Göttingen Dogmatics: Instruction in the Christian Religion*, Volume 1, trans. Geoffrey W. Bromiley (Grand Rapids: Eerdmans, 1991 [1990]), §10.III, 261.

sacrifice His will goes its own way as it did before. It is, surely, childish to suppose a May Day Procession to be itself the Labor Movement. It is a Demonstration.

So far so unsurprising. But, Barth goes on: 'Nevertheless, any class-conscious "worker" would feel bound to take part in it. Similarly, all ethical behaviour, even the primary ethic of the broken line, even the worshipper bowed before the merciful God, is not more than a demonstration: the demonstration is, however, necessary and obligatory.' Radically relativized as human action may be, Barth still insists on its necessity. In fact, human action relativized in this way as a 'mere' demonstration is precisely human action stripped of any pretence of divinity and therefore liberated to be genuinely human creaturely action. It is relativized so that it may be upheld with the dignity and integrity proper to it. Anything more is of the devil.

Paul's exposition of Romans 14–15 is particularly instructive here. It clearly displays some specific implications of this human-sizing effect of divine revelation upon human action. Summarizing the ideal human response to the revelation of grace in terms of 'free detachment', Barth says this constitutes the 'precise manner of life' demanded of those who are cognizant of the relativization effected by grace (503):

> So securely bound and chained to God that we can preserve a calm independence with regard to those many problems and requirements and duties of life which are not imposed upon us directly by God Himself and by Him only; loosed ... from the whole compulsion of authority and regimentation, from the whole multiplicity of godlike powers and authorities which make up our world – is not this the Pauline freedom and detachment?

With another self-critical twist, however, Barth pulls the rug out from under our feet here. Following Paul's argument that the 'strong' are not to use their freedom to destabilize the 'weak', he declares (504): 'Once again, as so often before, we are warned; once again the door is barred against us; once again our position is rendered critical and uncertain; once again our brokenness is broken. Paul against "Paulinism!" The Epistle to the Romans against the point of view adopted in the Epistle! The freedom of God against the manner of life which proceeds inevitably from our apprehension of it!'

As Barth construes him, Paul relativized the apparent spiritual strength of the 'strong' along with the moral rigourism of the 'weak'. Unlike contemporary New Testament commentators who debate the precise background and circumstances occasioning Paul's teaching about eating or refraining from eating,[31] Barth immediately generalizes away from the seemingly narrow frame of reference of

---

31. See, for example, John M. G. Barclay, 'Faith and Self-Detachment from Cultural Norms: A Study in Romans 14-15', *Zeitschrift für die Neutestamentliche Wissenschaft und die Kunde der Älteren Kirche* 104.2 (2013): 192–208.

Romans 14–15. Consequently, he regards as 'strong' not only those who literally 'have faith to eat all things', but all who insist on a radical freedom of conscience (507) – that is, those who tend to relativize moral issues as mere matters of taste. At the same time, Barth sees the 'weak' as those who, we might say, are ruled by a 'gastronomy' – a law of the stomach – and driven by disgust to police the boundaries of impurity.[32] This group includes a vast army of moral rigourists from ancient times to the present (508):

> Ranged behind the vegetable eaters at Rome we see the devotees of Orpheus and of Dionysus, the Neo-Pythagoreans, the Therapeutes, and the Essenes, of the Ancient World; the Monks of the Middle Ages; the Baptists of the Age of the Reformation; the Total Abstainers, the Open-Air Enthusiasts and the Vegetarians of the Present Day. But now we can understand also both the grandeur of the Catholic system and the dignity of the rigorous Reformation ethic; we can sympathize with Tolstoy as well as with some of the more religiously minded Socialists and Pacifists.

Barth is certainly not above taking a swipe at such rigourists. For example, he obviously savours the irony that 'the vegetable eater, in spite of his peaceable diet, lives upon secret and open protestation; he sighs and shakes his head over the folly of the world; he differentiates himself from others – because he is unaware of the real tragedy of human life, before which every mouth must be dumb' (509). Even more sharply, he registers the spiritual danger of rigourism (517): 'Before God everything is impure; and therefore nothing is especially impure. All notions of particular impurities arise from secret or open illusion; for they arise from hidden or open refusal to repent.' But it is the self-satisfied, self-reflexive attitude of the supposedly 'strong' for which he reserves his most withering commentary. To begin with, Barth highlights the grim irony of their position, which boasts a remarkably thin vision of belief – the 'strong' believer 'believes magnificently in the conception of the unfettered conscience of the believer' (507). What is more, they perversely turn their grasp of grace into grounds for opposing those with whom God graciously maintains fellowship: 'at the very moment that the "Pauline" Christian *sets at nought* the moralists and becomes an anti-pharasic Pharisee, he himself is also found to be unrighteous' (510). They too are ultimately beholden to a 'gastronomy', responding in disgust to the rigourism of the 'weak'. As a result, they step into the place of God with respect to the 'weak', contradicting their own deepest insight that God is God (519):

> No triumphant freedom of conscience, no triumphant *faith to eat all things* justifies me, if, at the moment of my triumph, I have seated myself upon the

---

32. The classic anthropological treatment of such an approach to morality is, of course, Mary Douglas, *Purity and Danger: An Analysis of Concepts of Pollution and Taboo* (Abingdon: Routledge, 1966).

throne of God and am myself preparing *stumblingblocks and occasions of falling* instead of making room for God's action. Gone then are my faith and my freedom; and all my knowledge is as though I knew nothing.

Ultimately, the tendency of the supposedly 'strong' towards self-referential and self-contradictory judgementalism runs aground against the utterly relativizing reality of God's self-revelation in Christ. The KRISIS that is the living and active lordship of Christ cuts across every human endeavour, judging and levelling the field in the same movement as that in which it holds out hope for all – moral rigourists and champions of conscience alike. 'Rigourism and free detachment are … both under KRISIS. But both are also directed towards life' (512). It may well be, Barth grants, that the 'strong' perceive this whereas the 'weak' are ignorant of it. But that does not put them in a position of advantage or superiority. 'The great critical truth' under which we all stand as human beings 'is no reason to disrupt the community', Barth maintains; 'on the contrary [it] is every reason to maintain fellowship' (514).

The relativization of human morality by the revelation of God not only provides grounds for the sharp rebuke Barth administers to the 'strong' alongside the 'weak'. It also points towards a positive vision of communal relations in which maximal freedom is granted to one another because what truly counts is each person's relation to God (518): 'The possibility of repentance depends upon every man following his own path to the end. For, as the goal of men and as their new beginning in God, repentance is an action of which no man should deprive another, since it is entirely particular, individual, and takes place once for all.' To borrow language that Bonhoeffer would come to popularize in *Life Together*, no relationships between people are direct but all are indirect, for all are mediated by Christ.

So, as Barth puts it, we relate not to the self in the other, but the One – that is, Christ – in the other. Applied to the 'strong' (525):

> This is the sacrifice, the renunciation, the journey into the wilderness, which is demanded of the strong. The strong man always has his neighbour in mind – and we remember that the neighbour is the One in every man. Here is the end of rivalry, the end of all particularity and superiority of behaviour. The strong man, because he is strong, is in opposition to no one; rather, he lies behind all men. He does not hurry ahead, he waits; he does not criticize – for that he is far too critical – he hopes; he does not educate, he prays or rather he educates through prayer. He does not stand out, he withdraws; he is nowhere, because he is everywhere.

Christ is not only the supreme reality who relativizes moral rigourism and freedom of conscience, taste and taboo. Christ is also the template for this way of relating to each other. For all believers – weak or strong, avoiding meat or eating it, moral rigourists who feel the tug of taboo or those whose freedom of conscience makes all things a matter of taste – are to receive and welcome one another as Christ has them, and this to the glory of God (Rom. 15.7). As Barth puts it, 'God does not merely instruct us: he GIVES us the incomprehensible, in order that in all our differences and in all our brokenness we may be – like minded; in order that we may, in all the play of our thoughts, look up to the One, and in order that we may, in the disharmony of the community, hear the voice of fellowship' (526). It is in Christ-shaped community – loving one another across and in spite of our differences rather than obliterating them – that Christians give a 'demonstration' of the relativization of human action by revelation.

This is what repentance looks like in the messy and thoroughly human reality of life together under the Word of Christ. Repentance that makes space for the other to also repent – not in response to pressure and judgement we apply to each other, but in response to the KRISIS effected by revelation and the disclosure of the 'infinite qualitative difference' between us and God. In other words, the grace of revelation humanizes us, and in doing so our repentance becomes not so much a channel for grace as an occasion for God to graciously invite others to embrace their true humanity in repentance too.

6.2.2 Discipleship, difference and disruption in The Christian Life

In *The Christian Life*, according to Webster, Barth 'succeeds in combining his unqualified insistence upon [human] dependence on grace and his assertion that the covenant is "a covenant which God did not just establish between himself and man but in which man was called and impelled to play his own free and active part."'[33] Many contest Webster's judgement that Barth is successful here. Certainly, Barth strains the images he employs in combining human dependence and freedom almost to breaking point. For example, in §76.1, the imagery of free covenant partnership presses precisely towards a notion of spiritual maturity and progress. But in the immediately following subsection, the imagery of childlike dependence dominates and drives out any thought of such maturity or progress. In this way, *The Christian Life* alternates from one image to the other with abandon. The result is a dizzying kaleidoscope or, perhaps better, a sequence of experimental variations on the key themes of Barth's mature theology, the dogmatic equivalent of 'free jazz' improvisations that trust that insight (if not beauty and harmony) will emerge from dissonance.

Indeed, it is possible to see *The Christian Life* as a whole – albeit a rough and unfinished whole – as a living signpost to the necessarily incomplete and unfinishable nature of Barth's project. Evidence of this is readily forthcoming in Barth's well-known revision of the framework for the ethics of reconciliation it contains. Barth initially chose the unifying theme of faithfulness for the ethics of reconciliation. It is in terms of the human faithfulness evoked by God's faithfulness in Christ that the only part of *The Christian Life* to be included in *The Church Dogmatics* (as IV/4) is framed. The implications of this framing for his theology

---

33. 'The Christian Life' in *Barth's Ethics of Reconciliation*, 184.

of baptism are well known. But by the time he was drafting the material for the envisaged central section – organized around the petitions of the Lord's Prayer – human invocation of God has displaced faithfulness as the unifying theme. And we can only speculate about an eventual final arrangement.

Fittingly for a theologian who believed theology must always be starting again ever afresh – in response to God's mercies which are new every morning – Barth's ethics of reconciliation could only ever have ceased and never been finished or completed. And the similarities between what we do have of the posthumously published *The Christian Life* and those works of art – and particularly music – that fit Theodore Adorno's designation 'late style' is suggestive.[34] As Edward Said glosses Adorno, 'late style' works offer a contestation and problematization of the artist's or composer's project. They resist the harmony, synthesis, closure and serene comprehensiveness of vision to which a life's work purportedly gives access. Instead, they shatter it into fragments, exposing its aporias and incoherences as they turn the mature achievements of the artist or composer against themselves.[35]

In much the same way, many of the sharpest tensions and most unsettling motifs of *Romans* II return again to the fore in *The Christian Life*. In returning to Romans 14–15, for example, Barth's reflections orbit around a similar cluster of themes – albeit expressed in a different conceptual vocabulary. Barth repeatedly broaches the topic of Christian unity in *The Christian Life*, drawing on Romans 14–15 alongside other key texts. Again, he shows how Christian discipleship deals with difference – even difference over significant moral issues – by resisting both the reification of these issues and their total relegation as matters of mere taste. Reflecting the complex and polyvalent Christology that lies at the heart of *The Christian Life*, Barth's mature ethics dialectically enacts a vision of 'kingdom disruption' in which God's grace in Christ does two things. First, it energizes a proactive approach to disagreement that sets it within a familial frame and takes Christ's other-regard as its template. Second, it radically relativizes this very approach – for God's action in Christ remains definitive for the reconciliation to which Christian love corresponds.

Within Barth's reading of the Lord's Prayer as a paradigm for Christian ethics, the issue of differences among believers posed by Romans 14–15 is treated in two closely related ways. First, it is placed alongside many other occasions Christians have to exercise familial responsibility towards one another. It is, in other words, an opportunity to enact the common identity we share as those who address God as 'Our Father' by embracing each other as sisters and brothers across our differences. Barth emphasizes both the concreteness and the dynamism of the New Testament summons to brotherly affection and solidarity. This summons is concrete because

---

34. See, for example Theodore W. Adorno, 'Late Style in Beethoven, 1937', *Essays on Music*, ed. Richard Leppert, trans. Susan H. Gillespie (Berkley: University of California Press, 2002), 564–8.

35. Edward W. Said, *On Late Style: Music and Literature Against the Grain* (New York: Vintage Books, 2007), especially chapter 1.

the '"weak" is not just any fellow man, although Christ undoubtedly died for all men, but a fellow Christian, a member of the people united by faith in Christ' (84). It is dynamic because without endorsing a generic conception of human 'brotherhood', Barth is careful to point out that the familial solidarity of Christians does not mean that they are to adopt 'a narrow indifference towards others' outside the community. Instead, they are called to pursue familial solidarity 'not for its own sake, but … "so that the world may know that we are thy disciples."'

The familial imperative of Romans 14–15 is not an end in itself. Communal solidarity and Christ-like willingness to embrace one another across our differences does not imply a strict exclusivity – its concreteness notwithstanding. Instead, it serves the wider imperative of mission (84–5):[36]

> The apparent exclusiveness with which the New Testament, when it speaks of the children of God, of brothers, brotherhood, and brotherly love, refers only to members of the community, is, then, only the reverse side of the comprehensiveness with which (Rom. 8.21) it regards the manifestation of the glorious freedom of the children of God as the hope of all humanity and indeed of the whole of sighing creation. Only this narrow place can offer a vista of the wider sphere which includes those who are still outside, who are not yet the children of God, who are not yet brethren, but who one day may become and be so.

In light of this, Barth is understandably pleased to note that the modern ecumenical movement is rooted in the missionary movement. In this vein, the ethical summons to concrete discipleship enacting familial love in the face of difference is set in the widest possible frame as it takes its bearings from the relationship implicit in the defining invocation of God as 'Our Father'.

The second way in which Barth treats the issue of difference posed by Romans 14–15 in *The Christian Life* appears to contradict this first way, with its great expectations regarding Christian action and integrity. When Barth again refers to the call for Christians to embrace each another as sisters and brothers across their differences, he does so in the context of registering our recurrent failure to display the 'zeal for the honour of God' that is to mark those who pray the Lord's Prayer. Indeed, failure is perhaps too weak a word. Barth treats this lack of zeal as evidence not merely of 'the trivial contradiction between our theory and our practice' but of 'the fatal split in the whole of our lives' (151):

> We see clearly the need to handle weak, confused, and curious fellow men in the church and the world with special patience and solicitude, to 'receive' them as

---

36. Mark Lindsay provides an excellent examination of this missional theme in Barth's late ethics, focusing on the baptism fragment, in his 'The Abandonment of Inauthentic Humanity: Barth's Theology of Baptism as the Ground and Goal of Mission', *Pacifica* 26.3 (2013): 229–45.

Romans 14.1 puts it, to bear with them (Rom. 15.1); and yet we do not bear with them, we are quickly at odds with them again, we take their strangeness amiss as though we had to do with bad healthy people instead of poor sick people.

Concatenated with the other matters he treats here, Barth climactically observes (152–3): 'This is how the Christian looks, at once righteous and sinner, from a few among many possible angles. This is the ambivalence, vacillation, and division in our personal Christian lives. This is our notorious knowledge of God accompanying our equally notorious ignorance of God. We fill up the measure of our desecration of the name of God if we will not at least openly admit this.' The chronic inability of Christians to carry out the moral exhortation, not only of Romans 14–15 but of the New Testament as a whole, underscores our radical need for deliverance – and along with this the radical relativization of creaturely agency that is such a persistent feature of Barth's ethics in *The Christian Life*, notwithstanding his strong emphasis on the Christian's participation in a cosmic 'revolt' against the 'lordless powers'.

Generating these two dialectically related approaches to the exhortation of Romans 14–15 is a foundational recognition of the critical and liberating 'kingdom disruption' that the Lord's Prayer announces as the literary and theological centrepiece of the Sermon on the Mount.[37] There are glimmers of this recognition already in the two moments in *The Christian Life* we have already examined, but Barth's next references to Romans 14–15 put this 'kingdom disruption' clearly on display. Specifically, as Barth turns to the second petition of the Lord's Prayer, he emphasizes the inexpressibility of the kingdom Christians pray would 'come' (237–8):

> The kingdom of God is the great new thing on the margin – yet outside and not inside the margin of the horizon of all the perceptions and conceptions of us people, who are people of disorder, who have fallen wholly and utterly under the lordship of the lordless powers … The kingdom of God defies expression. It is real only as God himself comes as King and Lord, establishes righteousness in our relationship to him and to one another, and thus creates peace on earth. It is true, that is, it may be known to be real, only as God himself reveals himself in this his coming, speaking to people and being received by them. Our own experiences, pictures, thoughts, and concepts may relate to this reality and truth of his. It is as well for us if they do. In and of themselves, however, they are all empty shells.

Just as in *Romans* II, it is the self-revealing action of God that is decisive. It is decisive in that it generates all Christian 'experiences, pictures, thoughts, and concepts', which at their best correspond to the reality of the kingdom in Christ.

---

37. Oliver O'Donovan argues persuasively for this way of seeing the Lord's Prayer in 'Prayer and Morality in the Sermon on the Mount', *Studies in Christian Ethics* 22.1 (2000): 21–33.

6. Discipleship and Analogy from Romans II

At the same time, however, it renders them 'empty shells' – at most parables rather than the reality in itself. Again as in his commentary on Romans, it is eschatology that makes this so. Barth understands the kingdom precisely in eschatological terms as the 'royal dominion of God, or, more precisely, his royal dominion which comes, which will break in, but which has already come and broken in' (239).

According to *The Christian Life*, the theological heart of Romans 14–15 is the disruptive, liberating and relativizing presence of the kingdom. For it 'is indeed among us in supreme and incontrovertible reality and truth, yet not in eating and drinking (Rom. 14.17), not in the observance or non-observance of ordinances, but in righteousness, peace, and joy in the Holy Spirit' (239). Relativization means joy, the establishment and upholding of human life and action in righteousness, peace and joy by the power of the Spirit. Alongside this, Barth insists that the disruptive 'presence of the future' in the kingdom, which judges and relativizes all human kingdoms and lordships, 'may be confused with a rigorous or liberal attitude to some observance' according to Romans 14.17 (248). That is to say, the very verse that announces the life-giving spiritual freedom of the kingdom of God is the verse that also warns us of the ease with which we can confuse it with either a rigourist insistence on certain moral matters as taboo or a libertarian relegation of these same matters as mere questions of taste. The confident assurance and joy the kingdom offers Christians can never become a complacent self-assurance and presumption. The very reality that generates Christian freedom – the living reality of Christ, whose kingdom disrupts and reconfigures human life – is also the reality that judges all human activity, including the properly ethical activity of discipleship undertaken in recognition of and correspondence with this divine disruption.

In all this, the discipleship-shaped correspondence between divine and human action stabilizes and secures Barth's daring improvisation in *The Christian Life*. The improvisation we have observed retains the analogical structure of the correspondence between Christ and his people dictated by the dialectics of discipleship. As a result, it consistently points back to the generative and criteriological 'true reality' of Christ rather than to aporia and undecidability. Christ is the Master, Christians his followers. In following him, they encounter the personal presence of the kingdom that brings the joyful disruption that reverberates out from the Lord's Prayer into the moral action of Christians, as a community – a family – bound together in love for the sake of the world.

I now turn my investigation to the consequences of Barth's use of the motif of discipleship to shape human correspondence to God in Christ. In Chapter 7, I attend to Barth's analogical redescription of the experience of moral agency in relation to the ecclesiological implications of his discipleship-shaped account of personal conversion (§66.4). In Chapter 8, I examine his exploration of moral activity in relation to the implications of discipleship for good works (§66.5) and ultimately love (§68). And in Chapter 9, I return to his discussion of moral passivity in relation to a discipleship-shaped approach to experiences of suffering and victimhood (§66.6). I will then articulate my constructive vision of discipleship – with, against and beyond Barth – for the contemporary context.

Chapter 7

THE IMPLICATIONS OF DISCIPLESHIP FOR MORAL AGENCY

Any account of the visibility of the church that does not take account of the church's sin is inadequate both empirically and theologically. At the same time, any ecclesiology that is not simultaneously Christology is in danger of being merely sociological.

—William T. Cavanaugh, *Migrations of the Holy*

I have established that discipleship has rich theological significance in Barth's treatment of sanctification. Barth turns to discipleship as a concrete means of tethering the church and the Christian life to Jesus. This reflects the 'dogmatic location' of sanctification within Barth's exposition of the reconciliation effected in Christ. One consequence of this is the 'actualization' of sanctification: holiness is concentrated decisively in Christ, who represents and includes all people *de jure* as 'passive participants' in his history. In the present time, this *de iure* reality is only experienced *de facto* by those whom the Spirit awakens to become 'active participants' in Christ's holiness. Such 'active participants' look to Christ as the living centre of their holiness, receiving present direction from him. This present direction takes shape in discipleship as they hear and respond to his call. As the form of sanctification takes in lived experience, discipleship therefore displays the christological determination of Christian community and ethics. Discipleship manifests Barth's conviction that creaturely holiness only 'lives' insofar as it maintains a living connection to the Lord who is sanctified in his being and action. As the Johanine Jesus insists, his disciples only live and bear fruit by remaining connected with him, the true vine (Jn 15). The centrality of discipleship in Barth's account of sanctification manifests the fact that it is a *Christology* rather than simply a *theology* of sanctification.

This chapter will begin to interrogate the implications of this turn to discipleship for Barth's vision of the church and Christian living. Specifically, it will investigate the 'actualistic concreteness' of the ecclesiology Barth develops on the basis of the theology of sanctification articulated in §66. The focus of this chapter will therefore be on the understanding of moral agency implied by Barth's discipleship-shaped theology of sanctification. Discipleship enables Barth to tether the church to Christ both formally and materially. What is more, it does this in such a way as to uphold, establish and set proper limits to its agency. In this discipleship-shaped vision, the identity and agency of the church manifests its 'paradoxical identity' with Christ. The church is relative to Christ, who retains irreversible priority over it – he remains its Master. At the same time, it is real, displaying its genuine agency as it responds to his call and follows after him.

In the following two chapters, I will complete my interrogation of the consequences of Barth's turn to discipleship by focusing on the account of moral activity and moral passivity (or suffering) it entails. I will therefore approach each chapter in a similar way. To begin with, I outline Barth's account of the church and Christian living as he develops them in §67 and §68. Then I analyse their connections to §66.4-6. To anticipate: Barth's discipleship-shaped approaches to conversion (§66.4), work (§66.5) and suffering (§66.6) each establishes decisive trajectories that are then followed in his accounts of 'The Holy Spirit and the Upbuilding of the Community' (§67) and 'The Holy Spirit and Christian Love' (§68). In the final part of each chapter, I will evaluate the consequences of Barth's turn to discipleship in conversation with some of his significant critics.

7.1 The 'actualistic concreteness' of the church in CD IV/2

Barth's vision of the church is undoubtedly 'actualistic'. While this actualism merely reflects its Reformed theological provenance at one level, this is no shield against the barrage of objections it has faced.[1] Some object that Barth's account of the church is 'occasionalist', believing his reliance on the language of 'event' yields 'an insufficiently concrete account of the church as something that [merely] "happens" when baptized women and men gather together to hear the proclaimed Word as sealed by the sacrament'.[2] Others detect a lack of concreteness in Barth's ecclesiology, especially compared with the 'practical Christocentrism' associated with the Anabaptist tradition and its neo-Anabaptist appropriation. This tradition tends to emphasize the visible practices and existence of churches. As Stanley Hauerwas memorably puts it: 'it is the church of parking lots and potluck dinners that comprises the sanctified ones formed by and forming the continuing story of Jesus Christ in the world'.[3] Similarly, the New Ecclesiologies (which Nicholas Healy describes) find concreteness in the community and liturgy of the church.[4] More recently, the robust and energetic 'ecclesiology and ethnography' conversation

---

1. Christopher R. J. Holmes, 'The Church and the Presence of Christ: Defending Actualist Ecclesiology', *Pro Ecclesia* 21.3 (2012): 268–80. Holmes explicitly contrasts this with both Anabaptist and Anglican approaches.

2. Holmes, 'The Church and the Presence of Christ', 268.

3. Hauerwas, *The Peaceable Kingdom: A Primer in Christian Ethics* (Notre Dame: University of Notre Dame Press, 1983), 107.

4. See Nicholas M. Healy, 'Practices and the New Ecclesiology: Misplaced Concreteness?', *International Journal of Systematic Theology* 5.3 (2003): 287–308.

thematizes reflection on concrete church practice and lived experience.[5] In contrast to this, Barth is accused of allowing Christology to swallow ecclesiology.

In response to such objections, one scholar points out that 'the church cannot, in Barth's mind, exist only occasionally, spasmodically' because 'it exists concretely as a function of the identity and presence of Jesus Christ who is never without his witnesses'[6] – or, in the terms of this thesis, who is never without his disciples. Christology decisively determines ecclesiology for Barth. Yet in doing so, it upholds and grants the agency of the church rather than abolishing it. Barth himself underscores this point in its wider application to creaturely being in IV/3.1 (153): God 'problematizes and *relativizes* the truth of His creature' in an action that at once 'integrates and institutes that truth'. Barth goes on to explain the two sides of this relativization (163): 'to relativize means critically to set something in its limited and conditioned place. But it also means positively to set it in the relationship indicated by the limits of this place.' Nevertheless, Bender points out that the objections are not without merit: 'The reality of the church is ... the product of divine will rather than human desire, and for Barth the church must be described theologically as a divinely established community in relation to Christ before it is described sociologically as a historical society.'[7] Bender argues that Barth prioritizes theological description like this for reasons of context and polemics. However, this results in a tendency to neglect the concrete description of the social and historical reality of the church. All the same, we can appreciate the reasons Barth resists engaging in any kind of independent theological or sociological description of ecclesial agency in abstraction from Christ. As I will show, his turn to discipleship provides significant theological resources for maintaining a christological emphasis while providing a relative but not unreal account of the church. In this account the church's agency is characterized by 'actualistic concreteness'.

The dynamics of Barth's Christology of church are most clearly on display when he sets forth his vision of the church's concreteness against the twin temptations of secularization and sacralization in *CD* IV/2 §67. In this context, Barth develops a version of the classic doctrine of the *totus Christus* – Christ seen in the fullest sense along with and including his people. He does this without for a moment denying the church's thoroughgoing humanity (and therefore its finiteness, fallibility and failure). Barth insists that the church's concrete identity, existence and agency must be located within the sphere of divine activity – in Christ and by the power of the Spirit. 'The true Church truly is and arises and continues and lives in the twofold sense that God is at work and that there is a human work which He occasions and fashions' (616). The import of this becomes evident in the programmatic statement early in §67 (616–17):

---

5. For two recent summaries of the ecclesiology and ethnography conversation see Ward, *Liquid Ecclesiology*, 1–36, and Smith, *Awaiting the King* 188–97.
6. Holmes, 'The Church and the Presence of Christ', 280.
7. Bender, *Karl Barth's Christological Ecclesiology*, 128.

Thus, to see the true Church, we cannot look abstractly at what a human work seems to be in itself. This would not be a genuine phenomenon but a false [one]. The real result of the divine operation, the human action which takes place in the true Church as occasioned and fashioned by God, will never try to be anything in itself, but only the divine operation, the divine work of sanctification, the upbuilding of Christianity by the Holy Spirit of Jesus the Lord, by which it is inaugurated and controlled and supported. To the extent that it is anything in itself, it is the phenomenon of the mere semblance of a Church, and it is only this semblance, and not the true Church, that we shall see when we consider this phenomenon.

For all its human reality, any consideration of the church in abstraction from Christ necessarily fails to penetrate the depths of its identity, existence and agency. Such a consideration neither reveals what the church really is nor discloses anything decisive about how Christian community should be seen and understood. As Webster puts it, 'the being of the church is not identical *simpliciter* with a human historical project'.[8] Bender draws attention to the way a kind of one-sided sociological reduction of the church characterized the Neo-Protestantism against which Barth was reacting.[9] Against this backdrop, Barth's tendency towards an equal and opposite one-sidedness in focusing on the divine determination of the church is at least comprehensible – although it does risk putting Barth's ecclesiology out of step with the concrete reality of the church.[10] Nevertheless, an insistence that something decisive or essential is missing from any account of church that abstracts it from the context of the divine activity centred on Christ does not necessarily lead to one-sidedness.[11]

The Christian community cannot be understood apart from the divine determination it receives by being centred on Christ, but correctly locating the church with respect to Christ is important not only for theological reflection on its nature and identity. According to Barth, it is also essential for rightly engaging in the church's defining activity – gathering to worship the God revealed in Jesus

---

8. John Webster, '"In the Society of God": Some Principles of Ecclesiology', in *Perspectives on Ecclesiology and Ethnography*, ed. Pete Ward (Grand Rapids & Cambridge: Eerdmans, 2012), 201.

9. Bender, *Karl Barth's Christological Ecclesiology*, 24–44.

10. Nicholas M. Healy, 'The Logic of Karl Barth's Ecclesiology: Analysis, Assessment and Proposed Modifications', *Modern Theology* 10.3 (1994): 253–70. Joseph L. Mangina, 'Bearing the Marks of Jesus: The Church in the Economy of Salvation in Barth and Hauerwas', *Scottish Journal of Theology* 52.3 (1999): 269–305. Peter Ward, 'Ecclesiology and Ethnography with Humility: Going through Barth', *Studia Theologica – Nordic Journal of Theology* (2016): 1–17.

11. In *Church as Moral Community*, O'Neil convincingly argues this point with regard to the very strong prioritization of Christ in *The Epistle to the Romans*, such that the church is rendered in primarily negative terms.

Christ. In §67 the gathering of the Christian community as a congregation-at-worship is *the* site of the true Church – 'its centre', the site 'where it continually begins and is directly palpable and perceptible' (638). This site is dynamic rather than static, taking shape in the work of corporate worship, in which the community aims at communion or 'integration' (*Zusammenfügen*) with one another and with God. Here, Barth is characteristically relentless in insisting on the priority of divine action. Yet this insistence evokes and underwrites the collective human agency of the church community rather than cancelling it out. Christians who see the church's agency this way both rightly view their collective work of worship and properly engage in it: 'In all its elements ... Christian worship is the action of God, of Jesus, and of the community itself for the community, and therefore the upbuilding of the community' (639). In, with and under the human activity of Christian worship, Christ is at work sovereignly in the midst of his people to build his church. This is *totus Christus* with an 'actualistic' twist. The being-in-action of the church is a reality that dynamically corresponds to the Christ whose identity, existence and agency define it. As a result, it is discipleship-shaped.

For Barth, secularization occurs when the Christian community departs from this dynamic by surrendering to the temptation to settle down in the world in which it is scattered. As such, secularization happens when the community 'allows its environment, or spontaneous reference to it, to prescribe and impose a law which is not identical with the Law of the Gospel, with the control of the free grace of God and with the will of Jesus as the Lord and Head of His people' (667). The community does this, according to Barth, 'when it wants to be a Church only for the world, the nation, culture, or the state' and in the process 'loses its specific importance and meaning; the justification for its existence' (668). Secularization therefore simply is the 'churchly' tendency identified by Ernst Troeltsch in his magisterial *Social Teaching of the Christian Churches*. Troeltsch famously structures his analysis around Weber's distinction between a 'church' and a 'sect' as two ideal types.[12] One scholar summarizes Troeltsch's construal of this distinction as follows: 'The church will affirm the "world"; the sect will deny the "world" by retreating from it or occasionally attacking it. The church will seek power in the world, and to achieve it, make the necessary compromises; the sect will insist on undiluted purity and remain on the margins.'[13] These differences are arguably explained by an underlying divergence when it comes to the sanctification of the Christian community. The 'church' expects sin to persist; the 'sects' expect members to strive for moral progress and purity. 'Churches' tolerate sin; 'sects' seek to eradicate it. In each case, different expectations about sin's persistence and the corresponding sanctification of the community prove decisive for the concreteness of the community's identity. In the case of the 'churchly' emphasis, its concrete identity is sacrificed in the name of solidarity with the world or some

---

12. Ernst Troeltsch, *The Social Teaching of the Christian Churches*. Two Volumes (London, UK/New York, NY: Allen & Unwin/Macmillan, [1921]1931).

13. Volf, 'Soft Difference', 16.

part of it – a particular nation, for instance. Seen from another angle, the church's concreteness is secured by correlating it with a particular society – the German Church, the English Church, and so on. In contrast, 'sectarian' rigourism fuels a drive towards distinctiveness from the surrounding society. The concreteness of the 'society of the saints' is purchased at the cost of disengagement, renunciation and (often enough) denunciation.

Of course, Troeltsch's typology has dated – as has desire to vindicate the stance of Neo-Protestantism towards nineteenth-century European society by claiming the mantle of the historically dominant and socially productive 'churchly' form of Christianity.[14] But the way he correlates expectations about sanctification and sin's persistence with differing 'stances' towards the world remains remarkably contemporary. 'Churchly' and 'sectarian' tendencies continue to be visible today. For example, in James Davison Hunter's landmark survey of contemporary North American Christianity, *To Change the World* (2010), the political Christianities of both Right and Left may be characterized in ways thoroughly reminiscent of Troeltsch's 'church'.[15] Both affirm (different) parts of the world. Both are tolerant towards (different) sins – within the Christian community as well as outside it. And both make the necessary compromises to pursue worldly power.

In contrast to this 'churchly' tendency towards secularization, Barth discerns the possibility of the church's sacralization. Sacralization occurs when the Christian community illegitimately 'thickens up' its distinctiveness by locating its concreteness in some aspect of its life – its doctrine, liturgy or polity – as though it were separable from Christ. This is how Barth describes a church that has fallen prey to sacralization (668–9):

> Its aim is ... to develop and maintain itself in the world. But in this case it tries to do it, not by self-adaptation, but by self-assertion. It now has a highly developed consciousness of itself in the particularity of its being and action in the world.

The problem here is what Nicholas Healy calls 'misplaced concreteness'.[16] Ironically, just as with secularization, sacralization leads the Christian community to mimic the world in its self-assertion. If Neo-Protestantism was Barth's polemical target when considering secularization, Roman Catholicism is the pre-eminent historical example of sacralization in Barth's eyes – although, he is careful to leave room in his polemic for other, less immediately obvious instantiations. (This is in keeping with the self-reflexive instincts we have already seen him display in the critique of the religion of revelation that lies near the heart of his account of discipleship in §66.3.) The temptation of sacralization besets various 'sectarian' neo-Anabaptists inspired ecclesiologies. Such ecclesiologies take a rigorous attitude towards sin.

---

14. On the entanglement of European civilization and Christianity in Troeltsch's schema, see Kerr, *Christ, History, and Apocalyptic*, chapter 2.
15. Hunter, *To Change the World*, Essay II, chapters 3 and 4.
16. Healy, 'Practices and the New Ecclesiology', 289–96.

They call out compromise within the Christian community and prophetically denounce it in the world – especially in the forms of nationalism, consumerism and predatory capitalism. They openly renounce worldly power in order to set up an alternative *polis*. But in doing this, neo-Anabaptists ironically mimic the self-assertion they condemn in others. Hunter, among others, highlights the overwhelmingly negative rhetoric and tone they employ in their 'prophetic' denunciations of North American society and politics.[17]

7.2 Mortification and discipleship-shaped moral agency

Barth's alternative to both 'churchly' secularization and 'sectarian' sacralization results from his discipleship-shaped vision of sanctification. For Barth, this is more than merely a pragmatic ecclesiological *via media*. Rather, it is a dynamic and principled application of the actualism at the Christology of church implicit in his account of sanctification in §66. Seen in terms of discipleship, his account of sanctification provides conceptual scaffolding and biblical warrant for the 'actualization' of the *totus Christus* we have observed in §67. Discipleship for Barth is firstly about Christ and only subsequently – and by an intensification of this – about the Christian community. This is the ecclesiological significance of his treatment of the biblical discipleship material under the heading of 'the *call* of discipleship' rather than simply 'discipleship'. Manifesting the 'actualization' of sanctification as it is focused in Christ – its determining centre – Barth gives the event of the call priority over any state that supposedly results from it, which Christians may (or may not) occupy. This dynamism functions to place the emphasis less on those who are called and more on the one who issues the call in freedom and sovereignty. To borrow the metaphor Barth uses for the 'true religion' in §17.3, like the earth in its orbit around the sun, the church and the Christian life are only 'lit up' insofar as the light of Christ falls on them (353). Sanctification resides in Christ; and yet it 'lights up' human communities when by the power of the Spirit, Christ is present to call people to follow after him. This corresponds to Barth's emphasis on the freedom of *Christ* throughout §66.3, such that human freedom takes shape in response to his free direction and call to participate in his 'kingdom onslaught' against the idolatrous and imprisoning distortions of the created structures of human life – including relationships, possessions and religion.

The shape of this conceptual scaffold emerges more clearly as Barth begins to draw out and make explicit the existential implications of his vision of sanctification as discipleship in §66.4. At a crucial point in this explication, Barth deploys the classic Reformed theological trope of mortification in order to calibrate expectations about the persistence of sin in the church in light of the gospel's announcement of the triumph of Christ. Barth's use of mortification

---

17. Hunter, *To Change the World*, 162–6.

takes us to the heart of his dynamic vision of the sanctified identity, existence and agency of the church. It is this vision that undergirds his principled alternative to both 'churchly' and 'sectarian' tendencies.

Barth's discipleship-shaped theology of sanctification has three closely related consequences for our understanding of ecclesial agency. First, it demands we see the church as practically and not just theoretically Christ-centred. The church's holiness only 'lives' insofar as it keeps Christ central, looking to him as Lord and responding to his call of discipleship. Second, Barth's discipleship-shaped theology of sanctification prompts the church to dynamically coordinate its solidarity with the world and its difference from it. Christians become 'creaturely reflections' of Christ's singular holiness insofar as they are bound to him, distinguishing themselves from others in the same movement as they echo him in identifying with others. Third, Barth's discipleship-shaped theology of sanctification presses towards concrete and active expression in ecclesiology. This takes shape in the Spirit's work of 'disturbing' – if not fully rousing – Christians from the slumber of sin to stand them on their feet and enlist them in Christ's 'kingdom onslaught' against idolatry. This movement of 'raising up' that the Spirit activates in Christians is the emblem of their participation in the humanizing activity of the elevation and glorification of the Son of Man that is the overarching theme of *CD* IV/2.

These three aspects of sanctification's distinctive shape as discipleship explicitly frame §66.4, in which Barth deploys the language of mortification (554): 'The call to discipleship is existentially realized only as the Holy Spirit awakens people to conversion' – that is, to turning from self to Christ as living Lord. This conversion is both complete and continuous. It is complete in that it involves nothing less than a 'falling out with oneself' in which the old self, which is done away with in Christ, is to be made war upon in the name of the new. There are no part measures (563): 'In conversion we have to do with a movement of the whole man. There are in his being no neutral zones which are unaffected by it and in which he can be another than the new man involved in this process.' But this Spirit-wrought disturbance is also continuous. Or, rather, it is the total character of a person's life renewed moment by moment (as opposed to merely its punctiliar starting point or repeated pattern of conversion and reconversion). As Barth construes it, Luther's *simul iustus et peccator* applies 'strictly to sanctification and therefore conversion if we are to see deeply into what is denoted by these terms, and to understand them with the necessary seriousness' (572). This is because 'the same [person] … is both the old man of yesterday and the new man of tomorrow, the captive of yesterday and the free man of tomorrow, the slothful recumbent of yesterday and the [upright] man of tomorrow' (572).

This is where mortification comes in. In Reformed thought, mortification displays the unity of the complete and the continuous in conversion. Consider John Owen's classic statement in chapter 5 of his *Of the Mortification of Sin in Believers* (1656). Here, Owen vividly describes the aim of mortification in terms of the complete eradication of sin: 'There is no man that truly sets himself to mortify any sin, but he aims at, intends, desires its utter destruction, that it should leave neither root nor fruit in the heart or life … Its not-being is the thing aimed at.'¹⁸ Having said this, Owen harbours no illusions about total victory. He expects mortification to be continual. This side of glory, sin will continue to be present in the life of even the most saintly believer. While mortification aims at 'a wonderful success and eminency of victory against … sin' – even 'almost constant triumph over it' – Owen concedes that 'an utter killing and destruction of it, that it should not be, is not in this life to be expected'.¹⁹ In this respect, Owen displays a similar optimism to the Westminster Confession (see especially Chapter XIII.III). This relative optimism contrasts with the insistence of the Heidelberg Catechism that 'In this life even the holiest have only a small beginning of … obedience' (Lord's Day 44).²⁰

Of course, optimism would hardly be an apt description of Owen overall. He goes to great lengths to stir his readers to continual effort and constant vigilance in mortifying sin – painting vivid (some would say lurid) pictures of the spiritual dangers of tolerating sin, and giving remarkably detailed directions for combatting it. Such efforts bespeak an urgent sense of sin's threat and destructive power. In addition, Owen's overwhelming emphasis on mortification may be at least partly a function of his particular pastoral context – and potentially also the genre in which he wrote.²¹ At root, however, Barth would argue that it reflects an imbalance evident in the Reformed tradition overall, going back to the relative weighting Calvin gives to mortification over vivification: 'the doctrine of Calvin obviously suffers … from a curious over-emphasizing of *mortificatio* at the expense of *vivificatio*' (575).

Tellingly, Barth deploys mortification in a way that is steeped in Reformed thinking while seeking to correct its imbalances and mitigate any unwelcome pastoral consequences (much as he does in the case of election). So Barth approves of Calvin's insistence that mortification is inextricably linked with vivification. But he faults Calvin for so strongly accenting mortification – so much so that he circles back to it when he has supposedly moved on to vivification – that pessimism tends to eclipse any joy or confidence that the new has broken in and will triumph through the work of grace (574–6). Ultimately, Barth stresses the essential unity of mortification and vivification. While – effectively for Calvin and explicitly in Owen – mortification tends to overshadow vivification, Barth joins the two together in an attempt to more adequately emphasize the joyful and expansive note struck in the latter. For Barth, the direction to put sin to death is undertaken in the joy and freedom of resurrection life (577): 'It is because and as

---

18. John Owen, *Of The Mortification of Sin in Believers* (1656) in *Overcoming Sin and Temptation*, ed. Kelly M. Kapic and Justin Taylor (Wheaton, IL: Crossway, 2006), 69.

19. Owen, *Of the Mortification of Sin*, 69.

20. For a fuller discussion, see Willem Van Vlaustin, 'Personal Renewal between Heidelberg and Westminster', *Journal of Reformed Theology* 5 (2011): 49–67.

21. On these features of Owen's work, see Kelly M. Kapic's introduction, 'Life in the Midst of Battle: John Owen's Approach to Sin, Temptation, and the Christian Life', in *Overcoming Sin and Temptation*, 23–35.

God issues the command to proceed that He also issues the command to halt, and not conversely. He kills the old man by introducing the new, and not conversely. It is with His Yes to the man elected and loved and called by Him that He says No to his sinful existence, forcing him to recognize that we are always in the wrong before God.'

Barth's conviction that mortification must speak of the gospel underwrites this change of emphasis. And here his treatment of conversion is emblematic of his wider vision of Christian living. It is gospel in the form of law, but it is gospel no less. It is good, life-giving news. Specifically, mortification is for Barth the pre-eminently biblical way to characterize the 'putting to death' of the old self that goes hand in hand with 'putting on' the gift of a holy (and wholly) new identity in Christ. In this way, it is much more than a psychological prelude either to the initial moment of conversion or of each progressive step towards perfection. To reduce mortification to the merely psychological (and hence subjective) would qualify the radical antithesis between the old and new selves entailed by the biblical picture of conversion (574–5). Likewise, mortification is far more than the fear, misery and despair that arise as people confront the ruin sin brings upon them – including the prospect of judgement (as in Owen). Mortification is evangelical, eloquent of the gospel. It is an aspect of the Spirit-empowered implementation of the decisive victory won by Christ. Mortification may be the gospel's *command*, but it is no less the *gospel's* command for being so.

Barth's discipleship-shaped and gospel-infused presentation of mortification as an aspect of the existential activation of sanctification functions in a specific way with respect to the church. With respect to the church's identity, it demands that the Christian community make an honest confession of sin's persistence in its midst. Barth deploys the trope of mortification on the premise that the old identity – with all its destructive and self-destructive misery – continues to exist not just in part but completely in contradiction and radical antithesis to the new. This is just as true for the church as for the Christians who make it up. In recognizing the ongoing presence of sin in this way, Barth's discipleship-shaped vision allows no room for denying, minimizing, revising or otherwise relativizing sin. Sin stands entirely under God's condemnation. It does not belong where it persists in being found – even, tragically, among God's holy ones. Barth's use of mortification calibrates our expectations about the flawed and broken humanness of Christ's church. It humbles the church, demanding its confession – the admission that it falls short of Christ's holiness.

In demanding the church's confession like this, mortification combats the twin temptations of secularism and secularization. As such, it is both theological and practical. Barth is clear-eyed about the tragic gap 'between the great categories in which the conversion of man is described in the New Testament and the corresponding event in our own inner and outer life!' (583). This unflinching and humble realism is for Barth the only alternative to constant vacillation 'between a heaven-soaring spiritual optimism and a mortally despairing spiritual pessimism' – that is, between the idealism of the 'sectarian' tendency to sacralize the church and the permissiveness of more 'churchly' approaches with their secularism. Sin's persistence in the church need not lead Christians to compromise or disown their identity (secularization), just as owning their identity need not demand a denial of sin's persistence – either through falsifying the record or by rigorously policing the church's boundaries (sacralization). It need not do this because the church's sanctified identity does not reside in Christians or their ability to vanquish sin. It resides in Christ, who has conquered sin and rescued sinners.

With respect to the church's existence, mortification points to the status of worship – and the human participation in the divine activity that worship entails. Worship is the taproot of ecclesial existence. This flows directly from Barth's correction of Calvin on mortification. Mortification for Calvin appears to be the proper work of God in conversion and vivification his alien work – such is the priority and emphasis mortification receives. But with Barth it is the other way around. The broken incompleteness of the church that mortification marks is the flip side of the Spirit's vivifying work in breaking the church open to God. Webster observes that 'the primary mark of creaturely holiness is … its external orientation, its ordering towards God as its source and the object of its praises'.[22] And mortification for Barth is shot through with this Spirit-wrought joy and ordering towards God in praise. Barth sees mortification enacting a profound response to the decisive work of God in Christ – the response of worship.

Mortification ensures the sanctified church's God-ward orientation by drawing its eyes away from both its wretched insufficiency and its apparent self-sufficiency, and lifting them to Christ instead (583). In this it displays the mystery of the church's existence as a work of Christ's sovereign agency. Jesus graciously commandeers and sanctifies the church's creaturely and sin-riddled being so that by the power of his Spirit it is rendered 'paradoxically identical' with his being. Consequently, the mortified church confronts its sinful insufficiency. Instead of wallowing in its sin and misery or following the 'churchly' trajectory of tolerance and revisionism, it repents. Ever and again, it lays aside the sinful being and history that has been crucified with Christ. The church's distinctiveness therefore coalesces around the proleptic and prophetic glimpse it provides of the eschaton, echoing the truth of its being in Christ.

Mortification also summons the church to resist the delusion of self-sufficiency. If the church is broken open – constitutively dependent on the Lord's sovereign working – it cannot remain closed in on itself, whether defensively or passive-aggressively as in the 'sectarian' tendency to underplay the community's solidarity with the world. Instead, a mortified church recognizes that its being – insofar as it is transparent to Christ's being– must be dynamic, open to God and his gracious working at its heart and therefore 'open-ended' in its outworking. As Johnson puts it, 'just as God is identified as the one who is "for" and "with" us in Jesus Christ, so … human identity is grounded not in neutral separation or sameness but in

---

22. Webster, *Holiness*, 77.

concrete, engaged openness to the "other".[23] Jesus gave himself for the sake of the church and the world God loves. And the mortified church is likewise moved to self-giving in mission as it worships, sounding a joyful and divinely empowered echo of Christ in its very existence.

Finally, mortification displays how mission is stitched into the church's very agency and activity, giving it shape and direction. The mortified church affirms the world in service and blessing rather than demonizing it or seeking to remake it in its own image. This is another outcome of the way Barth unites mortification and vivification as the Yes that its No serves. In the context of mortification, the overriding Yes bubbles up in the joy and freedom of the christological determination of the church's holiness rather than its own attempts to pursue it. This release and joy is audible when Barth declares (583):

> Everything is simple, true and clear when these statements [about sanctification, conversion, mortification and vivification] are referred directly to Jesus Christ, and only indirectly, as fulfilled and effectively realized in Him for us, to ourselves. It is to be noted that they are indirectly, and therefore genuinely, to be referred to us: in virtue of the fact that He is the Head and we the members; in virtue of our being in and with Him; in virtue of the fact that by His Holy Spirit He has clothed us with that which properly He alone is and has; in virtue of the fact that He allows us to have a share in that which belongs to Him. What more do we want? We should have much less, indeed nothing at all, if we tried to demand and seize more.

In conclusion, Barth's discipleship-shaped theology of sanctification results in a vision of Christian living that offers a lively alternative to both 'churchly' and 'sectarian' approaches to ecclesial agency. This is clearly manifested in the way mortification enables the church to resist the temptation either to falsify the record with regard to sin (e.g. through revisionism) or to pit an idealized church against a demonized world ('At least we're not like them, Lord'). Insofar as the mortified church is shaped and animated by the new identity and existence it receives in Christ, it may start to untangle that ugly inclination to turn in upon itself (*incurvatus in se*) that lies near the heart of sin as Barth describes it in §65. This inclination infects even the good created structures of family, religion and possessions. It turns them into the toxic and idolatrous 'given factors' that disciples must join their Master in resisting. In doing so, the church is freed to serve and bless others rather than covertly or overtly seeking to serve and bless itself. Lest this too be twisted into a cause for pride and self-exaltation, mortification closes the circuit by reminding the church that it will only ever limp along this path; for its sufficiency is not in itself but in the grace of Christ, the one who is its life.

---

23. Johnson, *The Mystery of God*, 155.

7.3 Solidarity and difference in the discipleship-shaped church

Mortification manifests the 'actualistic concreteness' of Barth's discipleship-shaped ecclesiology. In order to evaluate this ecclesiology, I now engage Stanley Hauerwas as a significant critic of Barth on the church. To do this, I focus on how Barth and Hauerwas handle the tension between ecclesial solidarity with and difference from the world.

In his 2000–1 Gifford Lectures, published as *With the Grain of the Universe*, Hauerwas gives voice to what has become a fairly standard criticism of Barth. According to Hauerwas, Barth's theology harbours a deficient Pneumatology. Hauerwas connects this supposed deficiency with Barth's refusal to allow the church a role as the instrument or medium for faith to be formed in people: 'Barth is not sufficiently catholic just to the extent that his critique and rejection of Protestant liberalism make it difficult for him to acknowledge that, through the work of the Holy Spirit, we are made part of God's care of the world through the church.'[24] Barth, in short, has 'an overly cautious account of the role of the church in the economy of God's salvation.'[25]

Ironically, Barth remains the hero of the story Hauerwas tells in his Gifford Lectures because 'Barth's extraordinary achievement not only helps Christians recover a confidence in Christian speech, but also exemplifies how Christian language works.' It does this especially in the way that 'from beginning to end, Barth's theology is designed to make the reader a more adequate knower of God.'[26] For Hauerwas, Barth rightly upends the liberal theological project of offering an apologetic aimed at Christianity's modern cultured despisers and couched in terms that would make immediate sense to them. While Hauerwas considers Barth's ecclesiology deficient, he appreciates that Barth approaches theology in such a way as to demand that 'your conceptual machinery, to say nothing of your life' must be 'turned upside down.'[27] In fact, it is Hauerwas's appreciation of the 'eschatological realism' of Barth's theological method that opens the door for his own characteristically post-liberal turn to the concrete practices and lived reality of the church. For Hauerwas, these provide less an intellectual than a communal apologetic, demonstrating that the Christian story generates 'a habitable world exemplified in the life of the Christian community.'[28]

---

24. Stanley Hauerwas, *With the Grain of the Universe: The Church's Witness and Natural Theology* (Grand Rapids, MI: Baker Academic, 2001), 145.

25. Hauerwas, *With the Grain of the Universe*, 202. For the criticism as Mangina articulates it, see, Mangina, 'Bearing the Marks of Jesus', 294–5.

26. Hauerwas, *With the Grain of the Universe*, 141–2.

27. Hauerwas, *With the Grain of the Universe*, 141.

28. Hauerwas, *With the Grain of the Universe*, 214. Ironically, it is particular individuals that Hauerwas cites as exemplifying this – they are the products of the (shadowy and half-submerged) formative processes of churchly practice and participation.

For Hauerwas, the human agency evident in the practices and lived experiences of church must not be subordinated or relativized with respect to Christ – a strategy he argues would undermine its reality. As one scholar points out, the divergence between Hauerwas and Barth can be largely accounted for in terms of difference in focus: 'Hauerwas focuses his attention on the concrete church because it is there that the gospel is displayed in the lives of Christians.'[29] Consequently, ecclesiology must be made the theme of theology. The embodiment that the church gives to the story of Jesus is the essence of its witness. Consistent with Hauerwas's typical approach, a premium is then placed on the distinctiveness of the Christian community.[30]

As we saw in relation to mortification, such an emphasis on the purity and distinctiveness of the church can fuel some dangerous tendencies. One tendency is the drive to deny the presence of sin in the church. Hauerwas includes a paean to John Howard Yoder as a paragon of the church's faithful witness in *With the Grain of the Universe*. But by his later admission, Hauerwas already knew of the abuses of which Yoder had been accused and was in fact guilty.[31] Another tendency is a kind of revisionism that redefines sin out of the church. Ultimately, Hauerwas's focus on the faithfulness of the church – and Christians who exemplify this faithfulness – appears to display both tendencies. Nicolas Healy rightly notes that this results in a '(relative) lack of attention to God's action in [its] midst'.[32]

In contrast to this, the agency and action of God in Christ is Barth's overriding concern, in ecclesiology as elsewhere. For Barth, the primary focus of attention in relation to the church must be God's activity in it – and over against it. This does not so much abolish human agency as establish it, relativizing it in a way that sets it within its proper limits and defining relationships. The discipleship-shaped church provides a 'creaturely mirror' of the holiness of Christ. Nevertheless, it is God's faithfulness – the holiness of Christ rather than our own (as though we could possess it for ourselves) – that looms largest. In thematizing God's faithful, sanctifying presence and activity in the church like this, Barth's account makes space to acknowledge the solidarity of the church with the world in both

---

29. Nicholas M. Healy, 'Karl Barth's Ecclesiology Reconsidered', *Scottish Journal of Theology* 57.3 (2004): 295

30. His approach is often characterized as 'neo-Anabaptist', although Hauerwas has strongly contested this label – see, for example Stanley Hauerwas and J. Alexander Sider, 'The Distinctiveness of Christian Ethics: A Review Article on John Colwell, *Living the Christian Story: The Distinctiveness of Christian Ethics*', *International Journal of Systematic Theology* 5 (2003): 225–33.

31. Hauerwas reports that he knew of the catastrophic situation by 1992 – though he had heard (and dismissed or not been able to investigate) rumours earlier to that – in 'In Defence of "Our Respectable Culture": Trying to Make Sense of John Howard Yoder's Sexual Abuse', *ABC Religion & Ethics Online* (18 October 2017, http://www.abc.net.au/religion/articles/2017/10/18/4751367.htm).

32. Healy, 'Karl Barth's Ecclesiology Reconsidered', 295.

mortifying confession (where it is the result of sin) and joyful affirmation (where the church proleptically and prophetically announces the glorious destiny of all secured in Christ). Healy captures the texture of this dynamic coordination of solidarity and difference in Barth's vision – sponsored as it is by a robust focus upon God's sovereign agency and action in Christ:

> We can [learn from Barth to] trust God to act to preserve the body of Christ in its historical and Spirit filled form until the eschaton. And this leaves us free to concentrate on the important work assigned to us. It is work that requires us, in faithful and prayerful obedience, to turn cheerfully away from ourselves, away from earnest and anxious attempts at self-preservation, towards the God who alone preserves us. And, as Barth would insist, thereby we turn, too, towards the world which the Father so loved that he sent his only Son to be its Saviour, and sent the church, the body of the Son, to be his partner in the Spirit, and witness to that Saviour.[33]

This, almost more than anything else, qualifies Barth's discipleship-shaped approach to the church for serious consideration as making a substantial contribution to theological ethics – and to the contemporary discipleship conversation in particular. Within Barth's account, the church is not the centre – or even the goal – of God's activity. Yet God is active in it, making it reflect his own sanctifying presence in discipleship. As a result, the church is freed from the need to police its own boundaries, deny its solidarity in sin or otherwise assert itself over against the world. The distinctiveness of a discipleship-shaped church emerges as it embraces its determination by Christ – along with the twofold solidarity with the world that this determination entails, backwards in sin and forwards to the eschatological unveiling of the universal scope of Christ's reconciling work. Such a church embraces its christological determination as it responds to Christ's living direction, corresponding to him in missional self-giving for the sake of others. The church's responsive agency – enacted in 'following after' Christ – may be actualistic and entirely relative to Christ, but it is far from unreal or lacking concreteness. Instead, it has the concrete reality appropriate to it as the 'creaturely reflection' of the supremely active, sanctifying Lord who rules and sustains it.

---

33. Healy, 'Karl Barth's Ecclesiology Reconsidered', 299.

Chapter 8

THE IMPLICATIONS OF DISCIPLESHIP FOR MORAL ACTION

The truly human person is the person who is definitively recognized by God, and in that way one who cannot be discredited by anything or anyone, not even by him- or herself; a person who is, however, liberated by just this irrevocable recognition for ever more human activity.

— Eberhard Jüngel, 'On Becoming Truly Human' (emphasis in original).[1]

The consequences of Barth's integration of discipleship with sanctification in *Church Dogmatics* IV/2 §66 need further investigation. To what extent does Barth's use of the discipleship motif allow him to coordinate divine and human freedom without compromising his foundational theological intuitions? The previous chapter considered moral agency, focusing on the implications of Barth's discipleship-shaped vision for his account of the church. Together with the next chapter, this chapter examines moral action. I interrogate the results of Barth's location and treatment of discipleship with respect to Christian living, which I consider both 'actively' (addressing the theme of work in the current chapter) and 'passively' (examining questions of suffering and victimhood in the next chapter).

Barth's approach to moral action has been contested by many in the reception history of his theology.[2] Whether originating outside his own theological

---

1. Eberhard Jüngel, 'On Becoming Truly Human: The Significance of the Reformation Distinction Between Person and Works for the Self-Understanding of Modern Humanity', in *Theological Essays, Volume 2*, trans. John Webster (London: Bloomsbury, 2014), 239.

2. For a slightly dated overview see David Clough and Michael Leyden, 'Claiming Barth for Ethics: The Last Two Decades', *Ecclesiology* 6 (2010): 166–82. Slightly more recent – although focused on Barth's ethics of war and peace – is Matthew Puffer, 'Taking Exception to the *Grenzfall*'s Reception: Revisiting Karl Barth's Ethics of War', *Modern Theology* 28.3 (2102): 478–502. A broader consideration that seeks to bring Barth's ethics into fuller conversation with approaches to theological ethics that prioritize narrative, ecclesiology and formation is provided by Derek W. Taylor, 'New Directions in Barthian Ethics', *Theology* 118.5 (2015): 323–30.

tradition – as with Hans Urs von Balthasar – or from within it – as with Stanley Hauerwas, Rowan Williams and others – Barth's theological ethics is routinely censured. Even sympathetic interpreters of Barth (e.g. Hunsinger) have found Barth's ethics deficient when it comes to direct application to concrete, real-world historical matters.[3] Michael Banner puts the often-inchoate objection sharply: 'if dogmatic Christian ethics' of the kind practiced by Barth 'claims as its chief task turning the world upside down (that is, describing the new world and new form of life which corresponds to the action of God in Jesus Christ) can it have any other task at all?'[4] That is to say, if it is singularly focused on God's action in Christ, how can it have anything meaningful or direct to say about human action?

Here I advance and develop an argument – suggested by Biggar, Johnson and Taylor – that the indirectness of Barth's moral vision is deliberate, strategic and necessary.[5] To begin with, I outline the way in which Barth's treatment of discipleship in §66.3 implies an approach to the Christian life in which its indirectness is the secret of its directness. Noting Barth's vision of the correspondence between God's love and Christian love in §68, I highlight the way discipleship functions there to give concrete form to sanctified human action in §66. Returning to Barth's appeal to discipleship as providing 'formed reference' for sanctification in §66.3, I analyse the connections between this indirectly direct vision of Christian ethics and Barth's account of 'the praise of works' in §66.5. Discipleship shapes and anchors active Christian living, ensuring it unfolds with responsive and joyful (but chastened) attention to the living presence of Christ. The call to discipleship enacts Christ's freedom as the living Lord, directing and governing his disciples in the power of the Spirit, while also enabling and energizing their freedom.

I then turn to some of the criticism levelled against Barth's account of moral activity. Engaging with Nigel Biggar's criticism in particular, I argue that in Barth's discipleship-shaped vision the active Christian life is rendered with rich and satisfying attention to its reality as well as its relativity. The 'indirect directness' of Barth's discipleship-shaped theology of sanctification enables it to achieve this rendering of Christian living, which is fundamentally a matter of a Spirit-enabled responsiveness to the determining 'direction' of the living Lord Jesus, resulting in human freedom that joyfully bears witness to Christ.

---

3. This is the conclusion of his argument that Barth attempted to integrate a Lutheran *simul* with a Calvinist one – *simul iustus et peccator* and simultaneously justified and sanctified. 'Unlike both Calvin and Luther', he writes, 'Barth clearly devotes little attention to the possibility of growth and progress in the Christian life'. Hunsinger, 'A Tale of Two Simultaneities,' 337.

4. Michael Banner, *Christian Ethics and Contemporary Moral Problems* (Cambridge: Cambridge University Press, 1999), 27.

5. See Biggar, 'Barth's Trinitarian Ethic', in *The Cambridge Companion to Karl Barth*, ed. John Webster (Cambridge: Cambridge University Press, 2000), 212–27; Johnson, *The Mystery of God: Karl Barth and the Postmodern Foundations of Theology* (Louisville: Westminster John Knox Press, 1997); Taylor, 'New Directions in Barthian Ethics'.

For Barth, Christian living is relative to Jesus, who is recognized as living, present and active to it. As such he is the determining reality – the 'true reality' – as far as moral action is concerned. The christological and 'eschatological realism' of Barth's discipleship-shaped vision allows for more directness in terms of Christ's relation to Christian living than does Biggar's proposed modification of Barth's ethics – and particularly his proposed retrieval of casuistic reasoning. I argue that the determining reality of Christ does not eclipse but makes space for and underwrites the very exercise of practical reasoning Biggar prizes. However, it does this in a subsidiary rather than a primary manner. Human moral activity takes its proper place as it 'follows after' Christ, whose action remains primary and determinative. This does not undermine human agency or compromise its integrity – for example, by rendering it indistinguishable from the kind of moral 'occasionalism' characteristic of situation ethics. Far from it! Rather, this vision puts human action in its proper place, allowing it to be itself – free to praise God and be praised by him – without needing to imagine itself as decisive, perfect and complete. As one Barth scholar puts it, 'for Barth the ethical question, "What ought we to do?" is itself the question about what Jesus Christ has already done' – and the freedom to which he calls us.[6]

8.1 The 'indirect directness' of moral action in CD IV/2

The correspondence between God's love in Christ and the Christian life of love dominates §68. Christ is the pattern of the active life of love because in his love he represents and includes all. Therefore, Christians correspond to Christ in love. Barth's notion of correspondence has yet further refinements and expansions to undergo – not least in *The Christian Life*. However, it is hard to overstate the importance of the way in which it is filled out and specified at this point in Barth's project. Barth's vision of the contours and possibility of Christian love is firmly grounded in its dialectical relation to the prior reality of divine love and the subsequent relativity of responsive human love – especially in the entanglement of *agape* with *eros*, which Barth treats at great length and with some subtlety (if not in an entirely satisfactory manner).[7] Nevertheless, the consequences of Barth's discipleship-shaped vision of correspondence are clearly on display here, as is its connection with his underlying emphasis on humanity's exaltation to covenant partnership with God in Christ.

---

6. Matthew Puffer, 'Taking Exception to the *Grenzfall*'s Reception: Revisiting Karl Barth's Ethics of War', *Modern Theology* 28.3 (2012): 480.

7. Oliver O'Donovan's reflections on the experiential – if not theologically logical – unity of love for God and the world and love for self read as implicit criticism of Barth's attempt to disentangle *eros* as self-love from *agape* as intrinsically other-regarding. O'Donovan, 'Sanctification and Ethics', 157–9.

For Barth, love both crowns the sanctified Christian life and bestows coherence on it. Christian love is located in, directed by and therefore corresponds to Christ. Towards the start of §68, Barth makes the following programmatic statement that sets the Christian's active life of love in relation to Jesus' work of reconciliation (729):

> In Jesus Christ a new man, the true man, has dynamically entered the human sphere, not merely demanding conversion and discipleship, but in the quickening power of His Holy Spirit calling and transposing into conversion and discipleship. Christians, then, are the men to whom Jesus Christ, and in Him their own completed sanctification, is revealed and present as this new, true man, and who know that they are co-ordinated with Him as their first-born Brother and subordinated to Him as their King instituted from all eternity.

Barth goes on to reframe this as a two-act drama. In the first act, Christians 'purely and totally receive' Christ's self-giving in faith. But in the second act, the Holy Spirit enables them to engage in a 'pure and total giving, offering and surrender corresponding to this receiving' (730). This Spirit-enabled correspondence is the essence of love; for in it, human beings align themselves with God's movement towards humanity in Christ's own love. The grace of Christ's movement of self-giving and self-surrender in love establishes its absolute priority and the corresponding relativity of human love. God's love brooks no comparison with human love. Indeed, it relentlessly exposes our corruption and compromise. Nor is it merited or conditioned by anything on the human side. Rather, it displays the sovereign freedom of God. At the same time, in that freedom it paradoxically creates, evokes and energizes a human response that by grace does, in fact, echo and correspond to the self-giving of divine love. 'Love', as Oliver O'Donovan puts it, 'is the leading out of restored agency in worldly activity' – which is why it is the capstone of Christian living.[8] Hence, Barth can go on to describe the dimensions of the Christian life of love in terms that mirror God's holy love in Christ – giving due attention, of course, to imperfection of our love and of the absolute priority of God's love.

Christian love corresponds to God's love in Christ in a way that aligns with the pattern of 'paradoxical identity' that I previously established. As we have seen, Barth increasingly refuses to configure the relation between divine and human action either in terms of parallel activity or of instrumentality. Setting human action and God's in parallel mistakenly implies an ontological parity between the two. For Barth, in contrast, there is an irreversible asymmetry between them, which he typically highlights by drawing on the anhypostatic–enhypostatic clarification of Chalcedonian Christology. In the case of love, God's action is always sovereign – it is without peer or competitor – and unconditioned by anything outside of Godself. Likewise, conceiving of human action as a mere instrument of divine action either threatens the integrity of the human – jeopardizing its reality – or ironically also

---

8. O'Donovan, 'Sanctification and Ethics', 158.

entails an ontological parity between them, treating them as parts of a larger whole that encompasses both. In contrast, the 'paradoxical identity' of divine and human action ensures that the relativity and reality of human action are not compromised.

Barth treats three aspects of Christian love in which the pattern of 'paradoxical identity' can be seen in §68.3. First, it can be seen in love's orientation towards God. God's love initiates. Christians respond in turn by loving God. Obedience is therefore the signature of Christian love. By obedience, Barth is careful to clarify that he does not mean rigidity or invariant duty. Instead, he envisages an active and living 'continual readiness and willingness to *follow* [God's] action' in relation to concrete and particular others (802, emphasis added). Second, Christian love is paradoxically identical with God's in that it turns towards our neighbours to accompany, witness and embrace them: 'with all the imperfection of what one man can be and do for another, there is a true reflection and imitation of what takes place between God and man, so that while there is no replacement of the latter, or identity with it, there is a similarity, and what is done is calculated to give a necessary reminder of it' (815–16). Christian love is a human echo and reflection of God's love in Christ. Third, Christian love corresponds with God's love in giving and even sacrificing itself for others, even when those others are unlovely. 'It resembles God's love and love for God in the fact that it is self-giving; the self-giving which reflects and therefore guarantees to the other the love of God and the freedom to love him' (819–20). Such love therefore takes the form of service and mission rather than self-assertion or attempted conquest. The term Barth uses for it is *Einsatz*, which is rendered 'interposition' in *Church Dogmatics* precisely because he goes on to identify Jesus as the 'secret and … revelation' of the human act of love in correspondence to God. Christlike self-giving and interposition for others is essential to Barth's vision of sanctified relationships, especially relationships within the family of God, sisters and brothers in Christ. There is no room here for rivalry, judgementalism or self-exaltation.

Christ is the pattern of the active life of love because he represents and includes all. That is why Christians may correspond to Christ in love. The presence of Christ is crucial to this, once again. Christ does not stand at a distance showing Christians an inspiring example or handing down invariant laws to govern and direct their moral action. Instead, he is present to them as they are present in him – by the power of the Spirit. The Christian's correspondence to Christ, in other words, is a matter yet again of discipleship – of living, active and free response to the living, active and free 'direction' of Christ in the power of the Spirit. Indeed, at the conclusion of §68, Barth explicitly invokes discipleship as the model for this (824):

> The clearer the relation of discipleship in which 'He is the Head and we His members' and not vice versa, the more forceful the reflection of the original in the copy, the greater the impress of similarity made by the action of the Master on that of the disciple, the more certain it will be that even among disciples there will be not merely a little love but much love, not merely little acts of love but great acts, and in any case a genuine actualization of love.

8.2 Good works and discipleship-shaped moral action

The discipleship-shaped account of sanctification that Barth develops in §66 provides the 'theological substructure' for the vision of correspondence that supports his treatment of love. This account 'finds its focus in a close description of what living the sanctified life looks like on the ground', as Bruce McCormack observes.[9] This close description begins with Jesus – the uniquely Holy One – and then moves to those who by the Spirit participate in Christ, corresponding to him in sanctified Christian living. Because Barth's account of sanctification is christologically determined, Christian moral action is narratively rendered in terms of correspondence with Christ and his love.

Previously I established that Barth's discipleship-shaped vision of sanctification yields an approach to Christian holiness as real but relative. For Barth, the Christian's relative but still real holiness has a particular shape, stretched between distinction from the world and solidarity with it. On the one hand, Christians stand shoulder to shoulder with all others. Along with all others, they are mired in the sloth and misery of sin (§65). In solidarity with the world, Christians find that Jesus stands over against them in his singular holiness – even though he also graciously includes them in it with all others *de jure* and activates it in them existentially *de facto*. What is more, in participating in Christ's holiness, Christian living and acting points forward to a future solidarity with all. Because all are included 'by right' in Christ's holiness, all may anticipate sharing in it *de facto* as their eschatological destiny and *telos*. On the other hand, the Christian life is distinctive. Christians are not simply sinners but 'disturbed sinners' (*gestörte Sünder*), whose slumber the Spirit has broken partially – if not yet decisively. In response to Christ's call, in the 'disturbing' power of his Spirit, Christians really do begin to correspond to Christ. Their sanctification mirrors Christ's holiness in proleptic and prophetic anticipation of the *telos* and eschatological destiny of all[10] (511):

> It is the witness of the love with which God has loved the world. What has come to it *de facto* has come to all men *de iure*. But in so far as it is only to it that it has come *de facto* (with the provisional task which this involves), it is concretely differentiated and separated from the world and all men … Among those who *de facto* are not holy it is the creaturely reflection of the holiness in which God confronts – not indolently but actively – both itself and the world, addressing it even as He is distinct from it.

---

9. McCormack, 'Sanctification After Metaphysics', 120.

10. Barth does not consistently disentangle 'natural' from 'historical' telos. That Christ represents and includes all de jure implies that all should ultimately experience holiness in him, actively as well as passively. That is their *telos* by 'nature'. Yet it does not automatically follow that all will *de facto* experience this holiness, although that is the conclusion towards which his conceptual scheme presses.

8. Discipleship and Moral Action

Corresponding to the real but relative status of sanctification, the vision of Christian moral action entailed here is both direct and indirect. It is direct insofar as it is orientated towards reality – the reality which Christ has created and unveiled through his self-sanctification. In this, Christian moral action concerns itself with the most concrete and decisive reality in any given situation, setting itself against any abstraction from Christ. Barth proceeds directly from this to discipleship. In other words, relativizing sanctification with respect to Christ takes Barth directly to a consideration of Christ's personal, living and present 'direction' (*Weisung*) as Lord. It is this 'direction' to which the Bible witnesses and which it mediates in depicting Christ's call to discipleship. Barth highlights the connection between attending to Christ and the direct implications of sanctification for the active, concrete reality of life at the beginning of §66.3: 'looking to Jesus Christ as … Lord is not an idle gaping. It is a vision which stimulates those to whom it is given to a definite action' (533). 'Direction' is Barth's way of holding together call and correspondence. The dynamic, living lordship of Christ is expressed supremely in his *call*, which breaks through the sloth and misery of sinners to awaken them. This call lifts them up to stand in freedom. Its effect in the lives of those Christ calls is their active *correspondence* to him. They echo in their being and action what is decisively true, active and real in his. Christ's 'direction' is therefore both the occasion and the outcome of Christ's determination of human life in the power of the Spirit. Sanctification thus conceived cannot lead away from real, concrete history into eternity or pure abstraction. It must lead into it.

At the same time, Barth's vision of Christian moral action remains indirect and necessarily circumscribed. As discipleship, it is necessarily limited and provisional. The activity undertaken in the process of following is relative to the one being followed. His moral 'direction' can point the way and prepare Christians, summoning and leading them by the hand towards concrete action. But it cannot take the step for them. Nor can it relieve them of their responsibility to do so. As disciples they must follow. Far from rendering their moral action irrelevant or dissolving it in Christ's prior, initiating action, this discipleship-shaped vision upholds its reality. Moral action taken in response to the 'direction' of Jesus must be tangible and real rather than merely notional or 'inward'. Barth puts it like this (539–40):

> Self-denial in the context of following Jesus involves a step into the open, into the freedom of a definite decision and act, in which it is with a real commitment that man takes leave of himself … without looking back or considering what is to become of him, because what matters is not now himself but that he should do at all costs that which is proposed and demanded, having no option but to decide and act in accordance with it – cost what it may.

As previously established, Barth holds together the directness and indirectness in his treatment of sanctification by insisting that the New Testament discipleship texts provide 'formed reference' for Christian living. Barth's interpretation of the New Testament discipleship texts along these lines has two implications that are worth reviewing. To begin with, it opens a space for disciplined and imaginative engagement with the hermeneutical task of attending to the text and our situation in order to discern Christ's 'direction'. This task is disciplined because it demands that we answer to Christ, refusing to substitute any human factor for the encounter with him: 'It is now our affair to render obedience without discussion or reserve, quite literally, in the same unity of the inward and outward' as those addressed in the Gospels 'and in exact correspondence to the New Testament witness to His encounter with them' (553). But discipleship is also an imaginative task. This is because the New Testament texts function generatively. We cannot be content with merely imitating what we glimpse in the Gospels: 'There is ... no reason why He should not ask exactly the same of us as He did of them. But again – along the same lines – He may just as well command something different, possibly much more, or the same thing in a very different application and concretion' (553). I explored the difference between this and the hermeneutic operative in both fundamentalist and post-liberal visions of the role of Scripture in the Christian life in Chapter 4.

The second implication of Barth's interpretation of the New Testament discipleship texts in terms of 'formed reference' is that attending to them is primarily formative. To borrow a distinction from the 'theatrical turn' in theological ethics, it is less a script (to be memorized and reproduced exactly) than it is a repertoire of exercises (to prepare for the improvisation required in actual performance).[11] Given the various contexts Christians inhabit, their 'performances' of discipleship will differ from those they read about in the New Testament. However, they will follow the lines and trajectories established there. In particular, they will never involve a lessening of Christ's demands – demands that, as always, enclose and give form to the freedom and joy of the gospel. As demanding as the path of discipleship can be, Barth insists that it is the path of freedom and renewed humanity. Combining Christ's call with the Christian's active correspondence to him, discipleship invites Christians into an ever-deepening experience of their full and sanctified humanity disclosed in Christ.

The trajectory established here reaches its apex in Barth's treatment of 'the praise of works' in §66.5. In calling this section 'the praise of works', Barth deliberately plays with two senses in which human works result in praise. Both senses are significant, as is the order in which Barth treats them. The first sense in which a Christian's works result in praise is the sense in which they attract God's recognition and acceptance: 'God praises them, affirming and acknowledging and approving them' (584). Such works are pleasing to God. God takes delight in them. In part, Barth explains, such works please God because they differ from the organic and 'automatic' results of natural processes like fruit-bearing. They imply a genuine history of significant human willing

---

11. Perhaps the most comprehensive study of the 'theatrical turn' to date is Wesley Vander Lugt, *Living Theodrama: Reimagining Theological Ethics* (London: Routledge, 2016).

and acting (or refraining from action). But primarily, Barth sees God taking pleasure in such works because by grace they participate in the pleasing work of Jesus in the reconciliation of the world – a work which itself fulfils the covenant that provides creation with its 'internal basis', that is, its goal, significance and ultimate coherence (585–9). The second sense in which the works of those called to discipleship result in praise is in bringing glory to God. The works that God praises in turn 'praise God, affirming and acknowledging and approving Him' (584). They glorify and exalt him.

Having distinguished between these two senses, Barth immediately insists that both 'meanings converge in the fact that the works to which they refer are obviously good works' (585):

> If they were not good – in a sense still to be fixed – they would not be praised by God, nor praise Him. If He praises them, this includes the fact that He finds pleasure in them as good works. And if they praise Him, this includes the fact that as good works they are adapted and able to do this.

Christian good works, Barth is quick to admit, are weak, faltering and incapable in themselves of winning or meriting God's favour. Yet they are *good*. However, he concedes that the sense in which they are good is 'still to be fixed'.

This way of framing the subsequent material on the goodness of good works invokes the famed Euthyphro dilemma – the ancient philosophical puzzle concerning the goodness of the deity: Is the deity good because, as the deity, it defines goodness? Or is the deity good because it corresponds to a pre-existing and external standard of goodness?[12] The first seems to imply a certain arbitrariness on the part of the deity. The second avoids that implication by subjecting the deity to a higher standard. Either way the claim of the deity to worthiness of praise is lessened – either because its goodness or its deity is jeopardized.

In a sense Barth is dealing with the flip side of this dilemma, although his discussion has implications for the classic problem. Barth's formulation focuses on the status of the human works that may or may not declare the worthiness of the God being praised. Are these works good because God praises and accepts them as such? Or are they good because something about them intrinsically praises and glorifies God? The first appears to entail nominalism (reflecting the arbitrariness of the deity on one answer to the Euthyphro dilemma). The second suggests that good works possess a free-standing goodness that appears to bind God to praise them. That is to say, the relativity of all good works – measured as they must be by God's decisive standard – and the reality of these works' goodness are not immediately able to be reconciled with each other. This problem animates Barth's discussion in §66.5.

---

12. See Plato, *Euthyphro*, trans. Benjamin Jowett (Charleston, SC: CreateSpace, 2016).

Barth approaches the 'still to be fixed' goodness of Christian good works by first emphasizing their obligatory nature. Good works are obligatory because they are the goal of Christ's reconciling work and included in its scope as the tangible manifestation of the 'real alteration of the human situation effected in the death of Jesus Christ and revealed in the power of His resurrection by the Holy Spirit' (585). Barth does go on to stress the absolute and utterly relativizing priority God's gracious working must claim. But at this point he underscores that God's gracious working claims this priority in order to raise up genuinely responsive covenant partners who correspond to Christ. According to Barth, the relativization of good works undergirds their reality and moral significance. It does not cancel them out. 'Just because God alone is righteous and holy, not remotely but in His acts among and to men, there are also righteous and unrighteous, holy and unholy men, goodness and evil, good works and bad, in the life of each individual man (including the holy and righteous)' (586).

Nevertheless, the 'real' goodness of good works remains strictly circumscribed within the moral vision of §66.5. In the discursive section on pages 586-7, Barth delimits the way in which works can be considered good. To begin with, they cannot justify before God the person who does them. 'Works which we may try to do with this intention and claim are as such works of an unbroken pride, and are not therefore good works but bad' (587). In addition, they cannot claim to be exempt from the need for grace, which not only persons but each and all of their works require in order to be praised and accepted by God and therefore to praise him. 'Because man exists in the sequence of his works, each of his works, as well as he himself, stands in need, as the work of a sinner, of justification, and therefore of forgiveness, and therefore of the unmerited recognition of God' (587). Some degree of nominalism seems inescapably entailed by the Protestant conception of God and God's free acceptance of sinners and their work as holy and righteous. Finally, Barth insists that good works cannot claim direct and immediate recognition as good or bad but must await the eschatological disclosure of their true significance: 'the final word concerning our right and wrong, and that of our works, is reserved for the universal and definitive revelation of the judgment of God' (587). As such, the goodness of good works cannot be apprehended directly, for they are only good in Christ and in the hope and expectation of faith in him.

Barth's negative demarcation of the goodness of good works appears to produce an unusually sharp version of the legal fiction problem that afflicts classic Protestant views of justification. The result is that indirectness – and even indifference to moral action – appears to lie at the heart of the Protestant moral vision. How we live appears not to matter. Grace appears to relativize human action a way that empties it of reality and significance. Of course, the Reformers were aware of this problem, and Roman Catholic polemics repeatedly brought it to their attention. McCormack analyses Calvin's riposte to the accusation, focusing on his insistence on the simultaneity of justification and sanctification:

> He could ... say that God does not merely impute Christ's righteousness to us; God makes us to be in ourselves what he declares us to be in justification: upright

and holy persons. So God does not lie when he pronounces us 'just'; he renders a judgment that looks forward to the completion of his work in us – an eschatological judgment.[13]

Barth takes a different approach. First, he refuses to ascribe to human works any kind of proleptic participation in the eschatological verdict. Second, he insists that the goodness, righteousness and holiness of sanctified works still needs justification. According to McCormack, the problem with Calvin's formulation is that 'it looks away from the ground of our justification in the alien righteousness of Christ and directs our attention instead to what God is doing in us' at this point. Barth will not do this. Good works are only good in Christ.

Barth's answer to the legal fiction charge – and the indirectness that his vision of justification seems to entail for ethics – is to insist on a christological directness. Our good works may only be good *in Christ*. But they *are good* in Christ – and all the more securely for being so. This is the ultimate resolution of the ethical version of the Euthyphro dilemma that animates Barth's discussion here. The positive insistence that accompanies the negative delimitation of good works is that God's work is primary, and therefore omnipotent and certain in guaranteeing their goodness (587): 'Primarily and properly it is His works which praise their Master. If there are human works of which this can be said, we have to seek them in the context of the work or works of God.' The goodness of any human works must be located in the context of the divine working, the economy of grace. Barth expounds this in terms of creation's 'internal basis' in the covenant concluded in Christ; the climax of this covenant in the definitive work of God – revealing God's glory and saving humankind – is the true meaning of that whole cosmic history. Therefore, 'this history of the covenant is the work of God which all His other works serve and to which they are subordinate' (588):

> It is the good work of God. He proves Himself to be good by nature, and therefore the source and norm of all goodness, by the fact that this is His work and therefore His will. It is the will of His goodness which is here at work. God ordains that in all His holiness, righteousness and wisdom, in all His omnipresence, omnipotence and glory, He Himself should be active in this work which has man as its aim and goal. He did not need to do so. He does not do it for Himself. He gives Himself up to it. In this work He is good in Himself only as He is good to man, actualizing His own glory only with man's salvation. He has to do with man in this work. He has turned wholly to man. He has even given Himself up to him. In a relentless compromising of His own case, He has addressed Himself wholly to the cause of man.

For Barth, Christ gives definitive access to the work of God as well as establishing its fundamental nature. In Christ, we see that God's work is

---

13. McCormack, 'Sanctification after Metaphysics', 114.

essentially a self-giving – even a giving-up of Godself – for it accepts the 'relentless compromising of His own case' in order to address and take seriously the human situation. Because of this, God's primary, initiating work necessarily produces and calls forth secondary, responsive human works.

The 'christological directness' of Barth's moral vision becomes clear in the context of this discussion of the goodness of good works. Rather than turning away from the messy and compromised historical reality that characterizes human action, Barth's ethics addresses it directly. Human action is not emptied of significance by being located in the context of God's primary and decisive working. It is filled to overflowing with it (589): 'What man does and achieves is thus in some sense bright and powerful in the light and power of what God does and achieves.' According to Barth, this takes place only in and through Christ. Here as elsewhere, the directness of Barth's account is christologically determined. The goodness of good works is constituted by the way in which, determined by and located in the context of God's work in Christ, they 'declare the occurrence of the good work of God.' And this is not exclusively a matter of verbal declaration; rather, good works speak as they 'reflect' and correspond to the holiness of Christ, which they may even do in the midst of sin as Christians point away from themselves to Christ. Indeed, Christians always reflect Christ's holiness in the midst of sin and brokenness to some extent. As a result, 'works can be good only as they declare what God has done and accomplished – the goodness in which He has turned to man and given Himself for him' (590). As these works declare the goodness of God, God accepts and praises them – and they in turn praise him because 'their goodness comes down from above into the human depths ... in the human depths it can only magnify the majesty of God to which it originally and properly belongs'.

Good works actively participate in Christ, manifesting the Christian's correspondence to him as they enter more deeply into an experience of the true, exalted humanity of Christ. This is the invitation of discipleship: to echo in human being and action, Christ's own being-in-act in good works. The dimensions and dynamism of this humanizing vision of moral action are on display at the heart of §66.5. There, Barth emphasizes how this vision humbles Christians (592): 'They are not differentiated from others by the fact that they are not transgressors in the judgment of God, or that even their good works are not full of transgression' (592). Christians and their good works 'are differentiated only (but genuinely) by the fact ... that they are sanctified in and by the Holy One; that they are called to His discipleship; that they are awakened to conversion by His Holy Spirit; and that they are engaged in conversion' (593). Nevertheless, what results is full of hope and energized rather than enervated or rendered hollow (593):

> [The Christian's] works are taken into service by God and are good works, quite irrespective of what they might be apart from this relationship in the eyes of men and above all in the eyes of God, and quite irrespective of the fact that even as good works they are full of transgression. What these men do as those who are in Jesus Christ, and in love to Him, and correspondence with the work of God, is well done.

Barth's unrelenting emphasis is that the grace of God shapes and energizes human activity in good works. We will and work for God's good pleasure only as God works in us (Phil. 2.13). As such, human moral action is most truly itself – most fully humanized – when it is cognizant of its utter, moment-by-moment dependence upon God's grace. A direct apprehension of the goodness of good works is neither possible nor desirable. Christological directness entails an inescapable indirectness, even in evaluating one's own work (594): 'As he cannot make himself one of the particular men of whom this is true, he cannot assume that any specific work really takes place in this correspondence, in the light and power of the divine work, and therefore that it is well done. He can only believe in the grace of God encountering and revealed to him.' The resulting destruction of presumption produces a 'radical claimlessness' (594). Good works do not entitle us to make claims on God, for they are properly God's own works and they attract God's praise as a matter of grace not desert. Yet this does not erode assurance so much as relocate it – existentially and dynamically – in Christ, producing joy, freedom and confidence. Freed from any aspiration to be or mean more than is humanly possible, the relativization of moral action by God's work in Christ liberates human action to be itself, with a reality and integrity appropriate to it. As a result, the modesty and indirectness of this ethics is the secret of its revolutionary significance and directness. As Barth puts it in §68, the holy love of God in Christ exposes and chases away the darkness of the unholy pretensions of human love, freeing it to witness and correspond to God's perfect *agape*. Such is the theological substructure of Barth's discipleship-shaped vision as it comes to expression in free human action that simultaneously attracts God's praise and brings praise to God.

Barth's discipleship-shaped vision therefore yields a distinctive approach to moral action. It takes moral action seriously without compromising either the sovereign freedom of God or the freedom of human agents. Barth will not compromise God's freedom by legitimizing human autonomy over against God. In this vein, his hostility towards casuistry is well known. For Barth, the operation of casuistry presupposes the autonomy of the human agent in ethical discernment as well as underplaying the present activity and direction of Christ. At the same time, Barth will not compromise human freedom. He refuses to take away our freedom for discernment and action – for instance, by prescribing some form of 'divine micromanagement'. As we have seen, his discipleship-shaped vision of sanctification does relativize human agency and action. But it does so in order to establish it properly. Barth conceives the lordly 'direction' of Christ in such a way as to maximize the freedom of human action (within its appropriate creaturely limits) rather than to obliterate it or render it beside the point. This enables Barth's discipleship-shaped vision to resist the tug of both casuistry and a formless situation ethics. Its indirectness is evident in that it prompts Christians to strive to correspond to Christ, who in his obedience embraced the compromise of living in a fallen creation without himself being compromised – although it ultimately cost him his life. Christ's obedient action is decisive. As a result, Barth feels no need either to provide general and exceptionless rules for action or to supply a moral calculus to generate an infallible method in every possible situation. Prayerful and biblically grounded intuition governed by the 'formed reference' of discipleship is the chief way to navigate the complexities and compromising situations in which we find ourselves.

At the same time, Barth's account of sanctification as discipleship is thoroughly direct and concrete as I have demonstrated. It is direct insofar as the free, active and authoritative 'direction' given by the living Christ is its centre. To hear Christ's present call in the biblical discipleship texts is entirely congruent with the nature and purposes of these texts. One scholar puts it particularly well: 'To know Jesus truly as Scripture attested is to know him as Lord, and so to follow him on his way, to be transformed.'[14] As Barth emphasizes, this lordship issues in the call to discipleship to which there must correspond the tangible, concrete action of love. The unity of Christ's living lordship and the disciple's correspondence to him in love is the converse of the frequent homiletical observation that the great paean to love in 1 Corinthians 13 is actually about Jesus. As the sum and crowning glory of the Christian's life in the freedom of discipleship, the life of love is a suit of clothes tailor made for Christ himself. And yet, in Christ, Christian living joyfully discovers love's unexpected fittingness for us – the disciples of the risen Lord. By the power of the Spirit, we are made to correspond to him not primarily as an example to imitate but as the environment in which we live and the 'effective presence' in every context and situation. As John Webster puts it, 'the human venture of obedient discipleship, both in its beginning and in its continuation, is wholly enclosed by one fact: Jesus Christ is in our place'.[15]

In this way, human moral action becomes 'paradoxically identical' with God's action in Christ, one at the same time as it is two – and asymmetrically so. As the person who is the living centre of the biblical text, Jesus is also the 'acting subject whose agency is never exhausted but continues to have its way by working what he is, by the power of the Spirit, into us'.[16] Christ's work underwrites active Christian living at every point. And although this relativizes human action – rendering ethics necessarily indirect – it upholds it at the same time. In this way, it safeguards the reality and creaturely integrity of moral action, leading into rather than away from the messiness of human life. Ultimately, Christ's relationship to Christian moral action in discipleship, good works and love is not illustrative or inspirational – or even something that stands on the far side of a hermeneutical gap waiting to be applied. Instead, it is direct by virtue of its very indirectness. Governed again by the logic of John 14–17, Christ is present in his absence to call his disciples as the one 'lifted up' for them.

---

14. Holmes, *Ethics in the Presence of Christ*, 143.

15. John Webster, 'Discipleship and Obedience', *Scottish Bulletin of Evangelical Theology* 24.1 (2006): 6.

16. Holmes, *Ethics in the Presence of Christ*, 23–4. Holmes gives a fuller exposition of this theme in chapter 1, drawing out its implications for our approach to Scripture and the church in chapter 5.

8.3 Discipleship and practical reasoning

Barth's discipleship-shaped vision of the 'indirect directness' of moral action has been found wanting by various critics. In this connection, Nigel Biggar's contention that Barth operates with too direct a way of envisaging the relation between Christ and Christian living must be considered. According to Biggar, Barth makes so much of the divine command – and of the corresponding human moral activity of mere attentive and responsive listening – that he leaves little room for the kinds of action that are central to more traditional conceptions of practical reasoning:

> Because God is not Man writ large; because God is active and personal subject; and because it is, therefore, proper for the human creature to act responsively, the first act of anyone who would know what he should do must be that of listening to what God commands here and now. It must not be that of engaging in abstract thought about the Good and about principles and rules. It must not be that of interpreting a normative text, theological or philosophical, objective or subjective, Scripture or Tradition, law-code or story. The first act of anyone who would know what he ought to do must not be one of reflection, but of hearing.[17]

Biggar is sympathetic to Barth's conception. Indeed, he sets out to defend it against the objections that 'it seems to betoken a moment of essentially private revelation' that is 'therefore irrational,' and that 'it precludes the formulation of precise moral guidance' because it excludes the appeal to trans-situational rules or principles.[18] Biggar regards these objections as mistaken. But he nevertheless seeks to rehabilitate an account of practical reasoning or 'normative ethics' that makes room for a more traditional casuistic appeal to principles and rules that can be brought to bear in reflection on particular cases. In doing so, he contends that – especially in Barth's much-maligned appeal to the *Grenzfall* or 'borderline case' in his ethics of creation (*CD* III/4) – Barth emphasizes the primacy of God's command in such a way as to render normative ethics pointless: 'If there is always the possibility that God may command an irreducible exception to my ethical rule, something that stands forever beyond the comprehension of my ethics; if my normative ethical reflection has no necessary or dependable connection with what God will or will not command, then why should I bother with it at all?'[19] In other words, Biggar sees divine directness eclipsing human indirectness.

Seeking to correct this imbalance, Biggar proposes a rehabilitation of 'normative ethics' that attempts to do justice to Barth's explicit criticisms of casuistry as well as his clear insistence on the determining reality of the living Lord Jesus. Ultimately,

---

17. Biggar, 'Hearing God's Commands', 102.
18. Biggar, 'Hearing God's Commands', 103.
19. Biggar, 'Hearing God's Commands', 114.

Biggar contends that it is possible and permissible on Barth's own premises to envisage 'normative ethics [as] preliminary to the moment of hearing' while insisting that 'the moment of hearing relativizes normative ethics'.[20] In the terms of my thesis, he insists that indirectness can exist alongside directness in the paradigmatic moral activity of practical reasoning.

In order to achieve his chastened account of practical reasoning, Biggar draws on Barth's own conceptual resources. In the process, he argues that Barth's theological project contains many examples of just such an exercise of practical reasoning: 'he practices a form of casuistry', Biggar claims, insofar as 'he formulates moral principles, derives rules from them, and connects these to cases'. (Barth's treatment of the New Testament discipleship texts in terms of the 'formed reference' they offer contemporary believers – as previously discussed – could well provide an example of this.) Biggar then offers a correction, claiming that the understanding of casuistry that Barth is hostile towards in fact deviates from the way practical reasoning is envisaged and practised in the tradition. Biggar contends that 'the rational movement from principles to rules to cases is not closed and mechanical and predictable – not rationalist', as Barth supposes, 'but open and vital and creative'.[21]

There is much to appreciate in this sympathetic and critical reading of Barth. Particularly salutary is the attention Biggar draws to the many and various ways in which practical reasoning plays an undeniable role, manifesting the indirectness of Christ's relationship to the Christian life in doing so. Practical reasoning plays this role despite Barth's strong insistence on open attentiveness and responsiveness to Christ's direct determination of Christian moral activity. However, as Puffer has demonstrated, the translation of *Grenzfall* as 'exception' upon which Biggar relies (following Ramsey and others) is inadequate.[22] Puffer points out that in *CD* III/4 §55 Barth consistently insists that the *Grenzfall* is not an *Ausnahme* ('exception').[23] Moreover, this confusion contributes to some concomitant failures

---

20. Biggar, 'Hearing God's Commands', 114.
21. Biggar, 'Hearing God's Commands', 116.
22. Puffer, 'Taking Exception to the *Grenzfall's* Reception', 484–7.
23. For example, Barth remarks, '*Ihm wird es auch an jenen Grenzen nicht um eine Beugung des Gebotes, nicht um eine Ausnahme von der Regel gehen können, sondern immer nur um die Beugung dessen, was er, indem er es als Aufforderung zum Lebenswillen vernahm, als Gehorsam ihm gegenüber verstehen und leisten zu sollen meinte*' (*KD* III/4 §55, 390). In the standard English translation this is rendered, 'Even on these frontiers they will not see a relaxation of the command or exception to the rule, but only a relaxation of that which they think they should understand and offer as obedience when they accept it as a summons to the will to live.' The translation of *Beugung* as 'relaxation' blunts Barth's clarity about the fact that at the 'frontiers', where we are dealing with 'borderline cases' (*Grenzfallen*, translated 'exceptional cases' in *CD* III/4), we are not permitted to find exceptions or to indulge in 'bending' (a better rendering of *Beugung*) God's commands. Rather, we are to bend and

to recognize important distinctions Barth makes – such as the distinction between 'the will to live' and 'respect for life' and that between the 'defence' and 'protection' of life. Taken together, the result is that critics like Biggar fail to reckon with the way 'Barth's ethics appear closest to casuistry until he arrives within the geography of the *Grenzfall*' where 'casuistry clearly fails'. This is ultimately a failure to grasp how ethics for Barth 'supplies neither exceptionless rules nor certainty in perceiving God's command but rather guidance in discerning how this command may give rise to acts that are congruent with, or correspond to, God's self-revelation in Jesus Christ.'[24]

Looming behind this failure is a lack of attention to the eschatological realism of Barth's method and the resulting 'paradoxical identity' between divine and human freedom. Barth does not grant the reality of human moral activity – in practical reasoning or any other aspect of Christian living – by placing it alongside the present and active command of Christ. This is because these are not two factors that must be coordinated, each one limited and qualified in relation to the other. The relation of divine and human action is not a zero-sum game. Instead, the determinative reality of Jesus relativizes human moral action. To be sure, this relativization does mean its limitation; but it also entails the *establishment* of human moral action in its proper creaturely relationship with God, which is to say, in discipleship-shaped correspondence to Christ. If human action and practical reasoning are underdetermined as a result of this, that is not so much crippling as liberating. As I have shown, Barth's underdetermination of human action sponsors a robust, creative and energetically real – though nonetheless relative and provisional – engagement in human activity. Christians are freed from attempting to bear the weight of the world (or even their own justification). Yet they are not thereby relieved of responsibility for moral action. Quite the contrary: they are liberated to pursue it with joy. Rather than trading directness for indirectness as in Biggar's account, Barth secures adequate indirectness – and with it space for human moral activity – by insisting that it take shape entirely in response to Christ. In this case, the *Grenzfall* is yet another way in which human moral activity – in very specific and unusual circumstances – witnesses its origin in and judgement by God's decisive action in Christ. In the discipleship-shaped Christian life, human moral activity follows *after* Christ – although it *follows* after him nonetheless.

The discipleship-shaped indirectness of Barth's vision of moral action provides a modest but also richly practical and pastoral resource for Christian living. Barth's emphasis on the determinative reality and living presence of Christ yields a confidence and joy that does not deny the all-too-human realities of Christian living.

---

reshape our understanding of how to pursue responsiveness to the Creator's commands for the sake of life.

24. Puffer, 'Taking Exception to the *Grenzfall's* Reception', 496.

Chapter 9

THE IMPLICATIONS OF DISCIPLESHIP FOR MORAL SUFFERING

> It is a vital and most beautiful fact that some members of Jesus' body may simply be called to bear witness to the powerful truth of being. In a world that has been seduced by the idolatrous power of speed, clocks, and busyness, bearing witness to the divine significance of simply being is indeed a noble vocation.
>
> —John Swinton, *Becoming Friends of Time*[1]

The third aspect of Barth's discipleship-shaped vision of Christian living that I will interrogate is suffering. To do so, I return to §66.6 and examine how Barth's distinctive approach to sanctification enables him to conceptualize the moral appropriation of suffering. This is a critical issue to investigate insofar as it bears on my evaluation of Barth's vision of Christian living. The significance that may be recognized in suffering is a litmus test for the theoretical coherence and practical utility of any moral vision. Accordingly, I will show that Barth's discipleship-shaped vision entails an approach to suffering that brings into conjunction and joint focus the questions of moral agency and moral activity underpinning the previous two chapters. Moreover, it raises a broader question with particular relevance to the contemporary discipleship conversation: namely, what status can be assigned to inaction and passivity when agency and action reach their limits? This question takes in a number of crucial moral issues not yet addressed in my theological investigation, including: suffering and victimhood, abstaining from action and being acted upon, rest and ultimately death itself. As Oliver O'Donovan points out, 'Suffering and dying ... are themes that belong with the concern of Ethics for life and action', although this is far from straightforward because 'we experience suffering as impotence, as the frustration and termination of our agency'.[2]

---

1. John Swinton, *Becoming Friends of Time: Disability, Timefullness, and Gentle Discipleship* (Waco, TX: Baylor University Press, 2016), 124.
2. Oliver O'Donovan, *Entering into Rest: Ethics as Theology. Volume 3* (Grand Rapids, MI: Eerdmans, 2017), 202.

In the first part of this chapter (9.1), I analyse how Barth wrestles with the status of moral passivity and inaction under the heading of 'The Dignity of the Cross' in §66.6. Barth develops an understanding of 'active passivity' in appropriating suffering and other experiences which befall Christians. In developing this understanding, Barth portrays human beings as fundamentally responsive and passively acted upon before they initiate or act. In the second part of this chapter (9.2), I compare the 'active passivity' of this account of suffering and moral agency with Hauerwas's emphasis on character. On this basis, I conclude the chapter (9.3) by arguing that Barth's discipleship-shaped approach to suffering provides a significant resource for grappling productively with 'the ambiguities of liberation.'[3] This will prepare for my final chapter, where I will indicate some further avenues in which working with Barth's discipleship-shaped moral vision must take us beyond him.

9.1 Discipleship, 'active passivity' and moral suffering

The material in §66.6 opens a fresh vista on Barth's moral vision. Specifically, it sheds light on the way in which 'active passivity' plays a crucial role in his moral theology. 'Active passivity' derives from his particular discipleship-shaped way of relating the various sufferings that Christians experience – including, ultimately, the suffering of death – to Christ's suffering. As I established in Chapters 5 and 6, the dialectics of discipleship structure the correspondence between the two – once again displaying Barth's characteristic 'eschatological realism' in terms of method, the christological form of the 'paradoxical identity' between Christ and his disciples and the 'christologized Pneumatology' that governs his account of sanctification. According to this discipleship-shaped vision of divine–human correspondence, human moral agents are primarily passive – or, perhaps better, receptive. They are acted upon before engaging in any activity of their own. Yet this passivity is not the last word on human moral agency, declaring it finished before it has even begun; rather, it is constitutive of it. It summons and sets in motion the properly creaturely and indeed *human* agency of humans as moral agents liberated by God's sovereign agency in Christ.

Barth brings together suffering and the active life of discipleship in a way that provides a primer for the moral appropriation not only of suffering but of all experience. According to Barth, Christians can bear suffering critically and constructively as disciples of their crucified and exalted Lord. Decisive for this critical and constructive appropriation of suffering is the distinction Barth makes between the 'dignity' and 'crown' of suffering (see 5.1). This distinction allows Barth to annex conceptual territory traditionally associated with virtue ethics – territory

---

3. Miroslav Volf, *Exclusion and Embrace: A Theological Exploration of Identity, Otherness and Reconciliation* (Nashville, TN: Abingdon Press, 1996), 101–5.

that is usually regarded as ceded by Barth to those indebted to Roman Catholic moral theology in particular. To this argument I now turn.

Barth further develops his christologically determined account of sanctification in §66.6 by showing how it enables Christians to appropriate the sufferings they inevitably experience. This even applies to the ultimate form of suffering that Christians encounter – namely, death. Barth emphasizes that following Christ is intrinsically active (see 4.1). It does not and cannot remain merely interior. It presses for visible expression in concrete action – action characterized by self-denial and participation in Christ's 'kingdom onslaught' in the name of freedom. However, making so much of active self-denial in response to the call to discipleship leaves a number of residual, unanswered questions: what becomes not only of what Christians actively do but of what happens to them, what they suffer and what afflicts and assaults them? What significance (if any) can we grant to such experiences? How does Barth's discipleship-shaped vision of sanctification make provision for those aspects of human moral agency that include 'passivity' in terms of suffering and victimhood as well as contemplation and rest? Barth wrestles with these questions in this final subsection of §66.

Fundamentally, Barth insists that the cross demands that suffering and the active moral life of discipleship be brought together – not kept apart.[4] At the head of his understanding of this conjunction between suffering and active discipleship in §66.6 is the distinction he makes between the 'dignity' and 'crown' of enduring suffering in discipleship: '[the] crown and the dignity which comes to the disciple in discipleship are two distinct things' (600). This distinction sponsors Barth's careful, dialectical and christologically determined treatment of the conjunction between suffering passivity and active discipleship here. It does this because it reflects both sides of his discipleship-shaped conception of the correspondence between Christians and Christ in suffering (see 5.1). That is, it reflects both the disciples' unlikeness to their Master – he calls, they follow – and their likeness to him. Suffering dignifies but does not 'crown' Christians in the same way it crowns

---

4. There are myriad ways of keeping suffering and the active moral life apart in moral and political theory. Hannah Arendt famously analysed the opposition in classical thought between the 'bare life' characterizing mere survival and household management on the one hand and the human and humanizing pursuit of politics available to Greek and Roman citizens on the other. Likewise, the medieval appropriation of this saw a disjunction between the vocation of contemplation (or rest) and the *vita activa* – although it inverted the classical evaluation of the relative value of each domain. In the contemporary discipleship conversation, things can operate more subtly. For example, Stanley Hauerwas's insistence that suffering is an essential aspect of character formation is common in the discipleship conversation. However, for Hauerwas and others, the hermeneutical and narrative effort required to enable the constructive moral appropriation of such suffering ensures that active human agency remains primary – notwithstanding his insistence that the two are mutually constitutive. See, for example, *Character and the Christian Life: A Study in Theological Ethics* (Notre Dame, IN: University of Notre Dame Press, 1994), 1–34.

Jesus. The disciples' cross is not identical with their exaltation as Christ's is with his. More than this, according to Barth, 'the crown of life, which the disciple is promised that he will receive at the hand of the King (Rev. 2.10), is the goal of the way which he may go here and now as the bearer of this dignity'. The crown of the disciples' willing bearing of suffering in correspondence with Christ is their final exaltation to the joy of unhindered covenant fellowship with God. This exaltation awaits the eschaton, when it will be given as the final gift from the risen King. But the anticipation of this exaltation bestows dignity on the suffering Christians endure here and now. As they await the crown, the cross Christians bear dignifies them as Christ's disciples. It is, so to speak, his signature. Their cruciform suffering shows that Christians are acted upon by Christ, claimed by and belonging to him.

In an important sense, then, all human beings are 'victims' according to Barth: all are passive and acted upon before they are active. And this being-acted-upon displays a dual reference. On one side, it looks backwards (so to speak), towards the universal determination of all humanity by virtue of their being mired in the sloth and misery of sin (see §65). This is a victimhood in which all are complicit, collaborating in it to a greater or lesser extent, although it remains an imposition from which they are unable to break free in our own power. On the other side, it looks ahead – or, rather, around – to its determination by Christ's work of reconciliation (in the shadow of which humanity's determination in sin also emerges). In his unique and unrepeatable history, the living Lord Jesus has roused and lifted up humanity. All are representatively included in his exaltation. On the basis of this history, Jesus works by his Spirit to 'disturb' (if not fully rouse) sinners from their slumber. In both these directions, then, Christians are primarily acted upon. This is the reality of Christian identity, which *de jure* is shared with all. This identity comes to expression in Christian sanctification, which takes concrete form as they hear and heed Christ's call to discipleship, and entails their Spirit-awakened *de facto* active participation in the *de jure* reality of all. Sanctification therefore does not mean escaping or rising above the moral passivity that is humanity's baseline condition – in some kind of moral exceptionalism. Rather, it means embracing it. Sanctified Christians are engaged in the human and humanizing activity of responding to Christ's direction and call, affirming their essential passivity in doing so – even as they are swept along and activated in his wake, corresponding to his freedom in their own.

The conjunction of suffering and discipleship here is both critical and constructive. It places Christ at the centre, refusing either to grant suffering (or its absence) a positive meaning in itself or to deny the meaning suffering (or its absence) might acquire in being received as a gift from Christ. For the disciple, suffering has no meaning in itself, although it can become meaningful in relation to the Master. This dynamic approach to suffering manifests the 'active passivity' of Barth's distinctive conception of human agency. Speaking of the way in which the cross determines the 'life-movement of the Christian' such that it is 'crossed through' as it is swept up in the movement of the exaltation of humanity in Christ, Barth contends (602):

9. Discipleship and Moral Suffering 193

The cross involves hardship, anguish, grief, pain and finally death. But those who are set in this movement willingly undertake to bear this because it is essential to this movement that it should finally, i.e., in its basis and goal, be crossed through in this way. We are necessarily outside the movement if we will not take up and bear our cross; if we try to escape the *tolerantia crucis* (Calvin).

While Barth strikes the note of willingness at the start of this quotation – granting the reality, integrity and significance of the agency and activity of those who 'undertake to bear' suffering – he situates this within a prior and determining 'passivity'. Those who willingly bear their suffering are 'set in this movement' by an agency and activity not their own. They are acted upon. What is more, this being-acted-upon is a necessity for Christian disciples: 'We are necessarily outside the movement if we will not take up and bear our cross.' However willingly disciples may embrace their sufferings, they have no choice but to do so if they claim to be following after Christ. Because discipleship entails taking up and bearing the cross, Christian suffering must fall within the scope of the activity characteristic of followers. Indeed, the activity of self-denial that lies at the heart of discipleship involves a decisive break with oneself that is nothing short of a death. But the extent to which this death is more than metaphorical comes into focus here in §66.6. It seems Barth would therefore endorse Bonhoeffer's famous provocation: 'Whenever Christ calls us, his call leads us to death.'[5]

Having insisted that the active life of discipleship and the suffering entailed in taking up the cross belong together, Barth immediately counters two potential misunderstandings. Confronting the first potential misunderstanding – in terms of the suffering entailed by the cross – Barth declares that 'it is not a matter merely of hardship, pain and death in themselves and in general' (602). Suffering is not 'baptized' by being included within his vision of active, willing discipleship. It has no positive significance in itself. It remains nothing but the enemy of God's good purposes. Accordingly, Barth emphasizes that it is simply ordinary self-care to avoid and seek to ward off suffering. This ordinary and perfectly valid impulse is underpinned by the intuition that suffering forms no part of God's original and ultimate intention for creation; rather, it opposes it (602):

> In themselves and as such, pain, suffering and death are a questioning, a destruction and finally a negation of human life. The Christian especially cannot try to transform and glorify them. He cannot find any pleasure in them. He cannot desire or seek them. For he sees and honours and loves in life a gift of God. And he is responsible for its preservation.

This echoes his framing of the ethics of creation in *CD* III/4 as a matter of preserving and promoting life. Barth argues that Christians 'cannot be … lover[s] of death'. To do so would involve a fatal paganization of Christianity. At the

---

5. Bonhoeffer, *Discipleship*, 87.

same time, unlike non-Christians who affirm life in itself – thereby idolizing it – Christians affirm it as a good gift of God: 'it is for [them] more than a matter of life'. As the gift of God, Christians gratefully receive and love life in obedience to God's call in Jesus Christ. That is to say, Christians affirm life as part of their discipleship. Viewing suffering through the lens of discipleship therefore safeguards the Christian affirmation of life (602): 'Because he does not love his life in itself and as such, he cannot love its negation and therefore pain, anguish and death as such.'

Barth argues that the Christian affirmation of life is anchored in the recognition that it is a gift from God to be cherished and preserved as he wills. Because of this, Barth also insists that Christians *can* affirm the negation of life – in death and in the tremors that warn of its coming. This negation too may proceed from God. The disciples recognize the lordship of Jesus not only in life but also in death. Belonging to Jesus and doing his will, therefore, becomes 'that which is more than dying in the dying of Christians' (602):

> To be the Lord's includes this alternative of dying. The Christian knows better than others – than those who for different reasons have lost their zest for life and long for its end and dissolution – what he is doing when he says Yes to the negation of life, to pain and suffering and death. He says Yes to these because his sanctification in fellowship with Jesus Christ, in His discipleship, in the conversion initiated by Him, in the doing of good works, ultimately includes the fact that he has to see and feel and experience the limit of his existence

In other words, Christ's sanctifying call to discipleship – and that alone – bestows positive meaning to the suffering involved with taking up the cross. Suffering is not something Christians should seek or wish for in itself, but something that they 'will not negate but affirm ... just as elsewhere and right up to this frontier [they] will not negate but affirm life' (603). Suffering and its absence are both received by disciples as gifts from the gracious hand of Christ.

Barth confronts a second potential misunderstanding of suffering by refusing to grant primacy to the disciple's moral agency and activity. While it may be true for every disciple that 'to save his life he must surrender and lose it', Barth maintains that this does not mean the disciple will 'seek or induce this loss' (603). Discipleship does not entail a death wish. Nor, might we add, does it coincide with a kind of 'persecution complex' in which the irritations and the indirect effects of policy changes in post-Christian societies are inflated in significance, feeding a narrative in which Christians must heroically bear persecution as they endure the loss of social position, power, privilege and comfort. Discipleship – with its necessary sufferings – refuses to imply that human agency or activity is primary. This includes the agency of Christians. Rather, the loss of life discipleship demands 'will come to [the Christian]' (603). Disciples are first of all passive in being acted upon in losing their life. Nevertheless, this passivity does constitute and call for their agency. Being acted upon presages and gives shape to the disciples' activity in not negating but affirming the suffering they receive, like their life, as a gift from Christ's hand. Suffering must not lead disciples to reverse this conception. Such a reversal occurs when they imagine that their activity is primary and their suffering secondary, undeserved and accidental. When this happens, discipleship becomes an inverted parody of itself as Christ's summons to take up the cross is twisted to serve a perverse desire for death and drive to experience persecution.

Recasting this discussion in more explicitly christological terms, Barth guards against either emptying out or romanticizing Christian suffering. Barth refuses to empty of significance the suffering Christians incur on the path of discipleship. He treats the conjunction between suffering and discipleship in correspondence with Christ in such a way as to avoid suggesting that it is swallowed up by Christ's suffering or otherwise stripped of value. Equally, Barth does not romanticize Christian suffering by giving it more weight than it can bear. Commenting on Calvin's treatment of cross-bearing, Barth speaks movingly of the filial confidence with which Christians can embrace their suffering (604):

> The Christian does not take up his cross, and yield to God, because it is quite futile to resist One who is so superior in strength. If we obey God only because we must, our secret thoughts are all of disobedience and evasion, and we refrain from these only because they are impossible. The Christian yields in recognition of the righteousness and wisdom of divine providence which rules his life. He obeys a living, not a dead, command. He knows that resistance or impatience is wrong. He understands that it is for his salvation that God lays his cross on him. He thus accepts it *grata placidaque anima*, not with his natural bitterness, but in thankful and cheerful praise of God.

Barth goes on to suggest that this picture would have been completed if Christ had been explicitly brought in as the premise of knowing that God loves and is favourably disposed towards us in this way. Since the Christian's cross is a matter of concrete fellowship between Christ and Christians, the suffering Christians experience in this way are far from being rendered inconsequential and empty of significance. Instead, it speaks to us of that fellowship and the welcome in God's family that it entails. This is the dignity Christ's cross bestows on the suffering of Christians: 'Christians are distinguished and honoured by the fact that the fellowship with Jesus into which He Himself has received them finds final expression in the fact that their human and Christian life is marked like a tree for felling' (605).

Nevertheless, Barth maintains that the suffering of Christians on the path of discipleship only receives this dignity indirectly. Disciples enjoy their fellowship with Christ and participation in God's family on the basis of Christ's suffering and obedience not their own (604):

> As Christians take up and bear their cross they do not suffer, of course, with the direct and original and pure obedience which for all its bitterness it was natural and self-evident for the Son of God who was also the Son of Man to render to His Father. Their obedience will never be more than the work of the freedom which they are given. It will always be subsequent. It will always

be so stained by all kinds of disobedience that if in the mercy of God it were not invested with the character of obedience it would hardly deserve to be called obedience. Nor is their suffering even the tiniest of contributions to the reconciliation of the world with God. On the contrary, it rests on the fact that this has been perfectly accomplished, not by them but by God Himself in Christ, so that it does not need to be augmented by their suffering or by any lesser Calvaries.

Barth excludes any possibility of over-investing Christian suffering with meaning by underscoring the graced nature of the disciples' obedience and suffering. In particular, he resists romanticizing suffering itself and the position of victim as such. While suffering does genuinely victimize human beings – as a demonic force opposed to God's purposes – Barth's vision admits of no 'pure' victims. Even when Christians face rejection as Christ did, their remain some significant differences between disciples and their Master. Not only will they not face God's rejection as Christ did, 'they will never be quite innocent in their suffering' either (605). Nor will they ever 'suffer merely through the corruption and wickedness of others, or through the undeserved decrees and buffetings of fate or the cosmic purpose'. Without surrendering to the paganization of suffering that Barth has identified as so difficult to resist if life is affirmed simply for its own sake, he does maintain that for Christians 'there is always a very definite (if sometimes disguised) connexion between the sufferings which befall them and their own participation in the transgression and guilt in which all men are continually implicated'.

Christian suffering derives its significance from Christ's cross and its liminal status from his grace, which both originates and mitigates it. Therefore, Barth's affirmation of universal guilt and deservingness – even on the part of Christians who suffer unjustly – functions less to 'blame the victim' than it does to underline how their suffering is overshadowed by Christ's, and will one day be overcome by it. Ultimately, this affirmation humanizes suffering rather than either demonizing or deifying it. As Webster argues, for Barth human action (in which we can include suffering) is not so much a channel of grace – as though God's grace could cause it to become in turn a cause of grace to others – as it is an occasion for grace to elicit an active human response.[6] From one angle, this humanization of suffering appears to diminish the significance of the disciples' suffering as they take up their cross: 'In the life of Christians it is not just a matter of themselves and the fulfilment of their sanctification, but ... of something far greater than themselves – of the glory and Word and work of God, compared with which they and all that they may become can never be more than dust and ashes' (605–6). From another angle, however, this is what lends their lives and sufferings genuine significance – the thoroughly human significance of witnessing to Christ, his singular holiness and its future universal revelation (606):

---

6. Webster, 'The Christian in Revolt', 144.

This is the limit which is set for the Christian especially, and as a sign of which he comes to bear his cross, not in identity but in similarity with the cross of Jesus. [The Christian's] cross points to fulness and truth of that which he expects, and to which he hastens, as one who is sanctified in Jesus Christ. It points to God Himself, to His will for the world, to the future revelation of His majesty, to the glory in which his Lord already lives and reigns.

The sufferings of Christians are assimilated by Barth to the logic of discipleship. This is how we correspond to Christ in following after our Master, actively receiving our suffering – critically and constructively – as meaningful because it is a gift from the one whose suffering is identical with his exaltation as our royal representative and head.

9.2 Grace, character and discipleship-shaped suffering

The sufferings of Christians point to their graced identity. Christian identity is undeserved, based in nothing disciples have done or could foreseeably do. As such, it is unshakeable, precisely because it is based on God's action not human action. But it also cannot be presumed upon as though it were the disciple's own possession or achievement – again because it depends on God's action not theirs. It is a gift that entails reciprocal obligations. With the putative notion of 'pure gift' advanced by Jacques Derrida and others, the graced identity of Christians shares an emphasis on the freedom of the event of giving. In giving, the giver is free from coercion and manipulation, never owing the gift but giving it freely. Likewise, the receiver cannot expect or presume upon the gift but only receive what is in fact given.[7] But in keeping with the cultural context of giving, receiving and exchange that provides the backdrop for the New Testament language of grace, the gift of Christian identity differs from Derrida's 'pure gift' in that it makes demands and expects a necessary return.[8] It is unconditional but not undemanding – and it is this precisely because it depends on God's action and initiative. The Christian's graced identity, which finds its centre and origin in the work of God in Christ, creates the demand for responsive action and suffering – that is to say, for discipleship – even as it relativizes it, refusing to valorize it or elevate its status beyond its creaturely reality.

In creating the demand for the very human activity and suffering that it also relativizes, the motif of discipleship allows Barth to annex terrain typically ceded

---

7. See, for example, Carl Olson's illuminating treatment of Marcel Mauss' foundational theorizing of gift giving and the 'transformations' it undergoes in the hands of Derrida and Georges Bataille, 'Excess, Time, and the Pure Gift: Postmodern Transformations of Marcel Mauss' Theory', *Method & Theory in the Study of Religion* 14.3/4 (2002): 350–74.

8. See John M. G. Barclay, *Paul and the Gift* (Grand Rapids, MI: Eerdmans, 2015), chapter 1.

to virtue ethics. This emerges sharply in comparison with Stanley Hauerwas's vision of character and virtue as he presents it in his early work, *Character and the Christian Life* (1994). For Hauerwas as for Barth, agency and suffering must be allowed to mutually illuminate and interpret each other. According to Hauerwas, character configures suffering as an essential concession to agency. Suffering is necessary. But our agency and activity remain primary even if being acted upon in suffering leads to the development of character: 'Though character may grow out of what we suffer, its main precondition must remain [our] agency.'[9] Hauerwas expounds the significance of suffering for the formation of character at length and in a variety of ways – not least as he returns to these themes in *The Peaceable Kingdom*.[10] But the priority of human agency is a constant feature of his thinking on this subject. Hauerwas does concede that 'we can never disentangle with confidence what we are given and what we do' – and that it is therefore 'difficult to maintain that we are agents, that is, that there is a fundamental distinction between what happens to us and what we do'. But he nevertheless maintains that 'an account of agency is indispensable ... to show how I am not without resources to make my life my own'.[11] As a result, suffering becomes productive of character only insofar as human moral agents make of it something positive and coherent with the story of their life.

Barth's understanding differs from this in an important manner – for the logic of discipleship as he expounds it entails that we are first acted upon. The call and summons of Christ take priority for Christians in their activity and suffering. What is more, being acted upon precedes and determines the disciples' activity in an essential sense. Christians follow after Christ. According to the dialectics of discipleship, this following constitutes their agency and activity in an ongoing way and not simply by initiating or inflecting it at a decisive point. Therefore, Barth could not concur with Hauerwas without significant qualification when he says, 'I am not an agent because I can "cause" certain things to happen, but because certain things that happen, whether through the result of my decision or not, can be made mine through my power of attention and intention.'[12] According to Barth, suffering – in both broad and narrow senses – shapes the identity of Christian disciples and makes them the kind of actors they are. It does this because disciples are acted upon in a way that occasions and underwrites all their subsequent activity. The oneness and identity Christians enjoy with Christ is paradoxical, a matter of two radically different orders of being brought together truly but without suggesting their interchangeability or compromising their asymmetry. The disciples' suffering – in the broad sense first of all of their passive receptivity

---

9. Stanley Hauerwas, *Character and the Christian Life: A Study in Theological Ethics* (Notre Dame, IN: University of Notre Dame Press, 1994 [1985, 1975]), 19.

10. See Stanley Hauerwas, *The Peaceable Kingdom: A Primer in Christian Ethics* (Notre Dame, IN: University of Notre Dame Press, 1983), chapter 3.

11. Hauerwas, *The Peaceable Kingdom*, 39.

12. Hauerwas, *The Peaceable Kingdom*, 42.

in being acted upon and consequently in the narrower sense of their following of Christ into the sufferings of the Christian life – is a matter of their subsistence in and relative to Christ's decisive activity, which acts upon them in order to free them for action.

Barth's discipleship-shaped vision renders suffering productive of character in a far more primary way than it does for Hauerwas. For Hauerwas as for the Roman Catholic moral theology he draws from, the appropriation of the classical notions of virtue and character formation requires that Christology be kept at a distance from human agency and activity, especially when it comes to suffering. Christology does have a role, but it builds upon and completes nature rather than defining the 'natural' to begin with.[13] For Barth, however, Christology is primary and determinative of the disciple's agency and activity. Suffering with and like Christ is not something alien to Christian identity. It is not an 'accidental' stimulus to the development of character – something that only becomes integral to them insofar as disciples creatively appropriate what happens to them. Rather, suffering in the sense of bearing the cross – which, in Barth's hands, unites both broad and narrow senses of suffering – is internal to discipleship. Indeed, it is necessary to and definitive of it. Discipleship shapes the 'paradoxical identity' Christians have with Christ. Character development is no 'accidental' outcome of suffering that Christians happen to have been able to creatively appropriate.[14] It is instead an unavoidable aspect of the call to discipleship.

In Barth's discipleship-shaped vision, the appropriation of suffering is far less heroic than in the virtue tradition Hauerwas represents. It is both more ordinary and less a matter of effort and achievement. It is more ordinary because it is essential and necessary for the identity of disciples; it is the 'fulfilment' of their sanctification. Bearing the cross is a demand placed on every Christian by virtue of their oneness with Christ. At the same time, appropriating suffering is less a matter of effortful – if chiefly interpretive – achievement. This is because suffering is something that is given to Christians in and with their union with Christ. It is, as we have seen, a gift. To be sure, it is a gift that summons disciples to a task as it presses for visible and practical actualization. But it is still primarily

---

13. My characterization of the theological substructure of virtue in the tradition of Roman Catholic theology (and especially in its appropriation of Aristotelian source) is reliant on the work of Nolan, *Reformed Virtue after Barth*, 72–4 and 90–9. Two important studies highlight the formative status of Barth's early encounter with criticisms from Roman Catholic moral theologian Erich Przywara: Amy E. Marga, *Karl Barth's Dialogue with Catholicism in Göttingen and Münster: Its Significance for His Doctrine of God* (Tübingen, DE: Mohr Siebeck, 2010) and Keith L. Johnson, *Karl Barth and the Analogia Entis* (London: T&T Clark, 2010).

14. If character development depended upon the ability to creatively appropriate suffering, it would be jeopardized by certain kinds of traumatic identity-fracturing suffering as well as being unavailable to actors lacking the kinds of resources needed for such creative interpretive effort.

received rather than achieved. Suffering is part and parcel of Christ's goodness to his people – both in the sense of being acted upon and in the narrower sense that takes in persecution, doubt and more mundane tangible reminders of our provisionality. As such, suffering is the foundation and stimulus of Christian activity in discipleship, not an independent object upon which Christians must labour in order to make something worthwhile out of it.

The gap between Hauerwas and Barth on Christian suffering prompts a further question: does Hauerwas's emphasis on the priority of agency in the appropriation of suffering to build character involve an unintended 'paganization' of the Christian attitude to life and death? We have already observed Barth wrestling with this theme (earlier in the text). Barth attempts to dialectically relate two intuitions. On the one hand, there is the intuition that life is best affirmed when it is received as the gift from God, which must not be emptied of meaning and value. This entails a critical stance towards suffering. As a force intrinsically opposed to life, it must be refused independent positive status. On the other hand, there is the intuition that receiving life as a gift demands that it not be totalized or confused with the Giver. This opens a space for a constructive approach to suffering and death, both of which can be received as gifts – although gifts with positive status entirely relative to Christ. Each of these intuitions in their own way points to Jesus the Lord, the Giver of every good gift. But the risk with Hauerwas's approach to character is that it affirms the second intuition in such a way as to violate the first – particularly as it opens up the possibility that suffering might be rendered positive through the creative interpretive effort of the human agent.

That this constitutes at least a potential 'paganization' of suffering arises from the fact that it bestows independent positive status on both suffering and human agency. Agency is primary for Hauerwas – even when he seeks to evade the implications of this, as when he acknowledges the kinds of complexities that mean we never purely determine who we are on the basis of what we do but must also always factor in what is done to us. In such instances, Hauerwas strains to move beyond a pagan, heroic notion of the self. He acknowledges, for example, that 'a man's agency and his character cannot be thought of as one external cause acting upon a pliable and passive material, for man's agency and character are internally related'. Yet he immediately reverts to his bedrock assumption that for a person 'to acquire character is to do so by the exercising of his ability to be an agent' – although he attempts to qualify this by maintaining that 'the actual determination of our being by our own agency is not different from our character'.[15] The tortuousness of Hauerwas's account suggests that while the language and concepts of character and virtue can be 'evangelized', Barth's reticence to do so may prove the safer course. Ultimately, Barth is more decisively christological as well as more able to do justice to the reality of lived experience – including suffering, struggle and failure. This is evident in the way he combines a reticence to employ traditional virtue ethics (avoiding notions like imitation, for example) at the same time as he annexes its

---

15. Hauerwas, *Character and the Christian Life*, 21.

conceptual territory by means of his discipleship-shaped account of the 'active passivity' of the Christian moral sufferer.

9.3 Discipleship and the 'ambiguities of liberation'

The final chapter will provide a fuller assessment of the extent to which Barth's distinctively discipleship-shaped account of human agency, activity and suffering can resource Christian ethics in contemporary, post-Christian contexts. To conclude this chapter and section, however, I provisionally evaluate the potential contribution of his discipleship-shaped approach to suffering. In particular, I establish the extent to which it can illuminate the restriction of human freedom that suffering frequently entails, taking disability as a test case. I have already demonstrated that discipleship thematizes freedom. But I have just argued that it also makes suffering essential to Christian identity. Consequently, one yardstick against which Barth's discipleship-shaped vision can be measured is how his handling of suffering in §66.6 helps navigate the 'ambiguities of liberation' highlighted by theological ethicists like Miroslav Volf. After providing an overview of these ambiguities, I consider Alexander Massmann's substantial criticism of Barth's approach to suffering as well as Amos Yong's brief appreciation.

In *Exclusion and Embrace* (1996), Volf points out that 'the categories of oppression and liberation provide combat gear, not a pin-stripe suit or a dinner dress; they are good for fighting but not for negotiating or celebrating'.[16] Volf highlights three of the most problematic aspects of the vocabulary of oppression and liberation – including the language of victimization. First, he acknowledges 'the paradoxical and pernicious tendency of the language of victimization to undermine the operation of human agency and disempower victims' particularly by 'imprison[ing] them within narratives of their own victimization'.[17] Second, he draws attention to the messy reality of every conflict situation, which undermines the attempt by any party to the conflict to claim pure victimhood or to portray their enemies as indisputably evil. On this basis Volf contends, third, that as 'categories "oppression/liberation" seem ill-suited to bring about reconciliation and sustain peace between people and people groups'.[18] In light of these ambiguities in the use of the language of victimization, oppression and liberation, Volf concludes that caution is necessary: 'Though the categories themselves are indispensable, we must resist making "oppression/liberation" the overarching schema by which to align our social engagement.'[19] Once our concerns move beyond simply combating oppression (as necessary as this is), a wider framework is needed.

---

16. Volf, *Exclusion and Embrace*, 103.
17. Volf, *Exclusion and Embrace*, 103.
18. Volf, *Exclusion and Embrace*, 104.
19. Volf, *Exclusion and Embrace*, 104.

Barth's discipleship-shaped vision can help provide this wider framework. For Barth, discipleship means freedom. The liberative thrust of the Barthian approach to discipleship fits well in the context of the indispensability of the categories of liberation and oppression. Christ enlists his disciples in the struggle against the idolatry and ideology embodied in the imprisoning 'given factors'. This includes a struggle against the disciples' own old self, which is always with them and to which Christ directs them to die – over and over again. In this way, there is at least a partial mitigation against the second of Volf's 'ambiguities' already built into Barth's approach. The sanctification of Christian disciples does not imply moral exceptionalism but rather manifests their graced identity. Moreover, the liberative thrust of Barth's view is tempered by his willingness to place moral passivity alongside – and even prior to – moral activity and agency. Especially significant is Barth's dual insistence that all are 'victims' – in the sense of primarily being acted upon rather than active agents, both in being mired in the sloth and misery of sin and in the work of Christ and the Spirit in lifting them up and 'disturbing' their sinful slumber. There are no pure victims in this way of seeing things. As Alexander Massmann argues, this dual insistence does risk entrenching Christians in their own victimhood – in the broad sense of being acted upon and subsequently of suffering, oppression and persecution more narrowly. Nevertheless, I have shown that Barth takes care with the analogical extension to Christ's disciples of the identity between suffering and exaltation. What is true of Christ – that suffering and exaltation, cross and crown, coincide – is not true of disciples in the same way. Barth also insists that the disciples' being-acted-upon does not so much efface their agency and activity as energize, direct and give definition to it. As a result, his approach makes space for notions of oppression, victimhood and liberation as necessary without setting them up as the exclusive or final word in his vision of Christian living.

In his close examination of Barth's ethics, *Citizenship in Heaven and on Earth* (2015), Alexander Massmann expresses some hesitation about the foundations of Barth's ethics of reconciliation as they are laid in *CD* IV/1-3. In particular, he rightly singles out Barth's thematization of discipleship and cruciformity as establishing the link between his Christology and his rendering of human moral agency and activity in this context. However, Massmann sees this not so much as a positive step as the introduction of a dangerous imbalance in his vision of human flourishing. Massmann remarks on Barth's apparent tendency to privilege apparently unilateral and hierarchical power relations among people – deriving from the way 'submission', 'subordination' and 'obedience' feature so prominently in Barth's account of Christ's identity and activity on his way into the far country (*CD* IV/2).[20]

Massmann rightly draws attention to the imbalance in Barth's presentation of male–female relationships chiefly in terms of female 'subordination' in IV/1.[21]

---

20. Massmann, *Citizenship in Heaven and on Earth*, chapter 4.
21. Massmann, *Citizenship in Heaven and on Earth*, 359–68.

Barth's attempt to give christological form to this aspect of human experience is comprehensible within his all-encompassing redescription of the world in light of the eschaton disclosed in Christ. But this is one point at which we must criticize Barth's success in doing so. Why does the suffering and unilateral submission of Christ map across to women's relation to men exclusively (with little awareness displayed of the potential for this to prime the relationship for abuse)? What has become of the essential 'alongside' as well as the 'order and sequence' he speaks of in CD III/4 §54.1 – where, as one Barth scholar puts it, a 'principle of reciprocity takes "absolute precedence" over any difference in order between male and female'?[22] And what has become of the christological form the New Testament suggests men's relation to women must take, in which the socially and culturally configured power differential between the two is to be an occasion for service and self-sacrifice on men's part rather than an immutable hierarchy and privilege to be insisted upon? So pronounced and troubling is this imbalance that it invites reflection on the possible presence of theological self-justification in Barth's correspondence with Charlotte von Kirschbaum between 1926 and 1932.[23] It is possible that Barth appeals to his theological formulations and their conceptual patterns – non-equilateral triangles, the relativization of created structures like marriage, and so on – in order to justify his behaviour. Likewise, his occasional stress on the importance of his theological work may have functioned to pressure Charlotte (and also his wife, Nelly) to persist with their tragic arrangement despite her misgivings and obvious pain.

Massmann claims Barth's identification of Christ's sufferings with the revelation of his glory and majesty is the root of the imbalance in Barth's theology of gender: 'Jesus Christ is true to his divine majesty precisely in the lowliness of his suffering.'[24] Massmann does not hesitate to underscore Barth's apparent application of this to Christians, resulting in his vision of cruciform discipleship:

> At some points in his *oeuvre* Barth reacts critically against the notion of repeating Christ's work or of actively seeking out the misery he experienced. Yet he also portrays cruciform discipleship in the sense of the *imitatio Christi* as a necessary manifestation of Christian freedom. In Christ's humility and his bearing of his suffering, Barth argues, we are faced with 'a binding law' for all Christians.[25]

---

22. Paul S. Fiddes, 'The Status of Woman in the Thought of Karl Barth', in *After Eve: Women, Theology and the Christian Tradition*, ed. Janet M. Soskice (Grand Rapids, MI: Zondervan, 1990), 153.

23. See Tietz, 'Karl Barth and Charlotte von Kirschbaum,' 86–111. Of course, caution must also be exercised, for even the new details that have emerged to light do not entirely obviate the fact that as Selinger observes, 'one must be careful not to think one can know' the precise nature or all the details of their relationship. Selinger, *Charlotte Von Kirschbaum and Karl Barth*, 13.

24. Massmann, *Citizenship in Heaven and on Earth*, 342.

25. Massmann, *Citizenship in Heaven and on Earth*, 345.

Massmann cites §66.6 as evidence for this contention. However, a closer reading may have made him more cautious. To be sure, a transfer of the unity of suffering and exaltation – cross and crown – to the Christian is present in Barth's thinking, especially in IV/1. But IV/2 focuses on the royal exaltation of humanity in Christ in a way that offers a distinct and dialectically complementary perspective to that of IV/1. In IV/2, as we have seen, Barth is careful to avoid making a direct transfer from Christ's suffering to that of Christians. Barth's discipleship-shaped portrayal of Christian agency and action does resonate with the self-sacrificial emphasis of IV/1. As McCormack rightly highlights, there is significant thematic interlocking between the vision of the Christian life as suffering obedience in IV/1 and the emphasis on self-denial and even death to self in IV/2.[26] However, as I have shown, Barth explicitly refuses to allow that the Christians' cross is identical with their crown in §66.6. At the very least, this opens up a gap between Christ and his disciples, calling for a halt in the effort to claim that disciples must relinquish any critical opposition to suffering.

What is more, Barth's climactic presentation of the cruciformity of discipleship in §66.6 – and specifically the dignity of bearing the cross – is bound together with his insistence that the suffering and endurance discipleship entails is penultimate. The ultimate goal and eschatological fulfilment of the sanctifying work of Christ in human life is not suffering. God's ultimate intention is not for Christians to suffer – as much as it dignifies disciples to follow after their Master in bearing their cross. Barth maintains that suffering has no positive value in and of itself. Rather, God's ultimate purpose is for disciples to share in the eschatological crown and triumph of Christ. Any dignity they receive in bearing suffering now simply anticipates the full experience of the reality promised in the acclamation of Revelation 21.3-4.

> Look! God's dwelling is with humanity, and He will live with them. They will be His people, and God Himself will be with them and be their God. He will wipe away every tear from their eyes. Death will no longer exist; grief, crying, and pain will exist no longer, because the previous things have passed away.

Ultimately, framing of sanctification in terms of humanity's exaltation achieves the opposite of what Massmann fears. Far from 'baptizing' suffering, Barth implicitly if not always explicitly contests and mitigates the possibility of abuse in bringing suffering and discipleship together. Indeed, Barth's approach can be mobilized as a resource to combat the first of Volf's 'ambiguities of liberation'. Barth affirmation of our 'active passivity' – which grants a foundational status and universality to suffering, victimhood and being-acted-upon – is set in dynamic counterpoint to his larger emphasis on Christ's liberation and humanization of his disciples. Affirming that people are victims may carry risks. But it remains indispensable. The liberative and humanizing emphasis in Barth's approach to suffering – and particularly the distinction he makes between the dignity and

---

26. McCormack, 'Sanctification after Metaphysics', 119–21.

crown of suffering – grows organically in the soil of his discipleship-shaped vision. Barth's emphasis on the exaltation of Christ and the corresponding dignity of discipleship bar the way to dehumanizing those who suffer or are victims; for the path that Christ trod – and which his disciples tread after him – is humanized insofar as it catches and refracts the light of eternity. At the same time, Barth insists that dignity and crown must be distinguished. The all-surpassing light of eternity will swallow up the darkness of suffering, ushering in the inexpressible experience of full covenant partnership with the living God. What Christ's disciples anticipate in this includes knowing as they are known, experiencing vindication and victory and walking in freedom as they reflect the glory of God in a properly human way. People who expect and begin to experience (indirectly) the restoration of their humanity are armed to resist anything that would corrode or corrupt it – in them or anyone else.

In contrast to Massmann's critique, Amos Yong's fleeting yet appreciative reference to Barth's christological identification of suffering and glory also calls for comment. In his book, *The Bible, Disability, and the Church* (2011), Yong undertakes a thoroughgoing critique of the 'normate' social and, unfortunately, ecclesial bias against suffering, illness, disease and particularly disability – and the people who experience these:

> By ['normate bias'], I mean the unexamined prejudices that non-disabled people have toward disability and toward people who have them. These assumptions function normatively so that the inferior status of people with disabilities is inscribed into our consciousness. Note, for example, how the rhetoric functions to describe people with impairments as *dis*-abled, *in*-capacitated, *in*-capable, *ab*-normal, and so on. In other words, non-disabled people take their experiences of the world as normal, thereby marginalizing and excluding the experiences of people with disabilities as not normal.[27]

In making this case, Yong draws on resources from ableist activism, biblical studies and theology. For instance, in re-examining key biblical texts employed in traditional theological reflection on the Christian eschatological hope, he contests the 'normate' assumption that Christ's return will mean the abolition of disability. According to Yong, this reads far too much into the promise that Christ will wipe away all tears and that the former things will have passed away. Rather than abolishing disability itself, Yong makes a case for the eschatological overcoming of all negative social and interpersonal implications of disability. In doing this, he seeks to defuse negative conceptualizations of disability itself here and now.

At a crucial moment in Yong's re-examination, he suggests that we 'extend in a disability direction Karl Barth's reflections on the Incarnation as the journey of the Son of God into a far country'.[28] While he stops short of claiming that Christ was

---

27. Amos Yong, *The Bible, Disability, and the Church*, 10–11.
28. Yong, *The Bible, Disability, and the Church*, 128.

disabled, he proposes to take seriously the New Testament witness to the fact that 'Jesus ... penetrated the depths of the human experience of weakness, exclusion, and marginality' such that he not only 'learned to empathize with people who have disabilities' but also that he 'came to recognize his own privilege as one who participated as a non-disabled person within a normate social order'.[29]

There is much to commend in Yong's proposal. His reading of God's presence in Christ in relation to suffering and disability is persuasive and theologically fruitful. This not only reflects the indispensability Volf has noted for the concepts of victimization and oppression – in this case employed in an analysis of the exclusions woven into the 'normate social order' that Jesus inhabited and challenged. It also very fruitfully mobilizes and develops Barth's willingness to follow through the theological implications of the fact that it is God in Christ who plunges into 'the depths of the human experience of weakness, exclusion, and marginality'. The resulting theological portrait of God's presence in, sympathy with and embrace of suffering and weakness – including the suffering and weakness of disability – holds remarkable potential to provide pastoral comfort. Just like Barth's emphasis on the dignity discipleship bestows on the experience of suffering, it prevents us from averting our eyes from the suffering we are confronted with or despairing at the thought of divine abandonment when we experience it ourselves.

Likewise, Yong's call to reimagine the future attested in the New Testament has much potential. Specifically, Yong contests the assumption that the restoration of humanity we anticipate in the new creation will involve the elimination of disability – as though we will one day leave behind all creaturely limitations (and therefore presumably resent them in the present). This suggestion, and the exegesis Yong provides to support it, is less persuasive than his analysis of God's embrace of suffering in Christ. In particular, it appears difficult to square with Jesus' healing of disabled people in the Gospels, which is consistent with the character of his ministry as an anticipation of the eschaton. Nevertheless, it rightly prompts a consideration of the wider perspective for which Yong argues. Jesus himself bears the scars of his crucifixion in his resurrection body – although they no longer impair him. Insofar as this is indicative of our future, Yong is right to call us to broaden our imagination. The crown of the life of discipleship may well mean the overcoming of suffering less in terms of its abolition than in terms of a social and communal healing in which the differences between people remain but are now 'evangelized', becoming occasions for service and self-sacrifice rather than exploitation and insistence on preserving the privilege of the powerful.

However, Yong risks too directly transferring the unity between suffering and glory – cross and crown – from Christ to Christians. Whereas Barth would caution that the (future) crown is to be distinguished from the (present) dignity of suffering in Christian experience, Yong implies that Christ's suffering – and transformative embrace of it – is exemplary for Christians in a way that potentially replaces the good news of the Incarnation with a moralistic call to be 'incarnational'. The

---

29. Yong, *The Bible, Disability, and the Church*, 128.

Incarnation is the decisive event of God's reconciling presence with us. As such it is determinative for Christian experience, including our experience of suffering and disability. Christ's living presence, direction and call enable us to receive suffering as a gift for ourselves and for those God brings into our lives. Christ's presence in and embrace of suffering – and ultimately his overcoming of it (while still bearing its scars) – bring comfort and hope. This is because they open up the prospect of our own crown and liberation from the negative impact of suffering as well as our present ability to find dignity in it rather than despairing at it in ourselves or turning away from those who suffer. In this way, Barth equips us to make common cause with Yong while protecting us from some of the risks to which his proposal is exposed.

In conclusion, Barth's discipleship-shaped approach to experiencing suffering – including at least potentially the suffering of disability as well as the whole gamut of experiences of passivity and being-acted-upon – offers a significant resource for navigating 'the ambiguities of liberation'. It does justice to the indispensability of the categories of oppression and liberation while refusing to turn them into 'the overarching schema by which to align our social engagement'.[30] It does this by dynamically coordinating a critical stance towards suffering – its overcoming *is* something to look forward to, however we envisage this – with a constructive stance by which we receive suffering as a gift, find dignity in the ways in which we may conform to Christ in it and draw comfort from Christ's knowledge of and sympathy with our experiences of it. Sponsored by the dialectics of discipleship, Barth's approach dynamically coordinates these around the living person and presence of Christ. Christ is not hermetically sealed in the past – leaving only his example to inspire our imitation. Nor is his transformative presence purely a future reality with no present implications. At the same time, Christ's presence and transforming power now is not all there is to the life of discipleship. The crown still awaits those whose discipleship-shaped sanctification dignifies their present sufferings. This critical and constructive stance towards suffering manifests the disciples' fellowship with Christ and primes them to be open to his determining agency and activity in the Spirit's power.

---

30. Volf, *Exclusion and Embrace*, 104.

Chapter 10

WITH, AGAINST AND BEYOND BARTH ON DISCIPLESHIP

My theological investigation into Barth's vision of discipleship is now able to identify and assess the distinctive contribution it can make to the contemporary discipleship conversation. I begin by highlighting the points of concurrence between Barth's approach and the wider conversation (10.1). Specifically, I indicate their convergence on the importance of the discipleship motif for the church and Christian living. I will also indicate how Barth might challenge or inflect some of the major trends in the contemporary conversation – particularly in elevating the importance of engagement and distinctiveness, which a number of the contributing voices in the contemporary discipleship conversation appear to be in danger of neglecting or relegating. I will focus on Barth's christologically determined dialectical coordination of distinctiveness and engagement on the one hand, and on the other hand his emphasis on realistic hope as the primary affective register that matches this.

After considering the potential of working with the grain of Barth's discipleship-shaped vision of Christian living, I identify some potential problems with it (10.2). I consider, first, its underdetermination in relation to others, which leaves it open to misunderstanding and misappropriation in relation to sociopolitical matters. A further problem is highlighted by the tragic and problematic interpersonal relationships in Barth's own household. Barth's own moral compromises raise questions about his vision – although I suggest that Barth's thinking about discipleship contains resources to assist in critically and constructively engaging him around these issues.

I then sketch how my reading of Barth's ethics of discipleship – with and against Barth – could be carried beyond Barth into two concrete concerns in the contemporary discipleship conversation (10.3). First, I outline a discipleship-shaped approach to theological education that seeks to move beyond the problematic framing of pedagogy as chiefly concerned with either belief (the mind) or behaviour (the habits). I draw attention to the resources Barth's vision provides to move beyond this binary towards a pedagogy uniting discipline and desire in worship. A doxological appropriation of our fundamental belonging to Christ nurtures a 'social imaginary' that can guide both belief and behaviour. Second, I examine the shape of discipleship when it comes to pressing social issues.[1]

1. A number of philosophers and social theorists – including Benedict Anderson, *Imagined Communities: Reflections on the Origin and Spread of Nationalism*,

Specifically, I outline the way in which it attunes us to 'wheelchair questions'.[2] A Barthian vision has implications not only for how Christians relate to those who suffer, as the objects of discipleship, but also for how those who suffer and may also be the subjects of discipleship.

I conclude the chapter – and the book – by drawing together the threads of these possible contributions based on Barth's account of discipleship (10.4). I highlight its theological significance more broadly, dwelling on its implications for Barth studies, and indicating its promise as a resource for Christian living in post-Christian contexts.

10.1 With *Barth on discipleship*

How does Barth contribute to the contemporary discipleship conversation? Where does he agree with many of the voices in it? Where does he challenge or inflect them? I will explore three key areas of convergence and contribution.

The first and most obvious area of convergence between Barth's discipleship-shaped vision of sanctification and the contemporary discipleship conversation concerns its importance. Barth affirms the importance of discipleship. Together with many of those accenting discipleship today, he sees that it is an under-appreciated theme historically and theologically. Discipleship is the distinctive form of the sanctified community and Christian life in Barth's christologically determined vision (Chapter 3). Barth's appropriation of the New Testament motif of discipleship displays the same kind of 'practical Christocentrism' that marks the Anabaptist legacy. Likewise, Barth takes seriously the concreteness of the church – although his emphasis and proposal about how to secure the church's concreteness and underwrite the integrity of its creaturely agency is distinctive (Chapter 7). Finally, Barth stands with those who commend the active life of distinctive works

---

rev. edn (London: Verso, 1991), Charles Taylor, *Modern Social Imaginaries* (Durham: Duke University Press, 2004) and Michael Warner, *Publics and Counterpublics* (Cambridge: Zone Books, 2003) – have fruitfully developed the notion of 'social imaginary' that was originally coined by Cornelius Castoriadis. There are important differences between these various theorizations of the 'social imaginary'. However, most agree on the importance of imagination as a 'third term' between the subject and the collective, the agent and those forces that act upon it. In addition, many do this in a more or less explicit attempt to escape the simplistic binary between idealism (in which beliefs and ideas drive social change) and materialism (in which experience and praxis are the engines for change).

2. Christopher Ash, *Job: The Wisdom of the Cross* (Wheaton: Crossway, 2014), 18–19, highlights the difference between two ways of asking hard questions about life and particularly about suffering. He says they can be asked from the safety of the 'armchair' at a distance from suffering or they can be asked from the 'wheelchair' by those intimately acquainted with suffering.

that unite doxology and an open-ended and costly commitment to the good of others (Chapter 8).

Importantly, however – and this is the second area of contribution – Barth reframes the importance of discipleship. Discipleship, on Barth's account, is more about Christ and less about us – the Christian community, ecclesial practices, obedience or even mission. Discipleship is the means by which Barth's actualistic and dialectical account of sanctification is dynamically coordinated with respect to the living presence of Christ. So it is not discipleship but Christology that is decisive in Barth's account of sanctification. In fact, the call of discipleship thematizes Christ's sovereign freedom, testifying primarily to him and only secondarily to the corresponding freedom disciples are summoned to in self-denial and enlistment in his 'kingdom onslaught' (Chapter 4). What is more, the dialectics of discipleship structure the eschatological realism, 'paradoxical identity', and governing christologized Pneumatology of his concept of correspondence (Chapters 5 and 6).

Discipleship provides Barth a way to resolve his preoccupation with correctly configuring the relationship between free and sovereign divine (initiating) action and genuine but dependent human (responding) action. The shaping of divine–human correspondence by means of the logic of discipleship safeguards the priority and non-interchangeable asymmetry between Christ and his people – even in their oneness and 'echoing' of him as they follow after him. Their freedom – and the integrity of their identity and action (and suffering) as his people – subsists in and exists only because of his freedom from and for them as their living Lord who calls and directs them by means of the 'formed reference' provided for them in Scripture. This is the key to its joyful character. In the freedom and power of the Spirit, disciples follow Christ – even in mortification and bearing their cross – not simply because they *must* but because they *can*. It is their privilege to correspond to their Master in discipleship.

Third, and as a result of this, Barth's approach to discipleship challenges and calls into question significant aspects of the contemporary turn to discipleship. Although neo-Anabaptists and those advocating various forms of new monasticism and the so-called Benedict Option differ significantly in their theologies and visions for the church and Christian life, they all share a tendency to accent the distinctiveness of Christian discipleship at the cost of engagement. Often they begin by registering the contemporary dislocation and loss of privilege the church faces as a social institution at the end of Christendom. But they then turn this (rightly named) social fact into a virtue. Discipleship is effectively defined by social or geographical distance from the surrounding culture – or, more usually, a particular aspect of it, whether consumerism or the military–industrial complex (in the case of neo-Anabaptism) or the 'agenda' of social progressives (as with the Benedict Option). As a result, the joy in following Christ in engaging with the world – and ultimately giving himself for its sake – which shines so clearly in Barth's discipleship-shaped approach, tends to disappear. In its place, there is the 'passive-aggressive ecclesiology', into which Hauerwas and others all too easily slip, and a sharp and totalizing negativity about present culture.

Discipleship leads to Christlike engagement with and self-giving for others when it is properly evangelical. It is evangelical insofar as it rises to the challenge of interpreting Christian distinctiveness in the light of God's action within the economy of creation and redemption. It can only do this by insisting that Christian distinctiveness is defined chiefly in relation to Christ rather than the culture (or cultures) in which Christians find themselves. In doing this, discipleship places self-giving at its heart. This contrasts with the tendency to self-assertion and self-protectiveness displayed by the neo-Anabaptists and others – a tendency that Hunter has shown frequently metastasizes into a negativity and inclination to demonize the prevailing culture (or aspects of it) that ironically mimics the prevailing cultural tone. At the same time, it contrasts with the kind of unintended self-betrayal that can befall Radical Orthodox and more 'missional' approaches to discipleship. The discipleship-shaped community and Christian life resists dissolving its distinctiveness by idolizing the culture of which it is a part, just as it refuses to artificially manufacture its distinctiveness by demonizing that culture – and, consequently, reifying its socially effected dislocation. Disciples receive their distinctiveness as a gift from Christ – and Christ's self-giving. What is more, Christ's holiness does not stand apart from unholiness but enters into it redemptively. He sanctifies himself as he engages with the world, giving himself in order to reconcile it. The church thus becomes a 'creaturely reflection' of his holiness as it echoes in its own being Christ's distinctive engagement in self-giving love.

10.2 Against *Barth on discipleship*

10.2.1 *The underdetermination of Barth's discipleship*

I need to offer a response to some problems with Barth's vision of discipleship – and with his own discipleship. My concern here is not so much the traditional objections to Barth's alleged lack of attention to the church and the Spirit, his supposed failure to do justice to human moral agency and his arguable inattention to the reality and structures of creation. I have already responded to a number of these. Nevertheless, some questions remain. The primary problem stems directly from the underdetermination of discipleship in Barth. While it is thoroughly determined by and anchored in Christ at one 'end', at the other 'end' – in relation to others in the church and the world – it is underdetermined. At one level, this underdetermination is an artefact of the unfinished nature of Barth's theological project in the *Church Dogmatics*, specifically in his development of an ethics of reconciliation to complete *CD* IV. Although Barth maintained that the decisions taken in the theological sections of the doctrine of reconciliation would necessarily work themselves out in the ethics, the task of translation is not simple. This is clear from the fragmentary nature of what we do have of *CD* IV/4 as well the tangible evidence of an unsatisfactorily concluded process of revision – as Barth continued wrestling to hold together various theological intuitions even in *The*

Christian Life. More than this, however, the underdetermination of discipleship for Barth actually follows from his stated conviction that dogmatics must remain intentionally circumscribed – even when it moves onto the terrain of Christian living. Theologians must not arrogate to themselves the work of God the Holy Spirit. This is the ultimate, theological reason why Barth is scathing about the expectation that he might give invariant answers – or an infallible mechanism for generating them – to the moral dilemmas thrown up in the ever-changing contexts and circumstances of life.

The underdetermination of Barth's discipleship-shaped vision of Christian living poses problems – especially when it comes to relating to others in a way that manifests the costly freedom to which Christ calls his people and for which the biblical texts provide 'formed reference'. His approach to discipleship is therefore open to misinterpretation and misappropriation. I have already explored how Barth was open to misunderstanding politically – precisely because of the kinds of convictions that shape his vision of discipleship (see 1.3 earlier). The more problematic aspect in the contemporary context concerns the way in which the underdetermination of discipleship may have left the door open to misappropriation in Barth's own interpersonal relationships. I need to explore this issue in order to establish the extent to which his theology of discipleship contains resources to mitigate this problem.

With regard to Barth's troubling and troubled interpersonal relationships, three potentially problematic aspects of Barth's account of discipleship are worth reviewing. First, Barth appears to privilege unilateral and hierarchical power relations – especially with regard to gender. Second, Barth's theological ethics allegedly fails to do justice to the concrete 'otherness' of others – assimilating them too quickly to the relativizing absolute otherness of Christ. Third, discipleship seems to lack specificity in rendering the commitment to other-regard at its heart.

10.2.2 Reading Barth against Barth on discipleship

Are there resources within Barth's own vision of discipleship that can help mitigate these three aspects of his own problematic discipleship?

To begin with, the treatment of discipleship in *CD* IV/2 can mitigate the tendency to privilege unilateral and hierarchical power relations. I have already discussed this (in 6.1 and 7.3), but it is important to register again what is achieved by means of the dogmatic location in which Barth places discipleship – namely, within his exposition of the exaltation of humanity in Christ. The note struck in his overview of the call in §66.3, and even more decisively in his exploration of bearing the cross in §66.6, resonates with the self-sacrificial emphasis of IV/1. This is evidence of thematic interlocking: the vision of the Christian life as suffering obedience in IV/1 aligns closely with the emphasis on self-denial and even death to self here in IV/2. However, I showed in the context of Barth's treatment of suffering that framing discipleship in terms of humanity's exaltation establishes a counterpoint to this. Barth's overarching emphasis in IV/2 falls on Christ's liberation and humanization of his disciples.

This liberationist and humanizing emphasis has been clear in the way Barth develops his discipleship-shaped account of sanctification. As we saw in the case of mortification, Barth is emphatic that putting sin to death belongs within and serves the wider, grander more obviously joyful cause of vivification. The old self is put to death by Christ's disciples not only because it is no longer their true self – for it is judged and condemned by Christ. More fundamentally, it is mortified because the new self given in Christ is their true self: 'So if anyone is in Christ, there is a new creation: everything old has passed away; see, everything has become new!' (2 Cor. 5.17). Likewise, Barth takes pains to underline the goodness of the works Christians have been called to do. It not just that they attract God's praise and approval as well as bring him praise and glory. It is also the case that the good works of Christians are suited and fitting for their being as creatures, making for life and peace in relation to their fellow creatures, fellow human beings and brothers and sisters in Christ. Finally, Barth's climactic presentation of the cruciformity of discipleship in §66.6 is bound together with his insistence on the penultimate status of the suffering and endurance discipleship entails. It is not God's deepest intention for Christians to suffer – as much as it dignifies disciples to follow after their Master in bearing the cross. Indeed, Barth maintains that suffering has no positive value in itself. Rather, God's ultimate intention for disciples of Christ is a share in the eschatological crown and triumph of Christ.

Framing discipleship as the penultimate form of Christ's sanctifying work takes in the lives and relationships of his people, and this is the first significant resource Barth's vision affords us for mitigating its underdetermination. In inculcating an eager anticipation of the eschatological restoration of humanity, it arms us to resist anything that would corrode or corrupt the humanity of human persons now – whether from the encroachment of political absolutism (of whatever stripe) or from Barth's own failures to specify and develop the oneness and mutuality of human persons in marriage (or anywhere else). To be clear: at this point, Barth failed to live out consistently his own vision of discipleship. He stood clearly against dehumanization at the political level in his post-War stance towards communism and capitalism just as he did in drafting the *Barmen Declaration*. But at the interpersonal level, his self-justifications and at times heavy-handed pressuring of Charlotte and Nelly to maintain their painful arrangement did not display the requisite resistance to dehumanization.

Another resource Barth's theology of discipleship makes available to mitigate its underdetermination stems from its actualization of Christ's living direction and call. Barth draws confession, worship and attentive openness to the disruptive grace of Christ into the heart of his vision of Christian living. Discipleship unites doxology and formation for tangible, distinctive Christian living within Barth's actualized vision of sanctification. Discipleship does this by de-centring the self of the disciple. The living Lord Jesus Christ, not the disciple, is at the centre of discipleship. Disciples are summoned to attend primarily to him, priming them to be surprised and challenged by his call to costly freedom – which will be consistent with but not limited by his call in the past and in other circumstances. Discipleship makes 'enlistment' in Christ's idol- and ideology-unmasking kingdom agenda fundamental to sanctification. The costly freedom to which Christ calls his disciples involves death to self as well as exposing the demonic distortion that comes with an idolatrous elevation of created things – even good things like wealth, reputation, power and belonging. In demanding that disciples take their bearings from the ultimate otherness of Christ, the self is not elevated or the otherness of concrete human others dissolved. Rather, they are reframed and 'right-sized'. Discipleship contradicts the self's tendency to adopt god-like proportions at the same time as it undermines the pretensions of others – including family and tribe – to divinity. Apart from Christ, an orientation towards either self or others is always potentially imprisoning: an ideology that licenses violence and dehumanization in its name. But discipleship issues a summons to freedom and resistance in the name of Christ. As a result, Barth's vision of discipleship inculcates an appropriate self-suspicion, alerting those who take it up to their own tendency towards self-assertion.

The final significant resource Barth's account of discipleship affords for mitigating its problematic underdetermination centres on how it refuses to play off a supposedly strict adherence to Christ against an allegedly more lax sensitivity to context. Discipleship structures the 'correspondence' between God's free action in Christ and human freedom in responding to his call in such a way that the open-endedness of Barth's moral vision with respect to others cannot be played off against its focused determination with respect to Christ. Discipleship may be underdetermined for Barth, but it is not formless or totally unspecified. In fact, Barth is willing to provide a great deal of specificity – or rather to allow Christ to do so. The 'narrative turn' in Barth's Christology is mirrored by the admirably concrete renderings of discipleship as we have seen in relation to the 'kingdom onslaught' against the tendency of good, created things to become imprisoning when idolatrously distorted. Furthermore, the 'formed reference' Barth sees the New Testament providing for Christian living is open-ended precisely in order to summon disciples to *more costly* and *more free* moral action. Applied to the problem of his own interpersonal relationships, even an appeal to the unfixed nature of discipleship cannot be used to excuse his conduct; if anything, it does the opposite – for discipleship is underdetermined so that Christ may ask more of his people not less.

In an important sense, this way of viewing the resources provided by Barth's use of the logic of discipleship to structure divine–human correspondence – and his resulting reticence to overdetermine other-regard – is actually what primes it to be truly other-regarding. Discipleship is open to others precisely because it refuses to dictate in too concrete terms how we should act towards them. Indeed, the disciples' correspondence with Christ is oriented to being with others rather than doing-for them. Structured by the logic of discipleship as it is, those who correspond to Christ relinquish the urgency to take the lead and occupy pride of place – or otherwise assert themselves – in acting for others. Instead, they turn to Christ, calling upon him as the Master and primary agent in working what is good for others. It is unsurprising therefore that 'invocation' provides the organizing principle for Barth's ethics of reconciliation in *The Christian Life*.

In summary, Barth must be read against Barth – especially in relation to the problematic areas where his vision of discipleship is open to misinterpretation and misappropriation. But when we do this with the grain of Barth's own theological instincts and resources, some of these problems can be successfully mitigated.

10.3 Beyond *Barth on discipleship*

The time has come to move beyond Barth, mobilizing the resources Barth provides to articulate a vision of discipleship that is important but not everything ethically, that is about Christ before it is about us and that strikes a note of evangelical joy in self-giving for the sake of others. As a sample, I will consider two key issues that take us well beyond Barth. The first issue is the perennial question about whether theological education is chiefly a matter of belief or behaviour, head or habits, theology or practice. The second is the question of the stance discipleship appropriately takes when it comes to those who suffer – such that it speaks not only to those with agency but also listens to those who appear to be deprived of agency. In the first, I consider the case of theological education. In the second, I consider the issue of ageing.

10.3.1 Discipleship, theological education and the 'social imaginary'

Is theological education chiefly about informing the mind or policing the performance of certain behaviours? Is its aim to shape beliefs and world view or to inculcate habits and ensure practical conformity?

Drawing on the resources identified in this book, I propose that a discipleship-shaped approach to theological education would attempt to access the 'social imaginary'. This proposal builds upon Geoff Thompson's advocacy of a reimagined relationship between systematic and practical theology, which abandons the oppositional approach resting on the discredited theory/practice binary in order to coordinate the two distinct disciplines in service to the church's 'social imaginary'. Thompson draws on the notion of the 'social imaginary' popularized by philosopher Charles Taylor to describe the 'largely unstructured and inarticulate understanding of our whole situation, within which particular features of our world show up for us in the sense they have'. Thompson acknowledges that systematic and practical theologies have differing emphases as well as their own disciplinary traditions and canons. Yet both disciplines require more than they can supply on their own terms to properly form the community's social imaginary. Systematics must reach beyond its traditional commitment to rational coherence and (attempted) finality, embracing correction and redirection by the impulse towards 'openness' embodied in practical theology. Likewise, practical theology must reach beyond its commitment to contextual 'openness to the particular work of God in given times and places' in order to anchor itself in the commitment to 'totality' that characterizes systematics.³ As a result, the two disciplines serve the church's social imaginary when they are dialectically related to each other, allowing their impulses towards 'totality' and 'openness' to critique, guide and shape each other.

I suggest that discipleship as I have developed it in this book can help coordinate systematic and practical theology in their mutual service of the church's social imaginary. Discipleship implies a methodological commitment to an eschatological realism that centres on Christ. Both the more characteristically systematic task of deriving dogmatic categories from the biblical witness to Christ and the more recognizably practical task of analogically redescribing human life and experience with reference to it are entirely relative to Christ. As such, discipleship summons both disciplines – systematics and practical theology – to the recognition of their limits upon which their fruitful coordination depends. A discipleship-shaped approach makes the reciprocity of systematics and practical theology intrinsic to each discipline; it is not something that must be imposed upon them from outside for it arises natively and organically as both are understood to stem from the same christological root.

Moreover, a discipleship-shaped approach entails the rendering of both systematics and practical theology in christological terms. This underscores their unity at a formal level, establishing their partnership in serving the church. It does this, by relating them not directly to the church but indirectly to it; for they are directly related to the one in whom the church subsists, who actively rules and governs his people as he creates, sustains and directs them in their correspondence to him. Such is the 'paradoxical identity' entailed by discipleship. This applies not only to disciples in their practical life as they (asymmetrically and non-interchangeably) follow after the Master with whom they are one. It also applies to their intellectual lives and the shared projects of systematics and practical theology. This not only secures their oneness – since both are oriented to and given form by Christ, and therefore serve him. It also upholds their integrity as disciplines and practices of the church. Crucially, this discipleship-shaped approach differs from any vision of systematics and practical theology that relate these disciplines directly to the church. On such accounts, these theological disciplines are either illegitimately enthroned or degraded and instrumentalized. They are illegitimately enthroned when they implicitly displace Christ as the living presence and voice dictating the church's true identity and proper activity. They are degraded and instrumentalized when they are made to answer entirely to the current preoccupations of the church – for instance to simply explaining or legitimizing them. In coordinating both around Christ, by contrast, a discipleship-shaped approach liberates the theological disciplines to serve the church by challenging and correcting it, its practices and its preoccupations just as much as by justifying and underwriting them. It does this because it insists that

---

3. Thompson, 'The Doctrines of Practical Theology', 32.

the disciplines of systematic and practical theology – like the disciples who both practice them and constitute the church – find their true life and centre not inside but outside themselves in Christ.

Ultimately, the approach I am advocating here summons systematics and practical theology to their most distinctive common work in response to the present direction of the living Lord Jesus. Discipleship does this by virtue of the christologized Pneumatology that materially governs Christian living. It demands more than simple cognizance of the static person and finished work of Christ in the past – looking back to him in his absence and seeking to apply his past achievement. It must be governed by more than a Christology that claims so much finality that there is no room left for Pneumatology and the present action of God; for Christ, as he promised, is present among his church in and through the Spirit. A discipleship-shaped approach to theological work must begin ever anew with attentiveness to the living Lord Jesus Christ. The one to whom it witnesses is living and present with his people (as he promised). At the same time, a discipleship-shaped approach to the theological disciplines demands nothing less than attention to Christ's unrepeatable history and action. It cannot be governed by a Pneumatology detached from and undisciplined by Christology; for the Spirit is the Spirit of Christ. As a result, the Spirit's free agency and activity is identical with that of the living Lord who is the same yesterday, today and forever. He is not only the beginning but also the end of theological work: the omega as well as the alpha. Any theological formulation – whether of practical or systematic theology – answers to and must be tested against the definitive status of Christ in his constancy. He is the one to whom theological work must witness, whether carried out in systematic or practical theological terms.

In the light of this discipleship-shaped vision, it becomes clear that the aspiration of systematics to 'totality' of description contains an unavoidable temptation to finality, to focus so exclusively on the past as to leave the present entirely undetermined theologically. Insofar as systematic theology remains oriented exclusively to the past – whether by ceding the present to an independent prophecy, or to a freestanding homiletics or to an unprincipled pragmatism – it fails to respond to the summons to witness. The merely intellectual work of informing the mind about what God has done in a hermetically sealed past can overshadow the present task of responding and corresponding to the living Lord Jesus. Equally, the aspirations of practical theology to 'openness' carry with them a temptation. This temptation is to treat attentiveness to what it supposes God to be doing in the present – typically by means of a 'de-christologized' Spirit – as sovereign, self-enclosed and all-encompassing. But it is precisely the Spirit's work to break open the self-enclosed circle of the present by mediating the presence of the future and establishing the penultimate status of the church in light of the eschaton, which is secured decisively not by the present but by the resurrection of Christ in the past. The practical work of shaping the present behaviour of the church in a contextually sensitive way can displace faithfulness to Christ's self-disclosure, sabotaging our witness. Theology thus conceived risks becoming a mere mirror to the contemporary culture rather than offering anything new or distinctive as it points to the Christ who sovereignly encloses and actively breaks into it in saving power.

In order to answer to this simultaneously more-than-merely-intellectual and more-than-simply-pragmatic vision, the disciplines of systematic and practical theology must be governed by a christologized Pneumatology in a manner consistent with their character as expressions of discipleship. Jesus, in his unique and unrepeatable history – as well as his surprising but thoroughly consistent contemporary agency and activity – must be the point of reference for both disciplines if they are to serve the church in a meaningful way. The fundamental ecclesial (and missional) service of any theological discipline is to witness to Christ, directing the church to him and priming it to attend to him and his call to join him in self-giving for the sake of the world. In other words, to function rightly, the disciplines of systematic and practical theology must be stretched between a worshipful orientation to Christ and a correspondence to him in other-regard. And it is their assimilation to the paradigm of discipleship that ensures this.

In this way, a discipleship-shaped vision of theological education not only coordinates the chiefly but not exclusively intellectual work of systematic theology with the chiefly but not exclusively pragmatic work of practical theology. It also moves beyond the popular opposition of head and habits – informing beliefs and world view on the one hand and dictating behaviour and specific actions on the other. A discipleship-shaped approach does this by virtue of its methodological, formal and material dimensions; for it attunes the disciplines of theology to the social imaginary of the church by summoning them to take their bearings from, serve and witness to Christ in his definitive and contemporary identity and activity. These disciplines serve the church insofar as they reflect Christ's call to follow him in being oriented not simply to the church but also to its Lord and the world he claims.

10.3.2 Discipleship and the 'evangelization' of generational difference

The second question I will answer – moving beyond Barth by utilizing the resources Barth's account of discipleship provides – concerns the status of those who suffer. The question is: what does discipleship mean not only for those who indisputably possess agency but also for those who are apparently deprived of it? How can discipleship contribute to the 'evangelization' of differences between people of differing socio-economic or political statuses, genders or ethnicities? This question has been treated in relation to refugees – the prototypical 'victimized' figure in contemporary political discourse – with a similar sensibility to that which I am advocating here.[4] It has also been treated in substantially overlapping ways with regard to ethnic and gender differences.[5] Therefore, I will bring the resources

---

4. Luke Bretherton, 'The Duty of Care to Refugees, Christian Cosmopolitanism, and the Hallowing of Bare Life', *Studies in Christian Ethics* 19.1 (2006): 39–61.

5. See, for example, Volf, *Exclusion and Embrace*, chapters 1 and 4.

of this vision of discipleship to bear on the social category of intergenerational relations.

The question of intergenerational relations is one about which traditional theological ethics has not been entirely silent – although much of its energy has been directed to the moral issues and quandaries surrounding the beginnings and ends of life. In contrast to such traditional approaches, contemporary social and anthropological research highlights the significance of the unprecedented reality of the 'long dying' that faces those who are ageing in the late-modern West.[6] One anthropologically engaged Christian ethicist points out that the two most 'highly visible cultural forms' of dying – the hospice and euthanasia – share much in common, notwithstanding the way they are 'typically presented as in deep contention with each other'.[7] Both share a 'critique of medicalization', for example, as well as a 'concern for the preservation of a self-conscious narrative and agency in dying'. In addition, they both share a 'joint inapplicability to the "long dying" which is increasingly characteristic of the affluent West'.[8] We lack adequate social 'scripts' for slow dwindling in physical and mental capacities. And far more abrupt scenarios are presupposed by the discourses of hospice care and euthanasia. Attention to the actual lived texture of dying suggests that we draw upon traditions and resources that have largely been absent from the discussion of end-of-life issues in ethics – resources such as the reconfiguration of the Christian imagination of the human that accompanied the 'discovery of Christ's sufferings' in iconography, art and devotional literature.[9]

The discipleship-shaped vision I have developed could further resource this insofar as it displaces the intellect from its traditional tyranny.[10] Christ's call to discipleship addresses not only those who for the moment retain full command of all their faculties (which all of us more or less inevitably forfeit in time), but also all whose inclusion in his sanctifying work is actualized by his call to follow him. This accommodates the recognition that the 'scriptless deaths' of late modernity 'seem to be fated to be preceded by "death before death", whether that death is decreed by a supposed medical necessity (Alzheimer's), or by current patterns of social exclusion (as in the old people's home)'.[11] Having recognized this, a discipleship-shaped approach might draw on the resources Christian liturgy and theology offer – gathering around a common and inclusive table, witnessing to a unique and universal Lord, and so on – to facilitate 'a ministry to the bitterness and despair and loneliness of many in the long dwindlings to death which mark our late modern

---

6. Michael Banner, *The Ethics of Everyday Life: Moral Theology, Social Anthropology, and the Imagination of the Human* (Oxford: OUP, 2014), chapter 5.

7. Banner, *The Ethics of Everyday Life*, 114.

8. Banner, *The Ethics of Everyday Life*, 107.

9. Banner, *The Ethics of Everyday Life*, 109.

10. Swinton explores the resources discipleship offers along such lines in *Becoming Friends of Time*.

11. Banner, *The Ethics of Everyday Life*, 133.

dyings'.¹² In this way, the difference between those (temporarily) retaining their agency and integrity and those who have lost it – or are in the process of losing it – becomes an opportunity to witness to the good and life-giving news of Jesus' work and lordship. Life and inclusion thereby replaces death and exclusion.

What is more, discipleship summons Christ's people to a solidarity and an underdetermined openness to others that prepares them to be with and learn from others and not only to serve and do for them. This includes learning from those who suffer and are socially excluded – including those facing the 'long dying'. As such, discipleship primes those adopting this approach to difference to embrace the perspective Oliver O'Donovan offers on ageing at the end of *Entering into Rest* (2017). There, O'Donovan names the characteristic temptations facing those who are ageing in the late-modern West, moving beyond seeing it simply as 'an individualized, biological/medical experience' towards also understanding it as 'a social phenomenon of oppression, marginalization, and exclusion' much like disability.¹³ Consequently, O'Donovan addresses the temptation faced by those who are ageing to cling to economic and social position as well as the tendency to either reify the differences between generations (thus obstructing the possibility of intergeneration communication) or to obliterate them by exploiting every technological, medical and cultural resource in a quest to deny death.

In light of such tendencies and temptations, the approach to discipleship I have developed recognizes that those suffering the 'long dying' are genuinely entitled to claim at least some degree of victimization – especially if a systematic and social reading of the phenomenon is adopted alongside an individual and medical one. Discipleship summons us to humanize those who suffer by granting dignity to their suffering rather than denying or demonizing it. However, a discipleship-shaped approach grants this dignity in light of eternity, hoping for the ultimate consummation of the exaltation of humanity when Christ returns to crown his own and wipe away every tear. It is this hope that can pull the sting from intergenerational differences without denying that they are real and (relatively) significant. It can do this because it declines to universalize the experience and context of one generation against another. As a result, discipleship teaches us what following Jesus means for and from those facing the 'long dying' as well towards them. This resists the tendency to insist that the older generation's way is infallibly right and everything new constitutes a falling away from it, therefore calling us to avoid digging in to defend our generational turf. At the same time, it summons us not to give up on the task of intergenerational communication – even if we have to cede control and stand to one side. Disciples cannot absolutize their generational context. Christ is the reference point for discipleship, not 'my' generation (or any other). Equally, a discipleship-shaped vision resists treating the experience and perspective of the upcoming generation as normative. While ageing disciples must not close themselves off from seeking to learn from and understand the world

---

12. Banner, *The Ethics of Everyday Life*, 134.
13. Yong, *The Bible, Disability, and the Church*, 126.

of younger people – changed as it inevitably is – neither need they wish away the differences between their generation and the next. No generation's context is absolute, but neither is it unreal. Indeed, it is one venue within which following after Jesus takes concrete shape. Under God, different generations live alongside one another – amidst all their differences – as a gift of grace in order to bring life to each other, whether through the 'energy' younger people bring to the tasks and projects of life or through the 'experience' borne by older people (with all its potential to bestow wisdom on others).[14]

In the case of intergenerational relations as in that of theological education, discipleship affords significant resources to address concrete concerns raised in the contemporary context. It offers clarity by anchoring moral agency, activity and passivity in Christ, from whom all must take their bearings in approaching such concerns. Likewise, it primes us for contextual sensitivity through its deliberately underdetermined and circumscribed approach. Corresponding to Christ in discipleship, Christian living is 'evangelized' and set free; for Christ breaks into its self-enclosed circle and breaks it open towards others in self-giving love.

10.4 The theological significance of discipleship

Discipleship provides a theologically rich, materially christological and consequently deeply practical resource for Christian living in post-Christian contexts. Crucially, it upholds and reframes Barth's notorious emphasis on the definiteness of the divine command or 'direction'. Put provocatively, the central claim of this book is that what many fault in Barth is the key to the promise of his discipleship-shaped theology of sanctification. My argument may thus be read as a contribution to the project of clarifying and sympathetically restating Barth's vision in order to deflect such criticisms. At a deeper level, however, I simply concur with his critics in their descriptions – or, perhaps better, with the essential intuitions these descriptions express – while nevertheless dissenting from their evaluation.

Barth relentlessly refuses to privilege human action, interpretation or reflection in construing sanctification in terms of discipleship. Nevertheless, in relativizing human action and interpretation like this, Barth upholds its creaturely reality rather than abolishing it. In insisting that it follows *Christ*, discipleship-shaped human agency, action and suffering *follow* Christ all the same. Chapter 3 established that Barth's turn to discipleship grows organically in the soil of the lively Christology that dominates IV/2, towering over his theology of sanctification. According to Barth, discipleship is first about Christ and only secondarily – and by an intensification of this – about us. The burden of that chapter was therefore to indicate how the turn to discipleship is the consummation of Barth's revision of

---

14. O'Donovan's discussion of the 'energy' of youth and 'experience' of age draws on Proverbs 20.29.

sanctification rather than a departure from it. Chapters 4 and 5 developed this – first by showing how Barth's account of discipleship in §66.3 thematizes freedom, for both Christ and his people, and second by analysing how the dialectics of discipleship explicitly structure Barth's important concept of 'correspondence' in §66.6, enabling him to properly configure the divine–human analogy that is one of his enduring preoccupations (as we saw in Chapter 6). Discipleship begins with the recognition that Christ is *the* exalted human being. At the same time, Christ represents and includes us. We are exalted in him, participating in the perfection of our humanity as it is raised to covenant partnership with God, responding and corresponding to Christ in the power of the Spirit. Discipleship therefore proves to be deeply consistent with Barth's mature theological vision. This is because it entails a turning to the God who has already decisively turned to us.

Chapters 7, 8 and 9 found that a distinctive account of moral agency, moral activity and moral passivity (or suffering) emerged from Barth's discipleship-shaped theology of sanctification. Once again, discipleship's theological significance for Barth is the way it keeps Christ at the centre of sanctified Christian living (as the Master) while simultaneously upholding the human reality and integrity of those who are united with Christ (as his disciples). The brief interventions earlier in this concluding chapter suggest some ways in which this discipleship-shaped theology of sanctification can take us with and beyond Barth into contemporary conversations. A christologically determined and evangelical account of discipleship can also work against Barth, mitigating the problems evident in his own personal discipleship, as well as taking us beyond him into some key challenges brought into focus by the contemporary discipleship conversation.

10.4.1 Discipleship in Barth studies

In light of my focus on the theological significance of discipleship in Barth's doctrine of sanctification, it is appropriate to consider the contribution of this to Barth studies. Three key areas have emerged.

First, I have provided a thoroughgoing appreciation of the integration of the discipleship theme with Barth's theology of sanctification. The existing English-language literature on Barth's theology of sanctification does at times acknowledge the prominence of discipleship in this context. However, it tends to either invest Barth's turn to discipleship with undue significance – for example, in seeing it as a basic departure from his otherwise more recognizably Reformed thinking (whether as part of a 'Free Church' turn or in some sort of post-metaphysical rapprochement with Weslyianism) – or underestimate the positive importance of this moment – for example, treating it as primarily polemical or defensive in ensuring that participation in Christ is interpreted ethically rather than mystically or sacramentally. In contrast to both of these tendencies, I have shown that discipleship plays a positive role within Barth's vision of sanctification. Specifically, it develops the 'theoretical Christocentrism' of §66.1-2 in the direction of a far more 'practical Christocentrism' that overlaps conceptually with more Anabaptist and Wesleyan accounts of sanctification, accommodating their concerns with human agency and tangible action, without abandoning its Calvinian and Lutheran heritage – particularly their shared emphasis on divine initiative and the completeness of Christ's reconciling work.

My emphasis on the integration of discipleship with Barth's wider theology of sanctification speaks to one of the most controversial issues in Barth's moral theology – namely, the issue of the definiteness of the divine command. Barth's elaboration of the discipleship image beyond its very brief treatment in *CD* II/2 §37.2 upholds the freedom and presence of Christ at the same time as it does justice to the relative reality of the Christian's responsive moral agency. This bears on the definiteness of the divine command because the discipleship theme as Barth develops successfully supplements the explicitly ethical material in the *Church Dogmatics*. Unlike other proposals – which seek to leverage other moments within Barth's comprehensive redescription of human experience in an attempt to counterbalance his perceived lopsidedness with regard to Christ's authority[15] – discipleship does not smooth the sharp edges of Barth's emphasis on the definiteness of the divine command, itself a by-product of his relentless and polemical thematization of the sovereign freedom and presence of Christ. Rather, it reframes it. What is more, it accomplishes this dual task coherently and with an overt biblical anchor.

The second contribution my book makes to Barth studies centres on its characterization of Barth as a theologian. My book confirms and extends the consensus in Barth scholarship about the ethical character of his theology and the theological character of his ethics. Discipleship for Barth addresses Renaissance questions about ethics and what it means to be human on the terms of the Reformation. This theological approach to the questions of ethics and the human is especially evident when it comes to Barth's handling of Bonhoeffer and the precedent set by his work on discipleship. I have shown that Bonhoeffer's work on discipleship is catalytic for Barth. While it is more than simply the occasion for him to articulate his own characteristic concerns, Barth does not take over Bonhoeffer without critical modification. In particular, he is careful to reframe Bonhoeffer's emphasis on the costliness of discipleship within a larger vision of the freedom of Christ and the (corresponding) freedom into which Christ calls his disciples. Barth engages with the biblical discipleship texts to fill out his vision in a way that accommodates Bonhoeffer's ethical emphasis as part of his more expansive, liberative and ultimately theological vision of sanctification. Paradigmatic in this regard is the way Barth construes the New Testament discipleship texts as providing 'formed reference' for contemporary Christian living. Barth's turn to discipleship ensures that his thinking about sanctification remains both theological and ethical, reflecting his prioritization of faithfulness to the *Sache* of the biblical witness – specifically, to God's gracious and authoritative self-revelation in the Christ, the holy one – as well as his seriousness about the human and ethical arena in which sanctification must be lived.

---

15. Both Massmann and Sonderegger advance versions of this solution.

Third, the theological significance of discipleship in Barth's theology of sanctification contributes to the emerging conversation around how to read and evaluate Barth in light of his own mixed record of discipleship. On the one hand, it clarifies a frequently misunderstood aspect of his political theology. Barth was consistent in opposing all forms of ideology – whether fascist, communist or liberal. Christ's call to discipleship enlists his people in the 'kingdom onslaught' against all idolatrous 'given factors', including political authorities and systems that implicitly or explicitly divinize themselves. On the other hand, Barth's thinking about discipleship – especially as it is situated within the overarching emphasis of IV/2 on the exaltation of humanity in Christ – provides a standard against which his own discipleship can be measured (and found wanting) at the same time as it offers resources for resisting his own theology's openness to misappropriation and abuse. In the context of the ongoing, public conversations about the intersection of gender relations and power both within and outside the church, Barth's thinking about discipleship can be drawn on to mitigate to the problematic construal of gender relations in his mature theology. According to Barth, discipleship demands death to self, and this death to self cannot be limited to one gender or be twisted by the other gender to bolster its power and privilege. At the same time, the way in which Barth brings together the intrinsically active response to Christ that discipleship demands, and suffering as an inescapable and constitutive aspect of human moral agency, attunes it to the concerns and questions of those who need liberating (including women) without implying that any are pure victims or pure oppressors. In both of these ways, Barth's thinking about discipleship is intrinsically humanizing, resisting attempts to dehumanize others – and therefore implicitly criticizing Barth's own interpersonal compromise.

10.4.2 Discipleship and Christian living

Regarding the final and constructive task of mobilizing Barth's theology of discipleship to inform contemporary practice, what can be learnt from Barth when it comes to talking about and pursuing discipleship? Or, more sharply, what questions may we pose to the contemporary discipleship conversation now that we have listened carefully to Barth? After considering these questions, I close by offering several observations about how a theology of discipleship constructed along similar lines to Barth's can resource Christian living in 'post-Christian' contexts.

The first significant aspect of Barth's theology of discipleship for the contemporary discipleship conversation is counterintuitive: discipleship is *not* everything for Barth. He does not allow discipleship to swallow up ecclesiology or Christian living – let alone the theme of sanctification. It is important to learn from this. Discipleship, according to Barth, belongs within the economy of God's dealings in creation and redemption, which attain their climax and point of focus in the living Lord Jesus. As such, discipleship must not speak of itself but rather of Christ, his freedom, his presence and his call to correspond to him in freedom. Discipleship is properly evangelical – and therefore practical – when it is properly theological. This is because it is only when it is properly theological that it resists being pressed into service as a covert means of smuggling moralism back into the Christian life, even in the name of the urgent need to take action. All the same, discipleship is not an open door for licence. Rather, the freedom to which Christ summons his people in discipleship has a concrete form and a definite shape, which it gains in reference to him. Supremely, discipleship means corresponding to Christ in bearing the cross – that is, suffering in 'paradoxical identity' with him: like him and yet unlike him. Such correspondence is an echo and aftershock in human life of the seismic shift effected in our place by Christ. Even in suffering, then, discipleship speaks above all of Jesus.

The second significant aspect of Barth's theology of discipleship complements the first aspect: while discipleship is not everything it *is* something. Discipleship sheds fresh light on sanctification, proving more than merely illustrative. It is not the case that everything that needs to be said about sanctification is already said when themes from Paul and John have been considered. Its proper theological stress on Christ – and the living, present Christ in particular – demands a practical human correspondence. He calls in sovereign and life-giving freedom; we answer and are set free to follow after him. Discipleship therefore opens up new vistas on sanctified moral agency, activity and passivity. Specifically, it binds the church and Christian living to Christ, insisting on our attentiveness to his living presence as the determining factor in the moral landscape. In doing this, discipleship does not leave us with nothing to do; rather, it mobilizes our responsive agency and activity – including our interpretive activity in discernment. Discipleship moves beyond a fundamentalist concern with mere fidelity to Scripture. Discipleship is not a matter of aping the actions we read of in the New Testament. Nor is it a matter of attempting to establish the relevance of the New Testament vision for our contemporary contexts, either ignoring or declaring morally insignificant any aspects that do not fit. Equally, discipleship moves beyond the post-liberal desire to allow the story of God – especially as it is embodied in the community, liturgy and practices of the church – to 'absorb' the world. Even if it is not morally decisive, the hermeneutic labour of reflecting on our context cannot be short-circuited within the logic of discipleship – just as the responsibility for obedient, responsive action cannot be abdicated because Christ is the primary, initiating agent. The theological significance of discipleship in Barth is that Christ's agency as Master, calling his people to follow after him, entails the responsive agency of his disciples, who hear and heed his call – even as they discern what in their life and context must be put to death and resisted in the name of the life and freedom he grants them.

Barth's theology of discipleship, understood in the terms of this book, provides a resource for Christian living in contemporary post-Christendom contexts such as Australia. It can do this in a number of ways. For instance, this approach to discipleship can prompt churches to seek their point of reference in Christ when it comes to cultural participation, rather than either a trend within or aspect of the culture they are drawn towards or – as is often the case – repulsed by. In 'post-Christian' contexts, in which churches have lost social position and privilege (just as the Christian faith has lost discursive supremacy and shaping power on the social imaginary), churches face a twin temptation. They may either seek to recoup lost prestige by trumpeting their conformity with some aspect of the culture or they may boast in being countercultural for its own sake – effectively demonizing the culture in whole or in part. In contrast, discipleship-shaped churches will turn to the Lord Jesus who gave himself – and even gave himself up to death out of love for his enemies. In doing this, such church will resist the twin temptations of the context by engaging in confession and the honest admission of their brokenness and entanglement with sin. Discipleship-shaped churches do not seek to commend themselves or condemn the culture, but instead look to Christ, acknowledging their failure and need for him – and also for each other – as it speaks to and shows others what they are discovering to be true in the presence of their living Lord and in the company of his disciples. They will, in short, adhere to the theological orientation of the *Barmen Declaration*: 'Jesus Christ, as he is attested for us in Holy Scripture, is the one Word of God which we have to hear and which we have to trust and obey in life and in death.'[16]

Likewise, as Christians seek to discern what kinds of activities to engage in and what projects to pursue, a discipleship-shaped approach will insist that worship, prayer and attentiveness to Scripture belong at the heart of their ethics. Even if such things are not sufficient, they cannot be dispensed with by any community or Christian longing to be faithful in discipleship. Such a 'Barthian' approach can resource Christian living in a post-Christian context for it will prepare the church to suffer. Barth's discipleship-shaped vision of suffering never allows the church a persecution complex, in which any instance of perceived hostility is magnified to cosmic proportions. Rather, Barth's approach again focuses attention on the Master, who suffered as the representative (and therefore the substitute) for his people. His suffering did have cosmic significance. Barth insists that Christ's suffering was unique, unrepeatable and enduring in its effects. At the same time, his 'lively Christology' means that the Christ who suffered like this for all calls his disciples to follow after him and share in his suffering as they walk in his footsteps. Discipleship ensures that Christ remains the reference point for all of Christian living. Christ forgives and frees us so that we can correspond to him in joyful, liberated conformity to his self-giving. Again, the *Barmen Declaration* captures this: 'As Jesus Christ is God's assurance of the forgiveness of all our sins, so in the same way and with the same seriousness is he also God's mighty claim upon our whole life. Through him befalls us a joyful deliverance from the godless fetters of this world for a free, grateful service to his creatures.'[17] This is how Barth's theology of discipleship provides a richly theological, materially christological and consequently profoundly practical resource for Christian living.

---

16. 'The Theological Declaration of Barmen', Article 1, in Arthur C. Cochrane, *The Church's Confession Under Hitler* (Philadelphia: Westminster Press, 1962), 240.

17. 'The Theological Declaration of Barmen', Article 2, in Cochrane, *The Church's Confession Under Hitler*, 240.

BIBLIOGRAPHY

Adorno, T. W. 'Late Style in Beethoven, 1937'. In *Essays on Music*, edited by Richard Leppert. Translated by Susan H. Gillespie. Berkeley: University of California Press, 2002.
Allison, D. C., and W. D. Davies. *The Gospel of Matthew 8-18*. London: T&T Clark, 2004.
Anderson, B. *Imagined Communities: Reflections on the Origin and Spread of Nationalism*. Rev. edn. London: Verso, 1991.
Arendt, H. *The Human Condition*. 2nd edn. Chicago: University of Chicago Press, 1998.
Ash, C. *Job: The Wisdom of the Cross*. Wheaton: Crossway, 2014.
Augsburger, D. *Dissident Discipleship: A Spirituality of Self-Surrender, Love of God, and Love of Neighbor*. Grand Rapids: Brazos, 2006.
Balke, W. *Calvin and the Anabaptist Radicals*. Translated by William Heymen. Grand Rapids: Eerdmans, 1981.
Balthasar, H. U. *The Theology of Karl Barth: Exposition and Interpretation*. Translated by Edward T. Oakes. San Francisco: Ignatius Press, 1992.
Banner, M. *Christian Ethics and Contemporary Moral Problems*. Cambridge: Cambridge University Press, 1999.
Banner, M. *Christian Ethics: A Brief History*. Chichester: Wiley-Blackwell, 2009.
Banner, M. *The Ethics of Everyday Life: Moral Theology, Social Anthropology, and the Imagination of the Human*. Oxford: Oxford University Press, 2014.
Barclay, J. G. M. 'Faith and Self-Detachment from Cultural Norms: A Study in Romans 14-15'. *Zeitschrift für die Neutestamentliche Wissenschaft und die Kunde der Älteren Kirche*. Volume 104.2 (2013): 192-208.
Barclay, J. M. G. *Paul and the Gift*. Grand Rapids: Eerdmans, 2015.
Barns, I. 'Towards an Australian Post-Constantinian Public Theology'. In *Faith and Freedom: Christian Ethics in a Pluralist Culture*, edited by David Neville and Philip Matthews, 175-94. Adelaide: ATF Press, 2003.
Barth, K. *Der Römerbrief*. 1st edn. Zürich: Theologischer Verlag Zürich, 1919.
Barth, K. *Theological Existence Today: A Plea for Theological Freedom*. Translated by R. Birch Hoyle. London: Hodder & Stoughton, 1933.
Barth, K. *The Knowledge of God and the Service of God according to the Teaching of the Reformation: Recalling the Scottish Confessions of 1560*. Translated by J. L. M. Haire and I. Henderson. London: Hodder & Stoughton, 1938.
Barth, K. *The Epistle to the Romans*. 6th edn. Translated by Edwyn C. Hoskyns. London: Oxford University Press, 1968.
Barth, K. *The Christian Life: Church Dogmatics IV, 4. Lecture Fragments*. Translated by Geoffrey W. Bromiley. Grand Rapids: Eerdmans, 1981.
Barth, K. *The Göttingen Dogmatics: Instruction in the Christian Religion*. Volume 1. Translated by Geoffrey W. Bromiley. Grand Rapids: Eerdmans, 1991.
Barth, K. *The Theology of John Calvin*. Translated by Geoffrey W. Bromiley. Grand Rapids: Eerdmans, 1995.

Barth, K. *The Word of God and Theology*. Translated by Amy Marga. New York: T&T Clark, 2011.
Barth, K. 'The Christian in Society, 1919'. In *The Word of God and Theology*, 31–69. Translated by Amy Marga. New York: T&T Clark, 2011.
Barth, K. 'The Word of God as the Task of Theology, 1922'. In *The Word of God and Theology*, 171–98. Translated by Amy Marga. New York: T&T Clark, 2011.
Bartholomaeus, M. 'The Place of Growth in Karl Barth's Theology'. *International Journal of Systematic Theology*. Volume 21.2 (2019): 157–81.
Bartholomaeus, M. *Karl Barth's Doctrine of Sanctification: An Exploration of Church Dogmatics* 66. Washington, DC: Rowman & Littlefield, 2021.
Bauckham, R. *The Gospel of Glory: Major Themes in Johannine Theology*. Grand Rapids: Baker Academic, 2015.
Bender, K. J. *Karl Barth's Christological Ecclesiology*. Aldershot: Ashgate, 2005.
Berkouwer, G. C. *The Triumph of Grace in the Theology of Karl Barth: Introduction and Critical Appraisal*. Milton Keynes: Paternoster, 1956.
Biggar, N., ed. *Reckoning with Barth: Essays in Commemoration of the Centenary of Karl Barth's Birth*. London: Mowbray, 1988.
Biggar, N. 'Hearing God's Commands and Thinking about What's Right: With and beyond Barth'. In *Reckoning with Barth: Essays in Commemoration of the Centenary of Karl Barth's Birth*, 101–18. London: Mowbray, 1988.
Biggar, N. 'Barth's Trinitarian Ethic'. In *The Cambridge Companion to Karl Barth*, edited by John Webster, 212–27. Cambridge: Cambridge University Press, 2000.
Biggar, N. 'Karl Barth's Ethics Revisited'. In *Commanding Grace: Studies in Karl Barth's Ethics*, edited by Daniel L. Migliore, 26–49. Grand Rapids: Eerdmans, 2010.
Bonhoeffer, D. *Discipleship*. Dietrich Bonhoeffer Works. English edn. Volume 4. Translated by Barbara Green and Reinhard Krauss. Minneapolis: Fortress Press, 2001.
Bonhoeffer, D. *Ethics*. Dietrich Bonhoeffer Works. English edn. Volume 6. Translated by Reinhard Krauss, Charles C. West and Douglas W. Stott. Minneapolis: Fortress Press, 2005.
Bornkamm, K. 'Die reformatorische Lehre vom Amt Christi und ihre Umformung durch Karl Barth'. In *Luther und Barth*, edited by Joachim Heubach, 127–59. Erlangen: Martin-Luther-Verlag, 1989.
Breen, M. *Building a Discipling Culture: How to Release a Missional Movement by Discipling People Like Jesus Did*. Greenville: 3DM Publishing, 2016. Kindle edition.
Bretherton, L. 'The Duty of Care to Refugees, Christian Cosmopolitanism, and the Hallowing of Bare Life'. *Studies in Christian Ethics* 19.1 (2006): 39–61.
Brock, B. 'Bonhoeffer and the Bible in Christian Ethics: Psalm 119, the Mandates, and Ethics as a "Way"'. *Studies in Christian Ethics*. Volume 18.3 (2005): 7–29.
Brock, B. 'Living in the Wake of God's Acts: Luther's Mary as Key to Barth's Command.' In *The Freedom of a Christian Ethicist: The Future of a Reformation Legacy*, edited by Brian Brock and Michael Mawson, 65–92. New York: T&T Clark, 2016.
Bromiley, G. W. *Introduction to the Theology of Karl Barth*. Grand Rapids: Eerdmans, 1979.
Broughton, G. *Restorative Christ: Jesus, Justice, and Discipleship*. Eugene: Pickwick, 2014.
Brown, C. G. *The Death of Christian Britain: Understanding Secularization, 1800–2000*. London: Routledge, 2001.
Burnett, R. E., ed. *The Westmister Handbook to Karl Barth*. Louisville: Westminster John Knox Press, 2013.

Busch, E. *Karl Barth: His Life from Letters and Autobiographical Texts*. Translated by John Bowden. Eugene: Wipf & Stock, 2005.

Busch, E. *Karl Barth and the Pietists: The Young Karl Barth's Critique of Pietism and Its Response*. Translated by Daniel W. Bloesch. Downers Grove: InterVarsity Press, 2004.

Busch, E. *The Great Passion: An Introduction to Karl Barth's Theology*. Translated by G. Bromiley. Grand Rapids: Eerdmans, 2010.

Busch, E. '"Doing Theology as if Nothing Had Happened" – The Freedom of Theology and the Question of Its Involvement in Politics'. Translated and edited by Martin Rumscheidt. *Studies in Religion*. Volume 16.4 (1987): 459–71.

Busch, E. 'Pietism'. In *The Westminster Handbook of Karl Barth*, edited by Richard E. Burnett, 163–5. Louisville: Westminster John Knox, 2013.

Camp, L. C. *Mere Discipleship: Radical Christianity in a Rebellious World*. 2nd edn. Grand Rapids: Brazos, 2008.

Capper, J. M. *Karl Barth's Theology of Joy*. PhD dissertation: University of Cambridge, 1998.

Carter, E. C. 'The New Monasticism: A Literary Introduction'. *Journal of Spiritual Formation and Soul Care*. Volume 5.2 (2012): 268–84.

Cavananugh, W. *Migrations of the Holy: God, State, and the Political Meaning of the Church*. Grand Rapids: Eerdmans, 2011.

Clough, D., and Michael Leyden. 'Claiming Barth for Ethics: The Last Two Decades'. *Ecclesiology*. Volume 6 (2010): 166–82.

Cochrane, A. C. *The Church's Confession Under Hitler*. Philadelphia: Westminster Press, 1962.

Cortez, M. 'What Does It Mean to Call Karl Barth a "Christocentric" Theologian?' *Scottish Journal of Theology*. Volume 60.2 (2007): 127–43.

Crisp, O. D. *Retrieving Doctrine: Explorations in Reformed Theology*. Milton Keynes: Paternoster Press, 2010.

Crisp, O. D. 'The *Anhypostasia–Enhypostasia* Distinction'. In *Divinity and Humanity: The Incarnation Reconsidered*, 72–89. Cambridge: Cambridge University Press, 2007.

Dalferth, I. U. 'Karl Barth's Eschatological Realism'. In *Karl Barth: Centenary Essays*, edited by Stephen Sykes, 14–45. Cambridge: Cambridge University Press, 1989.

Davidson, I. J. 'Gospel Holiness: Some Dogmatic Reflections'. In *Sanctification: Explorations in Theology and Practice*, edited by Kelly M. Kapic, 189–211. Downers Grove: InterVarsity Press, 2014.

Douglas, M. *Purity and Danger: An Analysis of Concepts of Pollution and Taboo*. Abingdon: Routledge, 1966.

Doyle, R. C. *The Context of Moral Decision-Making in the Writings of John Calvin: The Christological Ethics of Eschatological Order*. PhD dissertation: University of Aberdeen, 1981.

Dreher, R. *The Benedict Option: A Strategy for Christians in a Post-Christian Nation*. New York: Sentinel, 2017.

Ebeling, G. *Lutherstudien: Begriffsuntersuchungen – Textinterpretationen – Wirkungsgeschichtliches von Ebeling, Gerhard*. Volume 3. Tubingen: Mohr Siebeck, 1985.

Fergusson, D. 'Reclaiming the Doctrine of Sanctification'. *Interpretation*. Volume 53.4 (1999): 380–90.

Fiddes, P. S. 'The Status of Woman in the Thought of Karl Barth'. In *After Eve: Women, Theology, and the Christian Tradition*, edited by Janet M. Soskice, 138–55. London: Marshall Pickering, 1990.

Flett, J. G. *The Witness of God: The Trinity, 'Missio Dei', Karl Barth, and the Nature of Christian Community*. Grand Rapids: Eerdmans, 2010.

Frei, H. W. 'Scripture as Realistic Narrative: Karl Barth as Critic of Historical Criticism'. In *Thy Word Is Truth: Barth on Scripture*, edited by George Hunsinger, 49–59. Grand Rapids: Eerdmans, 2012.

Frei, H. W. *The Identity of Jesus Christ: The Hermeneutical Bases of Dogmatic Theology*. Updated edn. Eugene: Cascade, 2013.

Galli, M. *Karl Barth: An Introductory Biography for Evangelicals*. Grand Rapids: Eerdmans, 2017.

Gibson, D. *Reading the Decree: Exegesis, Election and Christology in Calvin and Barth*. New York: T&T Clark, 2009.

Gollwitzer, H. 'Kingdom of God and Socialism in the Theology of Karl Barth'. In *Karl Barth and Radical Politics*. 2nd edn, 50–86. Eugene: Cascade, 2017.

Greggs, T. 'The Influence of Dietrich Bonhoeffer on Karl Barth'. In *Engaging Bonhoeffer: The Impact and Influence of Bonhoeffer's Life and Thought*, edited by Matthew D. Kirkpatrick, 45–64. Minneapolis: Fortress Press, 2016.

Grieb, A. K. 'Living Righteousness: Karl Barth and the Sermon on the Mount'. In *Thy Word Is Truth: Barth on Scripture*, edited by George Hunsinger, 86–110. Grand Rapids: Eerdmans, 2012.

Gutiérrez, G. 'Theology from the Underside of History'. In *The Power of the Poor in History*, translated by Robert R. Barr, 169–221. New York: Orbis Books, 1983.

Hare, J. E. *God's Commands*. Oxford: Oxford University Press, 2015.

Hattrell, S., ed. *Election, Barth, and the French Connection: How Pierre Maury Gave a 'Decisive Impetus' to Karl Barth's Doctrine of Election*. Eugene: Pickwick, 2016.

Hauerwas, S. *Character and the Christian Life: A Study in Theological Ethics*. Notre Dame: University of Notre Dame Press, 1994.

Hauerwas, S. *The Peaceable Kingdom: A Primer in Christian Ethics*. Notre Dame: University of Notre Dame Press, 1983.

Hauerwas, S. 'Discipleship as Craft, Church as Disciplined Community'. *The Christian Century* (October 2, 1991): 881–4.

Hauerwas, S. 'Preaching as though We Had Enemies'. *First Things*, May 1995, accessed 13 February 2017. http://www.firstthings.com/article/1995/05/003-preaching-as-though-we-had-enemies.

Hauerwas, S. *With the Grain of the Universe: The Church's Witness and Natural Theology*. Grand Rapids: Baker Academic, 2001.

Hauerwas, S. 'In Defence of "Our Respectable Culture": Trying to Make Sense of John Howard Yoder's Sexual Abuse'. *ABC Religion & Ethics Online*, 18 October 2017, accessed 15 January 2018. http://www.abc.net.au/religion/articles/2017/10/18/4751367.htm.

Hauerwas, S., and J. Alexander Sider, 'The Distinctiveness of Christian Ethics: A Review Article on John Colwell, *Living the Christian Story: The Distinctiveness of Christian Ethics*'. *International Journal of Systematic Theology*. Volume 5 (2003): 225–33.

Healy, N. M. 'The Logic of Karl Barth's Ecclesiology: Analysis, Assessment and Proposed Modifications'. *Modern Theology*. Volume 10.3 (1994): 253–70.

Healy, N. M. *Church, World, and the Christian Life: Practical-Prophetic Ecclesiology*. Cambridge: Cambridge University Press, 2000.

Healy, N. M. 'Practices and the New Ecclesiology: Misplaced Concreteness?' *International Journal of Systematic Theology*. Volume 5.3 (2003): 287–308.

Healy, N. M. 'Karl Barth's Ecclesiology Reconsidered'. *Scottish Journal of Theology*. Volume 57.3 (2004): 287-99.

Hirsch, A. *Disciplism: Reimagining Evangelism through the Lens of Discipleship*. Orlando: Exponential Resources, 2014.

Hitchcock, N. *Karl Barth and the Resurrection of the Flesh: The Loss of the Body in Participatory Eschatology*. Eugene: Pickwick, 2013.

Holmes, C. R. J. *Ethics in the Presence of Christ*. London: T&T Clark, 2012.

Holmes, C. R. J. 'On Becoming Aligned with the Way Things Really Are'. In *Apocalyptic and the Future of Theology: With and Beyond J. Louis Martyn*, edited by Joshua B. Davis and Douglas Harink, 219-35. Eugene: Cascade, 2012.

Holmes, C. R. J. 'The Church and the Presence of Christ: Defending Actualist Ecclesiology'. *Pro Ecclesia*. Volume 21.3 (2012): 268-80.

Horton, M. *The Christian Faith: A Systematic Theology for Pilgrims on the Way*. Grand Rapids: Zondervan, 2011.

Hunsinger, G. *How to Read Karl Barth: The Shape of His Theology*. Oxford: Oxford University Press, 1991.

Hunsinger, G. 'Truth as Self-Involving: Barth and Lindbeck on the Cognitive and Performative Aspects of Truth in Theological Discourse'. *Journal of the American Academy of Religion*. Volume 61.1 (1993): 41-56.

Hunsinger, G. 'What Barth Learned from Luther'. *Lutheran Quarterly*. Volume 13.2 (1999): 125-55.

Hunsinger, G. *Disruptive Grace: Studies in the Theology of Karl Barth*. Grand Rapids: Eerdmans, 2000.

Hunsinger, G. 'Karl Barth and the Politics of Sectarian Protestantism: A Dialogue with John Howard Yoder'. In *Disruptive Grace*, 114-28.

Hunsinger, G. 'Karl Barth's Christology: Its Basic Chalcedonian Character'. In *The Cambridge Companion to Karl Barth*, edited by John Webster, 127-42. Cambridge: Cambridge University Press, 2000.

Hunsinger, G. 'A Tale of Two Simultaneities: Justification and Sanctification in Calvin and Barth'. *Zeitschrift für dialectische Theologie* 37 (2001): 316-38.

Hunsinger, G., ed. *Thy Word Is Truth: Barth on Scripture*. Grand Rapids: Eerdmans, 2012.

Hunsinger, G. 'Sanctification'. In *The Westminster Handbook of Karl Barth*, edited by Richard E. Burnett, 193-8. Louisville: Westminster John Knox, 2013.

Hunsinger, G. *Reading Barth with Charity: A Hermeneutical Proposal*. Grand Rapids: Baker Academic, 2015.

Hunsinger, G., ed. *Karl Barth and Radical Politics*. 2nd edn. Eugene: Cascade, 2017.

Hunter, J. D. *To Change the World: The Irony, Tragedy, and Possibility of Christianity in the Late Modern World*. Oxford: Oxford University Press, 2010.

Jehle, F. *Ever Against the Stream: The Politics of Karl Barth, 1906-1968*. Translated by Richard and Martha Burnett. Grand Rapids: Eerdmans, 2002.

Jenson, R. W. *Systematic Theology. Volume 1: The Triune God*. Oxford: Oxford University Press, 1997.

Johnson, K. L. *Karl Barth and the Analogia Entis*. London: T&T Clark, 2010.

Johnson, W. S. *The Mystery of God: Karl Barth and the Postmodern Foundations of Theology*. Louisville: Westminster John Knox Press, 1997.

Jüngel, E. 'Humanity in Correspondence to God: Remarks on the Image of God as a Basic Concept in Theological Anthropology'. In *Theological Essays, Volume 1*. Translated by John Webster, 124-53. London: T&T Clark, 2014.

Jüngel, E. 'On Becoming Truly Human: The Significance of the Reformation Distinction between Person and Works for the Self-Understanding of Modern Humanity'. In *Theological Essays, Volume 2*. Translated by John Webster, 216–40. London: Bloomsbury, 2014.

Käsemann, E. 'The Freedom to Resist Idolatry'. In *Theologians in Their Own Words*, edited by Derek R. Nelson, Joshua M. Moritz and Ted Peters, 103–11. Minneapolis: Fortress Press, 2013.

Kerr, N. R. *Christ, History, and Apocalyptic: The Politics of Christian Mission*. Eugene: Cascade, 2009.

Köbler, R. *In the Shadow of Karl Barth: Charlotte von Kirschbaum*. Translated by Keith Crim. Eugene: Wipf & Stock, 2013.

Lewis-Anthony, J. *If You Meet George Herbert on the Road, Kill Him: Radically Rethinking Priestly Ministry*. London: Mowbray, 2009.

Lindbeck, G. A. *The Nature of Doctrine: Religion and Theology in a Post-Liberal Age*. Louisville: Westminster John Knox Press, 2009.

Lindsay, M. R. 'The Abandonment of Inauthentic Humanity: Barth's Theology of Baptism as the Ground and Goal of Mission'. *Pacifica*. Volume 26.3 (2013): 229–45.

Luther, M. *Commentary on the Epistle to the Galatians (1535)*. Translated by Theodore Graebner. Grand Rapids: Zondervan, 1949.

Mangina, J. L. 'Bearing the Marks of Jesus: The Church in the Economy of Salvation in Barth and Hauerwas'. *Scottish Journal of Theology*. Volume 52.3 (1999): 269–305.

Mangina, J. L. *Karl Barth: Theologian of Christian Witness*. Burlington: Ashgate, 2004.

Mangina, J. L. 'The Stranger as Sacrament: Karl Barth and the Ethics of Ecclesial Practice'. *International Journal of Systematic Theology*. Volume 1.3 (1999): 322–39

Marga, A. E. 'Jesus Christ and the Modern Sinner: Karl Barth's Retrieval of Luther's Substantive Christology'. *Currents in Theology and Mission*. Volume 34.4 (2007): 260–70.

Marga, A. E. *Karl Barth's Dialogue with Catholicism in Göttingen and Münster: Its Significance for His Doctrine of God*. Tübingen: Mohr Siebeck, 2010.

Marsh, C. *Reclaiming Dietrich Bonhoeffer: The Promise of His Theology*. Oxford: Oxford University Press, 1994.

Massmann, A. *Citizenship in Heaven and on Earth: Karl Barth's Ethics*. Minneapolis: Fortress Press, 2015.

McCormack, B. L. *Karl Barth's Critically Realistic Dialectical Theology: Its Genesis and Development, 1909-1936*. Oxford: Clarendon Press, 1995.

McCormack, B. L. *Orthodox and Modern: Studies in the Theology of Karl Barth*. Grand Rapids: Baker, 2008.

McCormack, B. L. 'Grace and Being: The Role of God's Gracious Election in Karl Barth's Theological Ontology'. In *Orthodox and Modern*, 183–200. Grand Rapids: Baker, 2008.

McCormack, B. L. 'Karl Barth's Historicized Christology: Just How "Chalcedonian" Is It?' In *Orthodox and Modern*, 201–34. Grand Rapids: Baker, 2008

McCormack, B. L. 'Sanctification after Metaphysics: Karl Barth in Conversation with John Wesley's Conception of "Christian Perfection"'. In *Sanctification: Explorations in Theology and Practice*, edited by K. M. Kapic, 103–24. Downers Grove: InterVarsity Press, 2014.

McFadyen, A. I. 'The Call to Discipleship: Reflections on Bonhoeffer's Theme 50 Years On'. *Scottish Journal of Theology*. Volume 43.4 (1990): 461–83.

McFarland, I. A. 'Present in Love: Rethinking Barth on the Divine Perfections'. *Modern Theology*. Volume 33.2 (2017): 243–58.

McGrath, A. E. *Iustitia Dei: A History of the Christian Doctrine of Justification*. 2nd edn. Cambridge: Cambridge University Press, 1998.

McKenny, G. *The Analogy of Grace: Karl Barth's Moral Theology*. Oxford: Oxford University Press, 2010.

McMaken, W. T., and D. W. Congdon, eds. *Karl Barth in Conversation*. Eugene: Pickwick, 2014.

McMaken, W. T. 'Election and the Pattern of Exchange in Karl Barth's Doctrine of the Atonement'. *Journal of Reformed Theology*. Volume 3 (2009): 202–18.

McMaken, W. T. 'Definitive, Defective, or Deft? Reassessing Barth's Doctrine of Baptism in Church Dogmatics IV/4'. *International Journal of Systematic Theology*. Volume 17.1 (2015): 89–114.

Migliore, D. L. '*Participatio Christi*: The Central Theme of Barth's Doctrine of Sanctification'. *Zeitschrift für dialektische Theologie*. Volume 37 (2001): 286–307.

Migliore, D. L. 'Commanding Grace: Karl Barth's Theological Ethics'. In *Commanding Grace: Studies in Karl Barth's Ethics*, edited by Daniel L. Migliore, 1–25. Grand Rapids: Eerdmans, 2010.

Muggeridge, M. *The End of Christendom*. Grand Rapids: Eerdmans, 1980.

Muller, R. A. *Christ and the Decree: Christology and Predestination in Reformed Theology from Calvin to Perkins*. Grand Rapids: Baker Book, 1986.

Muller, R. A. *The Unaccommodated Calvin: Studies in the Foundation of a Theological Tradition*. New York: Oxford University Press, 2000.

Muller, R. A. *After Calvin: Studies in the Development of a Theological Tradition*. Oxford: Oxford University Press, 2003.

Muller, R. A. 'A Note on "Christocentrism" and the Imprudent Use of Such Terminology'. *Westminster Theological Journal*. Volume 68 (2006): 253–60.

Nation, M. T. 'Discipleship in a World Full of Nazis: Dietrich Bonhoeffer's Polyphonic Pacifism as Social Ethics'. In *The Wisdom of the Cross: Essays in Honour of John Howard Yoder*, edited by Stanley Hauerwas, Chris K. Huebner, Harry J. Huber and Mark Thiessen Nation, 249–77. Grand Rapids: Eerdmans, 1999.

Neville, D. 'Grace Elicits Correspondences: The Theologian as Peacemaker'. In *Embracing Grace: The Theologian's Task*, edited by Heather Thomson, 119–33. Canberra: Barton Books, 2009.

Nation, M. T., A. G. Siegrist and D. P. Umbell. *Bonhoeffer the Assassin? Challenging the Myth, Recovering His Call to Peacemaking*. Grand Rapids: Baker Academic, 2013.

Niebuhr, H. R. *Christ and Culture*. New York: HarperCollins, 2001.

Niebuhr, R. 'We Are Men and Not God'. In *Essays in Applied Christianity*, edited by D. B. Robertson, 168–75. New York: Meriden Books, 1959.

Nimmo, P. T. *Being in Action: The Theological Shape of Barth's Ethical Vision*. London: T&T Clark, 2007.

Nimmo, P. T. 'Karl Barth and the *Concursus Dei* – A Chalcedonianism Too Far?' *International Journal of Systematic Theology*. Volume 9 (2007): 58–72.

Nimmo, P. T. 'Actualism'. In *The Westminster Handbook of Karl Barth*, edited by Richard E. Burnett, 1–3. Louisville: Westminster John Knox, 2013.

Nolan, K. J. *Reformed Virtue after Barth: Developing Moral Virtue Ethics in the Reformed Tradition*. Louisville: Westminster John Knox, 2014.

O'Donovan, O. 'How Can Theology Be Moral?' *Journal of Religious Ethics*. Volume 17.2 (1989): 81–94.

O'Donovan, O. *Resurrection and Moral Order: An Outline for Evangelical Ethics*. 2nd edn. Leicester: Apollos, 1994.

O'Donovan, O. *Desire of the Nations: Rediscovering the Roots of Political Theology.* Cambridge: Cambridge University Press, 1996.
O'Donovan, O. 'Prayer and Morality in the Sermon on the Mount'. *Studies in Christian Ethics.* Volume 22.1 (2000): 21–33.
O'Donovan, O. *Self, World, and Time: Ethics as Theology 1.* Grand Rapids: Eerdmans, 2013.
O'Donovan, O. *Finding and Seeking: Ethics as Theology 2.* Grand Rapids: Eerdmans, 2014.
O'Donovan, O. 'Sanctification and Ethics'. In *Sanctification: Explorations in Theology and Practice*, edited by Kelly M. Kapic, 150–66. Downers Grove: InterVarsity Press, 2014.
O'Donovan, O. *Entering into Rest: Ethics as Theology 3.* Grand Rapids: Eerdmans, 2017.
Olson, C. 'Excess, Time, and the Pure Gift: Postmodern Transformations of Marcel Mauss' Theory'. *Method and Theory in the Study of Religion.* Volume 14.3/4 (2002): 350–74.
O'Neil, M. D. *Church as Moral Community: Karl Barth's Vision of Christian Life, 1915–1922.* Milton Keynes: Paternoster, 2013.
Owen, J. 'Of the Mortification of Sin in Believers (1656)'. In *Overcoming Sin and Temptation*, edited by Kelly M. Kapic and Justin Taylor. Wheaton: Crossway, 2006.
Pangritz, A. *Karl Barth in the Theology of Dietrich Bonhoeffer.* Translated by Barbara and Martin Rumscheidt. Grand Rapids: Eerdmans, 2000.
Plato. *Euthyphro.* Translated by Benjamin Jowett. Charleston: CreateSpace, 2016.
Puffer, M. 'Taking Exception to the *Grenzfall*'s Reception: Revisiting Karl Barth's Ethics of War'. *Modern Theology.* Volume 28.3 (2012): 478–502.
Puffer, M. 'Dietrich Bonhoeffer in the Theology of Karl Barth'. In *Karl Barth in Conversation*, edited by Travis McMaken and David Congdon, 46–62. Eugene: Pickwick, 2014.
Roberts, R. H. *A Theology on Its Way? Essays on Karl Barth.* London: T&T Clark, 1992.
Said, E. W. *On Late Style: Music and Literature Against the Grain.* New York: Vintage Books, 2007.
Schweizer, E. *Lordship and Discipleship.* London: SCM Press, 1960.
Selinger, S. *Charlotte von Kirschbaum and Karl Barth: A Study in Biography and the History of Theology.* University Park: Pennsylvania State University Press, 1998.
Siggelkow, R. O. 'The Nothingness of the Church under the Cross: Mission without Colonialism'. *Anabaptist Witness.* Volume 1.1 (2014): 103–19.
Smith, J. K. A. *Desiring the Kingdom: Worship, Worldview, and Cultural Formation.* Grand Rapids: Baker Academic, 2009.
Smith, J. K. A. *Imagining the Kingdom: How Worship Works.* Grand Rapids: Baker Academic, 2013.
Smith, J. K. A. *You Are What You Love: The Spiritual Power of Habit.* Grand Rapids: Brazos, 2016.
Smith, J. K. A. *Awaiting the King: Reforming Public Theology.* Grand Rapids: Baker Academic, 2017.
Snyder, C. A. *The Life and Thought of Michael Sattler.* Scottdale: Herald Press, 1984.
Sonderegger, K. 'Sanctification as Impartation in the Doctrine of Karl Barth'. *Zeitschrift für dialektische Theologie.* Volume 37 (2001): 308–15.
Sonderegger, K. 'Barth and Feminism'. In *The Cambridge Companion to Karl Barth*, edited by John Webster, 258–73. Cambridge: Cambridge University Press, 2000.
Stassen, G. H. *A Thicker Jesus: Incarnational Discipleship for a Secular Age.* Louisville: Westminster John Knox Press, 2012.
Swain, S. R. *The God of the Gospel: Robert Jenson's Trinitarian Theology.* Downers Grove: InterVarsity Press, 2013.

Swann, C. 'Discipleship on the Level of Thought: the Case of Karl Barth's Critique of the Religion of Revelation'. In *Revelation and Reason in Christian Theology: Proceedings of the Theology Connect Conference*, edited by Christopher C. Green and David I. Starling, 166–81. Bellingham: Lexham Press, 2018.

Swann, C. 'A Tale of Two Bedrooms? The Problem and Promise of Karl Barth's Theology of Discipleship'. *St Mark's Review: A Journal of Christian Thought and Opinion*. Volume 251.1 (2020): 20–36.

Swann, C. 'Karl Barth on the Dignity and Crown of Suffering: Reimagining the Fourth Age for Discipleship'. In *Embracing Life and Gathering Wisdom: Theological, Pastoral, and Clinical Insights into Human Flourishing at the End of Life*, edited by Stephen Smith, Edwina Blair and Catherine Kleeman, 145–70. Macquarie Park: SCD Press, 2020.

Swinton, J. *Becoming Friends of Time: Disability, Timefullness, and Gentle Discipleship*. Waco: Baylor University Press, 2016.

Taylor, C. *Modern Social Imaginaries*. Durham: Duke University Press, 2004.

Taylor, D. W. 'New Directions in Barthian Ethics'. *Theology*. Volume 118.5 (2015): 323–30.

Thompson, G. 'The Doctrines of Practical Theology and the Practice of Doctrine: Re-imagining the Relationship between Practical Theology and Systematic Theology'. *Pacifica*. Volume 26.1 (2012): 17–36.

Tietz, C. 'Karl Barth and Charlotte von Kirschbaum'. *Theology Today*. Volume 74.2 (2017): 86–111.

Tilley, T. W. *The Disciples' Jesus: Christology as Reconciling Practice*. Maryknoll: Orbis, 2008.

Torrance, T. F. 'The Problem of Natural Theology in the Thought of Karl Barth'. *Religious Studies*. Volume 6 (1970): 121–35.

Troeltsch, E. *The Social Teaching of the Christian Churches*. London: Allen & Unwin, 1931.

Vander Lugt, W. *Living Theodrama: Reimagining Theological Ethics*. London: Routledge, 2016.

Van Vlaustin, W. 'Personal Renewal between Heidelberg and Westminster'. *Journal of Reformed Theology*. Volume 5 (2011): 49–67.

Volf, M. 'Soft Difference: Theological Reflections on the Relation Between Church and Culture in 1 Peter'. *Ex Auditu*. Volume 10 (1994): 15–30.

Volf, M. *Exclusion and Embrace: A Theological Exploration of Identity, Otherness, and Reconciliation*. Nashville: Abingdon Press, 1996.

Volf, M. 'Theology, Meaning, and Power: A Conversation with George Lindbeck on Theology and the Nature of Christian Difference'. In *The Nature of Confession: Evangelicals and Postliberals in Conversation*, edited by Timothy R. Philips and Dennis L. Okholm, 45–66. Downers Grove: InterVarsity Press, 1996.

Volf, M. *A Public Faith: How Followers of Christ Should Serve the Common Good*. Grand Rapids, MI: Brazos, 2011.

Volpe, M. A. *Rethinking Christian Identity: Doctrine and Discipleship*. Oxford: Wiley-Blackwell, 2013.

Ward, P. 'Ecclesiology and Ethnography with Humility: Going through Barth'. *Studia Theologica—Nordic Journal of Theology* (2016): 1–17.

Ward, P. *Liquid Ecclesiology: The Gospel and the Church*. Leiden: Brill, 2017.

Warner, M. *Publics and Counterpublics*. Cambridge: Zone Books, 2002.

Webster, J. B. 'The Christian in Revolt: Some Reflections on *The Christian Life*'. In *Reckoning with Barth*, edited by Nigel Biggar, 119–44. London: Mowbray, 1988.

Webster, J. B. *Barth's Ethics of Reconciliation*. Cambridge: Cambridge University Press, 1995.

Webster, J. B. *Barth's Moral Theology: Human Action in Barth's Thought*. Grand Rapids: Eerdmans, 1998.

Webster, J. B., ed. *The Cambridge Companion to Karl Barth*. Cambridge: Cambridge University Press, 2000.

Webster, J. B. 'The Dogmatic Location of the Canon'. In *Word and Church: Essays in Christian Dogmatics*, 9–46. Edinburgh: T&T Clark, 2001.

Webster, J. B. *Holy Scripture: A Dogmatic Sketch*. Cambridge: Cambridge University Press, 2003.

Webster, J. B. *Holiness*. London: SCM Press, 2003.

Webster, J. B. *Barth's Earlier Theology: Four Studies*. London: T&T Clark, 2005.

Webster, J. B. 'Discipleship and Calling'. *Scottish Bulletin of Evangelical Theology*. Volume 23.3 (2005): 133–47.

Webster, J. B. 'Discipleship and Obedience'. *Scottish Bulletin of Evangelical Theology*. Volume 24.1 (2006): 4–18.

Webster, J. B. 'Theologies of Retrieval'. In *The Oxford Handbook of Systematic Theology*, edited by J. Webster, K. Tanner and I. Torrance, 583–99. Oxford: Oxford University Press, 2007.

Webster, J. B. '"In the Society of God": Some Principles of Ecclesiology'. In *Perspectives on Ecclesiology and Ethnography* edited by Pete Ward, 200–22. Grand Rapids: Eerdmans, 2012.

Werpehowski, W. 'Karl Barth and Politics'. In *The Cambridge Companion to Karl Barth*, edited by John Webster, 228–42. Cambridge: Cambridge University Press, 2000.

Williams, R. *Why Study the Past? The Quest for the Historical Church*. Grand Rapids: Eerdmans, 2005.

Willis, E. D. *Calvin's Catholic Christology: The Function of the So-Called Extra Calvinisticum in Calvin's Theology*. Leiden: Brill, 1966.

Wilson, J. R. *Living Faithfully in a Fragmented World: Lessons for the Church from MacIntyre's 'After Virtue'*. Harrisburg: Trinity Press International, 1997.

Winn, C. T. C. *'Jesus Is Victor!': The Significance of the Blumhardts for the Theology of Karl Barth*. Eugene: Pickwick, 2009.

Woodard-Lehman, D. A. 'Reason after Revelation: Karl Barth on Divine Word and Human Words'. *Modern Theology*. Volume 33.1 (2017): 92–115.

Yocum, J. *Ecclesial Mediation in Karl Barth*. London: Routledge, 2016.

Yoder, J. H. 'The Basis of Barth's Social Ethics'. In *Karl Barth and the Problem of War, and Other Essays on Barth*, edited by Mark Thiessen Nation, 133–48. Eugene: Cascade, 2003.

Yong, A. *The Bible, Disability, and the Church: A New Vision of the People of God*. Grand Rapids: Eerdmans, 2011.

Ziegler, P. G. 'Discipleship: Militant Love in the Time that Remains'. In *Militant Grace: The Apocalyptic Turn and the Future of Christian Theology*. Grand Rapids: Baker Academic, 2018.

INDEX

action
 divine 3, 13, 28, 30, 51, 56–7, 86, 100, 109, 144–5, 158–9, 211
 human 3, 28, 30, 79, 100–1, 137, 145–6, 171–3, 177–9, 183–4, 189, 211
 relation of human and divine 27, 35, 36 n.56, 100, 109–10, 113, 118–19, 121, 153, 174–5, 184, 187, 211, 215
actualism 14, 25, 51–6, 85–7, 130–1, 156–61, 211
ageing. *See* intergenerational relations
agency
 divine 3, 25, 36 n.56, 55–6, 98, 100, 113, 168–9, 184
 human 22–7, 32, 56, 77, 79–81, 84–5, 102–3, 113–14, 119–20, 125–6, 131–3, 138–46, 155–62, 166–8, 189–90, 197–207, 222–7
analogy. *See also* correspondence 27, 34–6, 111–12, 117, 127–53, 223
Augsburger, David 4 n.11, 8

Balthasar, Hans Urs von 115–16, 127–8, 172
Banner, Michael 4 n.11, 116, 172, 220–1
Barmen Declaration 6, 33–4, 36, 38, 214, 227
Barns, Ian 11–12
Barth, Karl
 and Charlotte von Kirschbaum 39–41, 203, 214–15
 'The Christian in Society' (Tambach lecture) 34–5
 The Christian Life 36 n.56, 58 n.34, 113–14, 123, 126, 127–9, 130–5, 149–53
 Church Dogmatics II/2 15, 20, 27, 48–9, 65–6, 73, 77–8, 79–80, 99–100, 128, 224
 Church Dogmatics III/2 94

 Church Dogmatics III/4 40 n.75, 77, 80, 185–6, 193–4, 203
 Church Dogmatics IV/1 18, 85–6, 114, 120, 136–41, 202–4
 Church Dogmatics IV/2 17–19, 21–8, 43–61, 70, 73–7, 79–81, 84–91, 122–6, 140–2, 157–66, 171–84, 204, 222–3
 Church Dogmatics IV/3 142–4, 157
 Church Dogmatics IV/4 72, 149, 212
 eschatological realism of 97, 105–6, 114–20, 167, 173–87, 190, 211, 217
 moral theology of 13, 27, 70–1, 92–3, 114, 130, 171–3, 185–7, 190–7, 224–5
 Der Römerbrief (first edition) 35, 114
 Romans II (second edition) 35–6, 125, 127, 130–5, 144–9
 socialist sympathies 33–6
 theological method of 32, 53, 71, 97 n.25, 106, 114–17, 120–1, 167, 187, 217
 The Theology of John Calvin 28
 and women 39–41, 120, 202–4, 214, 225
Bartholomaeus, Michael 22 n.14, 52 n.17, 70–1, 141
Bender, Kimlyn J. 12–13, 105 n.2, 128–9, 132, 135, 137–9, 142–3, 157–8
Bigger, Nigel 78 n.87, 93 n.21, 123, 172–3, 185–7
Bonhoeffer, Dietrich 6–7, 19, 31–3, 84, 88, 90–5, 124, 148, 193, 224
Brock, Brian 4 n.11, 70–1
Brown, Callum 9
Busch, Eberhard 29 n.36, 37–8, 117 n.31

Calvin, John 18–23, 28, 45–6, 49–55, 59–74, 83, 91, 165, 180–1, 193, 195
Camp, Lee 4 n.11, 5 n.14, 10–11
Capper, John Mark 52 n.16
casuistry. *See also* discernment; practical reasoning 93, 183–7
character. *See* ethics, virtue

Index

Christian ethics. *See* ethics
Christocentrism 14, 43–7, 56–69, 61–73, 83–4, 105, 108–9, 156, 210, 223–4
Christology
    Chalcedonian 18, 92, 109, 114, 117–20, 139, 174–5
    enhypostasis–anhypostasis 117, 119, 124, 135, 139, 174–5
    historicisation of 85, 92, 102, 118–19, 124
    'lively' 46–7, 71–2, 74–81, 120–1, 222, 227
Church (doctrine of)
    agency of 130–2, 137–40, 143–4, 157, 167, 219
    concreteness of 85, 130–1, 143, 157–60, 167, 169, 210–11
    and ecumenism 48, 141–2, 151
    and mission 31, 47–8, 57, 72–3, 80, 133, 140–1, 151, 166, 169, 175
    ministry of 142–4
    moral formation of 7–8, 125, 133, 171 n.2
    relativization of 130–5, 137–9, 145–6, 152–3, 157
    sacrilization of 131, 157, 160–1, 164–6
    secularisation of 157, 159–60, 164–5
    solidarity in sin 45, 57, 72, 133–4, 164–5, 167–9, 176
    totus Christus 140–1, 143, 157, 159, 161
Christian identity. *See* discipleship and Christian distinctiveness
Christian life, the. *See* Christian living
Christian living. *See also* ethics; discipleship 2–6, 9, 12, 26–7, 50, 60–1, 85–6, 88–91, 123–6, 225–7
Christian love 74, 124, 150–3, 172–6, 184, 212, 222
Christian nonconformity. *See* discipleship and Christian distinctiveness
Collins Winn, Christian T. 29 n.26
correspondence (*Entsprechung*) 24, 30, 95, 105–26, 138, 153, 173–87, 191–2, 195–7, 215–17, 223, 225–6
Crisp, Oliver 13, 119 n.36
cruciformity. *See also* suffering. bearing the cross in 108–9, 130–5, 192, 202–4, 214

Dalferth, Ingolf U. 97 n.25, 114–17, 129 n.12
Davidson, Ivor 3, 6 n.20
deliberation 80, 93, 99–100
deontology 77–8
disability 201, 205–7
discernment. *See also* casuistry; deliberation; practical reasoning 79, 85, 92–3, 98–103, 183, 226
discipleship
    call of 2–3, 6–8, 16, 19, 28–31, 38, 43–4, 59, 84–6, 88–98, 101–3, 112–13, 123–4, 136, 161–2, 177, 184, 191–2, 194, 211, 215, 220, 225–6
    contemporary conversation about 1, 4–8, 44, 210–12
    and direction (*Weisung*) 19, 21–3, 25, 29, 43, 47, 55–6, 71, 75–81, 83–5, 93, 95–6, 98–103, 122–3, 126, 155, 169, 175, 177–8, 183–4, 222–3
    and Christian distinctiveness 7–8, 44–6, 56–8, 71–4, 176, 211–12
    dogmatic location of 30, 71–4, 155, 171, 213
    as formed reference 79, 92–8, 100–1, 123–4, 172, 177–8, 183–6, 211, 213, 215–16, 224
    and liberation 6, 23, 56–8, 75–7, 84–92, 95–6, 101, 124–5, 152–3, 187, 202–7, 213–15, 224
    motif in the New Testament 19, 29, 43, 49, 123, 210
    and participation 17, 19, 22–3, 76, 83, 107–9, 192, 223
    presence of Christ in 6, 47, 55–6, 70, 74–81, 86, 98–103, 120–5, 137–40, 143, 161, 175–8, 192, 218, 226
disgust 144, 147–8
divine action. *See* action, divine
divine command 74, 77–80, 100–1, 185–7, 222–4
Dreher, Rod 5 n.12, 9–10

ecclesial agency. *See* agency, human
ecclesiology. *See also* church (doctrine of) 12, 85, 130–44, 156–69, 225
election 15, 18, 26–7, 48–9, 53–4, 62–7, 72–3, 80, 93 n.20, 110–11, 128, 131–2

Index

ethics
　christological determination of 123–6,
　　166–9, 211–12
　relation to theology 6, 9, 29, 100,
　　144–5, 214–16
　underdetermination of 124–6, 187,
　　209, 212–16
　virtue 190, 197–201
Extra Calvinisticum 51 n.16

formation, moral. *See also* ethics, virtue 8,
　132–3, 191 n.4, 198–9, 214–15
freedom. *See* discipleship and liberation

gender. *See* Barth and women
Gibson, David 50 n.13, 61 n.39, 64–6, 73
Gollwitzer, Herman 13, 34–7
Gutiérrez, Gustavo 15–16

Hare, John E. 78 n.89, 80 n.94
Hauerwas, Stanley 4 n.11, 5 n.14, 32, 48,
　93 n.21, 156, 167–8, 172, 191 n.4,
　198–201, 211
Healy, Nicholas 85 n.3, 156–8, 160, 168–9
hermeneutics
　analogical 117, 120, 126
　Calvin vs Barth 66
　fundamentalist 97, 101–2
　liberal 97, 102
　and moral discernment 99–101
　post-liberal 97, 101–2
holiness. *See* sanctification
Holmes, Christopher R. J. 72 n.79, 86, 98
　n.26, 101 n.35, 121, 156, 157 n.6, 184
Horton, Michael 5 n.13
Hunsinger, George 14, 20–2, 52–60, 62,
　68, 74–5
Hunter, James Davison 160–1, 212

intergenerational relations 219–22

Jehle, Frank 33, 34 n.46, 37–9
Jesus Christ. *See* discipleship, call of;
　discipleship, presence of Christ in
Johnson, William Stacey 115 n.18, 124
　n.46, 165–6, 172
justification (doctrine of) 3, 17–18, 20,
　50–1, 54–6, 59–60, 62–6, 86, 91,
　132–3, 180–1

Kerr, Nathan 5 n.14, 86 n.5, 93 n.20,
　116 n.27, 160 n.14

Luther, Martin 14, 18, 20–1, 46, 60 n.38,
　67–71, 83, 89, 162

Mangina, Joseph 89, 136–7, 141–2,
　167 n.25
Marga, Amy 67, 69
Marsh, Charles 32
Massmann, Alexander 114, 120–1, 201–5,
　224 n.15
McCormack, Bruce 14 n.49, 15, 24, 26–7,
　51 n.15, 61–4, 65 n.57, 66, 92 n.19,
　128 n.5, 176, 180–1, 204
McFadyen, Alister 4 n.11
McFarland, Ian 74 n.81
McKenny, Gerald 13, 78 n.85, 79 n.90,
　95 n.24
McMaken, W. Travis 92, 109–10, 127 n.1
Migliore, Daniel 22–4, 52 n.17, 79,
　108 n.5
moral formation. *See* formation, moral
Muller, Richard 49 n.13, 61 n.39, 64–5,
　73 n.80

Niebuhr, Reinhold 33
Nimmo, Paul T. 15 n.52, 51, 78 n.87,
　79 n.90, 92 n.19, 94–5, 101 n.34,
　118
non-conformity. *See* discipleship and
　Christian distinctiveness

O'Donovan, Oliver 77 n.85, 99–101, 152
　n.37, 173 n.7, 174, 189, 221–2
O'Neil, Michael 35 n.54, 47, 125, 132–3,
　158 n.11

paradoxical identity. *See* action, relation of
　divine and human
participation 17–19, 21–4, 51, 54–5, 76,
　83, 107–9, 192, 223
pneumatology 18–19, 24, 55, 66, 72, 106,
　121–3, 135–6, 190, 211, 218–19
post-Christian 9–12, 194, 225–7
practical reasoning. *See also* casuistry,
　discernment 173, 185–7
Puffer, Matthew 32 n.41, 78 n.86, 79 n.91,
　186–7

repentance 6, 69, 133–5, 140, 145, 148–9, 165
retrieval, theological 13–14

sanctification (doctrine of) 3, 17–19, 21–2, 27–8, 61–74, 119, 121, 223–4
Schweizer, Eduard 2, 6
sin (doctrine of)
　in the church 159–60, 176
　confession of 164–6
　mortification of 161–6
Smith, James K. A. 5 n.13, 157 n.5
Sonderegger, Katherine 24–7, 40, 224 n.15
Stassen, Glen 4 n.11, 6
suffering
　bearing the cross in 110–13
　and dying 189, 194, 200–1, 220–1
　moral appropriation of 189, 191, 193–201, 226–7
　and moral passivity 190–5, 198–9
　and victimhood 192, 196, 201–4, 221

theological education 216–19
theological ethics. *See* ethics

Thiessen Nation, Mark 4 n.11
Tietz, Christiane 33, 37, 39–40, 203 n.23
Tilley, Terrence 4 n.11, 6
Torrance, T. F. 86, 128
Troeltsch, Ernst 159–60

Volf, Miroslav 3, 7 n.24, 44 n.2, 159 n.13, 201–2, 204, 206–7
Volpe, Medi Ann 8

Webster, John 2–5, 7–8, 13–14, 16, 19, 27, 30, 36 n.56, 53–4, 56, 58 n.34, 59, 71, 87–8, 105 n.2, 107, 113–14, 122–3, 128–9, 136, 149, 158, 165, 184, 196
Williams, Rowan 7, 172
Wilson, Jonathan R. 5 n.12, 11
Works, good 178–83

Yocum, John 14, 52 n.19, 129
Yoder, John Howard 20, 168
Yong, Amos 205–7

Ziegler, Philip 1, 2 n.5

www.ingramcontent.com/pod-product-compliance
Lightning Source LLC
Chambersburg PA
CBHW051520230426
43668CB00012B/1677